Lincolnshire
COUNTY COUNCIL

discover libraries

This book should be returned on or before the last date shown below. SA2

SA2 04114 31/05/2014	Bourne	

D0533173

'[In] this gripping, succinct and lethal book . . . Hurd
and Young have p:

04928133

such deft use of anecdote and quotation, that you do wonder whether there's any more to be said ... It is simply and beautifully written and always entertaining ... I believe Hurd and Young have understood, what made this person tick. I've never read a more intense or persuasive evocation of the child who was father to the man ... The outstanding insight of this book is to be found in the authors' bringing to life of a young exotic, crashing around from experience to experience, from debt to debt, from dandification and sexual ambiguity to womanising with other men's older wives, in search of an identity'   MATTHEW PARRIS, *The Times*

'Not only, they tell us in this vigorously debunking romp through [Disraeli's] political life, did he never use the phrases "One Nation" or "Tory Democracy", he was actively hostile to the concepts that they are now understood to represent ... This is an invigorating account, bracingly cynical and told with commanding ease – at least one of these authors has been around the political block a bit – and a lovely dry turn of phrase'   SAM LEITH, *Spectator*

'Less a biography than an unashamedly partisan, elegant and invigorating account of Disraeli the Tory. Hurd and Young navigate their way nimbly through the contours of Disraeli's life but are less concerned with exploring that story than with probing the contradictions in Disraeli's character, his role in the political landscape of the nineteenth century and his strange posthumous reshapings ... *Disraeli, or The Two Lives* has romance and enthusiasm in spades and as a result succeeds triumphantly'   DAISY HAY, *Literary Review*

'Conscientously researched and splendidly readable'

ANTONIA FRASER, *Financial Times*

'In this punchy and sparkling book, Douglas Hurd, one-time Conservative Foreign Secretary, and Edward Young skewer the myths that have grown up around Disraeli . . . Part biography, part polemic, this is an engaging, original and enjoyable book'

JANE RIDLEY, *The Tablet*

'Notably well written, even thrilling at times'

PETER CLARKE, *New Statesman*

'A highly enjoyable and thought-provoking book that convincingly makes the case that the real Disraeli is more extraordinary than the myth'

RICHARD ALDOUS, *Irish Times*

'In this highly absorbing biography . . . Hurd and Young ably chart Disraeli's two lives – the reality and the fantasy . . . It is a gripping read'

JESSE NORMAN, *Prospect*

'There is something lubriciously intriguing about the biography of a Victorian statesman subtitled "The Two Lives" . . . Hurd and Young are masterful in delineating the limited scale of Disraeli's actual achievements – they do so with dry wit, an ear and eye for telling detail and an elegant, economical, prose style. Yet they are even better when it comes to explaining Disraeli's one great real – and lasting – triumph, the second life of the subtitle . . . The memory of what Disraeli conjured up still captivates. He gave all who study and practise politics a vivid lesson in how to move men's and women's hearts, through dash, romance and – above all – courage'

'[Disraeli] remains the wonderfully entertaining political magician of legend, full of dazzling wit and tactical audacity, adored and distrusted in equal measure. Where Douglas Hurd and Edward Young succeed is in the beautiful style of writing, the pace of their narrative and their ability to condense complex political problems. Their enjoyment shines through, whether it be a lively analysis of Disraeli's early, rather flowery, novels or a gripping account of his achievement in pushing the 1867 Reform Bill through Parliament'

'Benjamin Disraeli remains the most colourful politician in English history . . . the book is well researched and written with the calm authority which was Hurd's hallmark when he was a minister'

'As Hurd and co make clear in this well-written history he never used the phrase ["One Nation"]. In fact, in this demolition of the Disraelian myth, we learn that this Victorian serial PM was a content-free zone, a flip-flopper, a shameless self-promoter, a jingoist, egomaniac. But still, what flair, charm and political savvy'

DOUGLAS HURD is a former diplomat, Member of Parliament, Secretary of State for Northern Ireland, Home Secretary and Foreign Secretary. He is the author of a number of works of fiction and history, including a much admired biography of Robert Peel and *Choose Your Weapons*, a history of British foreign policy. He lives in Oxfordshire and London.

EDWARD YOUNG gained a first-class degree in history from Clare College, Cambridge, and studied as a Mellon Scholar at Yale University. He has worked as a speechwriter for David Cameron and as Chief of Staff to the Conservative Party Chairman. He currently works at Brunswick Group LLP. *Disraeli* is Edward's third book in collaboration with Douglas Hurd. He lives in London.

By Douglas Hurd

Choose Your Weapons: The British Foreign Secretary
Memoirs
Robert Peel: A Biography
The Search for Peace: A Century of Peace Diplomacy
The Arrow-War: An Anglo-Chinese Confusion, 1856-1860
An End to Promises: Sketch of a Government, 1970-1974

By Douglas Hurd and Edward Young

Disraeli, or The Two Lives
Choose Your Weapons: The British Foreign Secretary

DISRAELI

or

The Two Lives

DOUGLAS HURD

and

EDWARD YOUNG

PHOENIX

A Phoenix paperback
First published in Great Britain in 2013
by Weidenfeld & Nicolson
This edition published in 2014
by Phoenix,
an imprint of Orion Books Ltd,
Orion House, 5 Upper St Martin's Lane,
London WC2H 9EA

An Hachette UK company

3 5 7 9 10 8 6 4 2

A CIP catalogue record for this book
is available from the British Library.

ISBN 978 0 7538 2832 8

Typeset by Input Data Services Ltd,
Bridgwater, Somerset

Printed in Great Britain by CPI Group (UK) Ltd,
Croydon CR0 4YY

The Orion Publishing Group's policy is to use papers that
are natural, renewable and recyclable products and
made from wood grown in sustainable forests. The logging
and manufacturing processes are expected to conform to
the environmental regulations of the country of origin.

www.orionbooks.co.uk

For Becky

CONTENTS

ILLUSTRATIONS

Engraving of Isaac D'Israeli by W.M. Miller and H. Wright Smith, c.1810 (*Getty Images*)

Sarah D'Israeli by Daniel Maclise, 1828 (*National Trust*)

Maria D'Israeli by J. Downman, 1805 (*National Trust/Thomas Boggis*)

Sketch of Disraeli by or after Daniel Maclise, c.1833 (*National Portrait Gallery, London*)

Henrietta Sykes, 1837, engraving after a drawing by Alfred Edward Chalon (*The Granger Collection*)

Hughenden Manor by Lord Henry Lennox, 1852 (*National Trust/John Hammond*)

Hughenden Manor (*National Trust/Matthew Antrobus*)

Mary Anne Disraeli by R.A. Chalon, 1840 (*National Trust/ John Hammond*)

Bulwer Lytton by Henry William Pickersgill, c.1831 (*National Portrait Gallery, London*)

Lord Lyndhurst by Alfred d'Orsay, assisted by Sir Edwin Landseer (*The Disraeli Collection, National Trust Photographic Library/Nick Pollard/Bridgeman*)

Lord George Bentinck by Samuel Lane, c.1836 (*National Portrait Gallery, London*)

Lord John Manners by Sir Francis Grant (*National Trust*)

Edward Stanley, 14th Earl of Derby, c.1860 (*Getty Images*)

Lord Palmerston by Francis Cruickshank, c.1855 (*National Portrait Gallery, London/Bridgeman*)

Edward Stanley, 15th Earl of Derby, c.1875 (*Getty Images*)

William Gladstone by Franz Seraph von Lenbach, 1879 (*Scottish National Portrait Gallery, Edinburgh/Bridgeman*)

John Russell by Sir Francis Grant, 1853 (*National Portrait Gallery, London*)

Sir Robert Peel by Henry William Pickersgill (*National Portrait Gallery, London*)

Robert Lowe, c.1873 (*National Portrait Gallery, London*)

Cartoon from *Punch*, 1867: The Derby, 1867. Dizzy Wins With 'Reform Bill' (*Punch Limited*)

Cartoon from *Punch*, 1872: The Conservative Programme (*Punch Limited*)

Peace with Honour: Queen Victoria with Benjamin Disraeli following the signing of the Berlin Treaty by Theodore Blake Wirgman, 1878 (*Forbes Magazine Collection, New York/Bridgeman*)

The Beaconsfield Cabinet by Charles Mercier, 1874 (*Crown Copyright, UK Government Art Collection*)

Benjamin Disraeli, Earl of Beaconsfield by Jabez Hughes, 1878 (*National Portrait Gallery, London*)

'Primrose Day': wood engraving featuring the statue of Disraeli in Parliament Square by W. Saull, 1886 (*National Portrait Gallery, London*)

TIMELINE

Date	General happenings	What happened to Disraeli
1804		Born on 21 December at 6 King's Road, Bedford Row, Holborn
1805	Battle of Trafalgar	
1815	Battle of Waterloo	
1817		Baptised into Church of England at St Andrew's, Holborn
1817–19		Attends Higham Hall School, Epping
1821		Articled as a solicitors' clerk
1824		Tours Low Countries with Isaac D'Israeli
		Writes pamphlets promoting South American mining shares
1825–6		Embarks on publishing venture with John Murray, *The Representative*
1826		Publishes first novel, *Vivian Grey*
		The Representative ceases publication
1826–9		Suffers a nervous breakdown, 'devoured by an ambition I did not see any means of gratifying'
1829–30		Writes *The Young Duke*
1830–31		Tours Near East with William Meredith and James Clay
1832	Great Reform Act	Stands as a Radical in High Wycombe but defeated

Date	General happenings	What happened to Disraeli
1832		Publishes *Contarini Fleming*
		Stands for a second time in High Wycombe, defeated again
1833		Publishes *Alroy*
1833–6		Embarks on affair with Henrietta Sykes, the inspiration for D's novel, *Henrietta Temple*
1834	Peel issues Tamworth Manifesto	Defeated for a third time in High Wycombe
		Becomes protégé of Lord Lyndhurst
1835		Fights Taunton as an independent Tory; defeated
		Challenges Daniel O'Connell's son to a duel
		Publishes *Vindication of the English Constitution*
1836		Writes 'The Letters of Runnymede' in *The Times*
		Elected to the Carlton Club
1837	Queen Victoria ascends throne	Publishes *Venetia*
		Elected as Member of Parliament for Maidstone; makes disastrous maiden speech
1839		Marries Mary Anne Lewis, widow of his former Maidstone colleague Wyndham Lewis
1841	Peel wins general election	D asks Peel for a place in Government
		Elected Member of Parliament for Shrewsbury
1842		Becomes leader of Young England group
1844		Publishes *Coningsby*
1845		Publishes *Sybil*
1846	Peel proposes Repeal of the Corn Laws	D leads onslaught on the Prime Minister, the 'burglar of others' intellect'

Date	General happenings	What happened to Disraeli
1847		Publishes *Tancred*
		Becomes Member of Parliament for Buckinghamshire
		Speaks in favour of Jewish Emancipation, 'Where is your Christianity if you do not believe in their Judaism?'
1848	Isaac D'Israeli dies	Purchases Hughenden Manor
1849		Becomes leader of the Conservatives in the House of Commons
1851		Publishes life of Lord George Bentinck
1852	Derby forms first minority Conservative Government (February)	D appointed Chancellor of the Exchequer
	Lord Aberdeen forms coalition Government (December)	D says that England does not love coalitions
1854–6	Crimean War	
1855	Palmerston becomes Prime Minister	
1857	Indian Mutiny	
1858–9	Derby forms second minority Government	D appointed Chancellor of the Exchequer again
1859	Italian Question	
1861–5	American Civil War	
1861	Death of Prince Albert	
1863		Inherits substantial legacy from Mrs Brydges Williams of Torquay
1865	Palmerston dies	
1866	Derby forms third minority Government	D appointed Chancellor for a third time
1867	Second Reform Act	D passes the Second Reform Act
1868		Becomes Prime Minister; 'I have climbed to the top of the greasy pole'

Date	General happenings	What happened to Disraeli
1868		Loses general election, but secures peerage for Mary Anne
1868–74	Gladstone as Prime Minister	
1870		Publishes *Lothair*
1872		Calls Government 'a range of exhausted volcanoes'
		Mary Anne dies
1873		Begins correspondence with Lady Bradford and Lady Chesterfield
1874		Wins large majority in general election and becomes Prime Minister again
1875	Government passes Public Health Act, two Trade Union Acts and Artisans Dwellings Act	D secures purchase of Suez Canal Company shares
1876	Queen Victoria becomes Empress of India	Becomes Earl of Beaconsfield
	Gladstone denounces Turkish atrocities in Bulgaria	These are dismissed by D as 'coffee house babble'
1877	Russia declares war on Turkey	D urges action to forestall Russia
1878	Congress of Berlin	From which D returns saying he has secured 'peace with honour'
1879	Zulus destroy British army at Isandlwana	
	Afghans massacre British delegation at Kabul	
1880	Tories trounced in general election	Leaves Downing Street for last time
		Publishes *Endymion*
1881	The myth of D begins	Dies (19 April)

INTRODUCTION

There are eighty-eight quotations by Benjamin Disraeli in the *Oxford Dictionary of Quotations*. Gladstone has twenty; Churchill just over fifty; there are a mere six by Sir Robert Peel. Like a supplier of greetings cards, Disraeli provides a message for every occasion. 'England does not love coalitions'; 'I have climbed to the top of the greasy pole'; 'A Conservative Government is an organised hypocrisy'; 'In a progressive country, change is constant'; 'A range of exhausted volcanoes'; 'Peace with Honour'; 'The Right Honourable Gentleman caught the Whigs bathing, and walked away with their clothes'.

Disraeli was not only the most quotable Prime Minister. Along with Churchill, he was one of only two who wrote novels – including a number written at the very peak of his career. Although these novels are now almost forgotten, for many years they were read widely and some were bestsellers. Disraeli's first novel, *Vivian Grey*, is thought to have been an inspiration for Oscar Wilde's *The Picture of Dorian Gray*. *Sybil, or The Two Nations*, which Disraeli wrote in the 1840s, was turned into a silent film in the 1920s. The £10,000 Disraeli received for *Endymion*, his last novel, published in 1880, was the largest sum ever advanced for a work of fiction.*

*The Bank of England inflation calculator tells us that £10,000 in 1880 would be worth around £1 million today.

And yet, for all this outpouring of words and ideas, one question remains, much discussed but never fully answered: how was it that Disraeli, a bankrupt Jewish school dropout and trashy novelist, came to exert such a hold on the Victorian Conservative Party, a hold which has stretched through to the present day?

At first, the record seems clear. In writing about the gulf between rich and poor in his novels, Disraeli inspired the idea of modern, compassionate, One Nation Conservatism. By passing the Second Reform Act, Disraeli paved the way for a new era of 'Tory Democracy'. Eventually, Disraeli became the first (and only) Jewish Prime Minister of this country. In delivering the first Tory majority for thirty years in 1874, Disraeli brought the modern Conservative Party into being. Once in government, Disraeli presided over a range of important social reforms, including the 1875 Public Health Act. At the Congress of Berlin in 1878, Disraeli scored a famous triumph, averting war and greatly enhancing British prestige. His rivalry with the Liberal Prime Minister, William Gladstone, was one of the great dramas of nineteenth-century politics, in which Disraeli built his reputation as a masterful Parliamentarian who repeatedly 'dished the Whigs'. He made Victoria Empress of India and became her favourite Prime Minister.

But on examination, none of these achievements is quite what it seems. Disraeli was not by any standard a One Nation Conservative; he rejected the idea of a more classless society. Nor was he a believer in mass democracy; the Second Reform Act was for Disraeli a way of regaining momentum for the Conservatives. Disraeli's Jewish origins were for him a matter of great personal pride throughout his career, but his views on race and religion were far from straightforward and he had been baptised as an Anglican before he was thirteen. Disraeli was hailed as the Conservative Party's saviour when he died in 1881, but he had himself broken the Party in the 1840s. It is true that his Government implemented important social reforms during the 1870s, but Disraeli had no hand in them and fell asleep when they were discussed in Cabinet.

In foreign policy, Disraeli achieved great popularity and made many rousing speeches, but his policies had a negligible impact on the balance of power. Although Disraeli is known for his rivalry with Gladstone, for a long time at the start of his career he was more obsessed with destroying his own Party leader, Robert Peel. He may have ended his career as Queen Victoria's favourite Prime Minister, yet in his own life Disraeli never behaved like a Victorian at all.

So what should we make of him? Many admirable books have been written about Disraeli. Any biographer must owe a debt to Robert Blake for his Life published in 1966. In wise, balanced and calm judgement he excels. Likewise, the work carried out by Disraeli's official biographers, William Monypenny and George Buckle, in the early twentieth century has been the foundation of much fine scholarship; their six volumes are almost an encyclopaedia of Disraeli's speeches and writings. We do not try to match or replace these scholars. We have a different purpose: we are struck by the extraordinary potency of the myth which surrounds Disraeli's career. How was it that Disraeli's career, remarkable but erratic, has become the subject of such an extravagant posthumous mythology?

Of course, to brand something as a myth is not to pass judgement on its truth or falsity. It is simply a way of describing how an idea or an individual surrounds itself with a cloud of rhetoric, some true, some false, which sustains it over the years and allows it to live longer and attract more followers than ideas and individuals which have no accompanying rhetoric. Such a myth surrounds Disraeli perhaps more thickly than any other politician of the last two hundred years.

For example, Disraeli was the only Prime Minister to be the focus of a posthumous political organisation, the Primrose League, which elaborately preserved his memory for over a century and at its peak in 1910 had two million members. Disraeli was also the hero of one of the first full-length talking pictures, *Disraeli*, starring George Arliss, in 1929. And within the world of Westminster politics, Disraeli's record of words and deeds came together after his death in a myth which he would have found delicious because of its irony. Every leader of the Conservative Party since Disraeli has worshipped at his shrine. Disraeli has been, and still is, hailed as the author of Tory Democracy, the original One Nation Conservative, a champion of Empire, the supreme parliamentary tactician, the maker of the modern Conservative Party and the most socially progressive Prime Minister of the nineteenth century. Indeed, in a 2005 *Weekly Standard* article the American writer David Gelernter pinned Disraeli up as a nineteenth-century neo-Conservative who invented modern Conservatism.

It appears that his influence now also stretches to the Labour Party. In October 2012, the Leader of the Opposition, Ed Miliband, delivered a panegyric to Disraeli in Manchester. 'You know 140 years ago, another Leader of the Opposition gave a speech,' he told the Labour Conference. 'It was in the Free Trade Hall that used to stand opposite this building. It's the Radisson now by the way. His name was Benjamin Disraeli. He was a Tory. But don't let that put you off, just for a minute ... let us remember what Disraeli was celebrated for. It was a vision of Britain. A vision of a Britain where patriotism, loyalty, dedication to the common cause courses through the veins of all and nobody feels left out. It was a vision of Britain coming together to overcome the challenges we faced. Disraeli called it "One Nation".'*

This is plain rubbish. Disraeli never used the phrase 'One Nation'. He held few principles which he was not ready to alter for the sake of immediate tactical gain. Nor did he advocate a national coming-together to overcome the challenges Britain faced. Adversarial politics, not consensus politics, was what ran through Disraeli's veins. Moreover, in Disraeli's personal life, the negative side of the ledger is piled particularly high. He married for money after abandoning women who adored him. He was persistently careless with the truth, for example inventing for himself a line of ancestry which had nothing to do with reality. He plunged into debts which he had no hope of paying. He mocked sycophants and toadies yet was won over by compliments and flattery. Added to all this is the oddity of the accolade that Disraeli was the greatest Leader of the Opposition who ever existed, yet he lost six general elections as a leader of the Party and won only one.

In these ways and others, it is easy enough without exaggeration to make the case against Disraeli. We have looked at each of the accusations and acquitted Disraeli of none. Yet at the core there remains a quality which explains the myth. In truth Disraeli's legacy is not political but personal. He was tolerant in an age when intolerance was normal. He was marvellously witty at a time when pomposity was treated as a

---

*The subject has since become the focus of much political knockabout. The day after Ed Miliband's speech, John Prescott was asked for his views on Disraeli. 'Who the hell is Disraeli?' he replied. One week later, the Prime Minister delivered an airy counter-attack: Labour were not the One Nation party but 'the one notion party – more borrowing'. Meanwhile, William Hague invented a new myth about Disraeli. He said: 'Disraeli believed in fiscal discipline . . . He was no deficit spender, but was careful to budget for a surplus.' Unfortunately, as we shall see, this is not the full story.

virtue. He emphasised the importance of individual and national character when others were concerned with the details of legislation. He made, and still makes, politics exciting to people who otherwise find it dull. He was imaginative to excess, and unstintingly brave.

This point about imagination is vital. Disraeli believed it was the guiding political quality. He rejected the spirit of the Victorian age, with its emphasis on science, technology, progress and steady reasoning. Disraeli preferred more ethereal forces – faith, religion, the social utility of belief. He despised the mathematical or utilitarian approach to politics. He attacked those who mistook comfort for civilisation. In his view real civilisation required deeper roots. A nation to be worthy of the name will build on its own history, customs and creed.

Here too the paradox reveals itself. Disraeli was not a religious man; he was a practising Anglican but it is hard to pin down any specific religious belief. In the ordinary coming and going of daily life he was a sceptic. He despised Gladstone's self-righteous, ostentatiously religious manner. He saw through the pretensions behind which most men concealed their ambition. Yet Disraeli argued that religion lay at the heart of the human spirit. His speeches and writings are full of phrases about the power of faith to heal the nation's ills.

Disraeli disliked intellectuals, but in his mind he developed a set of powerful ideas. They were like a collection of silver, proudly displayed, constantly polished, often added to, but only occasionally used in the course of daily life. His ideas were eccentric in the literal sense; they were distinct from the day-to-day activities of his political career. Every now and then Disraeli opened this storehouse, took out a handful of ideas and tested them as creatures of fiction or as deft phrases for a speech. After carefully perfecting and buffing them, Disraeli put the ideas back in the cupboard for another day.

In 1874, as Prime Minister of his country and now at last with a large majority in Parliament, Disraeli finally had the opportunity to test his ideas, not as literary characters, but in real life. He was tired and old by now, but he did his best. Sadly the six years of power which he was given were not enough to prove what he preached about the underlying character of the British people. He failed to establish Britain as a new Oriental power. He did not regenerate the aristocracy. There was no return to chivalry. He did not bridge the gap between rich and poor. When the general election came round in 1880 the British people rejected Disraeli and returned Gladstone to Downing Street.

If you had asked Disraeli what he had achieved during his political career, he would have diverted you, with a smile, by selecting an epigram from his cupboard of ideas. If pressed, he might have mentioned his European diplomacy or the crucial vote in the House of Commons where he had smashed the Opposition. He would not produce a list of legislative achievements as Gladstone would have done or indeed as almost every Prime Minister has done since. Disraeli did not deal in that currency unless he had to. It was enough that he had made the Queen Empress of India and that he had snapped up a decisive handful of the Suez Canal shares for her Government. The prestige of Britain was thus enhanced and, for him, prestige was the currency of politics.

Disraeli fooled many into quoting his words to keep his memory alive. In this bewildering modern world there will always be those who echo his words and claim to uphold his principles. We have called our book *Disraeli, or The Two Lives* because the life he lived was markedly different from the myths he left behind. These contradictions do not mean that he was phoney. At the heart of Disraeli's beliefs lay the thought that imagination and courage are the indispensable components of political greatness for an individual or a nation. That conviction, rather than any particular Bill, book, speech, treaty or quotation, is the true legacy of Benjamin Disraeli.

THE FUNERAL

It took three and a half hours for news of Disraeli's death to reach Gladstone at home in Flintshire. Memories of past conflicts must have crowded in. As Prime Minister, Gladstone now found himself leading a nation in mourning for a man he had detested. He at once sent a telegram offering his rival a public funeral.

The competition was over. In the months before his death on 19 April 1881, Lord Beaconsfield had been only a shadow of the Benjamin Disraeli who had destroyed Gladstone's mentor Peel and routed Gladstone himself in the battles round the Reform Bill of 1867. Something remained of the sense of humour and malice which had made Disraeli in his prime so formidable. But that remnant of ancient skill had latterly been reserved for conversation with old ladies at fashionable dinner tables rather than great speeches in the Commons or Lords. Gladstone at the age of seventy-one had been granted the gift denied to his rival, namely enduring physical strength. Gladstone cannot have felt any real grief at the news of Disraeli's death; the bitterness between the two men had been too strong. But the disappearance of his rival created a gap in Gladstone's life. A landmark, unloved but familiar, had been swept away.

The offer of a public funeral must have seemed a natural response. Convention would be respected and due honour paid to a remarkable man. Moreover, Disraeli had been noted for his respect for outward form and dignity. He would surely have relished the idea of a hushed, appreciative crowd gathered round his final appearance in London, providing a last theatrical gesture at the close of an essentially theatrical life.

But Gladstone did not know there had been another and simpler side to Disraeli. It had been his custom to wander alone, or with a friend, through the woods of his estate at Hughenden, not armed with an axe like Gladstone at Hawarden, admiring rather than attacking the oaks and beeches. His love of Hughenden was linked to his wife's happiness there and to an earlier letter to him, in which she had hoped that they would rest side by side in the local church. His will left definite instructions to the same effect and his executors did not hesitate in carrying them out.

So he was buried as he wished at Hughenden on 26 April in the presence of the Prince of Wales and an array of old colleagues. Crammed into the small church were all surviving members of Disraeli's last Cabinet except Cranbrook, who was in Italy. Hartington, Harcourt and Rosebery attended as Whigs with whom Disraeli had been friendly. Disraeli's near neighbour in Buckinghamshire, the banker Nathan de Rothschild, was present to pay his respects along with Disraeli's executor Sir Philip Rose and his long-serving Private Secretary, Monty Corry. The Ambassadors of France, Austria, Russia, Germany, Turkey and the United States all travelled from London for the service. Even the 15th Earl of Derby, despite the bitter end to their friendship, took a place in the stalls.

The two notable absentees were Gladstone and the Queen. The Prime Minister, keen to avoid an occasion at which he would have been conspicuous for the wrong reasons, claimed, absurdly, that he was prevented by the business of his office. The Queen respected the rule which prevented her attending the funeral of a subject, but she had every intention of playing her part. Four days after the funeral she drove through the nearby town of Penn on her way to pay royal respects at Hughenden. She organised her own tribute in the form of a marble monument with the following inscription:

To the dear and honoured memory of Benjamin,
Earl of Beaconsfield,
This memorial is placed by his grateful Sovereign
and Friend, Victoria R.I.
'Kings love him that speaketh right.'
Proverbs XVI. 13
27 February 1882.

Gladstone found the very simplicity of the occasion offensive. He remarked to his secretary Edward Hamilton: 'as he lived so he died – all display, without reality or genuineness'.

The Prime Minister's opinion was not widely shared, and he himself concealed it when the time came for parliamentary tributes after the Easter recess. But in death, as in life, ambiguity clouded discussion of Disraeli's life and career. What was it that the nation had lost?

If you had asked members of the congregation why they had gathered to say goodbye to Disraeli you would have gleaned many answers, all different and all true. He himself would have denied, with a smile which was half an admission, that the different facets of his character contradicted one another. But the combination was highly unusual, indeed unique.

Some would pick out, as Lord Salisbury would do later in his tribute to Disraeli in the House of Lords, the passionate concern for the prestige of his country. 'Zeal for the greatness of England was the passion of his life,' Salisbury observed. 'The people of this country recognised the force with which this desire dominated his actions, and they repaid it by an affection and reverence which did not depend on and had no concern with opinions as to the particular policy pursued.' To Disraeli national prestige was something definite and very practical. It could be obtained by military force, but that was a crude method, and clever, far-sighted men could do better. A bold speech, a deft phrase, a secret summit, a subtle gesture were the chosen tools of Disraeli's diplomacy. They provided the foundation of a myth which became mightier than the man.

Others such as Lord John Manners, his Cabinet colleague and political comrade, would remember Disraeli for the flamboyant rhetoric of the Young England movement and the entertainment provided by his novels – ranging from the boyish extravagances of *Vivian Grey* and *Contarini Fleming*, through to *Coningsby* and *Sybil* with their scathing attack on Peel's Conservatism, before ripening into the reflective fruits of his maturity in *Lothair* and *Endymion*.

To another group, Disraeli was noted as a social reformer who had defended the Chartists and whose Government had encouraged the growth of trade unions. They remembered his words about a country divided into two nations, the rich and the poor. If pushed they might mention some Act passed by his Government to improve public health or support slum clearance. The details were hazy, but the impulse was there.

To others again he was first and foremost the Party leader who outmanoeuvred Gladstone and steered through the Second Reform Act in 1867. Disraeli had proclaimed the importance of Party and Party unity as the necessary foundation of modern politics. Most of those attending Disraeli's funeral were therefore bound to him by ties of loyalty and affection. To them he was 'the Chief', the leader of a great party who had earned his position the hard way through more than thirty years of arduous slog.

To Nathan Rothschild, Disraeli had been a champion of the Jewish race and indeed a remarkable friend to his own family, risking his career by supporting the right of Jews to sit in the House of Commons. Paradoxically, Disraeli had based his argument not on the liberal case for tolerance and equality but on the bolder, more controversial claim that the Jews were in effect a superior race by virtue of their consistent faith and privileged role in the Old and New Testaments: 'Where is your Christianity if you do not believe in their Judaism?' he had asked the Commons in December 1847.

There was some truth in all these claims to fame, though they sat uneasily side by side. Disraeli made no pretence to consistency. Since politics was always a matter of chance and circumstance, it was not reasonable to expect a rigid consistency. A leader, even a Prime Minister, could not be expected to pursue a steady, unwavering course. On his way to the top Disraeli had become a master of manoeuvre and eloquent prevarication.

Even the most loyal supporters knew that Disraeli had many enemies, and even loyal supporters retained the residue of doubt. Lord Salisbury was the most famous of these doubters, but he was not alone. Even those who most genuinely mourned him acknowledged that there were characteristics of Disraeli and events in his past which raised question marks over his reputation. Gladstone was the leading, but not the only, sceptic.

So far as could be seen Disraeli had emerged into the public gaze by two devices pursued in parallel. He had written a number of novels which verged on the scurrilous; and he had launched himself into politics without clear allegiance to either of the two main parties. Any principled choice had been obscured by the overwhelming need for self-advertisement. So he had set himself to destroy Peel, the man with whom he had pleaded for a place in the Government, in order to make a name for himself. Having put himself at the head of those who opposed Peel on the repeal of the Corn Laws, he made no effort to return to Protection when he had the opportunity to do so. Having deserted his followers on this issue, he repeated the unfairness by imposing on them the Reform Bill of 1867 which ran against the principles which the Tories had consistently proclaimed over the years.

Even in foreign policy, where Disraeli had found greatest fame, it was not entirely clear what it was that he had achieved by his diplomacy. Certainly Lord Derby, who had been his Foreign Secretary, believed that Disraeli's foreign policy had been an elaborate, indeed a dangerous, sham.

This was a formidable indictment to which many critics added underlying dislike and distrust of the man and his methods. Of his wit and cleverness there could be no doubt, but for many these qualities increased their distrust. Anthony Trollope for example talked about Disraeli's wit as that of a hairdresser. Another contemporary described how Disraeli belonged 'not to the bees but to the wasps and butterflies of public work. He can sting and sparkle but he cannot work.' The great historian J.A. Froude wrote a critical biography which concluded: 'perhaps no public man in England ever rose so high and acquired power so great, so little of whose work has survived him'.

Yet the myth of Disraeli outlived and soared above such criticism. For his own party, Disraeli provided a necessary point of reference together with a flow of quotable remarks which no one in his century could match. Indeed by 1881 Disraeli, in any number of guises, had become indispensable to the Tories. As Salisbury wrote, 'he has been so long associated with the Tory Party, and of late his popularity has risen so much that the party will hardly believe in its existence without him'.

So the question lodged in the minds of Salisbury and his

Conservative colleagues as they gathered for the funeral was unsettling: what could glue the Conservative Party together now that Disraeli was gone? The solution to this conundrum came inadvertently from the Queen.

Covering the coffin that day in April 1881 was a wreath of primroses from the Queen's family home on the Isle of Wight, Osborne House. It carried a dedication in the Queen's hand which referred to 'his favourite flower'. No one actually heard Disraeli use these words to the Queen, but it is likely enough. He was a chronic abuser of superlatives. In his lifetime Disraeli had commended any number of flowers with similar praise. Nonetheless, it was true that when the Queen used to send Disraeli flowers each year to celebrate the arrival of spring, his letters of thanks more than once picked out the primrose as deserving special mention. For example in his letter of 28 March 1878, Disraeli paid the primrose a typically ornate compliment: 'Some bright bands of primroses have visited him today, which he thinks shows that Your Majesty's sceptre has touched the Enchanted Isle.' And on another occasion: 'He likes the primroses so much better for their being wild; they seem an offering from the Fauns and Dryads of the woods of Osborne.' The choice of a simple, fragile, English flower might surprise those who more readily associated Disraeli with some exotic bloom; he also referred to roses in a rather similar way; but no one presumed to question the judgement of the Queen Empress.

A year later, a senior official at the India Office named Sir George Birdwood wrote a letter to *The Times* which caught the popular imagination. After noting a sharp increase in the orders for primroses placed with West End florists ahead of the first anniversary of Disraeli's death, he went on: 'The purpose of my letter ... is ... to place on open record the small beginnings of what may gradually grow into a settled popular custom, more honouring in its simple, unbought loyalty

to Lord Beaconsfield's memory, and more truly English, than
the proudest monument of bronze or marble that could be
raised to his name.'

It later emerged that Sir George himself had contributed to
the increased sale of primroses. He also encountered pockets
of dissent. Neither the Carlton Club nor St Stephen's Club
displayed primroses that April. Predictably, Gladstone was
suspicious. He questioned whether Disraeli had any particular fondness for the primrose. 'The glorious lily, I think,
was more to his taste.' Doubts were stifled as the primrose
quickly became the emblem of Disraeli's life and convictions.
19 April became known as Primrose Day.

The cult of the primrose now began to attract attention
from the leadership of the Conservative Party. In 1883 a
row broke out over the new statue of Disraeli in Parliament
Square. Lord Randolph Churchill, a mercurial Tory, criticised
the choice of Sir Stafford Northcote, leader of the Conservatives in the House of Commons, to pronounce the oration
at the unveiling on Primrose Day. This was part of his campaign to denigrate Northcote and exalt his preferred choice
as leader of the Party, Lord Salisbury. He walked home from
the Commons that day in the company of his friend and ally
Sir Henry Drummond Wolff, who happened to remark that
every Conservative MP had worn primroses in the Chamber. Wolff suggested that the Party should start a Primrose
League; Lord Randolph encouraged him to draw up a plan.

Lord Randolph was then at the peak of his powers. He was
fast becoming the most popular public speaker of the day. Up
and down the country, he addressed huge audiences of a size
which matched those who heard Gladstone. He slashed at the
fading Liberal Government with an extraordinary mixture
of wit and venom. The political temperature rose sharply
and, with it, the appeal of the new Primrose League as the
meteor of Lord Randolph streaked across the sky. In 1885 it

numbered about 11,000; by 1886 this had risen to 200,000. In 1887, over half a million were enrolled in the League. This was a success without parallel in British political history.

In terms of popularity, Lord Randolph Churchill for a few years looked like Disraeli's natural heir. He shared the latter's wit, political courage and dislike of Gladstone. But the Conservative Party's new hero was wrecked by a combination of ill health and poor judgement. He succeeded in installing Lord Salisbury as the unquestioned leader of the Conservative Party. But he followed this success by picking an argument with Salisbury about the internal constitution of the Party. This was ground which Salisbury could not yield. Salisbury found it more and more difficult to work alongside Lord Randolph, whom he had made Chancellor of the Exchequer in August 1886. When Lord Randolph tried to force the issue by resigning he found to his great surprise that the Prime Minister accepted his resignation and had a new Chancellor ready and willing. Lord Randolph's meteor then fell rapidly from the sky. The League was confronted with a choice between its admiration for Lord Randolph and its loyalty to the Party. Without hesitation it chose and practised loyalty to the Party.

The League meanwhile was developing an array of ranks and titles designed to attract a generation brought up on the chivalry of Lord Tennyson's poems. Although the League made a point of appealing to all classes of society, the aristocracy set the pace. Women, still thirty years away from receiving the vote, were from the start prominent in the Primrose League. The first to become President of the Ladies Grand Council was Randolph Churchill's mother, the Dowager Duchess of Marlborough. Women were brought into the mainstream of politics for the first time. Young men and women were encouraged to join and were known as 'primrose buds'. For men, the apex of the hierarchy was the Grand

Master, the first of whom was Lord Salisbury, the last Sir
Alec Douglas-Home. The members of all branches, which
were known as Habitations, were requested to swear the following declaration:

> I declare on my honour and faith that I will devote my best
> ability to the maintenance of Religion, of the Estates of the
> Realm, and of the Imperial Ascendancy of Great Britain; that
> I will keep secret all matters that may come to my knowledge
> as a member of the Primrose Tory League; and that consist-
> ently with my allegiance to the Sovereign of the Realms, I
> will obey all orders coming from the constituted authority of
> the League for the advancement of these objects.

The Statutes of the League included a firm commitment to
campaign for the Conservative cause. It chose as its motto the
Disraeli phrase 'Imperium et Libertas'. A special hymn was
devised for young members:

> Children of the Empire
> Primrose Buds are we,
> Marching ever Marching
> On to Victory.

By 1910, more than two million members had been enrolled
in the League. It was by then the strongest political organisation in the country. The Liberals were envious and looked
for a counterpart, but somehow Gladstone did not fit the bill.
Herbert Gladstone, son of the Grand Old Man, was content to
mock the Primrose League as a snobbish outfit, only suitable
for duchesses and scullery maids. In fact, there was much to
be said for an organisation which brought together, even in
an artificial way, the Upstairs and Downstairs of Victorian
and Edwardian society.

After the Great War the Primrose League faded, but the myth of Disraeli remained and indeed became more powerful in the new century. The League had never established itself as a distinct element within the Party rallying behind a definite policy. Lord Randolph Churchill had made free with the phrase 'Tory Democracy', but had hardly attempted to give it meaning. Now, in the new century, the myth of Disraeli mutated and took on more immediately political overtones.

The high priest of this process was Stanley Baldwin. In December 1924, in a speech at the Albert Hall, Baldwin used a phrase which had never been uttered by Disraeli. 'I want to see the spirit of service to the whole nation the birthright of every member of the Unionist Party – Unionist in the sense that we stand for the union of those two nations of which Disraeli spoke two generations ago: union among our own people to make one nation of our own people at home which, if secured, nothing else matters in the world.' The reference to national unity made sense at a time when Britain faced deep social difficulties. But the words 'one nation' had never appeared in Disraeli's lexicon and certainly had never been developed as a meaningful political creed.

None of this mattered to Baldwin or indeed other Conservatives in search of ideas in these years. Baldwin contrived to develop and refine these arguments during the 1920s. 'One Nation' Conservatism became associated with social welfare and industrial relations. In his first speech as Prime Minister, Baldwin invoked Disraeli to lend credibility to his party's progressive credentials: 'We were fighting the battle of the factory hand long before he had the vote ... we were speaking in favour of the combination of working men, long before the Liberals had thought of the subject. It is more than 50 years ago that Disraeli was calling the attention of the country to housing and health questions.'

The idea soon took on a life of its own. For Lord Birkenhead and later R.A. Butler, Disraeli was a useful ally in the world of the Welfare State and the General Strike, in part because of Disraeli's policies on trade unions and factory reform. Thus Birkenhead wrote, preposterously, that 'if Providence could have made Disraeli a dictator in the early thirties, there would have been no social problem today'. Later, in 1950, Enoch Powell and others set up a dining club called the One Nation Group. In one of his first speeches in the Commons, Powell spoke admiringly of Disraeli's second Government, referring to 'the constellation of acts which made that administration a landmark in the social history of this country'.

The attraction between ambitious young Conservatives and the life of Disraeli was driven by the supply of ready artillery provided in his novels. Harold Macmillan wrote in his diary for 9 July 1943: 'It is curious how each generation in turn turns out with the sort of Young England idea. Disraeli left a great mark on England, and I am interested to find that the young men in the Tory Party now read his novels and study his life with the same enthusiasm as we did thirty years ago.' For a party which lagged behind Labour in numbers of university academics and fashionable intellectuals, Disraeli offered a supply of credible, and quotable, Conservative counter-beliefs. As Baldwin had said in the 1930s, 'I am quite sure that all those who look back, as every Tory must look back, to Disraeli for inspiration will never be afraid to go forward.'

Certainly, Disraeli's words breathed warmth and imagination into the prosaic world of twentieth-century politics. But his continued relevance cannot simply be explained by the quality of his quotations. Besides, Disraeli's usefulness was not limited to the Conservatives. As the British economy ground to a halt in the 1970s, Margaret Thatcher and a new generation of Tories abandoned Disraeli, allegedly an advocate of state intervention and public spending, in favour of the more modern discipline of monetarism. For Margaret Thatcher herself, there were also presentational problems. 'Disraeli's style was too ornate for my taste,' she wrote later, 'although I can see why it may have appealed to Harold Macmillan.' Subsequently, Disraeli became a code word for dissension from Thatcherite orthodoxies during the 1980s. In July 1982, the unsuccessful Labour candidate in the Beaconsfield by-election, Tony Blair, wrote a letter of protest to Michael Foot.* 'My opponent at Beaconsfield, in his speech of thanks to the Returning Officer quoted some lines of Disraeli. What was remarkable was that the Tory supporters present were completely disinterested in it [sic]. Not a cheer or a shout. There were even the rumblings of a suppressed jeer. The Tory Party is now increasingly given over to the worst of petty bourgeois sentiment – the thought that there is something clever in cynicism: realistic in selfishness; and the granting of legitimacy to the barbaric idea of the survival of the fittest.'

But it was not simply Labour politicians who referred wistfully back to Disraeli. His memory continued to be deployed by Conservatives who questioned the intensity and inflexibility of Margaret Thatcher's policies. Indeed, in a 1994 poll of Conservative MPs, Disraeli came top as the most popular source of inspiration, reflecting the shift away from Thatcherism within John Major's Conservative Party.

After the collapse of the Conservative Government in the 1997 general election, and three subsequent failed election campaigns, Disraeli was exhumed again. For a party searching for an identity, Disraeli seemed a useful starting point. After all, so the argument went, was not Disraeli the greatest Leader of the Opposition who had ever lived? Had he not invented One Nation Conservatism?

---

*In a parallel act of protest, Michael Foot named his pet dog 'Dizzy'.

In particular, it was the way in which Disraeli had managed to charm and persuade his party into adopting the centre ground which held greatest appeal for those now seeking to reinvent it. In 2007, following David Cameron's election as Conservative leader, Michael Portillo explained the changes he was making by invoking Disraeli. 'There is no shame in adapting,' he wrote. 'Parties that fail to evolve become extinct. In 1867 the Tories had already endured twenty-one years in the political wilderness. Widening the franchise was the issue of the day, and the Conservatives were known to be against it. But their leader, Benjamin Disraeli, took advantage of a brief spell as Prime Minister in a minority government to go well beyond even what his Liberal opponents were proposing, and gave the vote for the first time to many working-class men. The move was counter-intuitive and audacious. The Tories still had to wait till 1874 to enjoy a majority but Disraeli's "new" Conservatives had shed their reactionary image and were back in the political game. Cameron understands that history well.' David Cameron himself put Disraeli on a pedestal. 'My favourite political quote is by Disraeli,' Mr Cameron explained; 'he said the Conservative Party should be the party of change but change that goes along with the customs and manners and traditions and sentiments of the people rather than change according to some grand plan.'

And so the Conservatives persuaded themselves of the case for change again. Today, Disraeli is being flung into the debate on bankers' bonuses, with the Prime Minister invoking him as the author of responsible capitalism ('the idea of social responsibility is not a new departure for my party ... Under Disraeli, it led to the Factory Acts, which began to set working conditions'), and Ed Miliband arguing for a new 'one nation' banking ('We need banking serving every region, every sector, every business, every family in this country').

The myth of Disraeli continues to offer a seemingly inexhaustible supply of words, images, phrases and ideas which qualify him for entry into modern politics. There is no doubt that successive leaders will continue to quote him and seek to follow the example set by those quotations.

How is it that Disraeli has gained such a place in the political pantheon? Neither Pitt, nor Peel, nor Palmerston nor indeed any subsequent Prime Minister except perhaps Churchill has become the focus of such a posthumous mythology. The blurring of edges began early. The statues of Lord Beaconsfield which still stand in our squares are of the stately and heavily robed eminent Victorian statesman, not the foppish young Disraeli or the thrusting but frustrated politician of his middle age. But there Lord Beaconsfield stands in Parliament Square and market places and village halls across the country, impassive and dignified, with no hint of controversy in his stance or humour in his eye. Our aim in writing this book is not to pull down the solemn statues, for they have a firm foundation, but to explore the mystery of how the myth grew so strongly from the life of the man.

What would Disraeli himself make of it all? Without any flicker of emotion, he perhaps would pick out two skills which separated him from others in politics. The first was imagination. Neither at home nor abroad could Disraeli when in office realise the dreams which fill his novels. But the dreams survived the disappointment. Dreams are particularly important for a political party which prides itself on being practical and hard-headed. As Ian Gilmour once wrote: 'Disraeli was one of the few Tory leaders who has been able to bring warmth to Conservatism and to add to its basic common sense a degree of romance, generosity and excitement.' At the time of Disraeli's death, the Conservative Party was entering a period in which it was closely allied with the array of tough businessmen which multiplied under Victorian capitalism. The Forsytes were in the ascendant. Dreams were needed to breathe life into this more mechanical politics.

The Left are natural dreamers, and so they have a ready supply of heroes. Their supporters tend to believe in the perfectibility of man. For them, the role of the politician is to pursue elaborate schemes so that man might fulfil his destiny. The Conservative by contrast has no such illusions. Left to himself, he is likely to degenerate into selfishness and anarchy. There is no beneficent Whig tide carrying him forward to a better future. Institutions are needed to channel man's energy into areas where it may do good rather than harm. For the Conservative, the state is a regrettable necessity, but the ideal society relies to a great extent on voluntary effort and the natural coming-together of like-minded people. But this can become a dreary, plodding concept when set against the prospect of a New Jerusalem. Something more is needed and that something is what Disraeli offers. Disraeli infused his party and indeed the whole political profession with a sense of greatness, as a theatre where remarkable things could be achieved. That is what Stafford Northcote meant when he said after Disraeli's death, 'the sun has been taken out of our political system'.

For the second skill, Disraeli might, without any hint of irony, have directed you towards Gladstone or, more precisely, to the tribute Gladstone gave Disraeli in the House of Commons a few weeks after his death. This was a difficult ordeal for Gladstone. He had been ill for several days previously and was coming under heavy criticism for his failure to attend Disraeli's funeral. He needed to find a way of commending his opponent which maintained credibility. After agonising for several days, he selected as a quality for praise a characteristic that was central to Disraeli's career: courage.

In the Chamber, Gladstone spoke with sincerity. 'There

were certain great qualities of the deceased statesman that I think it is right to dwell upon,' he told the House. 'They were qualities not only written in a marked manner on his career, but possessed by him in a degree undoubtedly extra-ordinary. I speak, for example, of his strength of will; his long-sighted persistency of purpose, reaching from his first entrance upon the avenue of life to its very close; his re-markable power of self-government; and last, but not least of all, his great parliamentary courage – a quality in which I, who have been associated in the course of my life with some scores of Ministers, have, I think, never known but two whom I could pronounce his equal.' Disraeli would have appreciated and agreed with the assessment. All his life, Dis-raeli displayed courage. It was the courage of the outsider who believed himself worthy of a remarkable career.

CHRISTIAN AND JEW

On 31 July 1817 the Reverend Thomas Thimbleby of St Andrew's Church Holborn took without knowing it a step with momentous consequences for British political history. He baptised into the Christian faith a curly-haired twelve-year-old called Benjamin Disraeli. He thus opened the door for Disraeli's entry into political life that would otherwise have been barred by the law. Little is known about the circumstances of this decision by Benjamin's father and nothing at all of Benjamin's own attitude to the event. Voluble and explicit on most events in his life, Disraeli wrote nothing at all about one of the most important. For the rest of his life he joined, not fervently but consistently, in the life of a practising Anglican, taking Communion at regular intervals and abandoning the Jewish faith into which he had been born.

Seen from a distance, the decision by Disraeli's father Isaac to take his son out of the religion which he and his ancestors had practised for centuries appears a radical, indeed a traumatic step. But Isaac D'Israeli was not given to ostentatious dramatic gestures. He was known for his warmth and geniality, and was anxious always to avoid unnecessary conflict. Throughout his life, Isaac showed no appetite for the noisy encounters of everyday existence. Business and politics held no attraction for him. 'Nature had disqualified him, from his cradle, for the busy pursuits of men,' Disraeli wrote of his father in a memoir many years later. All surviving evidence supports this verdict.

As a teenager, Isaac D'Israeli had baffled his parents when, after running away from home, he was found lying on a tombstone in Hackney churchyard. His own father, a practical-minded businessman who had made a small fortune from the stock markets after dabbling in the straw bonnet trade, assumed that the correct response to this act of rebellion was to give his son a pony. Later he tried to place Isaac in business at a Bordeaux manufacturing firm. Isaac resisted, explaining that he had written a poem which he planned to publish, 'against commerce which was the corruption of man'.

And so Isaac had embarked on a literary career. Success was brief but early. Aged twenty-five, Isaac published a book called the *Curiosities of Literature*, an agreeable mishmash of anecdotes about literary personalities which ran to twelve editions and was followed by five more volumes in the same style. Thereafter Isaac settled down to life as an assiduous dilettante. With his big brown eyes entombed in round metal spectacles, Isaac spent his mornings pottering about the British Museum, collating fragments of information on thin scraps of paper. His evenings were passed in the comfort of his vast and expanding library at home. It is remarkable how little attention Isaac paid to earthly matters. As Disraeli's biographer William Monypenny points out: 'D'Israeli the elder lived through one of the most stirring periods in the history of the world, yet in all his correspondence there is hardly an allusion to passing events.' Isaac had no firm political allegiances. Indeed he was scathing about political parties, remarking that where there was party there was also deception. But his instincts were patriotic and Tory, and he encouraged in his children a nostalgic affection for the House of Stuart and the Cavaliers.

Propped up by his father's finances and a wife named Maria Basevi, about whom we know surprisingly little, in 1802 Isaac took residence near Holborn in a street called Bedford Row. It was there, at half past five in the morning on Friday 21 December 1804, that Maria gave birth to her eldest son and second child, Benjamin. Two years earlier, she had given birth to a girl named Sarah, and after Benjamin three more boys followed – Napthali, who was born but also died in 1807, Ralph, born in 1809, and James, born in 1813.

What were the prospects for young Benjamin? In later years, Disraeli liked to say that he had been born in a library. This, although not literally true, captures the comfortable, literary environment into which he had been born. After his death, a myth emerged that Disraeli's ascent in British political life represented a triumph of social mobility, a back story of success against the odds. Financially speaking, this story does not work. The year before Disraeli was baptised his grandfather had died leaving the family £35,000 – the equivalent of many millions today. Although not in the same league as a Rothschild or a Goldsmid, the D'Israelis were nonetheless in the upper ranks of London Jewish families, on friendly terms with such names as the Lindos, Mocattas and Montefiores. Backed by relative wealth, Isaac and his family moved to a new and larger house at 6 Bloomsbury Square, cementing their position at the hub of London's literary society.* The publisher John Murray and the Poet Laureate Robert Southey both had places at the D'Israelis' dining table. Whatever trials Disraeli endured during his

---

* Quite by chance, as we were researching this book, we made a trip to Majorca to address the Conservatives Abroad branch and found ourselves seated on the easyJet plane next to a gentleman and his wife who had spent many years working in 6 Bloomsbury Square. Mr and Mrs Charles Durham had met in the import-export company which for a long time had its main offices in Disraeli's old home.

childhood, poverty and social exclusion were not among them.

Rather, the main impediment to Disraeli's progress was the simple fact of his Judaism. Writing many years later, Disraeli described in dramatic terms the situation facing a young Jewish child in nineteenth-century society. 'Instead of joyousness and frank hilarity, anxiety and a shrinking reserve are soon impressed upon the youthful visage. It is the seal of ignominy. The dreadful secret that they are an expatriated and persecuted race is soon revealed to them.' This was certainly an exaggeration in Disraeli's own case. Some 20,000 Jews lived in England in the early nineteenth century out of a total population of ten million. This was a smaller community than that in either Germany or France, but by most standards it was freer and more mobile. Persecution was rare, but discrimination still apparent. In the early nineteenth century a Jewish man could own land and trade in most professions. He could not however practise law, teach except in private schools, or serve as a magistrate or judge.

In one profession in particular, being Jewish meant the door swung shut at the entrance. Anyone elected as a Member of Parliament had to swear an oath of allegiance 'on the true faith of a Christian' before taking their seat. Of course this handicap could be circumvented by those who were prepared to convert to Anglicanism. Sampson Gideon, Sir Manasseh Lopes and David Ricardo all put aside their Judaism and successfully took seats in the House of Commons. But they still faced a society where soft bigotry against Jews, converted or not, was seen as fair game. On the hustings at elections or in *Punch* cartoons they would be mocked and caricatured, often taunted with the cry of 'Ole Clothes'. When Disraeli stood for election at Shrewsbury in 1841 a man arrived on a donkey saying he had come to take Disraeli back to Jerusalem.

All this gave strong grounds for abandoning Judaism and becoming immersed in the advantages of Anglican acceptability. But in Isaac's case the reasons behind his religious rebellion were more intellectual than in other men. Isaac had particular views about Judaism. He later articulated these views in a book called *The Genius of Judaism*, published in 1833. In this book Isaac explained at length why Rabbinic Judaism was a corruption of the true Jewish faith. In particular, he fiercely criticised the social practices and dietary laws through which the Rabbis had isolated their communities. To Isaac, schooled in the Enlightenment and the works of Voltaire, all ceremonial practices were a distraction from the true meaning of religion. The 'infinite multiplicity of customs, and gross superstitions' which the Rabbis perpetuated were 'as ridiculous as once were those of witchcraft'. After praising those Jews who challenged the Rabbinic authorities, Isaac concluded with a call for assimilation and good relations between Judaism and Christianity.

None of this would have been apparent when young Benjamin was a teenager. True, Isaac rarely attended his local synagogue, the Bevis Marks in Aldgate. True also that Isaac's mother had come to despise the religion into which she and her family had been born. But for the most part, Isaac was like many other London Jews, paying his dues, broadly conforming, and abiding by such practices as the circumcision of his three sons.

So when, in October 1813, the authorities of the Bevis Marks wrote to Isaac informing him that he had been elected as Parnass – or Warden – of the congregation, they might have been surprised by the strident reply. First came the refusal: 'I must own I feel surprised that the Mahamâd should nominate a person to this official situation at so late a period of his life [Isaac was not yet fifty]; and had they thought their choice worth a moment's consideration they would have

been aware of its singular impropriety.' Then came the compromise: Isaac would contribute in a limited way to annual
subscriptions, but not get involved any further. He pointed
to a friend, a Mr Prado of Grafton Street, as a precedent for
this approach. But the Elders resisted, insisting that a fine
of £40 would be payable if Isaac declined the position. This
prompted a further exchange of letters. By December Isaac
had gathered full theological steam in mounting his rebellion:

> A person, who has always lived out of the sphere of your
> observation; of retired habits of life; who can never unite in
> your public worship, because as now conducted, it disturbs
> instead of exciting Religious Emotions, a circumstance of gen-
> eral acknowledgement; who has only tolerated some part of
> your Ritual, willing to concede all he can, in those matters
> which he holds to be indifferent; Such a Man, with but a
> moderate portion of Honour and Understanding, never can
> accept the solemn functions of an Elder in your Congregation.

He implored the Elders to change their ways before the entire
congregation left the Synagogue.

> Many of your Members are already lost; Many, you are
> losing; even those whose tempers would still cling to you
> are gradually receding. But against all this, you perpetually
> plead your existing Laws ... Some of you boast that your
> Laws are much as they were a Century ago! You have Laws to
> regulate what has ceased to exist ...

But Isaac's trump card was the threat he now wielded, warning the authorities that if they pursued the matter he would
insist that they removed his name from the Synagogue list.
For a time this seems to have calmed the situation. But two
years later the dispute was still rumbling on. In a fifth letter,

dated 1 November 1815, Isaac took on the Elders once again, arguing that their own Rabbinic laws prevented him from becoming an Elder. Finally in March 1817, four years after Isaac's unwanted election, the Elders resumed their pursuit – and this time Isaac insisted that his name be removed from the Bevis Marks community list. The breach, long impending, was now complete.

And so Isaac and his family entered religious limbo. There they would have stayed had it not been for the intervention, decisive from the point of view of the young Disraeli, of Sharon Turner, a family friend. Turner, a solicitor who had recently written a history of Anglo-Saxon England, lived near the Disraelis in Bloomsbury Square. He seems to have impressed strongly on Isaac D'Israeli that whatever his own personal complaints against organised religion, it did his children no good to be shut off from both the Jewish community and the mainstream Anglican majority. He persuaded Isaac to arrange his children's baptism, which he duly did in the summer of 1817.*

As for Isaac, he was content to live in religious exile, never converting and indeed criticising conversion in *The Genius of Judaism*. He was eventually buried in the churchyard at Bradenham in Buckinghamshire, where he had moved with his family in 1829. The legend among followers of the Reform Judaism movement that Isaac D'Israeli travelled to

---

*It took several years for Isaac to rid himself of the Rabbinic authorities. In October 1821 he discovered that in his fierce theological quarrel he had forgotten to ask the Bevis Marks for his sons' birth certificates. To enrol Disraeli as solicitors' clerk a birth certificate was a necessity. A frosty letter was dispatched to the synagogue. An even frostier reply followed informing Isaac that he owed £100 and 2s to the synagogue; until the debt was paid no certificates would be released. Isaac exploded. Eventually in December a compromise was reached. Isaac made a payment of £17.19.6 through an intermediary in exchange for the birth certificates of his children.

London aged seventy-five to attend the consecration of the new Reform synagogue is a plausible coda to this protracted spiritual crisis.

After Benjamin Disraeli's baptism, his parents decided to enrol him in a new school. His education so far had been scratchy. A stint at a school in Islington run by a woman called Miss Roper had been followed by four years at a place in Blackheath under the care of a nonconformist Minister named John Potticany. At Blackheath, Disraeli had received separate Hebrew lessons on Saturdays and had been excused morning prayers. Both schools were tiny. Indeed it seems that Potticany's school may have closed down around the time that Disraeli left. But now Disraeli, at the age of thirteen, found something different as he was enrolled in a large Unitarian school at Higham Hall near Walthamstow. He described this change in his autobiographical novel *Contarini Fleming*. 'For the first time in my life I was surrounded by struggling and excited beings ... Light laughs, and bitter cries, and deep imprecations, and the deeds of the friendly, the prodigal, and the tyrant, and the exploits of the brave, the graceful, and the gay, and the flying words of native wit, and the pompous sentences of acquired knowledge – how new, how exciting, how wonderful!' That search for excitement and wonder lasted almost to the end of his life.

As it happens, there is scant evidence to suggest that Disraeli found his new school either exciting or wonderful. He lasted less than three years. A Unitarian minister called Eli Cogan ran the establishment and seems to have been relatively capable. Disraeli wrote of Cogan later: 'Nothing was thought of but the two dead languages, but he was an admirable instructor in them as well as a first rate scholar.' But by his own admission Disraeli did not shine at either Latin or Greek. He never rose to the first class at Higham Hall and 'was not eminent even in the second'. By 1820, Disraeli had returned home to Bloomsbury Square and spent the remainder of his school years teaching himself the classics in his father's library. The following year, Disraeli was placed by his father as a solicitors' clerk at a firm in Old Jewry. He was not yet seventeen.

This was not the standard start in life for a Victorian statesman. The early lives of Gladstone, Palmerston, Peel and Stanley all look very different – indeed more like something from *Tom Brown's Schooldays*. In sport, study, social life and even dramatic pursuits, these men carried all before them at one of the leading public schools. Usually they went on to study at Christ Church, Oxford, where Peel and Gladstone achieved Double Firsts. By contrast Disraeli's early life is beset by interruption and mediocrity. Three schools in seven years; none of them prestigious; a mixed academic record – this was not a glittering school career and quite different to that of Disraeli's two younger brothers, who were both sent to study at Winchester.

Why was his early progress so erratic? Disraeli leaves clues in his novels. *Vivian Grey* and *Contarini Fleming* are stories of precocious, talented young men let down by a system which fails to foster their geniuses. In both novels, the heroes get into frenzied, indeed almost fatal, physical conflicts with other pupils in which they beat their opponents to a pulp and are then promptly expelled from school. These fight scenes are described in such detail and with such electricity that the reader is left to suspect that only personal experience could have added such authenticity to the prose. Certainly, we know that Disraeli took boxing lessons as a teenager at home – inspired by Jewish boxing heroes such as Daniel Mendoza.

Were Disraeli's Jewish roots the flashpoint for this feuding? Was he particularly sensitive to anti-Semitic slurs? Two pieces of evidence suggest opposite interpretations. On the one side, we have an anecdote which implies that Disraeli regarded all religion rather casually. On arriving at Higham Hall, Disraeli discovered that those boys who were Anglicans faced an immediate disability, in that the local church was some distance from the school. The boys therefore had to trek long distances on Sunday mornings and were invariably late for lunch and missed much of the food. To Disraeli, who had experience of converting between religions, the solution was perfectly simple: the Anglican students should become Unitarians when they were at school.

The other morsel of information we have from these years creates a contrasting picture. Curiously, the date of Disraeli's baptism is different by a month from that of his two younger brothers. What was the reason for the delay? We cannot know, but Disraeli was certainly ambivalent about his conversion in later years. His novel *Alroy* deals unfavourably with the concept and many years later Disraeli complained: 'I was not bred among my race, and was nurtured in great prejudice against them.'

What is certainly clear is that Disraeli, like his fictional heroes, was a precocious and unsettled youth wrestling with identity issues. He looked different, he felt different; he certainly was superior and unique. But was he a Christian or a Jew? In Disraeli's mind the answer had nothing to do with religion. As a Jew, he faced discrimination, difficulties, a life on the margins of society. As a Christian, he faced the prospect – abhorrent to Disraeli – of becoming the same as everyone else.

Disraeli's solution to this quandary was to turn his unusual identity from a source of uncertainty into a source of immense strength. In 1821 Disraeli, aged sixteen, for the very last time signed his name with an apostrophe before the Israeli. Thereafter he was simply Disraeli, part English, part Italian, simultaneously Christian and Jew. He was the first one in his family to make this change. Disraeli had not stopped being a Jew because he was now a Christian; every so often in later years he would refer to 'my race' or talk of Christians as 'you'. But now he began an elaborate process of self-styling in which he exaggerated his exoticness. As Blake puts it: 'Throughout his life people remarked upon the indefinable but indubitable impression that he gave of being a foreigner, whether it was the pride of a Spanish grandee, the ingenuity of an Italian juggler, or the plausibility of a Levantine on the make.'

There were several components to this self-styling, each one carefully crafted. Physically Disraeli took great pride in his appearance and nurtured his curls of black hair. Occasional panics about strands of grey were solved by regular dying, a cosmetic treatment Disraeli continued through to his death. To this Disraeli added an extravagant wardrobe – blue bottle frock coats, green pantaloons, purple waistcoats, white gloves with rings worn on the outside. Taken together with his dark eyes and pale skin, the effect was exotic and confusing. Indeed, Disraeli liked to cultivate the confusion, entering fashionable drawing rooms in his late twenties and early thirties with his thumbs in his waistcoats and exclaiming: 'Allah is Great'.

Next came the invented ancestry. Not content with his grandfather's steady rise from Jewish immigrant hat maker to stock market millionaire, Disraeli forged an elaborate genealogy which he later published as a family history. He concocted a belief that he was descended through his father from an aristocratic Jewish family who had been expelled from Spain in 1492 and taken refuge in Venice, where they had prospered as merchants. There is no evidence to support this claim. His grandfather's papers show that he came from Cento, a town in the Papal States of Italy, before moving to England in 1748. If Disraeli had seriously investigated his ancestry he would have discovered a link on his mother's side with the Cardoso family, who had settled in Britain as long ago as the end of the seventeenth century. He might even have realised that his mother's family was in all likelihood descended from Isaac Aboab, who in the 1490s led some 20,000 Jews into Portugal following their expulsion from Spain. But it was enough for Disraeli to be able, without support from the facts, to pretend that he came from an aristocratic Jewish family. The true details held no interest for him.

The third pillar of the myth was the novels. Time and again, Disraeli in his literature placed on a pedestal good-looking young noblemen with a link to the East and an interest in the exotic. In one novel, Disraeli dealt exclusively with these issues. *Alroy* is the story of the young Jewish leader who frees his people but then falls into the temptations of worldly power. It was published in 1833 while Disraeli was still in his twenties. With the help of an austere priest called Jabaster, Alroy stirs his people and quickly becomes master of Baghdad and all the Arab lands. He then falls in love with and marries the Khedive's beautiful daughter, who plots the old priest's death. Alroy gives his life over to pleasure, but the Arabs revolt and he is captured. He is offered his life in return for confessing loyalty to the Prophet. In the resulting argument, the Arab leader loses his temper and kills Alroy with a stroke of his scimitar. Alroy dies with a victorious smile on his face; in the end he has kept to the true faith.

Disraeli described *Alroy* as his 'ideal ambition'. No doubt in his dreams Disraeli fancied himself as the good-looking liberator of the Jewish people and felt a tension between this and his life as a fashionable novelist. Certainly, the turmoil inside Alroy is vividly described and we become genuinely interested in guessing whether the sexy and treacherous

Queen will prevail over the austere Jewish priest. But otherwise the book is preposterous, indeed unreadable at times, and it often descends into blank verse. One quotation gives a good impression of the whole: 'Pallid and mad, he swift upsprang, and he tore up a tree by its lusty roots, and down the declivity, dashing with rapid leaps, panting and wild, he struck the ravisher on the temple with the mighty pine.'

In *Alroy* and his other novels Disraeli invented and perfected the most potent part of his mythology. Half comically, half seriously, Disraeli described a hierarchy of races and religions ... in which he placed the Jewish race and religion at the top. His writings and later his speeches are filled with extraordinary epigrams to make this point vividly. 'The Jews are humanly speaking the authors of your religion.' 'God never spoke to a European.' Arabs were 'Jews on horseback'. 'Christianity is Judaism for the multitude.' 'How can English bishops know anything? A few centuries back they were tattooed savages.' At great length, he spelled out the debt which Christianity owed to Judaism, using terms which turned into a paradox the traditional Christian denunciation of the Jews as the murderers of Christ. If Christ had not been crucified the doctrine of atonement would have been meaningless; Christians therefore owed their faith to what the Jews had done. Separately, he traced a racial argument that the Semitic race was superior because it was largely composed of unmixed blood.

For a Victorian audience these were bizarre, indeed incomprehensible, arguments. They were not the stolid fodder which people were used to hearing from the pulpit. But Disraeli was not writing to persuade others. He was seeking to define his own identity. Equipped with an aristocratic ancestry, a pure bloodstream and a religion without which Christianity could not exist, Disraeli could in his own mind compete and excel in Victorian society. His difference gave him the edge. Both Christian and Jew, Disraeli was in a position of unchallengeable strength in this deeply devotional century. 'I am the blank page between the Old Testament and the New,' he explained.

One comment in *Punch* captures the mix of bewilderment and curiosity with which Disraeli's arguments were received in later years. Reviewing *Tancred* in the 1840s, *Punch* made a joke about Disraeli's new racial hierarchy: 'Look at the old clothes man ... who would think that the unmixed blood of the Caucasus runs through the veins of that individual who has just offered us nine pence for our hat?' But this cynicism would not have concerned Disraeli. Never the dupe of his own mythologies, Disraeli knew that middle-class mid-Victorian Britain would not swallow such extravagant theories. Winning the argument mattered much less to Disraeli than building up an armoury and convincing himself he was right.

And so in the privacy of his home and the luxury of his imagination Disraeli indulged and cultivated the main elements of this fantasy. His notebooks are scattered with comments about religion and race. At one point he had the idea of writing a life of Jesus from a Jewish point of view. At another, he considered creating an essay competition on the following subject: 'What w'd be the position of the Hebrew race in universal History, with reference to their viewed influence on man?' The judges could be Gladstone, Canon Stanley and Disraeli. He would dedicate £500 or even £1,000 for the best essay on the issue – 'Not bound however to award the prize unless satisfied with the performer.' Occasionally he liked to dabble in complex German philosophy: 'Anthropomorphism: a great cry against it by the Philosophes – But if the Hegelian principle be true, that man is the first organisation in which God is conscious, then the old legend of Genesis, that God made man in his own image, comes to the same thing – This is curious, & might be pursued.'

Particularly telling are Disraeli's bookshop accounts from the 1840s and 1850s. Alongside the standard Victorian fare of works by Aeschylus, Cicero and Thucydides we find such lustrous publications as Bainer's *Hebrew Mythology*, Giles's *Hebrew and Christian Records*, Marmont's *The Present State of the Turkish Empire* and Helous's *Pilgrimage*. In 1856 Disraeli bought Munk's *Palestine* and Salvador's *Jésus Christ*. A decade later he sent in for binding Dean Stanley's *Sinai and Palestine*, Delvette's *Old Testament* and Strauss's *Life of Jesus*. His interest toppled into racialism, buying Cox's *The Mythology of the Aryan Nations* and Pickering's *The Races of Man*. Only occasionally were the ideas imbibed from these works of academia deployed by Disraeli in the public arena, perhaps in a new novel or a particularly erudite speech. For the most part, they took their place beside many others, glittering and occasionally polished, in his storehouse.

Inevitably, these ideas left their imprint on Disraeli's wider views of politics in the nineteenth century. The long, complicated process of racial and religious self-fashioning left a residue. In three key areas we can detect this residue from the distance of two centuries.

One such imprint was noted by Disraeli's long-term political companion and ultimately his enemy, Edward Stanley, the 15th Earl of Derby, in his diaries. There is no repetition anywhere of the conversation which Disraeli held with Stanley in 1851 in which he expounded the advantages of creating a Jewish homeland in Palestine. But it is clear that Disraeli had given the concept detailed thought: 'the country, he said, had ample natural capabilities; all it wanted was labour, and protection for the labourer: the ownership of the soil might be bought from Turkey: money would be forthcoming: the Rothschilds and leading Hebrew capitalists would all help'. According to Stanley, Disraeli concluded: 'A man who could carry this out would truly be hailed as the next Messiah, the true Saviour of his people. He saw only a single obstacle: arising from the existence of two races among the Hebrews, of whom one ... look down on the other, refusing even to associate with them. "Sephardian" I think he called the superior race.'

Second, and more alarmingly, we can trace Disraeli as an unwitting contributor to the pseudo-science of late-nineteenth-century racialism. This was partly a matter of believing, as Disraeli and countless others did, that race was important and indeed could be decisive as the driver of history. Writing in 1870, Disraeli looked back on how he had developed these ideas in his early novels: 'the general influence of race on human action being universally recognised as the key of history, the difficulty and hazard of touching for the first time on such topics cannot now be easily appreciated'. He explained that in asserting the doctrine of race, his novels 'were entirely opposed to the equality of man, and similar abstract dogmas, which have destroyed ancient society without creating a satisfactory substitute'. This was vague stuff, but Disraeli's basic rule of thumb nonetheless was straightforward: 'the decay of a race is an inevitable necessity, unless it lives in deserts and never mixes its blood'.

Disraeli's purpose in dabbling in such dodgy territory was to turn on its head the traditional hierarchy of races and creeds. In this way he was an inverter, rather than an inventor, of popular prejudices. Instead of placing Jews at the bottom of society, as had traditionally been their lot, Disraeli placed them in the prime, indeed the dominant position. What for Disraeli was a matter of justified Semitic pride was transformed into a very different myth, indeed a nightmare by those who followed him. Central to the controversy was the character of Sidonia which Disraeli created in his novels *Coningsby* and *Tancred*.

'All is race there is no other truth,' Sidonia explains. These words make us uneasy today, as indeed does the whole analysis which flows from this remark. Sidonia himself is unreal and disturbing; he is less a character in a novel than a phenomenon symbolising Disraeli's philosophical truth, namely the uniqueness and superiority of the Jewish race. Thus, in Disraeli's description, Sidonia 'was Lord and Master of the money market of the world and of course virtually Lord and Master of everything else'. He gives voice to some of Disraeli's boasts: 'you never observe a great intellectual movement in Europe in which the Jews do not participate. The first Jesuits were Jews; that mysterious Russian diplomacy which so alarms Western Europe is principally carried by the Jews'. But all this was to play straight into the hands of the enemy. What Disraeli meant as a harmless boast became for men such as Houston Stewart Chamberlain a sinister accusation and an excuse for persecution. Indeed Disraeli was cited by Chamberlain in his anti-Semitic writings as proof that Judaism should be treated as a matter of race rather than religion: 'In days when so much nonsense is talked concerning this question, let Disraeli teach us that the whole significance of Judaism lies in its purity of race, that this alone gives it power and duration.'

Of course, Disraeli had no patience for these attitudes. Later in life, he introduced into his novel *Lothair* a character called Mr Phoebus who preaches and practises Aryan thinking. But Mr Phoebus and his two lovely daughters are presented as genial though slightly ridiculous people, backing a good-humoured though nonsensical analysis of the world. For Disraeli, to the extent that Jews were successful in the world, this was a success which they deserved, a counterbalance to the prejudice which they often suffered. History had indeed made them a special people. Other people, and in particular Christians, whose faith was derived from Judaism, therefore owed them admiration and respect.

The third imprint from Disraeli's youthful search for identity was that it convinced him of religion's social utility. 'The connexion of religion with the exercise of political authority is one of the main safeguards of the civilisation of mankind,' he explained. This theory is found most strongly in *Tancred* but it resurfaces throughout his career. It was connected to a broader emphasis on imagination as a tool in the government of nations and in that sense was not associated with any one particular set of religious beliefs. What mattered was devotion, not doctrine. The people simply needed something to believe. Neither Liberalism nor Utilitarianism could satisfy this craving. 'Man is made to adore and obey; but if you give him nothing to worship, he will fashion his own divinities and find a chieftain in his own passions,' Disraeli explained.

In *Tancred* and the other Young England novels this thought grows into a specific proposal that the Church should become 'a main remedial agency in our present state'. Unfortunately, it never becomes clear what that means. It was sufficient for Disraeli to paint the problem with a few vague but striking phrases. Thus we are told that 'Europe is not happy. Amid its false excitement, its bustling inventions, and its endless toil, a profound melancholy broods over its spirit and gnaws at its heart. In vain they baptize their tumult by the name of progress: the whisper of a demon is ever asking them "Progress, from whence and to what?"' So what is the solution? Material prosperity is dismissed out of hand by the hero. 'I see nothing in this fresh development of material industry, but fresh causes of moral deterioration. You have announced to the millions that their welfare is to be tested by the amount of their wages ... You propose for their conduct the least ennobling of all impulses ... why are we to believe that people should become more pure, or that they should escape the catastrophe of the policy that confounds the happiness with the wealth of nations?' Instead the answer is a kind of moral elevation, which can only be secured by a mass religious awakening. After all, 'if there be no faith, how can there be duty?'

This was of course the age not just of liberalism and utilitarianism, but also of Darwinism. Twelve years before *On the Origin of Species* was published Disraeli had already rejected the main thesis of evolution: 'I do not believe I ever was fish.' In one sense his argument was both disprovable and unproven – in that he believed belief was intrinsic to man: 'instead of believing that the age of faith has passed, I hold that the characteristic of the present age is a craving credulity,' he argued. 'My Lord, Man is a being born to believe.' And yet the curiosity was that Disraeli himself held no particularly strong religious beliefs of any kind. Of course, he took Communion and attended church regularly. Like most Victorian politicians, he played his part in the ecclesiastical arguments of the time. But unlike Gladstone or Shaftesbury, Disraeli wore his own religion casually. We are left therefore with an oddity: a man who believed in nothing nonetheless believed very strongly that the public needed to believe.

Let us make one final observation before we return to Disraeli's early years. Many years later, in a life of Disraeli, the historian Froude wrote this of Britain's first Jewish Prime Minister: 'Though calling himself a Christian, he was a Jew in his heart.' This loaded comment was marked with a tick by Gladstone in his own copy, preserved at Hawarden. The accusation of crypto-Judaism never left Disraeli, and yet it does not hold up to scrutiny. Unlike his father, Disraeli simply had no firm views about the Jewish religion. He certainly was no religious doctrinaire. In a fairy-tale kind of a way, Disraeli probably believed in God and the idea of a divinity.

He certainly relished the concept of an afterlife and the potential pleasures of life eternal. But beyond that, he showed little interest in the details of what God's role on earth might be. Instead His message, like so many others, might be moulded to meet the needs of the supreme mythmaker of nineteenth-century England.

DOER OR DREAMER?

Benjamin Disraeli never doubted that he was capable of great-ness, but he could not be content simply with being great. His greatness had to be recognised. There was no question of his light being hidden under a bushel. Fame was the spur. 'I am one of those to whom moderate reputation can give no pleasure,' he wrote on one occasion. And on another: 'Fame, although not posthumous fame, is necessary to my felicity.'

The hunt for fame was linked in Disraeli's mind to the search for pleasure and excitement. Disraeli found a key to sustained excitement in the exuberance of words, both writ-ten and spoken. The taunt which Disraeli threw at Gladstone many years later could have been turned back on him: Dis-raeli was indeed intoxicated with his own verbosity. Later in life he specialised in epigrams, carefully polished before being thrown into conversation. But as a young man in his late teens and early twenties he dealt in superlatives. In his novels and other writings, descriptions abound to the point of tedium of dukes, banquets and castles. Every estate is mag-nificent, every meal superb, every woman overwhelming in her beauty.

We can trace Disraeli's love of superlatives in his early letters, meticulously edited by a team of Canadian scholars and published by the University of Toronto Press. The rep-ertoire was extensive in the summer of 1824 when Disraeli took his first trip to the Continent, travelling with his father and a friend called William Meredith who had just graduated from Oxford. In his opening letter back to his sister at home, Disraeli placed Bruges on an unlikely pedestal: it is the 'City of Cities', the streets are 'the handsomest and widest and the architecture the most varied and picturesque imaginable'. He reserved special praise for the sea: 'We came in with a very fresh sea, the night was most magnificent indeed I never witnessed a finer night.' In the next letter we hear of High Mass in Ghent Cathedral ('The service was sublime beyond conception') and the special quality of food in the Low Countries ('A Fricandeau the finest I ever tasted'). By the time they reached Brussels the torrent of words had become overpowering: 'Our living for the last week has been the most luxurious possible and my mother must really reform our table before our return.'

If words were to be the tools at Disraeli's disposal, what should be his chosen trade? In 1821, aged sixteen, Disraeli had been articled as a solicitors' clerk through his father's connections. The firm was well known and respectable: Swain, Stevens, Maples, Pearse and Hunt of Old Jewry were regarded as the chief rivals of Freshfields at the time. Disraeli worked hard at his apprenticeship, but he was not for a life of dry law books and methodical casework.* As he put it in one of his novels: 'To be a great lawyer, I will give up my chance of becoming a great man.' Disraeli sought fame, power, a dazzling reputation – and all three quickly. But none seemed available through a legal career. As a solicitor,

---

* Or so the evidence suggests. Many years later the son of Mr Maples wrote the following with the benefit of hindsight: 'I have heard my father say that Mr Benjamin Disraeli was very obliging and useful.' Disraeli himself regarded the years as not wasted and credited his legal experience as having given him 'great facility with my pen and no inconsiderable knowledge of human nature'.

there were no shortcuts to success. This was intolerable to
Disraeli, who could see his own way clearly. Aged nineteen,
and on his return from the Continent in 1824, he decided to
abandon the legal profession. For the next eighteen months
he pursued three very different projects intensively.

First came a crack at the capital markets. During his time
in the solicitors' office, Disraeli had come into contact with
a businessman called John Diston Powles. At that moment,
Powles was deep in plans for a canal through the Panama
Isthmus. He was also busy pumping up the bubble in South
American mining shares. The independence of various South
American republics had been a fillip for foreign investors;
businessmen were eager to make quick money from new
commercial schemes. Together with a man named Messer
and another legal clerk called Evans, Disraeli was encouraged by Powles to purchase the stock and publish pamphlets
in praise of the interested mining companies. The 'Inquiry
into the Plans, Progress, and Policy of the American Mining
Companies' was Disraeli's first work in print. It was followed
in the same year by two further publications, but all three
failed to convince. Within months, the prices fell and prof-
its began to deteriorate. So Disraeli shifted his focus to his
second project, this time in publishing.

One of the advantages of living at home was that Disraeli
could insert himself in his father's social life. In particular, he
was able to go with Isaac to John Murray's literary dinners
in Albemarle Street. Murray was the leading publisher of the
day, numbering among his clients Sir Walter Scott, Robert
Southey and, until his death, Lord Byron. Disraeli never
met Byron but heard a great deal about him – in part because Byron was a great admirer of his father's writings. In
dress and speech, Disraeli began to take Byron as his model.
The fashion of the 1820s was for men to dress in black. Disraeli used to appear at dinner parties hosted by the staid

solicitors in a black velvet suit with ruffles and red clocks.

John Murray had developed an affection for Disraeli and consulted him at the age of fifteen about a play which had been submitted to him for publication. Four years later, Disraeli had sent him in turn a novel of his own. Murray rejected the novel, but the relationship between them developed and Murray was persuaded to buy the fashionable mining shares. Indeed, Disraeli cast something of a spell over his senior and the two men began to plan a new venture which they could carry out as a team.

The Times newspaper in the early 1820s held a dominant position among the daily press. The editor since 1817 had been Thomas Barnes, but Barnes displayed a leaning towards radicalism which began to dismay the leaders of the Tory Party. Disraeli therefore convinced Murray, by nature a timid man, together with the banker Powles, to set up a Tory morning paper in rivalry to *The Times*. Improbably, Disraeli, aged twenty and still legally barred from borrowing money, was to supply a quarter of the capital.

What happened next defies logic. Murray, the forty-six-year-old world-famous publishing tycoon, was convinced to delegate to this unknown youth the task of creating the new newspaper. Disraeli, with no experience of journalism or politics, began to assemble a somewhat ramshackle crew of foreign correspondents for the paper. But the key was to find a good editor. They decided to approach the Scottish writer John Lockhart through his father-in-law, Sir Walter Scott. At the time, Scott was the most famous Tory writer living and already a client of Murray. Disraeli, who had never ventured north of the Trent, was commissioned to besiege the great man at his border stronghold of Abbotsford. He set forth in September 1825, stopping in York on his way north to stock up on superlatives ('York Minster baffles all conception; Westminster Abbey is a toy to it').

In Scotland, Lockhart and Scott had been prepared for
Disraeli's arrival by a letter from a lawyer friend, which informed them that the emissary was a 'sensible clever young
fellow; his judgement however wants watering down ... At
present his chief exertions as to matters of decision have been
with regard to the selection of his food.' Lockhart however
pretended to be surprised when it was Benjamin, not Isaac,
who arrived on his doorstep. But within hours, so Disraeli
reported, the two men completely understood one another.
The only difficulty was that Lockhart was reluctant to leave
Scotland. Disraeli therefore upped his offer without any
authorisation from his sponsors in London. It was no longer a
question of Lockhart becoming a lowly editor of a newspaper
which did not yet exist; the offer became far more splendid.
Lockhart was to become the leader 'of an immense organ at
the head of a band of high bred gentlemen and important
interests'.

Throughout his life, Disraeli believed in conspiracies,
and where they did not exist, as in this case, he was always
ready to invent them. He therefore began to conduct his correspondence in code. Sir Walter Scott became the Chevalier;
Lockhart was M; the Foreign Secretary, George Canning,
who was supposed to smile on the project, was referred to as
X; Disraeli christened himself Puck and was identified by the
letter O. He aimed high as was his wont and was not down-
cast by the coolness which at first greeted him. Thus Puck
wrote optimistically to Murray that if a seat could be found
for M in Parliament, 'I have no doubt that I shall be able
to organise in the interests with which I am now engaged a
most IMMENSE PARTY and a MOST SERVICEABLE one'.
Disraeli did his best to gift-wrap his offer, but unknown to
him the project was already beginning to unravel. Lockhart
was aiming at a higher prize. He wanted to become editor of
the *Quarterly Review*, the Tory magazine which Murray had

founded several years previously and which was already in successful rivalry with the Whig *Edinburgh Review*.

After a fortnight in Scotland, Disraeli and Lockhart travelled down to London together. In his notebooks written in later years, Disraeli looked back on his first trip to Scotland. 'When I was quite a youth I was travelling in Scotland, & my father gave me a letter to Sir Walter Scott. I visited him at Abbotsford. I remember him quite well. A kind but rather stately person: with his pile of forehead, sagacious eye, white hair & green shooting coat.' Unfortunately, the fond feelings were not reciprocated. Sir Walter Scott dismissed the young upstart in private as 'a sprig of the Rod of Aaron'. Meanwhile, behind the scenes, a battle was unfolding between a group of right-wing Ultra Tories who were resisting changes to the *Quarterly*. The leader of this group was John Wilson Croker, a Tory writer and Secretary to the Admiralty. It is not clear how deep Disraeli plunged into this argument, but the outcome was a success for Lockhart, who became the editor of the *Quarterly* and banished Croker from the magazine for several years. Lockhart agreed simultaneously to support Disraeli and Murray's new venture, although he stopped short of a formal editorial role.

Disraeli meanwhile was busy creating the newspaper. He even coined a name: *The Representative*. Yet still the newspaper had no management staff or printing machines. A publication date was set for January 1826. This timing was far from ideal. Right on cue, the stock market crashed four days before Disraeli's twenty-first birthday in December 1825. The investors in South America, including Powles, Murray and Disraeli, all lost large sums of money. Indeed, Powles now vanished from the scene. With Murray footing the bills, Disraeli was pushed out of the project. When *The Representative* finally came out it ran for less than six months and lost Murray £26,000, forcing him to sell his two smart

London homes and move back into his offices in Albemarle Street. In a rage, he took to the bottle and to his bed.

In terms of money and personal relationships this was for Disraeli a shipwreck. But Disraeli, true to character, turned the shipwreck to good effect. He wrote a novel about it – or, to be more accurate, he wrote a novel about himself as the brave and blameless survivor of the shipwreck.

Disraeli had begun writing *Vivian Grey* several months earlier and had drafted parts of the book in tandem with his financial speculations and publishing career. This might explain the comment by the father of the young protagonist: 'Vivian, you are a juggler'. The book was written as a silver fork novel, which meant that the author's identity was ostentatiously concealed while he crammed the novel with gossipy details about the high life of celebrities. The flaw in *Vivian Grey* is therefore from the outset obvious: Disraeli had no knowledge of high society. He had, however, something more important – namely a highly active imagination, which he used to cultivate the mystery.

Disraeli found as a partner in this project a pretty, clever, entertaining young lady called Sara Austen. Eight years older than Disraeli, Sara was married to a dull lawyer and family friend. She was on the hunt for entertainment and had already scored a literary triumph with an author called Robert Plumer Ward, whose own silver-fork novel she had rewritten and presented anonymously to a publishing firm with great success. Her boredom and Disraeli's needs now came together. Sara undertook to repeat her literary feat for the young bankrupt author. The relationship quickly grew in intensity, probably stopping short of a full love affair, but certainly spilling out into flirtation and excitement on both sides.

With Sara Austen's help, *Vivian Grey* was published in April 1826. Like all of Disraeli's novels, the prose is over-dramatic and there is no real plot. Like all of Disraeli's heroes, the protagonist is groping for the key to his personality. After leaving school, Vivian Grey is a hit in society, but thirsts for something more meaningful. He stumbles on the answer after reading a great deal of history and realises that his future lies in politics: 'a branch of study certainly the most delightful in the world; but for a boy, certainly the most perilous'. In this way, the hero made the same discovery as the author, namely that true fame could only be found in politics. We should note here that there is no suggestion of a vocation or higher calling. Had Gladstone written this passage the hero would have sunk to his knees thanking the Almighty for enlightening him. But Vivian Grey is driven by a different, almost sensual craving: 'and now everything was solved, the inexplicable longings of his soul, which so often perplexed him were at length explained, the indefinable want that he had so constantly experienced was at last satisfied ... he paced his chamber in an agitated spirit and panted for the senate'. While panting, Vivian Grey encounters an exhausted statesman, the Marquis of Carabas, whom he flatters into believing that he can rebuild his former position and create a new political party. Vivian Grey makes the running, already a master of manipulation, and brings together the great new party, which promptly falls to bits amid infighting.

The storyline is so thinly veiled that it is impossible to believe that Disraeli thought he would get away with it. Indeed he did not, as John Murray read the book and realised that he was the Marquis of Carabas. The Marquis is not an attractive character. He is vain and portentous – but above all, he drinks. If it were not for the bottle, Murray might have laughed off the whole episode, but he was notorious for tipsiness and the cap fitted him closely. Already cross with Disraeli over the *Representative* fiasco, he flew into a further rage and banished the Disraelis – father as well as son – from his offices in Albemarle Street.

Worse was to come. Disraeli had worked hard to limit knowledge of his authorship, resorting to ingenious tricks to throw critics off the trail. At first there was a gratifying and profitable period of curiosity while the literary world speculated on the identity of the self-assured individual who had produced such a knowing book. Sara Austen jealously guarded the secret, which for some time seemed secure. But then came the leak – and a highly hostile reaction. The literary world was furious to have been tricked by a young Jewish upstart of whom no one had heard. For Disraeli, exhausted after eighteen months of frantic activity, this blow was too much to bear. He collapsed and sank into a deep depression from which he did not emerge for three years.

In later years, Disraeli did not know what to make of his first novel. As a former Prime Minister writing in 1870, he observed that books 'written by boys, which pretend to give a picture of manners and to deal in knowledge of human nature must be affected. They can be, at the best, but the results of imagination acting on knowledge not acquired by experience. Of such circumstances exaggeration is a necessary consequence, and false taste accompanies exaggeration ... Vivian Grey is essentially a puerile work, but it has baffled even the efforts of its creator to suppress it.' But there was no apology and no pulling back from the obsession with politics which captured Vivian Grey's spirit and which in turn was to make a prisoner of Disraeli.

Besides, in writing *Vivian Grey* Disraeli had discovered a remarkable ability to write full-length novels at breakneck speed. According to one researcher, the first volume, which ran to 80,000 words, may have been written in around three weeks. Indeed, on reading, it bears all the hallmarks of such velocity. This useful skill never left Disraeli and over the years enabled him to stake out a reputation in the second rank of Victorian novelists.

Those who pick up a Disraeli novel in search of a detailed political philosophy may come away disappointed. As was inevitable, besides the enjoyable and liberal scattering of wit across the pages the first purpose of the novelist was to make money. Sometimes the need for money was pressing, sometimes in later life it was less insistent, but it was never absent entirely.*

Subject to that overriding aim, Disraeli's early novels fall into a number of categories. First came those novels which in essence are autobiographies. *Vivian Grey*, *Alroy* and *Contarini Fleming* (also known as *A Psychological Romance*) look at Disraeli from different angles and chart his future. They were all written before he was thirty. *Vivian Grey* was Disraeli's first published novel and brought him £700. By the standards of the times this was a respectable figure, although it did little to improve his overall indebtedness. In financial terms, neither *Contarini Fleming* nor *Alroy* came close, but for Disraeli there was compensation in that they reached for a higher purpose, namely 'the secret history of my feelings'. 'My works are the embodification of my feelings,' he noted. 'In Vivian Grey, I have portrayed my active and real ambition; in Alroy my ideal ambition; the Psychological Romance is a development of my poetic character.'

What are we to make of this? *Vivian Grey,* as we have seen,

---

*Disraeli also took an interest in the earnings of other authors. In his jottings he writes on this point with regard to Macaulay: 'I would like very much to know what was the amount that Macaulay made by the pen.' Curiosity eventually conquered his sense of propriety and one day Disraeli put the question directly to Macaulay's brother-in-law. The answer was £60,000. Disraeli reflected: 'I regret that I did not enquire whether this was the result of accumulated interest or of absolute payments.'

was about a young man's obsession with politics; *Alroy*, published in 1833, is a story centred on his pride in and lasting commitment to the Jewish race. *Contarini Fleming*, which was published in 1832, is certainly a better book than either of these, but covers much of the same ground as *Vivian Grey*. Disraeli regarded it as his best novel – 'the perfection of English prose'. It is hard to see how he reached this conclusion, except on the grounds that he attempts a vivid, indulgent, highly romantic self-portrait full of shifting moods of triumph and desire. It therefore appealed to the Narcissus which lurked at the back of Disraeli's self-consciousness.

The hero is the son of a Saxon nobleman who goes into exile and works his way into a high position in the service of the local ruler. At school, Contarini forms a passionate but non-sexual friendship with a boring boy called Musaeus. This friendship leads him into a fierce fight with a boy two years his senior whom he thrashes and tosses unconscious onto a dunghill. Contarini then leaves school and becomes his father's private secretary, quickly gaining promotion. After an unhappy love affair with a local girl called Christiana he produces a passionate novel under the title *Manstein*. This is reviewed in 'a new number of the great critical journal of the north of Europe' – and is a flop. 'With what horror, with what blank despair, with what supreme, appalling, astonishment, did I find myself, for the first time in my life, the subject of the most reckless, the most malignant and the most adroit ridicule. I was sacrificed, I was scalped ... I was ridiculous. It was time to die.'

Instead of dying, Contarini parts from his father and embarks on a series of voyages which take him across the Mediterranean and back again through the Ottoman Empire. In Venice he meets a distant relative and marries her, but she dies in childbirth. The story then peters out. The interesting characters are the hero's father and his tiresome stepmother, but neither reappears after the first few chapters, except when the father writes an affectionate dying letter to Contarini. There is plenty of other action, for example when Contarini leads a cavalry charge of the Turks against a rebel force as a result of which he meets the grateful Sultan in Constantinople and is suitably rewarded. But neither these events, nor the rest of the long travelogue which fills the second part of the book, are described with any real insight or passion. Contarini drifts from one site to another, indulging in many fits of introspection which are never clearly resolved. At some points the novel lapses into unconscious blank verse ('Like some lone Titan, lurid and sublime'); at others it becomes banal ('The Spanish women are very interesting'). In the end, Contarini's father leaves him his ample fortune and he sets about building a tower outside Naples which will be at least 150 feet high. 'This Tower I shall dedicate to the future, and I intend that it should be my tomb.'

Contarini Fleming is thus a combination of Flashman and Baron Münchhausen. Today any interest in the book is almost entirely autobiographical, as indeed Disraeli suggested afterwards: 'I shall write no more about myself.'

The second group of Disraeli's early novels are little more than fashionable light reading. Into this category we can place *Henrietta Temple*, *Venetia* and *The Young Duke*. Disraeli wrote *The Young Duke* between 1829 and 1830 to make money after his disaster on the stock exchange. In that limited objective, the book achieved its purpose, but otherwise it was an embarrassment even to Disraeli. 'What does Ben know of Dukes?' his father asked when he heard of the title; but, then as now, ignorance was no obstacle to books of this kind. Disraeli might be short on experience but he had a powerful imagination and this saw him through. The result was a slight, frothy work, preposterous though entertaining, and in later editions Disraeli cut large chunks from

the original text. *The Young Duke* was followed in 1837 by
Henrietta Temple and *Venetia*. *Henrietta Temple*, as we shall
see, is a long and passionate love story, in part a product
of his own experiences. *Venetia* meanwhile was the result of
Disraeli's youthful obsession with Byron and Shelley, their
lives improbably relocated to the 1770s and early 1780s. It
helped Disraeli to hold off the debt collectors, but did little
else to enhance his career.

Several observations are necessary at this point. In all his
novels, Disraeli found it much easier to ridicule than to commend. He was born with a gift for mockery which gleamed
through his political and literary careers. This is a precious
gift for a politician; the leader who can make men laugh is halfway to capturing their hearts. But unless strictly controlled a
ready wit can turn against its author. Disraeli subsequently
found himself fighting off old phrases which were flung at
him by opponents. Moreover this gift for mockery came at
the expense of other, arguably more vital, literary gifts. Disraeli's novels had no plots and weak protagonists. Except in
Henrietta Temple, he could not write romantic scenes. All his
works suffer from a surplus of spectacular buildings and extravagant meals. Almost everyone is titled and those who are
not wish to be. Disraeli aspired to a career like that of Byron,
Shelley and the other Romantics – yet disqualified himself
by preferring splendour to beauty. All of this means that we
are only occasionally moved or uplifted by a Disraeli novel,
even when we are entertained. Indeed this is what Anthony
Trollope meant when he slammed the early novels of Disraeli: 'the glory has been the glory of pasteboard, and the
wealth has been the wealth of tinsel. The wit has been the
wit of hairdressers and the enterprise has been the enterprise
of mountebanks.'

Such is the case for the prosecution. And yet Trollope's
attack does not quite ring true. This is not simply because

in Disraeli's later novels we find real jewels of cleverness. Rather, in all his novels, bad and good, mature and puerile, Disraeli was seeking something other than literary achievement. A conflict had emerged in Disraeli's early years which never fully resolved itself. On the one hand, Disraeli became a passionately ambitious politician, intriguing and manoeuvring with growing skill, choosing whatever tactics and relationships might take him up the greasy pole. On the other hand, through his interest in literature he developed a set of ideas to which he was devoted and which throughout his life he spent much time refining. He refused to give up either his career or his ideas; so how could they be reconciled? The answer was through his novels. For Disraeli, literary sparkle held the key to great leadership. Here was a man who had diagnosed the nation's ills and could supply the relevant imaginative remedies. Together with his Jewish stock and ancient ancestry, it gave him, as he later suggested, the feeling on waking each day that he could topple governments and shake dynasties.

But first Disraeli had to get started; aged twenty-two, and following the publication of *Vivian Grey* in 1826, he found himself adrift. As usual he analysed his own character with care. 'Whether I shall ever do anything which may mark me out from the crowd I know not.' These were the years of deep despondency. The difficulties spoke for themselves. Although baptised a Christian, he could not and did not wish to escape his Jewish ancestry. His education had been erratic though, in its own way, remarkable. He had no settled convictions, although waves of political and historical thought swirled round his brain. By now he had no money – indeed quite the opposite. He could earn a living of some sort with his pen but the reception given to his first efforts showed the pitfalls of this strategy. Meanwhile his sex life was becoming somewhat complicated. Sara Austen was more or less in love with him and Disraeli owed her husband money. He flirted and perhaps slept with the wife of one of his doctors, Clara Bolton.

Much panting would therefore be needed before our hero reached the senate. Through the combined calamities of *The Representative* and *Vivian Grey*, Disraeli had managed to smash the one connection he had to his credit, namely that to the literary world. In an effort to salvage her son's career, Disraeli's mother wrote to John Murray protesting at the rupture between their two families: 'for while you were expressing great friendship, we were constantly hearing of the great losses Mr Murray has sustained through the mismanagement and bad conduct of my son. Surely, sir, were this story truly told it would not be believed that the experienced publisher of Albemarle Street could be deceived by the plans of a boy of twenty whom you had known from his cradle.' Unfortunately this appeal had no effect and by October 1826 the situation was so serious that the Anglo-Saxon historian-solicitor Sharon Turner once again entered the fray. Having intervened once already in the young life of Disraeli, he now did so again, writing to both Isaac and John Murray to urge them to stop talking and writing about the row, which had become 'the football of all the dinner-tables, tea-tables, and gossiping visits of the country'. One way or another there was a calming between the families, although it was another three years before the breach was healed.

In the meantime, Disraeli wallowed in self-loathing. He spent his days in a dark room, sleeping for sixteen hours each day, complaining of a rushing of blood in his head together with a lack of springiness in his brain. Isaac described these years between 1826 and 1830 as a blank in his son's existence and indeed they were, as Disraeli shuttled about between town and country, spending time in Fifield, Lyme Regis and northern Europe in search of a remedy. Even his literary output dried up. He published a bland second volume of *Vivian Grey* in 1827 and a short novella called *The Voyage of Captain Popanilla* in 1829 which attacked utilitarianism, but little else during these long, dull years. His father seems to have persuaded him to go to the Bar in April 1827, and Disraeli duly ate the necessary meals at Lincoln's Inn, but his career as a barrister never got very far.

Disraeli had not solved his original problem: he must be great, but of what should that greatness consist? He had tried finance, newspapers, novels and publishing. He had thought about becoming a poet. Looking back on these years in old age, Disraeli admitted that he had been 'devoured by an ambition I did not see any means of gratifying'. His talent was for words; his appetite for action; he was increasingly drawn to politics. But lacking connections, confidence and a ready supply of credit, this was not a natural career path for a depressed Jewish writer in his early twenties.

Disraeli found a way out of the morass in his father's library. He discovered an account of David Alroy, the thirteenth-century liberator of the Jewish people from the Turkish Empire. As we have seen, Disraeli later turned this into a novel which he published in 1833, but initially the story awakened in him a deep desire to travel to the Orient. Together with William Meredith, his former travelling companion and now his sister's fiancé, he began to plan a great voyage of enlightenment round the Ottoman Empire. *The Young Duke* was duly written to pull in the necessary guineas. Within months, Disraeli had embarked on a turbulent and salacious journey. Gibraltar, Andalusia, Malta, Corfu, Albania, Greece, Constantinople, Jerusalem and Egypt were at great length and expense taken in during a tour which lasted seventeen months. The mingling of races, cultures and creeds left its mark on Disraeli and reinforced many of his idiosyncratic prejudices. The great issues of the day were the independence of Greece and the future of the Ottoman Empire; the fashion was to support the struggling Greeks. Disraeli, never a friend of nationalism except as regards England, strongly backed the Turkish Empire and at one point considered volunteering for the Turkish army to suppress an uprising in Albania. More importantly, the tour gave him the chance to perfect the dandyism which he had been developing. In Gibraltar he caused a sensation by using two canes each day, a morning and an evening cane, changing over at the sound of the midday gun. In Malta he made a point of embarrassing the stationed infantry by refusing to return a rackets ball which landed near him; instead he picked up the ball, handed it to a standing rifleman and 'humbly requested him to forward its passage into the court, as I really had never thrown a ball in my life'.

In this extravagant behaviour Disraeli found a well-qualified companion in the form of a notorious rake called James Clay. Clay had been at school with Meredith, but in Disraeli's eyes outshone his sister's fiancé. This was partly because Clay was more focused on finding sexual than intellectual awakening. As the trip wore on Meredith drifted apart from the other two men, and Disraeli and Clay made their own way round the Mediterranean in the comfort of Clay's sixty-ton yacht, the *Susan*. The three men eventually met up again in Egypt. It was here that catastrophe struck. In an alarmingly short space of time Meredith contracted smallpox. The doctors said that he would recover; instead he died. And so to Disraeli the task fell of writing to his sister back in England in order to break the terrible news. He offered by way of compensation an opportunity to share his own career. 'Live then for me' – on the surface the offer was another typical display of egotism; but for Sarah Disraeli, aged twenty-nine and unlikely to find another husband, it represented a sad but feasible reality.

In spite of Meredith's death, the trip to the East had raised Disraeli's spirits. On the return leg he wrote to his father from a ship moored off Cape St Vincent: 'If the Reform Bill passes, I intend to offer myself for the seat at Wycomb[e].' The date was 17 October 1831. In England, the supporters of reform were taking advantage of the collapse of the Tory Party to contemplate a new era of more inclusive politics. Indeed, within a year, the long era of Tory dominance was over as Lord Grey and the Whigs brought in and passed the Great Reform Bill. For an ambitious young man such as Disraeli, the new constellation of constituencies and franchises represented a quick way into politics. The springiness of his brain was now rediscovered. 'I was never more confident of anything than that I could carry everything before me in the House,' he informed his family.

So, his mind made up, Disraeli plunged into politics. He came up against the immediate question: to which party should he belong? Now the same inner struggle started again. He was not a Whig, but the Tories were crushed and exhausted. His first answer, 'as for Parties, I am for myself', was not entirely convincing. To clear his own mind he wrote a self-centred pamphlet simply entitled: 'What is He?' Of course, like the author, the answer was complicated. His ideas were vague and worthy, but with a special emphasis on the role of character in politics: 'Let us not forget also an influence too much underrated in this age of bustling mediocrity – the influence of individual character.'

Over the next three years Disraeli mounted a variety of political platforms but failed to find a steady perch on which to rest. He did indeed stand for Wycombe in 1832, both before and after the changes of the Great Reform Act. On both occasions he presented himself as an independent

Radical and lost to a recognised Whig, Colonel Grey, son of
the Prime Minister. The electorates were tiny: Disraeli lost
by twenty votes to twelve at the first outing, and came third
the second time around, winning only 119 votes compared
to Grey's 140 and the 179 votes won by another Whig called
Robert Smith.

In 1834, Disraeli tried for a third time in Wycombe, again
as an independent and again losing – but this time he was
supported with £500 from Tory campaign funds. Disraeli's
attraction to the Tories was almost entirely for negative reasons. He disliked the Whigs for their top-down, managerial
approach to politics and despised the utilitarians on similar
grounds. The Tories rejected all of this and showed more
respect for national institutions and the national character,
which Disraeli believed held the key to the well-being of the
country.

What Disraeli really wanted was a Tory leader with imagination. The leader of the Tory Party by this point was
Robert Peel and Disraeli had enough sense to pay lavish
tribute to Peel in his writings and whenever they met socially. Sometimes indeed he laid it on with a trowel which
he later reserved for royalty: 'In your chivalry alone is our
hope. Clad in the panoply of your splendid talents and your
spotless character, we feel assured that you will subdue this
unnatural and unnational monster [the Whigs].' But Peel was
the son of a cotton merchant. Peel spoke with a Staffordshire
accent. Peel supported the Whig Poor Law and thought for
the most part in pounds, shillings and pence. Above all Peel
lacked imagination. Disraeli also developed an admiration for
the Duke of Wellington, but the Duke was ageing and imagination had never been his strong point.

Disraeli eventually found the patron he needed in Lord
Lyndhurst. Lyndhurst, a brilliant lawyer who had already
served as Lord Chancellor, was a thrusting and ambitious

politician who felt ill at ease among Peel's more middle-class supporters. Peel watched carefully the slow decay of the Whig Government, waiting for the exact moment when he could strike with a reasonable expectation of an election which would give him a clear majority in the House of Commons. He was anxious above all to avoid a repetition of 1834, when he found himself compelled to take office without a working majority. Lyndhurst by contrast was in favour of seizing every opportunity to overthrow the Government and Disraeli egged him on. The two men at the time were also sharing a mistress, Henrietta Sykes, but this seemed to cement, rather than weaken, the alliance. Disraeli even invited Lyndhurst and Henrietta for the weekend to his father's house at Bradenham, which shocked the neighbours but otherwise was a success.

Lyndhurst meanwhile busied himself with finding Disraeli a seat in the Commons. Disraeli fought Taunton in the 1835 election; he was beaten again but reduced the Whig majority. More importantly at Taunton, Disraeli enjoyed a voluble exchange of insults with the Irish Radical Daniel O'Connell. Disraeli had originally sought O'Connell's support during his dalliance with radicalism. But now, a firm Tory, Disraeli attacked O'Connell in a speech at the hustings as a traitor and a violent rebel. The speech, and in particular the reference to bloodshed and treachery, was published in newspapers and O'Connell flew into a rage. At a meeting in Dublin O'Connell returned fire, calling Disraeli 'a vile creature', 'a miscreant' and 'a reptile'. He ended his speech with a burst of anti-Semitism: 'His name shows that he is of Jewish origin. I do not use it as a term of reproach; there are many most respectable Jews. But there are as in every other people some of the lowest and most disgusting grade of moral turpitude; and of those I look upon Mr Disraeli as the worst. He has just the qualities of the impenitent thief on the Cross, and I verily believe, if Mr Disraeli's family herald were to be examined, and his genealogy traced, the same personage would be discovered to be the heir at law of the exalted individual to whom I allude.'

Just as Peel had done twenty years previously, Disraeli decided that the only way to deal with O'Connell was to fight him. But, after killing a man, O'Connell had vowed never to fight another duel – so Disraeli approached his son instead, who understandably refused. Blocked with the sword, Disraeli turned to the quill and fired off a vast letter to all the newspapers. He also sent a private letter to O'Connell Junior: 'I fervently pray that you or someone of his blood, may attempt to avenge the inextinguishable hatred with which I shall pursue his existence.' At this point the police stepped in, arresting Disraeli and binding him to keep the peace. But the row had greatly enhanced Disraeli's reputation and notoriety (for Disraeli they were one and the same thing), and in his diary for 1835 he noted: 'Row with O'Connell in which I greatly distinguished myself.'

During this fracas, Disraeli had to explain how he had moved from standing three times in Wycombe as an independent Radical who had sought O'Connell's backing to his stance at Taunton as a full-blown Tory. He retorted that it was the Tories, not he, who had changed. In 1832 they had been discredited and beaten; by 1835 they had recovered. Underlying this riposte was a more fundamental point. Disraeli was working out in his own mind a theory of English history which proved that the Whigs had taken power by distorting the Constitution. They were the party of the Poor Law, of rigged elections, high finance and unnecessary wars. The Tories were the national party, often out of office, but preserving their independence. Disraeli, on the one hand, was a romantic Radical who sympathised with the Chartists. But on the other he was an instinctive Tory who trusted the underlying character of the English people. This combination baffled his opponents but otherwise stood him in good stead.

In 1835 Disraeli published his first serious work about politics. The *Vindication of the English Constitution* is dedicated to Lord Lyndhurst and for the first time Disraeli set out in full his political stall. He sent a copy to Peel with a short covering note, not expecting any commendation from the man who was notoriously stingy with praise. To his surprise (so he said, but Disraeli was in the habit of building a strong story on shaky foundations) Peel sent him a note of warm congratulation, although on closer inspection the wording is ambiguous at best. Peel was 'gratified and surprised to find that a familiar and apparently exhausted topic could be treated with so much original force of argument and novelty of illustration'. More importantly, Disraeli's father was delighted with the *Vindication*. For the first time, his eldest son had written something which could be taken seriously. More than that, he had for once shown sound sense. The hours spent in Isaac's library had not been wasted; the version of English history produced by Disraeli in the *Vindication* was quite close to Isaac's own, for example being mildly Cavalier in its account of the seventeenth century. In short, Disraeli had produced a Tory version of recent English history.

This history, as Professor Vincent points out, 'lurches wildly between the fanciful and the penetrating'. The sentences are too long and the arguments over-complicated, as if the author had some difficulty in believing them himself. Disraeli begins with an attack on utilitarianism and goes on to update Burke's *Reflections on the Revolution in France* by covering the reigns of Louis XVIII and Charles X. According to Disraeli, the French had made the mistake of trying to graft the English Constitution onto their own system, with which it had nothing in common. 'This innocent monarch

[Louis XVIII] seems to have supposed that the English Constitution consists merely of two rooms full of gentlemen who discuss public questions and make laws in the metropolis at a stated season of the year.' He leads on into a long essay on the growth of the English Parliament and the emergence of 'the gentlemen of England; a class of whom it is difficult to decide whether their moral excellence or their political utility be most eminent, conspicuous and inspiring'. The Tory Party is the truly national party, whereas the Whigs by a series of coups have seized political power and introduced a thoroughly mischievous Reform Act under which 'whole and important districts of the country, and considerable classes of the community, are not represented and the land, which originally formed the third estate, assumes only a secondary character in its present elements'.

Of course, when Disraeli talked about a 'national' party or indeed a 'national' anything at all he was dealing exclusively with England. The Welsh, the Scots and the Irish all pursued separate interests and the result was a Whig majority in the British Parliament whereas in England there was a solid Tory majority. According to Disraeli, this majority was composed of the natural followers of Bolingbroke and the Country Party as opposed to the Court. The squire and the parson had been outwitted by the Whigs in 1714 when the Whigs had installed George I as the equivalent of a Venetian Doge, a man with a title but no power. In 1832 the Whigs had, once again, manipulated the Constitution in order to advance their own interests and regain control of the levers of power. Disraeli ends with a rousing defence of the House of Lords and the hereditary principle. 'It is this great principle which has prevented the nobility of England from degenerating into a favoured and odious sect. It is this great principle which has placed the peers at the head of the people.'

This concept of a corrupt and illegitimate Whig oligarchy

hung in the background of Disraeli's thinking for the rest of his life. But it left several awkward questions unanswered. What about the Jacobites? How were the Tories supposed to feel about the accession of the latest Hanoverian monarch, Queen Victoria? What was the verdict on the younger Pitt, who proclaimed himself a Whig but whose war against France was supported by every red-blooded Englishman? The whole thing lacked the straightforwardness of the Whig interpretation of history, with its clear run of sympathy for Parliament, William of Orange, the Protestant religion and general belief in progress. Confronted with the dogmatic vehemence of Macaulay and the Whig version, this Tory history gradually withered or took refuge in detailed and scholarly criticisms of its Whig opponents.

None of this mattered to the young Disraeli, by now in his early thirties. He was a critic not a creator, built to attack not to applaud. Indeed this was the spirit in which he wrote a series of wild journalistic rants which were published in *The Times* under the name Runnymede in 1836. The *Letters of Runnymede* comprise two sections: a series of open letters addressed to leading politicians; and a short treatise on the Whigs and Whiggism. To the extent that there is one, the main argument is that the Whigs are factional and the Tories are national; again a somewhat odd version of history is deployed to support this case. But for the most part the letters are simply a set of fierce, rabid, witty hand grenades lobbed at the Whig Party.

Even by Disraeli's standards, the language is ridiculously florid. He uses words like 'eructating' and keeps talking about doges. Particularly fascinating is the sheer range of insults at Disraeli's disposal. Thus he labels Lord John Russell: 'cold, inanimate, with a weak voice, and a mincing manner, the failure of your intellect was complete'. On Lord Cottenham after his appointment to the Lord Chancellorship: 'this great

transition from Humbug to Humdrum. We have escaped
from the eagle to be preyed upon by the owl.' Meanwhile
Lord Palmerston was 'the Lord Fanny of diplomacy, cajol-
ing France with an airy compliment, and menacing Russia
with a perfumed cane!' His attacks on the Whigs never fall
short of the extraordinary: 'What a crew! I can compare
them to nothing but the Schwalbach swine in the Brunnen
bubbles, guzzling and grunting in a bed of mire, fouling
themselves, and bedaubing every luckless passenger with
their contaminating filth.'* His descriptions of the Irish are
simply extravagant bigotry: 'This wild, reckless, indolent,
uncertain, and superstitious race have no sympathy with the
English character. Their fair ideal of human felicity is an alternation of clannish broils and coarse idolatry.'

These are the words of a man high on life and low on proportion. Indeed, by this stage all aspects of Disraeli's life were
extreme. 'The two greatest stimulants in the world, Youth
and Debt,' Disraeli would later write in one of his novels;
and indeed he was heavily endowed with both. On the one
hand, he was the toast of society, a regular at fashionable
parties and the subject of portraits by D'Orsay and Maclise.
'There is not a party that goes down without him,' one host-
ess wrote. He lived in rooms off St James's where he flattered
his patrons and seduced his mistresses. Disraeli's father, for
example, wrote after visiting him in these years: 'There is no
calling on Ben without finding him engaged with Lords – or
others – I have just escaped by gliding thro' his bedroom
from Lord Strangford and the other day from Lord Eliot . . .'

---

* One phrase seems applicable to the last Labour Government: 'With peace,
reform, and retrenchment for their motto, in the course of five years they
have involved us in a series of ignoble wars, deluged the country with
jobs and placemen, and have even contrived to increase the amount of the
public debt.'

At the same time, Disraeli was being hunted. The debt collectors were closing in. By July 1836 the situation was precarious: 'Peel has asked me to dine with a party today of the late Government at the Carlton. Is it safe? I fear not ...' And in December he wondered whether he could risk a Buckinghamshire dinner. 'I trust there is no danger of my being nabbed as this would be a fatal contretemps inasmuch as, in all probability, I am addressing my future constituents.' There is even a story that at one point he had to hide down a well to escape the debt collectors. We can trace the escalation of Disraeli's debts in Lord Blake's biography. By this account, Disraeli had initially lost £2,000 or £3,000 on the stock exchange in 1825. Fifteen years later these debts had grown to over £20,000 – the equivalent today of around £2 million. Isaac was always a potential source of emergency bailouts and indeed had helped his son on several occasions, but Disraeli carefully concealed the full extent of his indebtedness from his family. The threat of debtors' gaol was therefore real.

And so, beset by debt but propelled to the top of society, the question was what would crash first: the debts or the social climbing? Becoming an MP held the key to a reprieve. An MP was not only immune from arrest, but also entitled to free postage, meaning that Disraeli might steadily continue his literary work from Parliament, paying off his debts gradually. By 1837, when a general election was made inevitable by Queen Victoria's accession, Disraeli had already stood four times unsuccessfully and was still waiting for a seat. But Lyndhurst and the Tory Party were now firmly on his side; he was a member of the Carlton Club, and in this election he was adopted for Maidstone. This was a two-Member constituency with a reputation for corruption. His fellow candidate in the Conservative cause was Wyndham Lewis, whose wife he had already met. Their opponent was a Radical Colonel called Perronet Thompson. Disraeli and Lewis were both elected, although Disraeli had to endure the usual cries of 'Old Clothes' and 'Shylock' in order to defeat Thompson by 200 votes.

At last, at the fifth attempt, Disraeli had entered Parliament. What happened next is well known. The story of Disraeli's maiden speech contains all the component parts of his youthful character in one episode: ambition; brashness; over-the-top rhetoric. Again the dreamer took over, as he aimed for a quick hit and ended up with a bloody nose.

Disraeli's initial mistake was to choose a poor subject, namely the validity of recent Irish elections. His choice of opponent was also unwise, setting his sights on O'Connell again. He must have expected a hostile reception but could not have predicted its ferocity. The Irish Members hurled abuse, obliterating Disraeli's rhetoric as he reached this description of Lord Melbourne: 'the noble Lord might wave in one hand the keys of St Peter, and in the other the cap of Liberty'.* Drowned out, Disraeli was forced to sit down, but before doing so emitted a cry which cut through all the noise: 'I will sit down now, but the time will come when you will hear me.'

A few days afterwards Disraeli was introduced through his friend Edward Bulwer-Lytton to an Irish MP called Richard Sheil. The older man spoke kindly to Disraeli as he emerged somewhat shaken from the ordeal. 'Now get rid of your genius for a session. Speak often, for you must not show yourself cowed, but speak shortly. Be very quiet, try to be dull ...' It was excellent advice and Disraeli followed it. His next speech was on a technical point about copyright.

*

* There is some question whether this phrase was audible. Gladstone in the margins of his copy of Froude's life of Disraeli wrote: 'I heard it'.

In following Sheil's advice, Disraeli completed his transition: from writer to politician; from political independent to Party man; from dreamer to doer. He changed what he wore and what he said. In his forties Disraeli admitted 'I get duller every day', but in his heart he was always the young man of frantic energy and wild ideas.

We have taken our time in charting this transition because we believe it holds the key to the true legacy of Disraeli. Disraeli was a master of words and indeed it was these rather than any policy that he refined most assiduously. As a writer, Disraeli injected imagination and even fantasy into politics. He gave it a unique literary quality which, in an age of slow communication and limited democracy, attracted and entertained thousands, indeed millions of people who were otherwise shut off from politics. Never a believer in democracy, Disraeli nonetheless made Parliament popular.

Here then is the ultimate paradox. By every standard of contemporary politics, Disraeli should never have had a successful political career. He was steeped in debt and sunk in controversy; he cheated and lied repeatedly. Yet over time and with great effort he lifted himself above all these indiscretions. He did so because he breathed life into politics. The writer Walter Bagehot, although a strong critic of Disraeli, was one of the first to observe this technique closely. Disraeli, 'devoid of constructive genius', nonetheless attempted to apply 'a literary ability in itself limited to the practical purpose of politics'. In this he was 'quick to hit, and so hard to be hit'. By some 'freak of nature' he was endowed with the quickness of a keen man and the impenetrability of an apathetic man.

Disraeli himself made no secret of what he was doing. 'We govern men with words', he wrote at one point; and at another, 'No people relish eloquence of the highest order so much as the lowest mob.' Indeed in his novel *Sybil* one of the chief discoveries the hero makes is about the power of words: 'He has not been at your schools and your colleges, but can write his mother tongue, as Shakespeare and Cobbett wrote it; and you must do that if you wish to influence the people.'

At times this effort to inspire took an eccentric twist. Disraeli's private notebooks display an affectionate interest in the standard of speeches and range of accents in the House of Commons. At one point he complains about the quality of quotations: 'Very few will venture on Latin – But it is not that the House has relinquished quotation, but that the new elements find their illustrations & examples in illegitimate means. It is not merely that they quote Byron & Tennyson before they have completed their quarantine – But Bright & Cobden and all those sorts of people are always quoting Dickens & Punch. These quotations are either tawdry or trashy. The privilege of Quotation sh'd not be too easy – It should be fenced in.'

But mainly Disraeli's focus was on the way words could mingle with ideas. He developed this point early while struggling to be elected in the 1830s. In a novel called *A Year at Hartlebury: Or, the Election*, written with his sister in 1834, Disraeli explained: 'It is the fashion now "to go along with the people", but I think the people ought to be led, ought to have ideas given them by those whom nature and education have qualified to govern states and regulate the conduct of mankind.' At around the same time he noted in his private diaries the chief problem with utilitarianism: 'The Utilitarians in Politics are like the Unitarians in Religion: both omit Imagination in their systems, and Imagination governs Mankind.' Later in *Tancred* he said a similar thing: 'Power is neither the sword nor the shield, but ideas, which are divine.'

The point is this: in an age of dull, worthy, free-trade economics; in a nation of merchants, manufacturers and industrialists; in a society governed by two parties that seemed to have been around for ever, presided over by a portentous Church of England and a cross-looking Queen, Disraeli sensed that people craved something more inspiring in their politics. To his mind, good government was not about Bills, balance sheets or people's pocket books. It should be a more divine enterprise. This was the task he set himself while still a young man in his thirties – lifting the mind of a mighty nation, then at the heart of an empire.

IV

MEN AND WOMEN

'You will not make love! You will not intrigue! You have your seat; do not risk anything! If you meet a widow, then marry!' Thus wrote Alfred, Count D'Orsay to Disraeli after his election at Maidstone in 1837. D'Orsay was a young French aristocrat who had scandalised society as the live-in lover of his stepmother-in-law, the Countess of Blessington. He was known across London as a decadent and a dandy; so naturally he was good friends with Disraeli. The two men could be seen, arm in arm, touring town together, on their way to a louche party or returning from an enjoyable session at the vapour baths.

Coming from such a source, the advice about marriage was worth noting; if even the wicked were recommending marriage, then surely the time for such a step had arrived. The difficulty, of course, was that for Disraeli marriage could never be a straightforward, conventional matter. It would have to fit in beside the myriad delights which now coloured his life. Disraeli in his early thirties was like a young boy who had bought a ticket into the huge, noisy fairground of nineteenth-century England. He spent his days pausing at the different stalls, deciding which could give him sustained pleasure.

With the daily delights of London life Disraeli was thoroughly familiar. He liked his champagne chilled and his rooms warm. He was quickly bored with the conversation of men talking among themselves about field sports in which he did not join. All his life he was a late riser; unlike other Victorians, he liked to saunter and lounge. In general, he dreaded the decanter moment at dinner parties when the ladies withdrew from the dining room and he was left to cope with his own sex. He found consolation at these and other trying moments by reaching into his pocket and lighting a cigar.

These were the years when Disraeli took special care over his clothing. He was a dandy and he wanted everyone to know. In 1835 he had stood as a Tory for Taunton. For this occasion he had chosen a bottle-green frock coat, a waistcoat overwhelmed by gold chains, and fancy pantaloons. As one contemporary described, he also combed his glossy black curls away from his right temple, so that they fell in abundance over his left ear. Meanwhile his behaviour was designed to fit his clothes. In Gibraltar, as we have seen during his long extended holiday, Disraeli started the fashion of carrying both a morning and an evening cane; in Malta he had excelled himself while watching a game of rackets, refusing to return a stray ball to the court. In Constantinople, Disraeli had found his favoured location: 'The life of this people greatly accords with my taste,' he wrote. 'To repose on voluptuous ottomans and smoke superb pipes, daily to indulge in the luxuries of a bath which requires half a dozen attendants for its perfection; to court the air in a carved caïque, by shores which are a perpetual scene; and to find no exertion greater than a canter on a barb, all this is, I think a more sensible life than all the bustle of clubs, all the boring of drawing rooms, and all the coarse vulgarity of our political controversies.'

In all this Disraeli was following his own principle: 'to govern men you must either excel in their accomplishments or despise them'. He was not trying to make friends but simply astonish those around him and give them something to talk about. At the same time Disraeli took great care to observe the character and behaviour of other men. His notebooks for these years are crammed full of lists of people, broken down into various categories. Page after page is filled with 'remarkable adventurers', 'eccentric characters', 'dandies', 'diplomatists', 'bastards', 'royal bastards' and 'party hacks'. These lists are not limited to contemporaries but range into the ancient and extraordinary. After carefully recording a number of 'eunuchs', Disraeli treats us to a list of 'Heroes, impotent or adverse to women'. These luminaries include de Gassion, Battori the Invincible, and Tilly.

But Disraeli was always less interested in other people than he was in himself. All the time he was artfully analysing his own character and looking for others who might also admire him. Disraeli did not just want to write about and talk to interesting people; he wanted to be read and to be listened to as well. The search for a sympathetic listener who acknowledged his genius and supplied affection and admiration in ample degrees was central to Disraeli's early life and career.

He looked for such a listener first of all in his own family. As we have seen, his relationship with his father, Isaac, was warm, generous and stimulating. In Isaac, Disraeli found much more than a genial source of emergency money. He was a man of letters, a thinker, a supporter of the Stuarts and the Cavaliers. But his father was ageing and in any case did not approve of his son's social life in London, so their connection was never quite as close as it might have been.

What of Disraeli's mother? Here we meet a mystery. Maria Disraeli is almost absent from Disraeli's life and numerous letters. Apart from one or two casual good wishes she is mentioned only in passing. His sister, Sarah, protested when he left his mother out of the memoir he wrote about their family; but no amendment was made to fill the gap. It is possible that Maria had prevented Disraeli from being sent to public school, perhaps due to doubts over his suitability. In her letter to John Murray during the row between the families she had described her eldest son as, 'tho a clever boy ... no prodigy'. For Disraeli, denying his genius was a misjudgement by anyone and by his own mother it ranked as a major betrayal. As it is, we are left with one elaborate cooking recipe which Disraeli sent to his mother during his tour of the Middle East.

The part which Disraeli's mother might have taken was largely assumed by Sarah. As we have seen, at the age of twenty-nine she had suffered the loss of her fiancé, Meredith. This event brought Disraeli much closer to his sister, forming a connection deeper and stronger than that with his other siblings. So far as can be seen, Sarah never again contemplated marriage and the help she gave Disraeli for the rest of her life was unique. He took her into his confidence and she brought to bear on each of his problems the advice of a shrewd, intelligent and devoted young woman. He trusted her entirely and told her details of his life and financial affairs which he confided to no one else. When she died in 1859 Disraeli was devastated; she had been the 'harbor of refuge in all the storms of my life and I had hoped she would have closed my eyes'.

Meanwhile Disraeli cast his net more widely for a sympathetic audience who could share in his genius and counsel him in his difficulties. At the start of his career Disraeli dressed and often behaved as if he were a homosexual. This was all part of being a dandy. Repeatedly in his novels, the lead is taken by a good-looking youth just launched into the world and finding his way around. The custom of that age was tolerant of affectionate behaviour between young men, provided that it stopped short of a sexual relationship. Indeed such affection was openly carried to a point which would certainly be called scandalous in our more prurient age. Here for example is the schoolboy friendship of Contarini Fleming in Disraeli's novel of the same name. 'There was a boy and his name was Musaeus ... I beheld him; I loved him; my friendship was a passion ... I gave up my mind to the acquisition of his acquaintance, and of course I succeeded. In vain he endeavoured to escape. O days of rare and pure felicity when Musaeus and myself with arms around each other's neck wandered together amid the meads and shady woods that formed our limits! I lavished upon him all the fanciful love that I had long stored up; and the mighty passions that yet lay dormant in my obscure soul now began to stir in their glimmering abyss.' Today we can have no doubt about the content of these mighty passions, but in the nineteenth century no conclusions were drawn, no climax reached, and the innocent love between the boys simply sputtered out.

And so it was in Disraeli's own life. As regards men there were whispers but no scandal. Disraeli seems to have profited as many did from the Victorian distinction between romantic friendships between men, which were widespread and acceptable, and sexual relations, which were criminal. He was attracted by the good looks of young men and sometimes allowed this attraction to distort his judgement. Thus in later years Disraeli became attached to Lord Henry Lennox, an entertaining, irreverent gossip and the younger son of the Duke of Richmond whose other qualifications were hard to find. Lennox can be found today in Disraeli's letters, hunting sometimes for an heiress, sometimes for a minor government job; there too is Disraeli's famous remark: 'I can only tell you that I love you.'

Prior to Lennox there was a string of similar sybarites, including the Count D'Orsay and later George Smythe. But in each case the relationship stopped short of a scandal. Not that Disraeli was particularly careful about these things. His journey to the East provided him with sexual as well as intellectual experience. His preferred companion on that trip had been the disreputable James Clay. The two men debauched their way around the Middle East and returned to London suffering from venereal diseases.

But for Disraeli, women rather than men were always the more compelling creatures. His attraction to women was sexual but, more importantly, cultural and conversational. Consistently Disraeli valued female relationships over those with his male friends. 'There is nothing in life like female friendship,' he wrote at one point, 'the only thing worth having.' In *Contarini Fleming* Disraeli wrote passionately about the role of women as a test bed for any political career: 'Talk to women, talk to women as much as you can. This is the best school. This is the way to gain fluency, because you need not care what they say, and had better not be sensible. They, too, will rally you on many points, and as they are women you will not be offended. Nothing is of so much importance and of so much use to a young man entering life as to be well criticised by women.' It is no coincidence that the last of Disraeli's published novels, *Endymion*, is a tribute to the role of women as the driving force in a great political career.

Only in one case did Disraeli form a male friendship which could compare to those with his women friends. Like Disraeli, Edward Bulwer-Lytton was devoted to the memory of Lord Byron. Like Disraeli, he wrote a silver-fork novel – his was called *Pelham* and sold well. The two men struck up a correspondence and got to know each other, gradually becoming firm friends. Bulwer held an added attraction for Disraeli in that he was well established in society and helped open many doors. He also helped Disraeli in his literary efforts, reading the manuscript of *The Young Duke* and advising Disraeli to tone it down. At last, Disraeli had found a companion who could counsel him in his various personal and political interests. Thus he wrote in his diary: 'I have not gained much in conversation with men. Bulwer is one of the few with whom my intellect comes into collision with benefit.'

The only obstacle to this relationship was Bulwer's wife, Rosina. As the friendship grew, she turned savagely against both men. Disraeli disliked her in part because she was Irish ('she is so thoroughly a daughter of Erin that I never see her without thinking of a hod of mortar and a potatoe'), but more serious were the accusations she hurled against the two men. In 1858, by now estranged from Bulwer, she appeared at his election hustings in Hertfordshire, making wild claims and ranting about her husband, who reacted by having her sectioned in Brentford Asylum. Shortly afterwards Disraeli wrote to his old friend: 'I thought you had tamed the tigress of Taunton – but unhappily this is not the case. She is writing letters to your colleagues and friends, of an atrocious description, such as, I thought, no women, could have penned, accusing you of nameless crimes, at least which can only be named by her, and threatening aggravated hostilities...'. In the end the aggravated hostilities never materialised; both men were able to continue their careers.

Whatever the truth behind Rosina's accusations, Disraeli had to some extent protected himself against such suspicions by a series of very public love affairs with married women during the 1820s and 1830s. After his early flirtation with Sara Austen, Disraeli's first mistress seems to have been the wife of the doctor who treated him during his mental breakdown. Clara Bolton was not a nice woman; her letters to Disraeli show her to be pretentious and possessive. In Disraeli's notebooks, Clara appears under the category 'Female Adventurers'. But for a brief time she was a source of great excitement to Disraeli and helped his re-entry into active life and society.

Disraeli in his twenties was not looking for love or lasting attachments. Half-heartedly he proposed to the sister of his dead friend Meredith, who rejected him. Otherwise he wrote scornfully of romance and marriage between women and men: 'all my friends who married for love and beauty either beat their wives or live apart from them. This is literally the case. I may commit many follies in life, but I never intend to marry for "love" which I am sure is a guarantee of infidelity.'

That letter was written in May 1833. Within a couple of months he was caught up in a full-blooded affair with another married woman. Henrietta Sykes was married to Sir Francis Sykes, 3rd Baronet and owner of Basildon Park in Berkshire, an intelligent but low-spirited man beset by ill health. Henrietta and Disraeli met in Henrietta's box at the opera and within a few weeks were deep in ... love? Or was it lust? From the letters it is hard to tell. In August Henrietta wrote her first letter to Disraeli. There is nothing guarded about the text:

12 o'clock Thursday night.
It is the night Dearest the night that we used to pass so happily together. I cannot sleep and the sad reality that we are parted presses heavily upon me – very very heavily. I love you indeed I do ... Good Angels guard my dearest. A thousand and a thousand kisses. Good night. Sleep and dream of – your Mother.

She was already cast in the role designed for her by Disraeli – that of the doting mother whom he had lacked.

Disraeli's letters to Henrietta have disappeared, but he went one better – he wrote her a novel which bears her name. 'There is no love but love at first sight. This is the transcendent and surprising offspring of sheer and unpolluted sympathy ... An immortal flame burns in the breast of the man who adores and is adored.' And so on for several hundred vivid pages. *Henrietta Temple* was published in 1837 but the first part had been written three years earlier at the height of his passion for the lady.*

No one who reads Henrietta's letters to Disraeli would stake any money on a happy ending. There is something feverish in her emotion which Disraeli does not match even when he is doing his best to describe passionate love. She was possessive and, as the relationship wore on, hysterical and neurotic. 'I cannot bear that your amusement should spring from any other source than myself,' she wrote on one occasion; and on another she protested, 'I will not be drawn off and on as you would a glove.' In one extraordinary and illiterate letter she panicked about a possible pregnancy: 'Do you think any misery can occur to us now from all the loved embraces? I fear we are very rash people & when I think I shake – answer please a little yes or no & I beseech you not to be angry with me for who have I to communicate all my thoughts and fears but you my Soul ...'

And yet for almost three years the relationship carried on. Even the most extravagant Victorian novelist would have been hard-pressed to describe its tortuous course. Sir Francis veered from tolerating the liaison to denouncing it. Henrietta gave Disraeli her own account of a crucial visit. Sir Francis had been foolish enough to entangle himself with none other than Clara Bolton, the doctor's wife with whom Disraeli had dallied only a few months earlier. Hearing of this, Henrietta decided to confront her rival. She marched unannounced into the drawing room where Sir Francis and Mrs Bolton were alone together. Her terms were harsh. She would continue to live under Sir Francis's roof and thus give sanction to

---

*In the revised 1853 edition the passionate element of the story is considerably reduced.

his adultery provided that he refrained from threatening Disraeli or criticising him in her presence. Sir Francis was silent and confused; he left Mrs Bolton to launch the rebuttal. She did her best, denouncing Disraeli as a heartless wretch. But the initiative remained with Henrietta. 'Madame cried and wrung her hands. F cried and begged me to be merciful. I did not cry and had apologies from both.' From then on Sir Francis accepted the situation but took his wife off on a tour of the Continent. Disraeli asked himself in his diary, 'How long will these feelings last? ... My life has not been a happy one. Nature has given me an awful ambition and fiery passions. My life has been a struggle – with moments of rapture – a storm with dashes of moonlight ...'

And so it went on. Sir Francis actually invited Disraeli to the Sykes home in Southend; the full party was composed of Sir Francis, Henrietta, Disraeli, Dr and Mrs Bolton. Disraeli was deep in debt and only with difficulty extracted a further loan from the Austens. Henrietta seems to have arranged for Disraeli to embezzle money from her husband; meanwhile Sir Francis paid a long visit to Europe, this time alone, leaving Henrietta and Disraeli to enjoy the London season from his house in Upper Grosvenor Street.

It was here that Disraeli first met Lord Lyndhurst in 1834. And now his relationship with Henrietta embarked on a more sordid course. As well as being an important Tory grandee, Lord Lyndhurst was a formidable womaniser. He was once asked by an inquisitive lady whether he believed in platonic love; he responded 'after, but not before'. We do not know what the exact arrangement was, nor precisely who was manipulating whom. But certainly Henrietta was soon sleeping with both men, with a view to helping Disraeli's career. 'Lyndhurst arrived in town last night. I can make him do as I like so whatever arrangement you think best *tell me* and I will perform it ...'

But there was a chill in Disraeli's heart which doomed all these adventures. He was genuinely attracted by Henrietta, enjoyed being seduced by Clara Bolton and was perfectly willing to receive love letters from Sara Austen. But none of them could satisfy what he knew by now was his main need, namely political fame and relief from the nagging burden of debt. Unlike his fellow Victorians, Disraeli had no romantic notions of love and marriage and indeed was sceptical of the entire concept. He thought that marriage was simply a comforting concept for the middle classes; indeed for them marriage was 'often the only adventure of life'. In *Vivian Grey* he had articulated his own attitude: 'He looked upon marriage as a certain farce in which sooner or later he was, as a well-paid actor, to play his part.' But for Disraeli, the consummate actor, this performance could nonetheless serve a purpose: a wife with a fortune could solve his financial worries and supply the affection which his mother had failed to give.

As he moved into the political world, Disraeli found that he no longer needed Sara Austen, Clara Bolton or Henrietta Sykes. So he dropped them from his life. Sara Austen had gone quietly, but Henrietta needed a lover to meet her emotional needs. She began to drift elsewhere, this time into the arms of Daniel Maclise, a handsome Irish painter with talent and a big heart. Unfortunately Sir Francis found them in bed together. This time her histrionics failed to calm him and he brought legal proceedings against Maclise. The case was eventually dropped, but it had ruined her reputation. She died on 15 May 1846, by chance the day of Disraeli's most famous and devastating attack on Sir Robert Peel during the debates on Corn Law repeal. But Disraeli had long ago moved into a world apart from hers and never mentioned her death. It was as if she had never been.

At the time of his election in 1837 Disraeli was unattached for the first time in five years. D'Orsay's letter about a wealthy widow was therefore timely; now at last an MP, Disraeli was free to focus on finding a wife who could help him advance his political career. It was at this moment that Mary Anne Lewis entered the scene. Disraeli had met Mary Anne five years previously, when he described her as a rattle and flirt. At the Bulwers', Disraeli had been asked to take her down to dinner; he responded: 'Oh anything rather than that insufferable woman, but Allah is Great.' Five years on she seemed less insufferable to Disraeli when he stood for Maidstone alongside her husband, Wyndham Lewis. Mrs Lewis already had a friendly eye for Disraeli and during the contest the couple loaned him money for his election expenses. Both men were elected, but Wyndham died suddenly several months later. From that moment on, the connection between Mary Anne and Disraeli grew in intensity.

Like all of Disraeli's women lovers, Mary Anne was older than he was, in this case by twelve years. As with Henrietta, Disraeli soon recast Mary Anne and himself in the roles of tender mother and child. But age was no obstacle to a steamy, erotic relationship. Ahead of one meeting, he told her to disembark from the carriage with her hand 'ungloved'. In one key respect, the relationship differed from those Disraeli had experienced before. Disraeli was the *demandeur* in this courtship – and Mary Anne was determined to keep it that way. She held all the cards: the income, the large house in Grosvenor Gate, the connection to Maidstone and, by now too old to have children, there was no rush for her to get married again. So she was able to keep Disraeli on a tight leash and refused to get remarried before the customary delay for a widow of one year had elapsed. This prompted arguments and at least at one fierce moment it looked as if the relationship might break down.

On 7 February 1839 they had a flaming row, at the end of which Disraeli stormed home and wrote her a long letter

of recrimination. He protested against the delay and complained that if their present unclear relationship continued it
would 'only' render Mary Anne disreputable; 'me it would
render infamous'. He then ventured onto even more dangerous ground: 'I avow, when I first made my advances to you, I
was influenced by no romantic feelings.' The marriage would
be convenient; he needed a wife; plus his father was urging
him to settle down. Mary Anne seemed to fit the bill. 'Now
for your fortune: I write the sheer truth. That fortune proved
to be much less than I or the world imagined.' Indeed, 'as far
as worldly interests are concerned, your alliance could not
benefit me'.

But by this point, Disraeli was no longer driven by money.
He had genuinely fallen in love with the ageing widow. He
told Mary Anne that he had 'devoted to you all the passion
of my being', and in case she had any doubts Disraeli spelled
out his feelings. 'My nature demands that my life should be
perpetual love.' He had found Mary Anne 'amiable, tender,
and yet acute and gifted with no ordinary mind – one whom
I could look upon with pride as the partner in my life who
could sympathise with all my projects and feelings, console
me in moments of despair, share my hour of triumph and
work with me for our honour and happiness'. This was the
prospect which she was throwing away; it was the same offer
he had made to his sister after Meredith's death: the chance
to be a managing partner in Disraeli's political career.

It was a great letter, monstrously frank, and Disraeli saved
the most savage point for the end. Mary Anne might reject
Disraeli's advances; she might for a few years 'flutter in
some frivolous circle'; but the time would come when she
would 'sigh for any heart that could be fond, and despair
of one that can be faithful. Then will be the penal hour of
retribution: then you will think of me with remorse, admiration and despair; then you will recall to your memory the

passionate heart that you have forfeited, and the genius you
have betrayed.' Many women receiving such a letter would
have torn it to pieces; not so Mary Anne, who replied immediately: 'For God's sake come to me.' They were married on
28 August that year.

Mary Anne was by no means the ideal wife for an ambitious politician. She dressed as if she were much younger
than her years and her conversation could be foolish. She
never could remember which came first, the Greeks or the
Romans, and would drop into conversation comments such
as: 'You should see my Dizzy in his bath.' But she was devoted to Disraeli and, as Robert Blake has pointed out, 'she
sank her existence in his'. Early in their marriage she drew
up a list of their contrasting qualities, Disraeli's on the left,
hers on the right. For a woman with a reputation for prattling
and silliness, the list is shrewd and touching:

Very calm	Very effervescent
Manners grave and almost sad	Gay and happy looking when speaking
Never irritable	Very irritable
Bad-humoured	Good-humoured
Warm in love but cold in friendship	Cold in love but warm in friendship
Very patient	No patience
Very studious	Very idle
Very generous	Only generous to those she loves
Often says what he does not think	Never says anything she does not think
It is impossible to find out who he likes or dislikes from his manner. He does not show his feelings	Her manner is quite different, and to those she likes she shows her feelings

No vanity	Much vanity
Conceited	No conceit
No self-love	Much self-love
He is seldom amused	Everything amuses her
He is a genius	She is a dunce
He is to be depended on to a certain degree	She is not to be depended on
His whole soul is devoted to politics and ambition	She has no ambition and hates politics

Clearly, this list was unbalanced by affection: for example, Disraeli was extraordinarily vain. But the truth is that they were made for each other, largely because Mary Anne had tapped into what was in Disraeli the supreme outward emotion, namely gratitude. When Disraeli's friend George Smythe once made a joke at Mary Anne's expense, Disraeli responded with a withering look: 'George, there is one word in the English language, of which you are ignorant ... Gratitude.' This gratitude rested on the firmest of foundations. A deeply self-centred man, Disraeli never lost the sense of how much he owed his wife. For the next twenty years she carried out exactly the programme which he had sketched for her in that letter. She coaxed, cared for and believed in Disraeli's genius. She used to scour books and pamphlets not for their own intellectual value, but to trace every possible mention of her husband. In 1865 she met a young Lord Rosebery and their conversation turned to Disraeli. 'Though I have many people who call themselves my friends,' she told the future Prime Minister, 'I have no friend like him.'

After his marriage, Disraeli's life settled down and the relationships he formed were steadier than those from his earlier years. Of course, he still had an eye for good-looking young aristocrats and continued to collect rich nobles around him, including his loyal, steadfast Private Secretary, Montagu Corry. Likewise, he enjoyed the flutter and frills of female conversation, particularly when supplied by statuesque, remarkable, older women. But increasingly he found his greatest thrills not so much in the heat of a new love affair, but rather in the techniques of courtship and romantic diplomacy, especially as they could be applied to his own political career.

Disraeli's preferred method of love-making was letter-writing. He was a born letter writer. It is a talent fast decaying in this century; Disraeli's letters show what we are missing. Indeed they are as a rule more skilful than his novels. Disraeli was not at ease with the plots of his own novels; there are inept and tedious passages in many of them, as the author tried to reassert mastery over the story he was telling. In the letters there is no such struggle. The recipient is always present to his mind, ready to receive a compliment or enjoy an anecdote. His letters stand in vivid contrast to those of Peel or Gladstone. All three men thought with a pen in their hand. When Peel or Gladstone took up the pen the natural product was a political letter or the draft of a state paper. For Disraeli the pen produced perhaps a note for Mary Anne, but more often a vivid account of some social event or a rhapsody describing the changing scenes in the woods of Hughenden. Disraeli's sister and his wife were keen correspondents and he made excellent use of both. But there was room for more. Particularly towards the end of his life he relished writing and receiving letters from elderly ladies whose acquaintance and friendship he cultivated with care amounting to devotion.

The first and strangest of these was Mrs Brydges Williams, a widow who, like Disraeli, was of Jewish origin but Christian belief. She wrote him several letters on the theme of this shared origin, and in 1851 Disraeli received a letter from her asking him to be the executor of her will; in return Disraeli would also stand to inherit a considerable sum of money. After taking a little time to consider, he accepted.

For the next twelve years, Disraeli rewarded his bene-factress with up to thirty letters annually. Although often invited, Mrs Brydges Williams never visited Hughenden, but Disraeli and Mary Anne visited the lady in Torquay almost every year, staying in a hotel and venturing out on country drives. Alongside his letters, Disraeli sent her many presents, often of fruit or game from his political friends. In 1852 for ex-ample he sent her a plate of raspberries which he had picked that morning, together with the relevant cuttings which had started life in Lord Salisbury's garden at Hatfield. She replied with a basket of prawns which he described characteristic-ally as the 'rosy coloured tribute of Torbay'. Her letters are short and matter-of-fact; he gave long and colourful accounts of rural life at Hughenden spiced with the latest political gossip. There is nothing to suggest that the correspondence was anything other than enjoyable and highly entertaining for both parties. In particular, his letters to her glow with en-thusiasm for the varied life which he was leading at the time. Before her death, Mrs Brydges Williams asked to be buried in the family vault at Hughenden. This turned out to be legally impossible but she rests alongside Disraeli and Mary Anne just outside the east end of the church at Hughenden. She died in 1863 leaving Disraeli a legacy of rather more than £30,000.

There remains one correspondent for whom Disraeli re-served a special style. His relationship with Queen Victoria was unique, not just in terms of his life and hers, but in the history of correspondence between British First Ministers and the Crown. The Queen's first Prime Minister had been Lord Melbourne, who treated the eighteen-year-old monarch as a court ward. He won her round with a boundless appetite for affectionate triviality; for example, they had bizarre conversations about sleeping too long ('Lord M thought 9 hours not too much. He said he was very sleepy of a morning'). Next came Sir Robert Peel, who gradually shed that clumsy awkwardness which had initially dismayed Victoria. Peel served her well, never shedding his formality, but attentive to her wishes and preferences on matters such as the Royal Yacht and the purchase of Osborne. By the time he left office, the Queen could not imagine life without him; she complained that his departure was like 'a very bad dream'.

Compared to these men Disraeli began with a disadvantage, in that the Queen detested him. As we shall see, she blamed Disraeli for the destruction of Robert Peel in the 1840s and complained violently in her journal of 'that dreadful Disraeli'. Yet Disraeli had a skill which was unique among Ministers; he was endlessly witty and entertaining. Quickly he grasped that the Queen was bored but had a taste for political excitement. And so, beginning when he served as Chancellor in 1852, and resuming when he became Prime Minister the following decade, Disraeli wrote Victoria entertaining, extraordinary, over-the-top, dramatic letters about each night's parliamentary debate. For example, in his first letter on 15 March 1852 he reported that Sir James Graham had made a great speech for the Opposition, 'elaborate, malignant, mischievous'. In March 1858 he described how Palmerston had given a 'mild and graceful speech, with a sarcastic touch'. He also liked to evoke the feeling of the Commons. Thus in the same letter of 1858 he told the Queen that 'the House is wild and capricious at this moment'. All this went down well with the monarch. To her uncle Leopold I of Belgium the Queen commented: 'Mr Disraeli (alias Dizzy) writes very curious reports to me of the House of Commons proceedings – much in the style of his books.' But she was hooked and Disraeli knew it. As one lady-in-waiting put it, 'She declares that she never had such letters in her life, which is probably true, and she never before knew <u>everything</u>.'

When Prince Albert died in 1861, Disraeli was quick to give his sympathy to the shattered Queen. 'The Prince', he wrote to Victoria, 'is the only person whom Mr Disraeli has known who realised the Ideal.' Disraeli was already putting into practice the advice he gave to others, namely that with royalty the flattery should be laid on 'with a trowel'. He had found the way to the Queen's heart and thereafter his grip on her affection only strengthened. The compliments and assurances of devotion poured in. To give one example, this is the tribute he paid Victoria on her birthday in 1879: 'Today Lord Beaconsfield ought fitly, perhaps, to congratulate a powerful Sovereign on her imperial sway, the vastness of her Empire, and the success and strength of her fleets and armies. But he cannot, his mind is in another mood. He can only think of the strangeness of his destiny that it has come to pass that he should be the servant of one so great, and whose infinite kindness, the brightness of whose intelligence and the firmness of whose will, have enabled him to undertake labours to which he otherwise would be quite unequal, and supported him in all things by a condescending sympathy, which in the hour of difficulty alike charms and inspires.'

At the same time, Disraeli invoked the majesty of Gloriana and borrowed from the poet Edmund Spenser the description of Victoria as the 'Faerie Queen'. Others, such as the 14th Earl of Derby, worried about Disraeli's approach; having dealt with her, they saw the Queen as not so much a force for great national prestige or glory as a source of deep emotional instability. But Disraeli was playing out a part he had sketched in his early novels, namely that of Grand Vizier to a Mighty Empress.

There is no missing the mockery with which Disraeli treated his plain and dumpy royal mistress. But she seemed to take seriously the homage and the compliments which he lavished upon her and the pretence that he depended entirely on her advice and support. She enjoyed the humour with which he reported government and parliamentary business. More importantly, Disraeli gradually rekindled in the Queen her interest in politics, helping to rehabilitate the monarchy at a time when it had sunk to a deep low. Without realising it she became a devoted partisan of her Prime Minister and his party, a process strengthened by her dislike of Gladstone.

By the time of Disraeli's death Queen Victoria, by now Empress of India, had pinned her colours firmly to Disraeli's mast. We do not know how much she fathomed of Disraeli's character, nor whether she was ever aware of the full extent of his outrageous behaviour in the 1830s. But she was devoted to him and there is no doubt that he was her favourite Minister. And so, in this way, Disraeli became the preferred Prime Minister of Queen Victoria without ever behaving like most other Victorians at all.

THE TWO NATIONS

In September 1841 Sir Robert Peel was in his prime. He had just fought and won a general election which gave the Conservatives a good working majority in the House of Commons. Now in his fifties, still handsome though rather plumper than the smart Home Secretary who had invented the Metropolitan Police, Peel dominated the political scene. As he began to assemble his Cabinet he might have been forgiven for looking ahead to an era of Conservative ascendancy under his stewardship. Peel was above all things a man of government; this surely would be the Age of Peel.

His had been a weary climb as Leader of the Opposition. Peel had found his party in the gutter after 1832 when the Tories had tried disastrously to resist the Great Reform Bill. During the next nine years, he had steadily rebuilt the Party's confidence and reputation in the country. Several times he was offered tactical opportunities to bring down Lord Melbourne and the Whig Government; several times he turned these opportunities aside. Peel was not interested in a rerun of the years 1834–5, when he had briefly served as Prime Minister without a majority in the House of Commons. Nor did he want a repeat of the fiasco of 1839 when the Queen, after inviting Peel to form a Conservative Government, refused to get rid of her Whig ladies-in-waiting, and he found himself back in Opposition. Peel knew that he needed a functioning Conservative majority to win over the Court and govern effectively for the good of the nation. His patience was rewarded in the summer of 1841 when he won a significant general election victory.

Peel had not simply waited for the Whig Government to fall to pieces. His success had grown out of an idea. In the Tamworth Manifesto of 1834 he had published what became the first national election manifesto, setting out his own Conservative philosophy about change. He drew a distinction between change for its own sake, which risked creating 'a perpetual vortex of agitation', and responsible and necessary changes which were based on a 'careful review of institutions, civil and ecclesiastical' and the 'correction of proved abuses and the redress of real grievances'. Peel had already applied this test while in Opposition, choosing to support measures proposed by the Whig Government such as the Malt Tax and the 1834 Poor Law which he believed were in the interest of the country. Now in government, with a strong majority in the House of Commons, Peel began to apply this philosophy to the great issue of the 1840s, namely the Condition of England Question.

The Condition of England was in fact not so much a question as a deep river of social unhappiness, swollen by a stream of tributary complaints. Poverty, disease, industrial strife, urban squalor, pollution and drunkenness all flowed with the miserable tide. Many in these years turned their talents to solving the various problems; taken together, they proposed a startling range of remedies. Friedrich Engels, the ally of Karl Marx, spent twenty months in and around Manchester and came to the conclusion that the inevitable outcome was a Communist revolution. The Chartists looked for a solution in radical political change. Lord Ashley, a strong Evangelical and Tory, strove mightily to pass Factory Acts limiting the hours children worked in factories. The historian Thomas

Carlyle wrote a pamphlet in which he coined the 'Condition of England' phrase.

Peel, as was his habit, fastened on one aspect and researched it in detail. He decided that the key concern which drove discontent across the country was the high cost of living. He concluded that it might be possible to improve the lot of the poor and head off any danger of sedition by reducing the tariffs which the Government levied on ordinary consumer purchases, in particular on food. The revenue which was thereby lost could be recouped by bringing in a new Income Tax. This tax had previously been used by Pitt as a way of raising emergency revenues during the wars with Napoleon, but it had never been levied in peacetime before. Would the measure be tolerable? And if so, what would be the best way of using Income Tax to reduce the cost of living on the poor? Peel began to write round and seek advice on these questions.

Peel was in no hurry and he was content to move stage by stage. But he saw that if he pursued this path he would eventually be confronted by the formidable obstacle of the Corn Laws. These tariffs on the import of foreign corn were the arch offenders in raising the cost of living for poor urban communities. But they were sacred to many of Peel's supporters and in rural constituencies they had been the cornerstone of the 1841 Conservative election campaign. Peel himself had already begun to insert escape clauses into his speeches about the Corn Laws, arguing that they must meet his test of bringing benefit to the nation as a whole. But few of his followers noticed these ambiguous reservations. The Throne, the Church and the Farmer had proved an excellent campaign cry. There seemed no need to delve into awkward details.

While Peel began to address the Condition of England Question with liberalising economic policies, one of his Tory supporters was already on the move and heading in quite a different direction. Disraeli had recovered well since his farcical maiden speech four years earlier. He had begun to carve out a niche as a Tory who took a special interest in the lot of the poor. In February 1841 he led a small cohort of fifty-four Tories and Radicals against the Whig Poor Laws, which he saw as heavy-handed and centralising: 'in making the government strong', Disraeli warned Lord John Russell, 'society might be made weak'. In the preceding years he had also made a point of urging greater sympathy for the Chartists and he was one of only a handful of MPs who voted for more lenient treatment of the arrested Chartist leaders. These activities caught the attention of the populist leader Charles Attwood, and the two men exchanged letters in 1840, giving Disraeli a chance to rekindle his youthful idea of a new national party based on an alliance between the aristocracy and the poor. 'I entirely agree with you', Disraeli wrote, 'that an union between the Conservative Party and the Radical masses offers the only means by which we can preserve the Empire.' As before, Disraeli said little about how such an alliance might be formed and even less as to what it might do. Nor was it clear what he meant by 'Empire'. But Disraeli plugged any gaps in his thinking with plenty of praise for the ancient character of the English people, and rousing diatribes against the 'denationalising' policies of the Whigs.

Armed with these arguments, Disraeli flung himself forward and tried to catch the eye of his Party leader. A difficulty had arisen in his seat at Maidstone as Disraeli was sued for unpaid election expenses, and by the time the 1841 election arrived he had given up the seat in favour of another two-Member constituency at Shrewsbury. After a boisterous campaign in which posters were pasted across town giving details of Disraeli's huge debts, the electors of Shrewsbury did their duty and both Tories were duly returned.

Now came the moment for which Disraeli had been waiting. He had steadily supported Robert Peel while in Opposition and had paid him extravagant praise in articles for the press. As others did, so Disraeli analysed every look and hint from his Party leader for a sign of special recognition. By 1841, Disraeli had every confidence that he had caught Peel's attention; he was particularly encouraged by an invitation to meet with Peel and other leading Conservatives in the spring of 1840. Surely, or so Disraeli decided, Peel would find a place for him in his Government.

Yet the relationship between Peel and Disraeli had never really got going. Contradictory accounts exist of an early dinner attended by both men in the 1830s. Disraeli was clear that Sir Robert had been genial and enrapt by his conversation; another eyewitness noted that Peel was vexed by Disraeli's importunity and brought their conversation to an end. Equally there was an ambiguity about Peel's reaction to Disraeli's maiden speech. Some said Peel had sat in silence, while others, notably Disraeli, thought they saw him cheering enthusiastically.* The gulf between the two men should have been obvious. Disraeli thought Peel lacked imagination and indeed told his sister so, remarking on a speech by Peel in 1837 that 'it appears to me both solemn and tawdry; he cannot soar and his attempts to be imaginative must be offensive to every one of taste and refined feeling'. For his part Peel, the reserved, gentrified, very Victorian Conservative leader, was never inclined to be impressed by a bizarre, irresponsible, overdressed bankrupt novelist who liked the sound of his own voice. He therefore found no difficulty in refusing Disraeli's request in 1838 to draft a general election manifesto.

---

*Gladstone many years later agreed that Peel had done his best to back Disraeli during this ordeal. He placed a tick of approval in his copy of Froude's biography beside the description of Peel's cheers.

By the time Peel took office in 1841, neither man was clear where the other stood. Had Disraeli done enough to convince Peel that he was worthy of office? Was Peel persuaded of Disraeli's genius? Disraeli was not one to leave these things to chance. Time was passing and no letter of invitation arrived. In his impatience he wrote a letter to the Prime Minister which is remarkable even by Disraeli's standards. 'I am not going to trouble you with claims similar to those with which you must be wearied,' he assured the Prime Minister, before doing exactly that. 'But there is one peculiarity in my case on which I cannot be silent. I have had to struggle against a storm of political hate and malice which few men ever experienced, from the moment, at the instigation of a member of your Cabinet, I enrolled myself under your banner, and I have only been sustained under these trials by the conviction that the day would come when the foremost man of this country would publicly testify that he had some respect for my ability and my character. I confess to be unrecognised at this moment by you appears to me to be overwhelming, and I appeal to your own heart – to that justice and that magnanimity which I feel are your characteristics – to save me from an intolerable humiliation.'

This was a preposterous argument. It verged on emotional blackmail. But it was backed up by a letter to Peel from Mary Anne Disraeli, her adjectives suggesting that her husband's hand gently guided her pen. 'Literature he has abandoned for politics. Do not destroy all his hopes, and make him feel his life has been a mistake. May I venture to name my own humble but enthusiastic exertions in times gone by for the party, or rather for your own splendid self? They will tell you at Maidstone that more than £40,000 was spent through my influence only.'

Nothing worked. The Disraelis had to swallow their disappointment. But the outcome should have been no surprise.

There was no political reason why Peel should have found a place for Disraeli; there were many fewer at his disposal in 1841 than there are to a Prime Minister today. Peel also owed debts of gratitude to many distinguished Tories who had helped him in Opposition and served in previous Tory Governments. Weighty voices behind the Prime Minister, including the Colonial Secretary, Lord Stanley, and the Party Manager, Francis Bonham, seem to have pushed hard against Disraeli whom they saw as a troublemaker. But in the end it is likely Peel made up his own mind. It was reasonable that Disraeli should write a begging letter; it was equally reasonable for Peel to turn it down. Peel was at fault only through an unnecessary quibble in his reply in which he misunderstood the phrase in Disraeli's letter about support that he had received from a member of the Cabinet.

So the Government was formed without Disraeli and Peel introduced his first Budget reviving the Income Tax. There was trouble from the Chartists and hardship in the northern cities; these were indeed 'the hungry forties'. But in the House of Commons, Peel reigned supreme. The sheer depth of his knowledge and breadth of his argument gave him, without any real eloquence or imagination, a notable superiority in each debate. Rich, happily married and by now on excellent terms with the Queen, he seemed to be as secure as any of his predecessors.

For about three years there was no serious tension between Peel and Disraeli. One reason for this was that Disraeli found an amiable avenue for his frustration as the leader of a small ginger group. The Young England movement, now almost forgotten, was for a few years a voluble force in the political life of our country. It was the political wing of a widespread nostalgia for the Middle Ages which had sprung up in the 1830s. This historical affection reached a peak in 1839 when the Earl of Eglinton hosted a huge Medieval Tournament at his castle in Ayrshire. In Parliament, Young England was chiefly composed of three good-looking young Old Etonians – George Smythe, Lord John Manners and Alexander Baillie-Cochrane – who were more or less convinced by the idea that the solution to England's present ills was a revival of feudalism. Smythe, for example, wanted to restore the royal practice of touching as a cure for scrofula; Manners wrote sonnets in support of the Spanish Legitimists; all three strongly believed that chivalry was a tried and tested social policy in which an active and dutiful aristocracy had built almshouses and tackled poverty in the spirit of Christian responsibility. Of course, that benevolent age had never quite existed, but this posed no problem for Disraeli. In the autumn of 1842 he made an extended visit to Paris where he was approached by Smythe and Baillie-Cochrane, who asked him to be their leader. Unlike other political compacts, this responsibility would not restrict Disraeli from accepting office should the opportunity arise. But for the time being Disraeli would sit with the other members of Young England, who would vote together under his leadership.

For the first time in his life Disraeli had attracted a following. More importantly, Young England gave him the ammunition he needed to resume his literary career. Life on the backbenches was not particularly demanding, and with long extended parliamentary recesses running from around July through to the end of the year, Disraeli had ample time on his hands. So, beginning in 1843, Disraeli embarked on a trilogy of political novels, *Coningsby*, *Sybil*, and *Tancred*. This trilogy is quite different from the earlier silver fork novels; all three aim to establish a meaningful Conservative philosophy. *Coningsby* is about what being a Conservative should mean according to Disraeli; *Sybil* is about what the Conservatives should do for the country; and *Tancred* sets out the social importance of belief.

Coningsby came first and was published in 1844. The first edition of 1,000 copies was sold out in two weeks. It is still the most popular of Disraeli's writings and the wit sparkles more strongly than in anything he had written previously. Disraeli took George Smythe as the model for the hero, Coningsby, and the plot flows from Coningsby's decision to refuse the demand by his grandfather, the icy and serene Marquess of Monmouth, to stand at his behest to become a Conservative MP. Coningsby is subsequently disinherited, but travels to the north and falls in love with a manufacturer's daughter. The story ends with Coningsby being triumphantly elected as an independent MP.

Such is the outline, but far more interesting is the string of supporting characters, in particular the manipulative Nicholas Rigby: 'Bold, acute, and voluble, with no thought but a great deal of desultory information,' Rigby was based on Disraeli's old enemy John Wilson Croker, who years earlier had helped to destroy *The Representative* newspaper. He is portrayed as an unscrupulous fixer: devious, deceitful and sycophantic. 'There is some portion of life which no one cares to accomplish but everyone wants to see,' wrote Disraeli, 'that was the portion of Mr Rigby.' Together with the two Tory apparatchiks, Tadpole and Taper, Rigby exposes the shallowness of Peel's new Conservative Party and, by implication, Peel himself. As Taper puts it: 'A sound Conservative government ... I understand: Tory men and Whig measures.'

One of the finest passages in the book is the exchange between Monmouth and Coningsby in which the hero attempts to explain why he cannot be a Conservative:

'I am sorry,' said Coningsby, rather pale, but speaking with firmness, 'I am sorry that I could not support the Conservative party.'

'By—!' exclaimed Lord Monmouth, starting in his seat, 'some woman has got hold of him, and made him a Whig!'

'No, my dear grandfather,' said Coningsby, scarcely able to repress a smile, serious as the interview was becoming, 'nothing of the kind, I assure you. No person can be more anti-Whig.'

'I don't know what you are driving at, sir,' said Lord Monmouth, in a hard, dry tone.

'I wish to be frank, sir,' said Coningsby, 'and am very sensible of your goodness in permitting me to speak to you on the subject. What I mean to say is, that I have for a long time looked upon the Conservative party as a body who have betrayed their trust; more from ignorance, I admit, than from design; yet clearly a body of individuals totally unequal to the exigencies of the epoch, and indeed unconscious of its real character.'

'You mean giving up those Irish corporations?' said Lord Monmouth. 'Well, between ourselves, I am quite of the same opinion. But we must mount higher; we must go to '28 for the real mischief. But what is the use of lamenting the past? Peel is the only man; suited to the times and all that; at least we must say so, and try to believe so; we can't go back. And it is our own fault that we have let the chief power out of the hands of our own order. It was never thought of in the time of your great-grandfather, sir. And if a commoner were for a season permitted to be the nominal Premier to do the detail, there was always a secret committee of great 1688 nobles to give him his instructions.'

'I should be very sorry to see secret committees of great 1688 nobles again,' said Coningsby.

'Then what the devil do you want to see?' said Lord Monmouth.

'Political faith,' said Coningsby, 'instead of political infidelity.'

The wise and slightly sinister figure of Sidonia glides through the book, giving Coningsby a lesson in history and philosophy by drawing attention to the moving power of Judaism. But the main point of the novel is the search for a unifying Conservative philosophy. What this creed should be remains elusive, but we are given a number of clues by Disraeli: a more enlightened aristocracy, a revered monarchy, a new guiding philosophy of community, national character and the leadership of great men, of which the last was the key.

A year later came *Sybil, or The Two Nations*. This struck quite a different note. Whereas in *Coningsby* Disraeli barely touched on industrial unrest and urban poverty, these issues lie at the centre of *Sybil*. Indeed the gritty and vernacular exchanges of dialogue in the northern slums of England are some of Disraeli's finest pieces of writing. For the first and only time in his literary career, Disraeli ventured beyond the genteel sphere of dukes and duchesses to give a flavour of what life was like on the bottom rung of society. In one bittersweet section, Disraeli summed up the tangled web of words and ideas which comprised working-class Christianity: 'I be a reg'lar born Christian and my mother afore me, and that's what few gals in the Yard can say. Thomas will take to it himself when work is slack; and he believes now in our Lord and Saviour Pontius Pilate, who was crucified to save our sins; and in Moses, Goliath, and the rest of the Apostles.'

Much of the inspiration for this and other passages came from an extended tour of northern England which Disraeli took in 1844. He gave a speech at the West Yorkshire town of Bingley which set out the central theme of *Sybil*: 'We are asked sometimes what we want. We want in the first place to impress on society that there is such a thing as duty ... if that principle of duty had not been lost sight

of for the last fifty years, you would never have heard of
the classes into which England is divided ... We want to
put an end to that political and social exclusiveness which
we believe to be the bane of this country.' These ideas run
through the novel and were the inspiration for its most
famous passage:

> 'Two nations; between whom there is no intercourse and
> no sympathy; who are as ignorant of each other's habits,
> thoughts, and feelings, as if they were dwellers in different
> zones, or inhabitants of different planets; who are formed by
> a different breeding, are fed by a different food, are ordered
> by different manners, and are not governed by the same
> laws.'
>   'You speak of—' said Egremont, hesitatingly.
>   'THE RICH AND THE POOR.'

Out of this passage has sprung the most tenacious example
of the myth which Disraeli bequeathed to the Conservative Party. The phrase One Nation is constantly paraded on
behalf of those who believe in the ideal of a fairer and more
classless society. On this basis books have been written,
dining clubs have been founded and the name of Disraeli is
used over and again as a sort of baptismal certificate for any
progressive Conservative. Disraeli himself set the direction
for future Conservatives in a later passage in *Sybil*. Toryism,
he wrote, would rise from the tomb when it announced that
power has only one duty – 'to secure the social welfare of the
PEOPLE'. This was of course the territory which Peel was
already venturing into.

The difficulty is that Disraeli never used the phrase 'One
Nation'. He believed in the existence of *Two* Nations, the rich
and the poor. Of course, it can be argued that there is no
contradiction; obviously those who believe in two nations

must, if they are men and women of principle, work for the reconciliation of these Two into One Nation. But the problem is not merely that Disraeli never used the phrase; he actively repudiates it. He argues that the Two Nations are fundamentally so different that there can be no meeting point. In many ways the storyline of *Sybil* offers a very specific way of bringing the two nations together. The main character, the aristocratic Egremont, meets and falls in love with a girl called Sybil whose upbringing has been among the People and whose father is a leader of the radical poor. He woos her extensively and plays down his family connections, but she repeatedly rebuffs him. Just as the novel appears to be heading towards an angst-ridden climax, the problem is magically solved. It turns out that Sybil is an heiress after all and the two lovers can be together. So in this novel about reuniting society, Disraeli's heroine ends up not crossing, but confirming, the class divides.

So far from believing in One Nation, Disraeli despaired of it. As the historian Jane Ridley points out, *Sybil* 'is profoundly and despairingly anti-democratic ... hell for Disraeli is the other nation. Hell is when the people rule themselves...'. The ideal solution for Disraeli would instead have been a renewed aristocracy presiding over a nation at greater ease with itself. That this was Disraeli's actual meaning is strongly suggested by a series of jottings in his private notebooks. The first mention of the Two Nations idea is not in fact *Sybil* but rather Disraeli's commonplace book from three years before. In the notebook, Disraeli scribbles the phrase 'The Two Nations' as if it were linked to 'The Five Great Forces' of political power. According to Disraeli, these driving forces were 'Dynasties and Governments', 'Nationality', 'Religious Opinions', 'Political Principles' and 'Material Interests'. There is nothing here to suggest that this was anything more than a description of the world around him – an analysis of what seemed to be an inevitable state of affairs. The challenge for Disraeli appears to have been not whether the two nations might be unified, but whether the relationship between them might be improved with more enlightened leadership. A few pages further on in the notebooks we find another clue which suggests the same thinking: 'The fusion of manners, classes & peoples diminishes national & individual character.' For a man who valued national character above every other political idea, it is not likely that he would have sacrificed it to a levelling policy. Disraeli simply was not interested in a classless society.

Tancred, as we have seen, was Disraeli's favourite novel. But it does not work. In many ways it falls furthest because it aims highest, taking as its theme the search for religious enlightenment. Blake holds that *Tancred* fails because Disraeli himself never went through a religious experience. This is probably true. The hero is another young man facing the annoying inconvenience of being pressured into becoming an MP. The story begins with a merry confabulation of Mayfair chefs and moves on to the coming of age of the young nobleman, Tancred. When Tancred's parents, the Duke and Duchess of Bellamont, present him with a parliamentary seat as a birthday present, he refuses and instead embarks on a long tour of the Middle East, where he falls in love with a Jewish girl called Eva. Tancred gropes for a cause which merits his allegiance and finds it in the social power of religion and the mysteries of racial superiority. For the first time Disraeli deploys in full his extraordinary conviction about the superiority of the Jewish race. After a series of mystical and military experiences, including an encounter with the Angel of Arabia, the novel descends into confusion. There is something almost provocative, because banal, in the very last sentence: 'The Duke and Duchess of Bellamont had arrived in Jerusalem.'

Tancred was published in 1847. Much of it was written during a curiously bleak holiday with Mary Anne in Flanders in the autumn of 1845. For almost the only time in his life, Disraeli rose early during the holiday, getting up shortly after dawn to write. His letters to his sister during these weeks show no particular concern with the Prime Minister. But within a few months he had returned to Westminster and turned his full focus to the complete destruction of Sir Robert Peel.

The first signs of a rebellion had come in 1843. Twice towards the end of the parliamentary session Disraeli had attacked the Government, first on Ireland then on foreign policy. Privately he boasted that he had an understanding with the Chief Whip, Sir Thomas Fremantle, which gave him a wide berth of independence, but he annoyed the Party hierarchy later in the year by asking for a job for his brother, which Peel and Sir James Graham, the Home Secretary, found no difficulty in turning down.

A few months later, Peel made his first serious mistake. In February 1844 he chose not to send Disraeli the standard circular letter he sent to all his supporters summoning them to attend the forthcoming parliamentary session. Disraeli protested strongly:

Private

Dear Sir Robert,

I was quite unaware until Friday night, when I was very generally apprised of it, that the circumstance of my not having received the usual circular from yourself to attend Parliament, was intentional.

The procedure admits, of course, of only one inference.

As a mere fact, the circumstance must be unimportant both to you and to myself. For you, in the present state of parties; which will, probably, last our generation; a solitary

vote must be a matter of indifference; and for me, our relations never much cultivated, had for some time, merged in
the mere not displeasing consciousness of a political connection with an individual eminent for his abilities, his virtues,
and his station.

As a matter of feeling however, I think it right, that a
public tie formed in the hour of political adversity, which
has endured many years, and which has been maintained
on my side by some exertions, should not terminate without
this clear understanding of the circumstances which it has
closed.

Disraeli went on to deny that he had systematically opposed the Government or that the Prime Minister was
entitled to cast him out of the Parliamentary Party. Indeed,
the fault lay with Peel himself, who had shown Disraeli a
frequent 'want of courtesy in debate'. 'Under these circumstances ... I am bound to say, that I look upon the fact of
not having received your summons, coupled with the ostentatious manner in which it has been bruited about, as a
painful personal procedure, which the past has by no means
authorised.'

Peel replied two days later. He explained that he had
honestly doubted whether Disraeli could still be counted
as one of his supporters, but expressed his satisfaction that
he had been proved wrong. He ended his letter by offering
a chilly apology for any offence he had caused Disraeli in
previous sessions: 'I am unconscious of having on any occasion treated you with the want of that Respect or Courtesy,
which I readily admit was fully your due. If I did so, the
act was wholly unintentional on my part.' But the damage
was done.

Over the next eighteen months Disraeli escalated his onslaughts on the Prime Minister. When Peel brought forward

policies to cut tariffs on imported sugar and to increase the grant to a Catholic College in Ireland Disraeli launched a string of highly personal assaults. Peel was the 'great Parliamentary middleman', a swindler and a conman, who had 'caught the Whigs bathing and walked away with their clothes'. Young England began to break apart as the good-looking young noblemen came under pressure from their families to detach themselves from Disraeli; indeed Smythe later accepted a job in Peel's Government. But Disraeli found no difficulty in leaving Young England behind.

One question is provoked again and again when reading Disraeli's speeches. His attacks are full of bitterness against Peel; hatred is not too strong a word. What was the cause? What was it about Peel that provoked an almost murderous reaction from his opponent?

Part of the answer is that Disraeli simply needed to accelerate his career. Self-advancement is no crime in a politician and it came as second nature to Disraeli. Many of Disraeli's peers and contemporaries were already in government and he lagged behind younger men such as Gladstone. All this meant that if Disraeli had aspirations ultimately to lead the Party, he would have to do something dramatic to elevate his own station. That this was Disraeli's overriding purpose is strongly suggested by his private jottings from later years. Sometimes a throwaway phrase reveals more than a long speech or careful letter. So it was with these brief words written down in a notebook in the 1860s: 'When I was establishing a reputation by attacking Peel...' There is no pretence of a higher mission. These attacks were about being noticed and making a name.

But there was also a genuine intellectual difference between Disraeli and Peel. They did not agree about the direction in which the country was going. Peel was hard at work, adapting the Tory Party to the spirit of the age. He was devoted to facts and figures, and used these to search for specific measures of national betterment. But for Disraeli this was to deny true Tory philosophy. True Tories should not adapt to the spirit of the age, but change it. They should restore the old order based on generous and stable relationships between classes which reflected the true character of the British people. Nowhere was this clearer than in their attitudes to free trade. Peel, as we have seen, became convinced during the 1840s that the correct solution to Britain's social problems was to cut tariffs on consumer goods in order to reduce the cost of living. By extension this meant supporting free trade. For Disraeli, this was a deeply unimpressive philosophy. He set out his own views in a lengthy speech long after Peel had fallen from grace: 'You set to work to change the basis on which this society was established. You disdain to attempt the accomplishment of the <u>best</u>, and what you want to achieve is the <u>cheapest</u>. The infallible consequence is the impoverishment of the people. But impoverishment is not the only ill consequence ... The wealth of England is not merely material wealth. It does not merely consist in the number of acres we have tilled and cultivated, nor in our havens filled with shipping, nor in our unrivalled factories, nor in the intrepid industry of our miners ... we have a more precious treasure, and that is the character of the people. This is what you have injured. In destroying what you call class legislation, you have destroyed the noble and indefatigable ambition which has been the source of all our greatness ...'

This was stirring stuff, but it still falls short of explaining the vastness of Disraeli's bitterness towards Peel. So where did this come from? Much is written about rivalry in politics. The implication tends to be that politics is driven by a series of antagonisms, if not between equals then certainly between opponents who despise each other with equal intensity. Such was the case, for example, between Castlereagh and Canning, who hated each other so much they ended up fighting a duel. But more often than not, the defining political rivalries tend to be of unequal intensity. So it was between Gladstone and Disraeli. As we shall see, Gladstone was driven to distraction by Disraeli. His books are full of obsessive jottings about a man he genuinely hated; but this hatred was not reciprocated by Disraeli, who until his very final years wrote in a more relaxed manner about Gladstone and his career.

In the same way, Disraeli's real driving obsession was Robert Peel, while Peel was far less irritated by Disraeli. Hostility to Peel was the decisive force in Disraeli's early political career. Everything about Peel grated on Disraeli. He disliked his manner, his speeches and his vocabulary. To Disraeli, Peel was like a second-rate schoolmaster, always lecturing and moralising in slow and plodding detail. Disraeli summed up his frustration in one verbal volley: 'He always traces the steam engine back to the tea-kettle. His precedents are generally tea-kettle precedents.' This priggish attention to detail irritated something deep inside Disraeli. Worse still, Peel spoke as a superior in knowledge and understanding of every subject, and this led him to treat his followers with a condescension which Disraeli found intolerable.

Disraeli's notebooks are full of notes and observations about Peel. These are quite different from those he wrote down about other Members of Parliament, noting and mocking Peel's habits, such as the way he tended to say 'We have the country with us', and his Staffordshire accent and tones: 'Peel always "pût" a question, & to the last said "woonderful" and "woonderfully". He guarded his aspirates with immense care. I have known him trip. The correctness was not spontaneous. He had managed his elocution like his temper: neither was originally good.'* By contrast, Peel's private letters and jottings contain remarkably few references to Disraeli. To evoke a mythical imagery, Peel was like a giant standing aloof from the mortals, while Disraeli darted about beneath the giant's feet, trying to find a way of felling the sturdy leader and nipping at his heels. In 1845, no one would have thought that the giant-like Peel would be felled by a negligible creature like Disraeli. But Disraeli, while biting, had found Peel's Achilles heel.

Over the previous eight years, Disraeli had changed the way he delivered speeches. He had more or less discarded the verbosity that marked his earlier rhetoric and developed a highly personal style in which cutting phrases were delivered from an almost expressionless face. The tone was one of biting sarcasm. Around this time, *Fraser's Magazine* published a telling portrait of Disraeli's speaking style: 'With his supercilious expression of countenance, slightly dashed with pomposity, and a dilettante affection, he stands with his hands on his hips, or his thumbs in the armholes of his waistcoat, while there is a slight, very slight, gyratory movement

---

*Not all of Disraeli's notes are hostile towards Peel. One of the best is his account of the two occasions when he saw Peel laugh uncontrollably. The first followed an unfortunate slip of the tongue by a Tory MP called Robert Inglis. 'Sir Robert Inglis ... brought forward once a case of grievance of some prisoner whose wife was not permitted in prison with free ingress ... He said: "Things have come to a pretty pass in this country when an Englishman may not have his wife backwards & forwards." The shout of laughter in the House was electrical. Sir Rob't Peel, who was naturally a hearty laugher, entirely lost his habitual self-control, & leant down his head in convulsions. I have only seen him once more overpowered in that way, & that was when Bickham Escott quoted three octavo pages & a half of Tacitus (literally) like a boy at Winchester (which he had been) at speeches. On this occasion, Peel, who had been quiet and demure for nearly a page, at last gave way. I sat behind him. I thought his life was in danger.'

of the upper part of his body, such as you will see ballroom
exquisites adopt when they condescend to prattle a flirtation. And then, with voice low-toned and slightly drawling,
without emphasis, except when he strings himself up for his
points, his words are not so much delivered as that they flow
from the mouth, as if it were really too much trouble for so
clever, so intellectual – in a word, so literary a man to speak
at all ... While all around him are convulsed with merriment
or excitement at some of his finely-wrought sarcasms, he
holds himself, seemingly in total suspension, as though he
had no existence for the ordinary feelings and passions of
humanity; and the moment the shouts and confusion have
subsided, the same calm, low, monotonous, but yet distant
and searching voice is heard still pouring forth his ideas,
while he is preparing to launch another sarcasm, hissing hot
into the soul of his victim.'

Disraeli had one negative target: the destruction of Sir
Robert Peel. The Prime Minister had no way of responding
to these attacks. His combination of ponderous speech and
detailed knowledge had been enough for years to hold the
Commons in submission. But here was a different kind of
adversary: agile, forceful and, above all, witty. Peel was pe-
culiarly sensitive to attacks on his honour and was helpless
in reply, pulling his hat down over his face to hide his reac-
tions to the gibes. There was nothing coarse or obvious about
Disraeli's attacks; they were lethal partly because they came
as a surprise.

Once Disraeli realised he had found a way to wound
the Prime Minister, his speeches became more abusive
and devastating. Indeed, the debates took on the feel of an
eighteenth-century blood sport. Peel had no hope of surviving this onslaught on his own. Survival for Peel became a
question of safety in numbers. So long as Peel commanded
enough support within the Conservative Party, Disraeli's

rebellion would remain guerrilla warfare – bloody but not overwhelming. But if Disraeli could find an issue around which more disgruntled backbenchers could form an alliance, then he would have a serious chance of isolating the Prime Minister and bringing down his Government.

That issue, inevitably, was the repeal of the Corn Laws.

It was wet weather that finally convinced Peel to repeal the Corn Laws – the weather and the failure of the Irish potato crop in the autumn of 1845. Taken together, the rain and the potato blight caused a famine in Ireland which created a crisis in Westminster leading to the repeal of the Corn Laws and the break-up of the Conservative Party.

The link between the Irish famine and repealing the Corn Laws was far from clear-cut. Certainly, there was a case for a temporary suspension in order to allow cheap foreign wheat into Ireland to relieve the starving people. But this was quite a different proposal to permanent Repeal. The truth was simply that Peel had changed his mind about the Corn Laws; and once he had convinced himself, Peel believed that nothing other than permanent Repeal was needed to lower the cost of living across the country.

Within weeks, Peel had informed the Cabinet that he had decided to propose the full repeal of the Corn Laws. Inevitably, the story leaked. At first it looked as if Peel would have to leave office immediately, but Lord John Russell and the Whigs were unable to form a government. And so Peel resumed his crusade against the Corn Laws, now fortified by a higher sense of purpose and believing that it was his patriotic duty to continue the Queen's Government.

Disraeli meanwhile was preparing to launch all-out warfare. In private he was vitriolic: 'Now I think it is a false famine and the question is not ripe enough for his fantastic pranks. He is so vain that he wants to figure in history as the settler of all the great questions; but a parliamentary constitution is not favourable to such ambitions; things must be done by parties, not by persons using parties as tools – especially men without imagination or any inspiring qualities, or who, rather, offer you duplicity instead of inspiration.'

At the same time, Disraeli fastened on a line of argument which might plausibly destroy Peel. Disraeli had never been a serious Protectionist. He had been rude about the Corn Laws in his earliest writings and as late as 1843 he had argued in favour of liberalising commerce so long as that liberalism was matched by reciprocal gestures from other countries. But the thrust of Disraeli's attack in 1845 and 1846 was different. Whatever the merits or failings of the Corn Laws, it was not for Peel to bring them crashing to the ground. Peel had repeatedly committed himself to the Corn Laws. His success in the 1841 election had owed everything to the support of the country gentlemen for whom the Corn Laws were an article of faith. He was using reports of famine in Ireland to disguise an act of betrayal. If he had changed his mind and was now a convert to free trade, he should resign.

At the back of Disraeli's argument was an assumption about political parties and their election promises which is familiar to us today. We are used to a world of policy pledges, carefully worded by a political party, binding all their candidates in a campaign – the breach of which is a serious matter, as we have seen over the last few years in the violent opposition to the otherwise justifiable Liberal Democrat decision to support increased tuition fees. But in 1845 this argument was relatively new. Those who study the 1841 general election in any detail find that, far from any coherent Conservative position on the Corn Laws, there was wide scope for local creativity as different pledges were made by different Tories fighting different kinds of constituency. However, once made, these local pledges were seen as sacrosanct. This is why there was a flurry of by-elections in 1846 as individual

MPs put themselves back in front of their local electorates in order to gain permission to support Repeal.

The reason why Disraeli's argument was so powerful was not that it raised questions about the inconsistency of Conservative policies in 1841, but rather that it shone a light on the inconsistency of Robert Peel himself. This was shaky ground for the Prime Minister. In his twenties and thirties, Peel had built his reputation as an Orange Protestant who opposed allowing Catholics into Parliament; in his forties, Peel had changed his mind and brought in the Catholic Relief Act of 1829. The fury of those who opposed Catholic Emancipation in 1829 had not been forgotten. When Peel proposed Corn Law repeal it seemed as though once again he was betraying the same wing of the Tory Party that he had betrayed in the 1820s. Once was unfortunate; twice was unforgivable. So when Peel stood up in the House of Commons on 22 January 1846 and proposed the repeal of the Corn Laws, Disraeli responded by focusing on the virtues of consistency. 'Let men stand by the principle by which they rise, right or wrong ... Do not then because you see a great personage giving up his opinions – do not cheer him on, do not give him so ready a reward to political tergiversation. Above all, maintain the line of demarcation between parties.'

Consistency is an overrated strength in a Prime Minister. There is no shame in changing one's mind in the face of new facts. Peel was probably right about the defects of Protection and, as we shall see, there was no serious attempt to reverse his decision in later years. But Peel's problem was that he had a history: he had changed his mind too many times. The landowners and squires now saw only a conman and a swindler – and this offered a way in for Disraeli. He knew that if he focused his fire on Peel's inconsistencies eventually the disgruntled backbenchers would unite against their chief.

And so it began. Night after night Disraeli and his allies

turned fire on their own Party leader. It is impossible to read Disraeli's speeches without admiration. They represent the high point of British parliamentary oratory. Gladstone at Midlothian in 1879 and 1880 was talking to a wider audience; so was Churchill in his broadcasts of 1940. Disraeli by contrast had one narrow political target: to bring down Robert Peel. But to bring down the Prime Minister, Disraeli knew that more than rhetoric was needed. What the Protectionists required above all was a leader who could rally the squires. Disraeli was too distrusted and, in the eyes of many Tories, frankly too weird. Lord Stanley, who had resigned from Peel's Cabinet, was the ideal candidate but he was not interested in leading such a rebellion. In February, Disraeli found the man he was looking for.

Lord George Bentinck was not known as a parliamentary orator. He had rarely spoken in the Commons since becoming an MP. As he himself admitted at one point, 'on general subjects I am much too ill informed and on a multitude of questions entirely ignorant'. To most people, Bentinck was better known as a King of the Turf, a racing fanatic who made a name for himself in exposing the Derby scandal of 1844 when a four-year-old horse won a three-year-olds' race. He is supposed to have used a racing analogy to explain his hostility to Peel in the 1840s: 'I keep horses in three counties, and they tell me that I shall save fifteen hundred a year by free trade. I don't care for that: what I cannot bear is being <u>sold</u>.' But what Lord George lacked in experience as an orator he made up for in pedigree. Rich, the son of a duke, and closely related to two Prime Ministers, Bentinck supplied what Disraeli was lacking – wealth, prestige, a noble name and therefore credibility among the Tory squires.

Disraeli and Bentinck quickly became allies. Both were driven by their determination to destroy Peel. In Parliament, Bentinck proved to be surprisingly effective. He refused to eat before giving his speeches. Hungry and angry, he proved hard to beat. He had a head for statistics, gained in a lifetime of betting on horses, which was a powerful weapon during the debates. To Bentinck, the supreme sin was swindling and dishonesty. So he rained down almighty tirades on anyone he suspected of being a cheat. The Prime Minister fell into this category, and so, together with Disraeli, Bentinck supplied much of the heavy ammunition for the nightly attacks on Peel.

Gradually it became clear that the Repeal Bill would be carried despite the rebellion, largely because of the support of many Whigs. So the Protectionists began to turn their target from victory to revenge. The key debate took place on 15 May during the Third Reading of the Repeal Bill. Disraeli landed some of his most stinging personal attacks on Peel that evening. 'When I examine the career of this Minister, which has now filled a great space in the Parliamentary history of this country, I find that for between thirty and forty years ... that right hon. Gentleman has traded on the ideas and intelligence of others. His life has been one great appropriation clause. He is a burglar of others' intellect ... from the days of the Conqueror to the termination of the last reign there is no statesman who has committed political petty larceny on so great a scale.'

Peel rose later the same evening. He returned to the Condition of England Question. 'I have a strong belief that the greatest object that we or any other government can contemplate should be to elevate the social condition of that class of the people with whom we are brought into no direct relationship by the exercise of the elective franchise.' This was almost an exact iteration of Disraeli's maxim from *Sybil*, namely that 'Power has only one duty – to secure the social welfare of the People', only that Peel uses forty-six words to Disraeli's thirteen. But Peel was not aiming at reconciliation. That night

Peel for the first and almost only time in his career responded
in kind to Disraeli's personal insults. He asked Disraeli why,
if he was so sure that Peel was a cheat and double-dealer, he
had been so keen to join his Government in 1841.

In reply, Disraeli took a great gamble: he lied. He flatly
denied that he had ever sought office under Peel: 'I can assure
the House nothing of the kind ever occurred. I never shall – it
is totally foreign to my nature – make any application for any
place ... I never asked a favour of the Government, not even
one of those mechanical things which persons are obliged
to ask ... and as regards myself, I never, directly or indi-
rectly, solicited office.' We do not know whether Peel had
Disraeli's begging letter of 1841 with him in the Commons
that evening; certainly had he used it the political situation
would have instantly changed; but as it was, Peel hesitated
and Disraeli wriggled free.

At four o'clock that morning the Repeal Bill was carried
by ninety-eight votes. Just over a month later, Disraeli and
the Protectionists exacted their revenge. In the Irish Coercion Bill they found a subject around which the rebels and
many Whigs could agree to vote tactically against Peel. Several years later, Disraeli wrote romantically of the almost
endless army of aristocrats who filed past Peel that night
to vote against him and bring down his Government, 'the
Manners, the Somersets, the Bentincks, the Lowthers and
the Lennoxes ... They trooped on: all the men of metal and
large-acred squires...'. This may have appealed to Disraeli's
sense of history, but the image was misleading. More Tories
voted with the Government that night than voted against it.
But it was not enough. When the Protectionists were added
to the Whigs and Radicals, the Government was defeated by
seventy-three votes. Peel resigned the following day.

Disraeli may have achieved his purpose, but from that
moment on he began to pay the price. With Peel's resignation

the Conservative Party broke in two pieces. It would not form a majority government again for almost thirty years. This may well have happened even without Disraeli's intervention. But either way he now found himself, in the words of the Duke of Argyll, 'like a subaltern in a great battle where every superior officer was killed or wounded'. The Party may have been broken, but for Disraeli the path to the top was now clear.

There was no tidy end to the feud between Disraeli and Peel, although one event brought them together in the very last days of Peel's life.

In June 1850 Lord Palmerston got into a scrape. As Foreign Secretary in the Whig Government, he ordered a British fleet to blockade Athens. This was because, three years previously, an anti-Semitic mob in Athens had pillaged a house belonging to a Jewish man called Don Pacifico. The victim had been born in Gibraltar and held a British passport; he therefore appealed to the British Government for assistance after failing to secure compensation from the Greeks. This assistance Palmerston duly provided in the form of the Royal Navy.

Naturally the policy provoked international outrage. More specifically, a motion of censure was carried in the House of Lords condemning Palmerston for basing his intervention on such a shaky case. The Whigs retaliated by tabling a countermotion in the Commons praising Palmerston's policies. This prompted a formidable array of parliamentary talent to assemble against the Government. Gladstone, Stanley, Peel and Disraeli all joined forces. The two broken wings of the Conservative Party – Protectionists and Peelites – came together as allies for the first time since 1845.

For the political connoisseur, the fascinating sub-plot was the relationship between Peel and Disraeli. Peel was anxious above all to prevent the Protectionists returning to office. Palmerston's aggressive policy was deeply offensive to him, but he had no wish to bring down the Whig Government. Disraeli had a different instinct. So far from rejecting Palmerston's policies he generally agreed with them. They did not differ greatly from those he would later follow when he held power. At this moment in 1850, Disraeli would have loved to draw Palmerston towards the Conservatives, but he was under rigid orders from Lord Stanley, by now the leader of the Conservative Party, to be strong and forceful. This also came at a tricky moment for Disraeli. He was the main contender for the leadership of the Party in the House of Commons, but the outcome was far from obvious. If he mishandled the moment, he might prejudice his now blossoming political career.

So Peel and Disraeli found themselves, reluctantly, on the same side. There was a muddle about the order in which they should speak. The initial plan was for Peel and Disraeli to speak on different evenings. But at the last minute Disraeli changed his plan and decided to speak on the last night of the debate. Peel was vexed, but it was too late to change his plans again. Peel spoke first and made a formidable speech, concentrating his fire on Palmerston's habit of interfering in other countries. Disraeli's speech was not one of his best, but Gladstone reported that as he finished, Peel gave a cheer of approval. Cheers come in all shapes and sizes in the House of Commons, varying from the enthusiastic to the perfunctory. We do not know which this was. In any case, Disraeli had not done enough to defeat the motion. Palmerston's own speech had been a masterpiece. His patriotic peroration, claiming that the 'watchful eye and strong arm of England' would protect every British citizen, had spoken to the burgeoning spirit of mid-Victorian assertiveness. He carried the House with him.

The following day Peel fell from his horse while riding in Hyde Park. He died in agony three days later. In his notebooks, Disraeli wrote two accounts of these final days which reveal much about the relationship between the two men. The final passage is particularly noteworthy:

Next morning, Peel was dead, or as good!

He seemed quite well in the House and spoke well – with none of the bitterness of his followers against Palmerston … Although he wd not have been in bed before 5 o clock, devoted to the Prince, he rose early to attend a Council about the projected 'Great Exhibition'. There was some financial question – He took it up, but not with his usual lucidity – Then he put pen to paper, but seemed confused, & finally said, he would think over the matter & send his results to the Prince.

He went home, & afterwards went out to ride, and it happened. Was it a fit? If so, it was brought on by unnecessary want of rest & repose. I know, as well as most men, what it is to get home at 4 or 5 in the morning after an exciting division. Sleep is not commanded under such circumstances, even by the philosophical. Had Peel taken his fair rest, would he have been saved? Bulwer-Lytton thought not, when we talked over these matters. 'He had done his work,' he said, 'no man lives who has done his work. There was nothing left for him to do.'

I did not rise, that fatal day, so early as Sir Robert Peel. And in the afternoon, my guardian angel persuaded me, instead of going to Clubs & House of Commons, to take a drive in our agreeable environs. We were returning thro' the Regent's Park & two gentlemen on horseback, strangers, stopped our carriage. 'Mr Disraeli,' they said, 'you will be interested to hear that Sir Robert Peel has been thrown from his horse & has been carried home in a dangerous state.' 'Dangerous?' I

enquired. 'I hope not. His loss wd be a great misfortune for
this country.'

It seemed a little uninspired, but I spoke what I felt.*

What are we to make of all this?

At one level, there need not have been a conflict between
the two men. Both were interested in the Condition of England. Both agreed that the nation was divided dangerously.
Both argued that improving the welfare of society was a political priority. Both rejected the notion that this could be
delivered by the Whigs. Disraeli's attachment to Protection
evaporated after the Repeal Bill had been carried. 'Search my
speeches through and you will not find one word of Protection in them,' he explained. And when it came to the point in
later years, Disraeli as Prime Minister acted in a similar way
to Peel. As Blake records, the electoral success which Disraeli
eventually achieved in 1874 'was more the result of winning
over the bourgeoisie than of any recurrence to the principles
of Young England. Many Conservative leaders have had a
hankering for Disraeli's precept, but they have usually followed Peel's practice – and so did Disraeli.'

Both Disraeli and Peel at times grumbled about their supporters. Peel did not conceal his low regard for those whose
priority in life was shooting pheasants or hunting the fox.
They had been elected to support him in carrying the Queen's
Government, and that should be their priority. Likewise,
Disraeli later complained about 'the apathy of the party:
they could not be got to attend to business while the hunting
season lasted ... They had good natural ability ... but they
wanted culture: they never read.' But whereas in the 1840s

---

* Initially Disraeli had written 'I spoke from my heart' but he crossed these
words out and replaced them with 'what I felt'. It was a telling alteration;
his heart was not involved.

Isaac D'Israeli instilled in his eldest son a love of books and a Tory interpretation of English history.

Disraeli's sister, Sarah. When her fiancé died, Disraeli advised her: 'live for me'.

Disraeli's mother, Maria, thought her son was clever but 'no prodigy'.

The dandy phase —
Disraeli in his late
twenties.

Henrietta Sykes — the most ardent of
Disraeli's lovers. Their relationship
was doomed from the start.

Disraeli bought Hughenden Manor in 1848; the purchase turned him into a country gent.

ver many years, he and Mary
nne transformed their new
sidence. While Gladstone felled
ees up in Flintshire, Disraeli
ked to plant them around his
uckinghamshire estate.

Mary Anne – dotty, devoted.
Disraeli told her she was more
like a mistress than a wife.

Lord Lyndhurst, with whom Disraeli shared a lover. Asked whether he believed in platonic love, he is said to have responded: 'after, but not before'.

The 14th Earl of Derby, with whom Disraeli had a rocky partnership. He served as Prime Minister three times but never won a general election.

Disraeli greatly valued his friendship with Bulwer Lytton. Bulwer's wife did not feel the same way and accused the two men of 'nameless' crimes; Disraeli responded by calling her the Tigress of Taunton.

Lord George Bentinck: Disraeli's chief patron and ally. Together they brought down a Prime Minister and broke up the Conservative Party.

Lord John Manners, Disraeli's long-standing comrade and co-founder of the Young England group.

Foes

Lord Palmerston, who
for decades delayed
Disraeli's climb up the
greasy pole.

Robert Lowe led the
'Cave of Adullam',
a gathering of
malcontents opposed to
Parliamentary Reform.

Lord John Russell
twice served as Prime
Minister but never
seemed big enough for
the role.

Gladstone:
the 'Arch-Villain'.

Disraeli hounded
Sir Robert Peel to
destruction but later
described him as the
greatest Member of
Parliament who ever
lived.

The 15th Earl of Derby:
Disraeli's long-standing
friend and later his
opponent. His views on
foreign policy were as
follows: 'If foreigners
can settle their affairs
without us, why should
we intervene?'

Nobody really understood the Second Reform Act, but passing it was deemed a great success.

THE DERBY, 1867. DIZZY WINS WITH "REFORM BILL"

Mr. Punch. "DON'T BE TOO SURE; WAIT TILL HE'S *WEIGHED.*"

Disraeli was bored by the details of legislation. He fell asleep when they were discussed in Cabinet.

THE CONSERVATIVE PROGRAMME.

"DEPUTATION BELOW, SIR,—WANT TO KNOW THE CONSERVATIVE PROGRAMME."
Rt. Hon. Ben. Diz. "EH?—OH!—AH!—YES!—QUITE SO! TELL THEM, MY GOOD ABERCORN, WITH MY COMPLIMENTS, THAT WE PROPOSE TO RELY ON THE SUBLIME INSTINCTS OF AN ANCIENT PEOPLE!!"
[*See Speech at Crystal Palace.*

With Queen Victoria. 'Everyone likes flattery,' Disraeli said, 'and when you come to royalty, you should lay it on with a trowel.'

Disraeli's Cabinet in 1874, after his great and only election victory.

Disraeli at sunset. 'There were days when I felt I could move dynasties and governments, but that has passed away.'

The Primrose League grew up shortly after Disraeli's death. The myth would become mightier than the man.

Peel was clumsy and sometimes ungracious in handling his supporters, Disraeli later bewitched and seduced the back benchers and Tory squires into backing a radical Reform Bill with which many of them did not agree.

Yet the difference between them was more than a matter of political skill. When researching a life of Peel, we were moved by the way Peel kept returning to the disaster that struck the weaving town of Paisley in the early 1840s. In 1841 the town had gone bankrupt. More than half the merchants and manufacturers failed. By 1842 some 17,000 were destitute. The situation was desperate. As one memorial which Peel received put it, 'there is a very general feeling of deep and settled discontent. Hopeless and worn out with either continued depression or often recurring distress, many have lost much of their wanted self respect ... Their homes are sometimes the picture of extreme wretchedness...'. Peel responded to the catastrophe with a highly unorthodox programme of relief and administration. Over time, the mills reopened and trade revived. But Peel never forgot what had happened at Paisley.

In letter after letter, Peel returned to the depression. Paisley took on a totemic significance as a sign of what was wrong with the economy. In particular, Paisley reinforced Peel's conviction that the aim of policy should be to increase the purchasing power of ordinary citizens. This was more important than protecting agricultural interests. So when stout, rural backbench Tory MPs wrote to Peel and complained about the low wheat prices which were the result of a good harvest and the cheapness of imported food, Peel exploded. One such letter from an MP called Sir Charles Burrell was given both barrels by Peel: 'If Sir Charles had such cases before him as I have, of thousands and tens of thousands in want of food and employment, at Greenock, Paisley, Edinburgh and a dozen large towns in the manufacturing districts, he would not expect me to rend my garments in despair if some excellent jerked beef from South America should get into the English market, and bring down meat from $7\frac{1}{2}$ pence or 8 pence a pound.'

The point is that Peel did not simply seek to alleviate poverty. He was genuinely moved by it. As the historian G.M. Young has written, 'his frigid efficiency covered an almost passionate concern for the welfare of the people'. The same simply cannot be said of Disraeli. We have scoured his notebooks and correspondence and found nothing resembling Peel's Paisley letters. Such letters do not exist. Poverty hardly appears. On the contrary, as we have seen, Disraeli's notebooks are littered with lists of famous people he had met and worked with. His letters are full of descriptions of dinners, diamonds and flowers. Nowhere do we find the same deepfelt commitment to relieving poverty which we find with Peel. Only in *Sybil* do we see Disraeli delve into these issues and write passionately about the problems of the north. This exception proves the rule, as we can never be sure when reading this novel whether these passionate passages about poverty are the result of genuine sympathy or rather a dazzling display of literary skill. More often than not, Disraeli's arguments are masked by an irony which barely conceals a sneer.

Of course, we can push this case too far. Disraeli was no thoughtless reactionary. He held a genuine belief that the aristocracy ought to behave in a more responsible and dutiful manner. While he rejected One Nation Conservatism, preferring an ancient and feudal social hierarchy to a more classless society, he nonetheless believed that the aristocracy should be open to new entrants and receptive to meritocracy. He was clear on this point in his later writings: 'The aristocracy of England absorbs all aristocracies, and receives every man in every order and every class who defers to the principle of our society, which is to aspire and to excel.' But none of this qualifies as sincere mission to improve society, and when it came to private philanthropy and charitable work, Disraeli was lax by comparison with many colleagues. As Professor Vincent records: 'Lord Derby (the Premier) set up a welfare state for his estate employees, and headed the relief operations in the Lancashire cotton famine of the 1860s. The younger Derby built public libraries and public baths, and ran the Peabody buildings trust. Sir Stafford Northcote was a great promoter of boys' reformatories. Sir John Pakington was a keen educational reformer. Cairns, the hard-headed Belfast man, who was Disraeli's Lord Chancellor, taught in a Sunday school ... For all his general kindliness of tone towards the indigent, Disraeli was simply not a very active man outside his ordinary parliamentary routine.'

Compassion is not everything in a politician and when it descends into sentimentality it can be actively corrosive. It would be unfair to make this the yardstick for any career. Indeed, cool, calm, unflappable and unemotional leadership, as shown by Lord Salisbury or William Pitt, can be more effective than any crusading visionaries. But politics is nothing if it has no purpose. It is simply not enough to be skilful and intelligent. Two of Disraeli's closest political allies were the 15th Earl of Derby and Lord Cairns; both found themselves worrying whether their chief sincerely believed anything that he said. They had a point. The reason why Peel ranks above Disraeli in the record of statesmanship is that he set himself a task of delivering a necessary change for the country, namely improving the economic condition of society. By repealing the Corn Laws, at the expense of his own career and even his party, this is what Peel ultimately achieved.

Shortly after Peel died, Disraeli wrote a life of Lord George Bentinck. This was a mark of gratitude and appreciation for Disraeli's old ally who had staunchly supported him in these

pivotal years. As with all of Disraeli's writings, the protagonist fails to come alive. But the centrepiece of the work, on
which Disraeli particularly prided himself, was the portrait
of Peel. This is indeed a masterpiece. Without withdrawing a word of his own bitter invective against his leader, he
works hard to strike a balance between Peel's merits and
his failings. In the background was a political need to win
back the Peelites to the remaining rump of the Conservative
Party. The conclusion Disraeli comes to is that Peel was not
an exceptional Prime Minister; this was because he failed Disraeli's test of leadership – 'he never could maintain himself
in power'. Instead, Disraeli says that Peel was the greatest
Member of Parliament who ever lived.

Disraeli does not offer an explanation for the accolade,
but by any standard the titles should be reversed. Peel, by
his achievements in office at the expense of his own party,
placed himself in the first rank of British Prime Ministers. But
he was not a particularly impressive Member of Parliament.
His speeches were cumbersome and wordy. That title instead
might be bestowed on the man who almost single-handedly
raised the profile and reputation of Parliament as a theatre of
imagination and rhetoric in the years before democracy and
mass media; that MP was Benjamin Disraeli.

Before we close this chapter, there is one final thread from
these years which is worthy of special mention here.

In 1849 Disraeli attended a Protectionist dinner at the Merchant Taylors' Hall. By chance, he found himself seated next
to Croker – a strong Protectionist but, more awkwardly, the
inspiration for the loathsome Rigby in *Coningsby*. This could
have been a difficult evening. Disraeli recalled the dinner in
a later note: 'It was rather embarrassing. But Mr Croker &
myself were not socially acquainted. I had never seen him
since I was a boy. For he was the person who ought to assume

that a character in one of my books, which he deemed odious, was intended for himself.'

Far from being appalled by this inveterate fawner, Disraeli was genuinely impressed by Croker. 'He behaved like a man of the world: informed me that he had had the pleasure of, he hoped, the friendship of my excellent father, talked generally about the political situation, warmed into anecdote, and made himself agreeable ... When I made my speech after dinner, I observed he nodded his head frequently in approbation, and gave other signs of sympathy, and perhaps stronger feeling. I thought all this on his part a very good performance, and that he had extricated himself out of an embarrassing position with dexterity and some grace.'

This was followed in Disraeli's notebook by the story of another encounter in later years. Disraeli had just opened and closed a notable debate. He was standing in the hall of the Carlton Club when Croker swept up and put his hand on Disraeli's arm, saying: 'The speech was the speech of a statesman, and the reply was the reply of a wit.' Disraeli then recounted a message which Croker sent as he was dying. Apparently, Croker sought a final reconciliation between the two men, but Disraeli declined an interview. 'It was too late, and my sensibilities ... too much required nursing.'

From these encounters, Disraeli drew a conclusion which tells us more about Disraeli than it does about Croker: 'The moral I draw from all this is that men of a certain age like the young ones who lick them.' We have a different view. Disraeli had Croker correct first time: he was indeed like Rigby and in these exchanges Croker appears at his most Rigbyesque – false, fawning and sycophantic. Yet Disraeli was completely won over by the display. Vanity was after all an all-conquering force with Disraeli. This was the triumph of the sycophant over the cynic.

THE GREASY POLE

Parliament returned after the collapse of Peel's Government for the new session on 19 January 1847. For the first time in his career, Disraeli took a seat on the Conservative front benches, alongside Lord George Bentinck and three places away from Sir Robert Peel. It would be many years of wearisome intrigue before he was generally accepted as the Party's unquestioned leader; but after the drama of the repeal of the Corn Laws, Disraeli had established himself as someone who could not be ignored. Just as he had forecast at the end of his maiden speech, they were listening to him now.

But what was he to say? Disraeli had burst upon the scene at a time when the political system was fast evolving. The influence of the Crown in deciding who should govern the country, and on what basis, was ebbing away, but the decisive power of political parties was not yet established. The result was a period of confusion in which parties and factions jostled angrily for position, operating under rules not yet clearly defined. The future of Ireland, the virtues of free trade, the authority of the Church and the wisdom of enlarging the franchise were some of the issues which divided the parties and brought about splits within Tories and Whigs.

As always in politics, clashes of personality cut across disputes over policy. The repeal of the Corn Laws provides the most striking example. Peel's determination to press on with Repeal had split the Conservative Party, but not symmetrically. The mass of squires and stalwart country gentlemen who had followed Disraeli and Bentinck into Opposition taunted a minority of Peelites who remained loyal to Sir Robert Peel. The trouble about the Peelites was that they were almost all chiefs and no Indians. They included a large number of Peel's senior Cabinet Ministers and many of the young men, such as Gladstone and Sidney Herbert, whom Peel had groomed for future leadership. No plausible Conservative government could form without some or all of these men, but they were too few in number to form a government on their own. So the question was whether the Tory squires could rebuild the Party by reaching some kind of acceptable compromise on free trade.

This was the task that fell to Bentinck and Disraeli as they took the lead of the Protectionist MPs. The difficulty for Disraeli was that his natural tendency was to divide rather than unite his Party. His successes so far had been entirely destructive. He had brought down a Prime Minister and helped break up the Conservative Party. The result was to put Lord John Russell and the Whigs back in power. To have any hope of holding office himself, Disraeli had to find a way of healing the wounds which he had opened in his own party, but his room for manoeuvre was extremely narrow. In foreign policy, Lord Palmerston carried all before him; his noisy patriotism appealed to the increasingly confident, mid-Victorian mood. In economic matters, free trade was fast becoming an established orthodoxy and a significant vote-winner in the key borough seats. And as for the religious debates which dominated these years, whatever his own views, Disraeli simply could not compete with Gladstone's passionate expertise.

The result was that, within a short space of years, the Whigs were able to establish themselves as the dominant force in British politics. The novelist Anthony Trollope compared the late 1840s and 1850s to the mythical conflict between the Gods and Giants. Up on Mount Olympus, the Whig Gods reigned over the Tory Giants beneath them. Every so often the Tories formed an alliance and managed to scale the mountain, but then the Whigs would bestir themselves and regain their rightful ascendancy.

Trollope was a Whig and a biased observer, but the Tory predicament was clear. For the next twenty years, which might have been his most productive period, Disraeli was confined almost entirely to Opposition. He searched in vain for a political combination which could provide the broken Conservative Party with a working majority. He tried one alliance, then another; he held private talks with the Whigs, the Radicals, even with what was known as the Irish Brigade. Paying little regard to political consistency, he twisted the key this way and that, but the door remained stubbornly locked. These manoeuvres gave him a reputation for duplicity, but he persevered because the prize was great. He was prepared to consider any rearrangement of positions or policies if it brought him a working majority.

There was one exception. The general election of 1847 produced no dramatic alteration in the balance of power in Parliament. The Whigs and Radicals were left with 325 seats in the House of Commons; the Protectionists and Peelites shared around 330. The Peelites were concerned above all that no alteration should be made to Peel's free trade settlement, so they were content to prop up Lord John Russell's Whig Government. The single dramatic outcome of the election was the success of the Jewish Lionel de Rothschild as a Whig MP for the City of London. He immediately ran up against the formidable obstacle of the Parliamentary Oath which prohibited non-Christians from taking up parliamentary seats. An impasse then developed, unresolved for eleven years, during which Rothschild could not take his seat despite being re-elected several times.

Initially in 1847, Lord John Russell brought forward a Bill to remove the disability and allow Rothschild and other Jews to take their seats. Any calculation of political self-interest would have led Disraeli to oppose the change, alongside the great majority of Tory MPs. But this was an issue of principle on which he was ready to stand firm. Other causes he was able to abandon or modify, as suited a politician of boundless ambition. But here was a rock-like conviction to which he must hold. He therefore repeatedly spoke and voted for Jewish Emancipation against the bulk of his own party.

What was remarkable was not just the way he voted but the argument that he used to justify that vote. The normal case for Jewish Emancipation was familiar. It was the same as the earlier argument in 1829 used in favour of allowing Catholics to enter Parliament. For anyone of even a mildly liberal frame of mind the case was impregnable, namely that it was indefensible that any of Her Majesty's subjects should be subjected to a test of faith as a condition of having a voice in Parliament. This was the case put in 1847 by Lord John Russell and thereafter by all those who advocated Jewish Emancipation. By contrast, Disraeli's arguments were so exaggerated as to be incomprehensible. 'Where is your Christianity if you do not believe in their Judaism?' he asked in one debate. And again later: 'I cannot, for one, give a vote which is not in deference to what I believe to be the true principles of religion.' He was greeted with almost total silence as he sat down. Few MPs had read his novels and were prepared for these arguments. To many they bordered on heresy. The stance won him few friends inside his own party and reinforced the general sense of suspicion towards him. Yet Disraeli stuck to his task and forcefully made his case. When finally a compromise was agreed in 1858 which allowed Jews to take their seats in the House of Commons, Rothschild made a point of pausing on his way to the Whig benches to shake hands with Disraeli.

Disraeli found a strong ally on this issue in Bentinck. In the confused and reduced state of affairs which existed in 1847, Bentinck was the default leader of the Conservatives in the House of Commons. But he had begun his political life as a Whig, and he argued for Jewish Emancipation on Whig grounds of individual liberty and religious toleration. Nonetheless, he took a significant gamble by making a public stand with Disraeli on this issue and his position as leader came under considerable pressure during the remainder of the year.

Meanwhile, Bentinck was playing a key supporting role in another aspect of Disraeli's political career. In March 1847 Disraeli had signed an agreement to purchase a large whitewashed house a mile north of High Wycombe, near the town of Beaconsfield. Hughenden Manor was on the market for £24,700 excluding the value of timber on the estate, the total cost coming to a cool £34,950. Of course, this was far more than Disraeli possessed. He still owed at least £15,000 to various creditors, despite Mary Anne's efforts to help settle his most pressing debts. The previous year he had hired a solicitor called Philip Rose of Baxter, Rose & Norton to handle his personal affairs and Rose helped raise funds for the new home. But the bulk of the bill seems to have been met by Lord George Bentinck's promise of a significant loan. The exact details are obscure, but a flow of letters in 1847 and 1848 make clear that Bentinck was prepared to provide a considerable sum of money to help Disraeli buy the house and become a country gentleman.

The decision to purchase Hughenden enabled Disraeli to move up the ladder of constituency seats. Disraeli's career as an MP so far had been far from ideal. Sued at Maidstone, abused at Shrewsbury, he required something more dignified and stable to support his claim to be a frontbench MP. He already had a strong connection to the county of Buckinghamshire, as his family were at this time still living in the constituency at Bradenham. Ahead of the 1847 general election he took his chance and offered himself as a candidate for this prized county seat. The electors accepted him and he was returned without contest as one of three Buckinghamshire MPs.

Three deaths in two years complicated these careful arrangements. First, on 21 April 1847, Disraeli's mother passed away aged seventy-one. Disraeli's relationship with his mother had not improved with age. He hardly mentioned her in his public writings or private letters. It is impossible to detect the cause of the coolness, but a moment of genuine warmth appeared right at the end of her life. In March 1847 Disraeli's sister wrote to Mary Anne about a particularly fine speech by Disraeli which had won over one longstanding doubter: 'Mama at last confesses that she never before thought Disraeli was equal to Mr Pitt.' Twenty years had passed since Mrs Disraeli had described her eldest son as 'tho' a clever boy, no prodigy'; it had taken Disraeli half a lifetime to convince his mother of what he had always believed. We do not know whether his mother's words of praise were passed on to Disraeli in March 1847. A month later, she was dead.

Isaac D'Israeli followed his wife nine months later, on 19 January 1848, aged eighty-one. For many years he had been blind and heavily dependent on Disraeli's sister Sarah who served as his intellectual companion and literary scribe. But he kept a close watch on his eldest son's political career as it developed and this gave him an immense source of pride in his infirmity. He particularly approved of Disraeli's speech on Jewish Emancipation, about which Sarah wrote: 'Papa thinks Diz's speech the most important ever delivered in the House of Commons.' His own views on Judaism remained strongly dissenting, but he and Maria never converted to Christianity. They were buried in Bradenham churchyard.

Of all the influences on Disraeli's life, Isaac had been perhaps the greatest. Isaac had supplied his son with a love of the Stuarts and a Tory version of English history. His library had been where Disraeli first assembled his own prized stock of ideas. Over the next two years, Disraeli paid handsome tribute to his father by working with his sister on a new edition of the *Curiosities of Literature*, together with an extended family memoir. Many years later Disraeli noted the continuing success of his father's literary work. He scribbled in his private notebooks that when a version of the *Curiosities* had been published in 1822, his father had gloomily predicted that science would supersede literature. 'My father lived more than a quarter of a century after this observation, & published before his death in 1848 more numerous & larger editions of the Curiosities of Literature than during his preceding life – and since his death, the Curs. & all his literary works have been stereotyped & are sold at every Railway stall of the Kingdom, & are the favourite reading in that kind of the bustling and toiling millions.'

Isaac's estate was valued at a little less than £11,000 at his death, of which both Ben and Sarah inherited a third and Disraeli's two younger brothers, Ralph and James, split the remainder. The four siblings also received a stream of income from investments of almost £12,000 on various government bonds, although Disraeli's share was significantly reduced as a result of the loans his father had made him prior to his death. Isaac had rented the house at Bradenham and there was no question of trying to keep it as a home for Sarah. So the remaining possessions were distributed and some 25,000 books belonging to Isaac were sold at Sotheby's; only a select few were transferred to Hughenden, including a number of volumes on Jewish history.

Two tricky questions remained. The first concerned Sarah. Ever since Meredith's death in Egypt, Sarah had lived a spinster's life and there was no prospect of that changing now. Initially she moved to live with friends, but her life became lonely and unhappy as she struggled to find a reason for her existence, with her beloved older brother now married and her literary father having passed away. A second and more unorthodox question concerned the fate of a manservant called Giovanni Battista Falcieri, or 'Tita' as he was known. Disraeli had picked Tita up during his tour of the Orient. He was something of a celebrity. Many years before, Lord Byron had taken on Tita as a manservant; indeed Byron had died in Tita's arms at Missolonghi during the Greek War of Independence. After returning to England in the 1830s, Tita had become Isaac D'Israeli's valet and had served the old man with distinction. But now, with no employer and doubtful job prospects, the future for this famous butler looked bleak. The situation was saved by John Hobhouse, the President of the Board of Control and a former friend of Lord Byron, who offered Tita a job as a Government messenger.

Disraeli completed the purchase of Hughenden on 6 September 1848. His contentment lasted two weeks. On 21 September Lord George Bentinck died dramatically, aged forty-six. He had spent the morning at his Nottinghamshire home of Welbeck Abbey, writing a letter to Disraeli, and had later set off on a walk to nearby Thoresby. Halfway there, he collapsed and died. Disraeli declared that the death was 'the greatest loss I have ever experienced', but it also raised the prospect of another loss of a quite different kind. Disraeli had relied on Bentinck's money to purchase Hughenden, but there was no guarantee that Bentinck's family, namely his brothers Lord Henry and Lord Titchfield and their father, the Duke of Portland himself, would honour the loan. Disraeli drafted an artful letter of condolence to Lord Henry which combined sadness with self-concern: 'It seems to me that the pulse of the nation beats lower after this ... All is unutterable woe! And I only write this because, when the occasion is fitting, there are reasons which make it necessary I should see you.'

Disraeli was duly summoned to an interview on 18 October. We do not know exactly what was agreed, but the meeting was a triumph for Disraeli. He laid his cards on the table, making clear to Lord Henry that if he was asked to pay back the loan he would have to sell Hughenden and resign his Buckinghamshire seat. 'This he declared to be utterly impossible,' Disraeli told Mary Anne later. 'Then I went on [to] the state of my affairs, observing that it would be no object to them and no pleasure to me, unless I played the high game in public life; and that I could not do that without being on a rock.' Lord Henry accepted this plea. 'Finally, he entreated me not to mention this to the Duke, or to anyone but himself: that the moment affairs were settled, he would himself see what he could do about my private affairs; that he was resolved that I should play the great game; and that I must trust him. He remained with me four hours, and appears more devoted than even Lord G.'

And so Disraeli remained on his rock. It was an old-fashioned arrangement, more resonant of a deal between Lord Rockingham and Edmund Burke in the eighteenth century than the more upright standards of Victorian times. But it facilitated the next step on the upward ladder of Disraeli's career. That is not to say that the rock never felt a little shaky. In 1857 Lord Henry's brother called time on the loan, once again throwing Disraeli's finances into considerable chaos. But by this time Disraeli had established himself at the top of the Conservative Party, and in any case Mrs Brydges Williams had appeared on the scene with her promise of significant future funds. The support provided by Lord Henry and his family had been critical precisely because it came at a critical moment. For the first time in his career, Disraeli could enjoy the same lifestyle as the gentrified Tory squires whom he sought to lead.

Disraeli never forgot what he owed Lord George Bentinck. In later years he would make an appropriate tribute to the Bentinck family, but at this moment he began to repay the debt in the only coin in which he was rich. He wrote a political biography of Lord George Bentinck, which he published in 1851. It is a strange book, too long because padded with speeches and arguments forgotten long ago. Yet it is compelling, at least for those who find the political drama real. In general he heaps praise on Lord George, picking out in particular his aptitude for hard work and his forthright support of all those who would suffer from Peel's conversion to free trade. The book was a surprising commercial success, going through four editions in six months. But the real value of the biography, apart from the portrait of Peel, is the tribute it pays to the alliance between Bentinck and Disraeli. No other political partnership has developed quite like it; it was a success precisely because it was unique.

Meanwhile, Hughenden had an effect on Disraeli which neither he nor Bentinck had considered when he signed the deeds. More than any other event in his private life, moving to this quiet, picturesque, comfortable, rural property opened up for Disraeli a hinterland beyond politics. The woods and streams which ran through the 750 acres of the estate had a calming effect on Disraeli, and he became a happier man when he was there. For example, in January 1849 Disraeli wrote to his wife after returning to London: 'Dear Lady of Hughenden. What would I not give to be with you in these almost spring mornings, surrounded by birds, flowers and running waters!' The pleasures of planting trees and roaming woodlands were all the more attractive to Disraeli because they were largely new to him; he had grown up in the city, around Holborn and Bloomsbury, and although his parents had moved to Bradenham in his early twenties, by this time his interests had taken him elsewhere, into stock markets and travels round the Middle East. It was only now, later in life, mellowed by marriage and middle age, that Disraeli saw the simple beauty of the countryside and began to cherish it deeply.

For the next thirty years Disraeli would divide his time between Hughenden and Mary Anne's house at Grosvenor Gate, moving up to the country for the long recess. For the first few days after his return to Hughenden he would do no work but walk round his estate, talking to the woodsmen and inspecting the greenery. A note written in 1860 gives a florid impression of these activities: 'I find great amusement in talking to the people at work in the woods and grounds at Hughenden. Their conversation is racy, and the repose of their natural manners agreeable ... I like very much the society of woodsmen. Their conversation is most interesting. Quick and constant observation and perfect knowledge. I don't know any men who are so completely masters of their business, and of the secluded, but delicious, world in which they live ... A forest is like the Ocean, monotonous only to the ignorant. It is a life of ceaseless variety.'

Disraeli was particularly fascinated by trees. In a previous book about Foreign Secretaries, we noted the strong links between plants and diplomacy. Lord Aberdeen, for example, planted fourteen million trees on his estate in

Scotland; the 15th Earl of Derby planted two million trees at Knowsley; Austen Chamberlain found plants more interesting than people. As it was for these Foreign Secretaries, so it was for Disraeli. Over the years he planted a countless number of shrubs and trees at Hughenden. Combined with the significant landscaping changes Mary Anne made to the estate, he transformed the grounds into a forest of firs and streams. Unlike Gladstone, who at this moment was pondering axemanship classes and would in later years fascinate large crowds by his steady slaughter of trees on his estate, Disraeli tended to overplant rather than overkill, and happily allowed his grounds to become cloaked in foliage.*

There was also another element to this transformation. Although, as we have seen, Disraeli always remained a willing outsider from society and lost no opportunity in blowing the trumpet of Judaism, he now took on the manners of an English rural gentleman. He was proud to be a magistrate and enjoyed attending Quarter Sessions. He paid close attention to the changing agricultural seasons and liked to wander down rural ways. Of course, Disraeli took this behaviour only so far: he hunted no foxes and shot no pheasants in these years. But now more than ever, he became part of landed society. He maintained these habits for the rest of his days.

It was here at Hughenden in the autumn of 1848 that Disraeli began to plot the next phase of his career. Lord George

---

*In his notebooks from 1860, Disraeli recorded a more extreme instance of this obsession. 'Old Lord Londonderry (the Minister's brother) told me that there used to be great discussions between his parents about cutting down trees. His mother was very opposed to this necessary and salutary process – when judiciously carried on. After her death, some verses were found in her papers, addressed to her husband, & they began: "Avaunt! Arboricide!".'

Bentinck's death had thrown open the Conservative leadership in the House of Commons. In the Lords, Lord Stanley was the most powerful Protectionist and any final decision on the Commons leadership rested with him. Rich, powerful, the heir to an ancient dynasty, Stanley had been marked out for great things ever since he entered politics in the early 1830s. A famous story survives of a conversation between Lord Melbourne and the youthful Disraeli in the 1830s during which Disraeli declared that he wished to become Prime Minister; Lord Melbourne brushed the ambition aside: 'No chance of that in our time. It is all arranged and settled. Nobody can compete with Stanley ...' In 1834 Stanley had switched parties over concerns about the growing radicalism of the Whigs. From his Lancastrian seat at Knowsley he had prepared a bold statement about the future of the Tory Party, but he was beaten to it by Peel's Tamworth Manifesto. For the next ten years he had operated under Peel's leadership, but broke with him over the repeal of the Corn Laws. By 1848 he was the recognised leader of the Conservative Party and one step away from winning the top prize. But, to fulfil his destiny, he needed an able lieutenant who could lead the Party in the House of Commons. Disraeli was determined to fill the vacancy.

That autumn Disraeli's friends, including Lord Henry Bentinck and Lord John Manners, struck up an unofficial leadership campaign. At one level Disraeli was unchallengeable. By sheer talent and debating skill, he was in effect already the leading Protectionist MP. He was quicker, cleverer and vastly more effective than any of the solid squires. For this reason Lord Malmesbury, a senior Conservative and future Foreign Secretary, noted after Bentinck's death that 'no one but Disraeli can fill his place'.

But there was something wrong with Disraeli. Like Canning before him, who could not take tea without a stratagem, so Disraeli inspired extreme feelings of distrust among his colleagues. Thus William Beresford, a Party Whip, observed he would sooner trust a convicted felon than Disraeli. Charles Newdegate reflected that 'I have been warned repeatedly not to trust Disraeli.' And Malmesbury himself, a shrewd observer, noted that there 'can be no doubt that there is a very strong feeling amongst Conservatives in the House of Commons against Disraeli. They are puzzled and alarmed by his mysterious manner, which has much of the foreigner about it, and are incapable of understanding and appreciating the great abilities which certainly underlie, and, as it were, are concealed by this mask.'

What made these suspicions more damaging is that they were largely shared by the Party's Commander-in-Chief. Lord Stanley had fallen out with Disraeli many years before. On the final leg of his voyage home from the Middle East, Disraeli had linked up with Lord Stanley's younger brother, Henry. The two men had travelled together to London from Falmouth. At this point, Henry Stanley fell off the radar and an elaborate manhunt was launched across London. He was eventually tracked down at the home of a notorious moneylender called Effie Bond, whereupon he claimed that it was Disraeli who had introduced him to the place. Whether or not this was true, Stanley Senior was convinced Disraeli had led his brother astray. Many years on, and this past had not been forgotten, although Stanley acknowledged that Disraeli's behaviour had generally improved: 'I have never seen, of late years, any reason to distrust him,' he cautiously noted, 'and I think he will run straight; but he would not be acceptable as Leader.'

For these reasons, and a host of others which filtered through to him from the Whips that autumn, Lord Stanley sat down on 21 December 1848 and composed a long letter of rejection to Disraeli. 'I am doing you bare justice when

I say that as a debater there is no one of our party who can pretend to compete with you; and the powers of your mind, your large general information, and the ability you possess to make yourself heard and felt, must at all times give you a commanding position in the House of Commons ... But, believing also, as I do, that, from whatever causes, your formal establishment in the post of Leader would not meet with a general and cheerful approval ... I pay you the much higher compliment of thinking that you have both the clearness of perception ... and the manliness of character ... as to be willing to waive [your] claim ...'

Only someone as sure of themselves as a Stanley could have written this letter. In essence, Stanley was saying that Disraeli would be the Party's star player but would be denied the captain's armband. It was an offer Disraeli was always going to refuse. This was his moment. He knew the longer he waited, the more likely it was that a talented rival would come along, unhindered by past controversies and thus more likely to be accepted by the Party rank and file. In particular, Lord Stanley's eldest son, Edward, was already making his way into politics and would certainly be a future leadership contender. But Disraeli held a wild card: he had already destroyed one Tory leader and could undoubtedly do it again if necessary. Disraeli received Stanley's letter on 26 December 1848 and replied the same day: 'I am gratified by the frank manner in which you have communicated with me, and I will reply to you with as little reserve.' He then proceeded to blow Stanley's proposal out of the sky. First, he said that politics did not interest him enough to play for such small rewards: 'I am no longer disposed to sacrifice interesting pursuits, health, and a happy hearth, for a political career, which can bring one little fame.' He then refused to serve under any other leader in the Commons: 'in the present distracted state of parties, it is my opinion, that I could do more to uphold the cause to which I am attached ... by acting alone and un-shackled, then if I fell into the party disciple, which you intimate.'

We do not know how Stanley reacted to this letter, but we might suppose that, after the initial irritation had faded, he felt a grudging respect at the boldness of the refusal. Stanley was a man whose wishes were rarely refused, so to be turned down in such a confident manner would have produced a certain startling effect. Certainly, Stanley's next letter to Disraeli on 6 January 1849 demonstrated a much warmer tone. Although he stopped short of withdrawing his initial proposition, he strongly requested that Disraeli maintain his attachment to the Party and suggested that they discuss the matter in London before Parliament met.

Eventually, after much manoeuvring, a compromise was reached the day before the new session opened, by which Disraeli would take the lead of the Commons jointly with Lord Granby and J.C. Herries, two nonentities. This was an entirely cosmetic arrangement. The wise old Lord Aberdeen shrewdly predicted the likely outcome when he was told about the pact the following day: 'Sieyès, Roger Ducos, and Napoleon Bonaparte,' he reflected with a dry smile. As it had happened with Napoleon, so it was for Disraeli. Within days he had established himself as the unchallenged leader of the Party in the Commons. On 22 February he wrote to his sister: 'After much struggling, I am fairly the leader.'

In taking the lead, Disraeli embarked on the third major alliance of his political career. As with his previous partnerships with Lyndhurst and Bentinck, Disraeli was the junior partner and he depended on Lord Stanley's reputation for his own authority. But unlike the previous two relationships, which had been underpinned by warmth and mutual respect, this was sustained by simple necessity. At no point over the next twenty years did this alliance ripen into a friendship. They were deeply different men. Stanley was as sure of himself and of his position as any man in England; for him politics was a duty, not a game. Disraeli on the other hand was one of the first career politicians – sharp, ambitious and eager to get ahead. Over time, the two men became frustrated with one another. But they needed each other and this kept the partnership going.

Disraeli was now near the top of the greasy pole. But he knew he could not reach the summit on his own. So he embarked on years of ceaseless intrigue, manoeuvring this way and that, in a futile quest to recruit new allies. Everything was open to repositioning. In particular, and with staggering speed, Disraeli began to drop the Protectionist principles with which he had dazzled and destroyed Peel. He had already warned against any fresh undertakings to bring back the Corn Laws, which he saw would be a blind alley for the Conservatives. In his own Buckinghamshire election address in 1847 he had rejected the idea of a repeal of the Repeal Act and said that free trade deserved a fair trial. He also made a specific point of avoiding further attacks on Robert Peel: 'Not in this hall, not on the hustings shall any word of criticism or captious comment fall from my lips as to the conduct of that eminent individual.' His objection to Peel all along had not been based on any conviction about Protection but rather Peel's wilful disregard of his party. His attack had been carefully crafted to preclude future promises. Indeed, in his private notebooks he stated pointedly that he avoided using the word 'Protectionist' in connection with the measures proposed in the late 1840s and 1850s. Now that Peel had been defeated there was no time to waste in irresponsible dreams.

As time wore on, his manoeuvring became more blatant. In the afternoon after Peel's death on 2 July 1850 Lord

Stanley's son Edward went up to Disraeli's rooms.* He found
him having breakfast. The contrast between Disraeli's behaviour and the melodramatic outpouring of grief which had
just taken place in Parliament is palpable from Stanley's account. Indeed, Stanley's version of events rather undermines
Disraeli's own elaborate and sober story of his response to
Peel's fatal accident a few days before. 'He made no parade
of regret, but seemed bewildered by the suddenness of the
event, and the prospect which it offered of new combina-
tions. He speculated on the possibility of recovering Graham
and Gladstone ... He also thought the time favourable for
definitively abandoning a protectionist duty.'

Only Disraeli could leap so nimbly from a national tragedy
to a dramatic political opportunity to refashion his party.
But for the time being the plan came to nothing. The leader
of the Party, Lord Stanley Senior, was opposed to any hasty
change. His concern above all was to maintain Party unity.
He knew that a sudden move from Protection would enrage
the squires. Disraeli was willing to offer the farmers compensation in some form for the loss of Protection, but he was
determined to steer clear of any undertaking which might
revive the fear that a Conservative Government meant an end
to cheap food. As Stanley's biographer has written, 'where
Disraeli proposed a contentious clarity, he restored a concili-
atory ambiguity'. Luckily for the Party, there was no second

---

*Studying this family can be confusing; it is not always clear who is who.
Lord Derby, the 14th Earl and Tory leader, and his eldest son, the 15th
Earl, were both named Edward Stanley. For many years during the 1830s
and 40s, the elder Derby was known by the courtesy title of Lord Stanley.
He was elevated to the Lords in 1844, but did not succeed to the earldom
until 1851. From then until his death in 1869 he was known as Lord Derby.
Meanwhile his son took on the courtesy title, Lord Stanley. From 1848 to
1869 he sat as an MP for King's Lynn before entering the Lords after becoming the 15th Earl on his father's death.

Disraeli lurking in the wings ready to punish him for betraying his principles as Disraeli had punished Peel.

Over the following months, the dark cloud of Protection grew heavier and hindered Disraeli's attempts to put his party back into power. At the end of 1850 the Whig Government looked set to collapse. Lord John Russell had weakened his own position by poking the ashes of ancient fears about Roman Catholicism. The Pope had just announced a revival of the old English bishoprics and Lord John Russell snarled defiance, hoping to fan the public's fury into a blaze. He successfully ignited such an explosion, but then the fire got out of control. The Whigs found they could do little to assuage the public's thirst for retaliation, and in any case they depended on Irish Catholic votes. In early 1851 the Whigs were defeated due to a Radical rebellion and Russell promptly resigned. The Queen called for Lord Stanley, who tried to piece together a Conservative Government. He failed. As he cast around for suitable candidates to take office, he is supposed to have uttered, 'these are not names I can present to the Queen'. From this disaster Disraeli concluded: 'One thing was established – that every public man of experience and influence, however slight, had declined to act under Lord Derby unless the principle of Protection were unequivocally renounced.'

In 1852 the chance came again. Lord Palmerston had got into a scrape with the Queen. In France, Louis Napoleon had carried out a coup and made himself Emperor, dissolving the National Assembly and arresting a number of Republicans. Palmerston's immediate reaction was to congratulate the French on such a decisive development, but he was forced to row back when the Cabinet took a more critical view. In the confusion, he fired off an unapproved dispatch which the Queen had wanted to change. She was furious and instructed Lord John Russell to remove Palmerston from the

Foreign Office. Lord John Russell happily obliged. But once again, Russell had started a fight which he could not finish. In February 1852 Palmerston exacted his revenge by moving an amendment to the Government's Militia Bill. The Government was defeated and Lord John Russell again resigned.

Once more, the Queen sent for Lord Derby. Once more, Derby sought out new allies, this time Palmerston himself. These attempts came to nothing, but Derby managed to cobble together a minority Government. The Government was not awash with great ability; only three members of the Cabinet had held office before. When the list of names was read out to the Duke of Wellington in the House of Lords he loudly and repeatedly interrupted: 'Who? Who?' His concerns were shared by the Queen, who said that it was 'a very sorry Cabinet', and she was obliged to supervise the semi-farcical scene of seventeen Conservative Ministers being summoned to Buckingham Palace in order to be sworn into the Privy Council.

For all these reasons, and the continuing confusion over the Party's position on free trade, the *Economist* called Derby's first Government 'The Great Unknown'. But the greatest unknown concerned the new Chancellor of the Exchequer. Disraeli's appointment as Chancellor had taken the world by surprise. Thackeray compared the improbable turn of events to a plot line from one of Disraeli's own novels, but no one was more surprised than Disraeli himself. Up to this moment his experience of high finance had been limited to the accumulation of large personal debts and his speculations in South American mining shares. When he pointed out the gap to the Prime Minister, Lord Derby brushed it aside as a humdrum irrelevance: 'You know as much as Mr Canning did. They give you the figures.'

Bolstered by this airy reassurance, Disraeli got to work in preparing a Budget. Disraeli believed in imagination as the mainspring of human activity, but, faced with the problems of managing an economy, other skills were also required. The role of the Chancellor had been transformed in recent decades, from a negligible post at the start of the nineteenth century to a commanding position of authority in the mid-Victorian years. As one newspaper put it in 1852, finance was 'more than ever the touchstone of political capacity'. Economic policy was a key test of credibility for the Government as a whole. But Disraeli saw the job in different terms. This was his chance to recast his party and find a fresh stock of allies. It offered, at a stroke, the opportunity to kill off Protection while also assuaging the rural interest. The result was a Budget of great courage, immense complexity, but no mathematics at all.

Over the next six months, Disraeli tried to turn every economic orthodoxy on its head. He paved the way with an interim financial statement on 30 April 1852. This was an extraordinary performance, chiefly because of his detailed defence of free trade. He focused at length on Sir Charles Wood's 1851 Budget, which had reduced tariffs on a range of imports and consumer goods, singling out these initiatives for praise. When Derby heard the performance he erupted in biblical rage: 'I called thee to curse mine enemies, and lo, thou has blessed them all together.' He wrote to Disraeli that it was 'one of the strongest free trade speeches I ever heard', and others formed the same view. As Derby left Parliament he overheard someone say that 'it was the eulogy of Peel by Disraeli'. At Windsor Prince Albert neatly summed up the overall mood: 'the Protectionists themselves (if one can any longer call them so. . .) are a great deal startled and don't know what to make of the triumph of Peel which the very man gives him who hunted him down'.

It was a dazzling performance which underlined Disraeli's reputation for political conjuring tricks. But behind the headlines something else was happening which Disraeli could not ignore. Free trade had not been the disaster for agriculture that Bentinck and others had predicted. Indeed agriculture had revived considerably over the previous years. Moreover, from the point of view of the whole nation, free trade seemed to be working and was proving economically prudent. As Disraeli made clear in his speech to the Commons, despite the reduction in tariffs on coffee, timber and sugar, there had been no corresponding decrease in the revenues received by the Exchequer. This was because the reduction in tariffs had been rewarded by an enormous increase in consumption. In other words, free trade was doing exactly what Peel had predicted: boosting consumption and lifting living standards across Britain. This was why Disraeli told his old friend James Clay in this period that Protection as a policy was not only as dead as Lazarus, but 'already stinketh' and could not be revived.

But Lord Derby could not smell the stench. In a separate speech a few weeks later in May, he put considerable distance between himself and Disraeli, reminding his audience of the important interests of the producer classes. He knew that there were still many in the Conservative Party, including Lord John Manners, who felt that dropping the principle of Protection would mean the Party would cease to exist. The decision was therefore taken to defer making a definitive statement on Protection until after the upcoming general election had given the public a chance to express their views.

Parliament was dissolved on 1 July. The general election which followed was, like the one that had brought Peel to power, a mass of confusion and contradictory pledges. Disraeli stoked things up by making statements which went much further than the agreed Party line. 'The spirit of the age tends to free intercourse, and no statesman can disregard with impunity the genius of the epoch in which he lives,' he declared in his Buckinghamshire election address. The election was a setback for the Conservatives, leaving them with fewer than 290 seats in the Commons.* In a letter to Derby's son, Edward Stanley, Disraeli concluded: 'We built an opposition on protection and Protestantism. The first the country has positively pissed upon' and the second seemed 'to have worked us harm'. When Parliament reassembled in the autumn Derby said as much as well. Free trade, he admitted, 'is now established and working more advantageously for the working classes than we anticipated ... on the part of myself and my colleagues, I bow to the decision of the country'.

So that was that. The Corn Laws were dead and there was no chance of resurrecting them. Disraeli began to look elsewhere for compensation for the disappointed farmers while trying to win over some Peelites. Although the election had failed to deliver a majority, there was still a chance that the Government could survive if enough Peelites voted for Disraeli's Budget or decided to join the Government. At Hughenden that summer, Disraeli applied himself to his task.

The Budget he produced bore all the hallmarks of his character: bold policies, sweeping gestures, a hint of radicalism, but no sense of detail. As a result, it was fatally flawed. In trying to appease so many different interests and factions, Disraeli broke the rules but failed to rewrite them. He proposed to halve the Malt Tax, which would please some farmers and all beer drinkers. He tried to lower the tariffs

---

*One notable side story from the campaign was the behaviour of the Secretary at War, William Beresford. He was dragged into a scandal about election bribery at Derby, and then made matters worse by bellowing at a crowd of his own constituents in Essex: 'I despise you from the bottom of my heart as the vilest rabble I ever saw.' Curiously, the rabble returned Beresford to Parliament, but he subsequently went before a parliamentary inquiry and was censured by a Committee of the House.

on tea. To pay for these changes, Disraeli planned to lower
the threshold of the House Tax while also doubling the rates.
But the key proposal concerned Income Tax. Disraeli was
the first Chancellor to try to distinguish between earned and
unearned income, by taxing the latter more heavily.* Unfortunately, he went about it the wrong way. At the time,
Income Tax was organised by several schedules under which
different kinds of income were categorised. Rather than sep-
arating out the different types of income, Disraeli simply
proposed altering three of the five schedules irrespective of
what these contained. The attempt to distinguish between
different sources of income was therefore beset by detailed
difficulties: were collieries earned or unearned sources of
income? What about quarries? What about a canal? Disraeli
dismissed such quibbles. In August he wrote to Derby with
characteristic over-optimism: 'My budget greatly expands
&, I hope, matures, & if we only had a majority to carry it,
shd give you the Govt. of the country as long as you liked.'
Meanwhile Derby's son, Edward, heard about the proposals and wrote to Disraeli: 'Great will be your glory ... but it
sounds too good to be true.'

And so it proved. On returning to London after the
summer, Disraeli's Budget was hit by a body blow. The
Navy needed extra money to counter the latest French invasion scare. Grudgingly, Disraeli agreed to provide funds
for 5,000 more sailors and another 2,000 artillerymen. But
the demands kept coming, and Derby was anxious that the
Navy should not be turned down. The Navy was the bugbear
of successive Chancellors during the nineteenth century. It
dominated the financial arithmetic as the NHS does today.
Total government spending during these years amounted to

*In those days, earned and unearned incomes were referred to as 'precar-
ious' and 'realised'.

around £50 million per annum, of which more than half went on servicing the national debt; the next two biggest items were the Army and Navy, which required around £8.75 million and £6.5 million each year respectively. Preserving naval superiority meant that all governments had to be on guard for any threats or technological changes which might puncture Britain's position – even when this meant the reallocation of significant sums. In this case, the alarm about the French was more invented than real, yet Disraeli had little choice and was pushed hard by the Prime Minister, who was himself under pressure from the Queen.

As Budget day approached, fresh demands came in from the Navy. On 30 November Disraeli received news that the Naval Estimates for 1853/54 would be about £1 million more than the previous year. Now his entire Budget was thrown into jeopardy. 'I ... must deeply regret ... that on the very eve of battle, I should be suddenly called upon to change all my dispositions,' he protested. Eventually he agreed a compromise of £350,000, but he was forced to fudge his figures in order to balance the Budget. As he put it to Derby: 'I fear we are in a great scrape & I hardly see how the budget can live in such a stormy sea.'

Meanwhile Disraeli had done himself considerable damage on an entirely separate matter. On 14 September 1852 the Duke of Wellington had died. For two months his body was refrigerated while a state funeral was arranged. On 15 November it fell to Disraeli as leader of the House of Commons to pay tribute to the fallen hero. For some reason – tiredness maybe, or perhaps a lack of preparation time – Disraeli's speech extensively plagiarised an obscure article by the French historian Adolphe Thiers. How Disraeli came to decide that a French article written twenty years previously could be copied at length on such an occasion is not at all clear. But whatever the reasons, the literary larceny was quickly discovered and Disraeli was heavily criticised.

By the time Disraeli rose to present his Budget on Friday 3 December he was in a sorry state. He was sick of numbers and in any case quite ill with flu. Once again Derby dismissed such trivial difficulties. 'Put a good face on it, and we shall pull through. L'audace – l'audace – toujours l'audace.' This was red rag to a bull. Courage was never in short supply for Disraeli, and so it proved as he spoke for five hours that evening, almost boring his audience into submission. As Macaulay commented afterwards, 'I could have said the whole as clearly, or more clearly, in two.'

For a while it looked as though Disraeli had got away with it. But over the following two weeks the Budget fell to bits. Gladstone told his wife that it was 'the least conservative budget I have ever known'. Ralph Bernal Osborne said it hurt the middle class. And Macaulay said that the 'plan was nothing but taking money out of the pockets of people in towns and putting it into the pockets of growers of malt'. The debate opened on 10 December and Sir Charles Wood denounced the Budget in detail. The House Tax, the Income Tax, the Malt Tax changes all came under heavy fire. A particular focus fell on Disraeli's proposal to abolish the Public Works Loan Board. This fund, which amounted to some £360,000, contributed the majority of Disraeli's overall surplus of £430,000. But as Gladstone eagerly pointed out, the fund had itself been created by borrowing – so Disraeli was in effect borrowing money to balance his Budget. It all seemed to confirm the impression that Disraeli was an unprincipled adventurer who could not be trusted with the public finances.

As the attacks grew louder so Disraeli's attempts to save himself became wilder and more improbable. Both he and Lord Derby had done their best in November to reach out to Palmerston and the Peelites to inquire whether they would join the Government. These overtures had come to nothing, so Disraeli took matters into his own hands. First he tried to do a deal with fifty Irish independent MPs by which he would secure their support in exchange for the introduction of new tenant rights in Ireland. Then Disraeli held two discussions with the Quaker Radical John Bright, the second of which took place late in the evening of 15 December at Grosvenor Gate and lasted one and a half hours. Bright recorded the conversation in his diary because it struck him as extraordinary. Disraeli, who was in his dressing gown, spoke to one of his oldest opponents with apparent frankness. He took Bright through the Budget calculations, dwelling on his determination to cut the defence budget where he knew he could rely on Bright's support. He explained that the Conservative Party had so far faithfully followed him and he thought they would stand a good deal more if necessary. He wondered whether Bright and Cobden might join Lord Derby's Government. Bright laughed at this, observing that, irrespective of the immorality of such a manoeuvre, their constituencies would not permit it. Disraeli replied that 'a man of genius . . . may do anything with a large constituency. I think I could represent Manchester, and be a very popular member.' Bright concluded: 'This remarkable man is ambitious, most able, and without prejudices . . . He seems unable to comprehend the morality of our political course.'

The final debate on Disraeli's Budget took place the following evening. Disraeli rose at 10.20 p.m. 'I was not born and bred a Chancellor of the Exchequer,' he told the Commons, 'I am one of the parliamentary rabble.' This was good, tub-thumping stuff, designed to get the backbenchers hooting. But as he went on he became more vicious and personal. One by one he turned on those individuals who had dared to attack his Budget. He said that Charles Wood had yet to learn that 'petulance is not sarcasm, and insolence is not invective'. He dismissed Sir James Graham as a man 'whom I will not say I greatly respect, but rather whom I greatly regard'. He labelled Peel's former Chancellor of the Exchequer, Henry Goulburn, 'that weird Sybil'. He even found time to mock Robert Lowe, the Liberal MP for Kidderminster, over his comments about emigration and productivity by making a seedy reference to the 'reserve of producing power' among the womenfolk of England. His closing lines have since passed into the reference books: 'I know what I have to face. I have to face a Coalition! The combination may be successful. A coalition has before this been successful. But coalitions, although successful, have always found this, that their triumph has been brief. This too I know, that England does not love coalitions.'

A thunderstorm had hit the House of Commons during Disraeli's speech. His words had been backed up by a battering of lightning, thunder and rain, reinforcing the sense that those listening were witnessing an epic struggle by a wounded titan. One observer noted that the Opposition had sat in silence, astonished, during Disraeli's speech. But now, as the House prepared to divide and vote on the Budget, Gladstone sprang to his feet and started speaking. The Prime Minister's son, Edward Stanley, noted the extraordinary scene: 'Gladstone's look when he rose to reply will never be forgotten by me. His usually calm features were livid and distorted with passion. His voice shook, and those who watched him feared an outbreak incompatible with parliamentary rules.' For some time Gladstone made no headway over the shouts and screams from the Conservative benches, but as the fury died away he launched a devastating counter-blast. His diaries for the previous two weeks are littered with detailed reading matter on Income Tax policies and biographies of William Pitt, who was the original author of that tax. As he finally made himself heard over the din, he made detailed use of this material and castigated Disraeli's Budget as 'the most subversive in its tendencies and ultimate effects that I have ever known'. Up in the Peers' gallery Lord Derby muttered 'dull', but he was helpless to prevent the relentless blows which fell on Disraeli. When at last Gladstone sat down after 3 a.m., a division was called and the Budget was defeated by 305 to 286 votes.

This was fatal for the Government. As Derby reflected afterwards, 'now we are properly smashed. I must prepare for my journey to Osborne to resign.' The Government had lasted a mere ten months, the shortest since the first Ministry of Robert Peel. But the vote did more than bring down the Government. A few weeks before, Lady Derby had hosted a party at which her husband had a long conversation with Gladstone. Derby had asked Gladstone if he was willing to join the Government. They discussed the matter and Gladstone made it clear that he and his colleagues looked to the forthcoming Budget as the moment when they would decide their future course. The lines were already shifting in the relationships between Tories, Peelites and Whigs. Peel's former Home Secretary, Sir James Graham, for example, was sitting with Lord John Russell. But Disraeli's reckless performance and Gladstone's intervention in the debate had reinforced the rift between the two parts of the Tory Party. Henceforth the Peelites began to drift into the ranks of the Whigs.

There was also a purely personal element to the contest. As Blake put it in a purple passage, the 'artist who wishes to immortalise, as if upon a Greek vase, an instant of time that would illuminate the political history of the mid-Victorian era would have done well to choose the moment when Gladstone rose to answer Disraeli at one o'clock in the morning of 17 December 1852; the faces of the members, pallid in the flaring gaslight, contorted, some with anger, some with delight, arms gesticulating in hostility or applause; Gladstone on his feet, handsome, tall, still possessing the youthful good looks, the open countenance, which had charmed his contemporaries at Eton and Christ Church; Disraeli seated on the Treasury Bench, aquiline, faintly sinister, listening with seeming indifference to the eloquent rebuke of the orator. It was a scene which was not easily forgotten.' This was indeed the beginning of a very public rivalry between Gladstone and Disraeli. For the next thirty years issues rose and fell, temporarily provoking outrage, but they were increasingly seen as weapons to be used by two mighty champions attempting to belabour one another. The relations between these two men came to dominate the political reckoning during the second half of the century. For much of the time they seethed silently at one another; occasionally, as in this case, their hostility erupted in dramatic explosions of rhetoric and rage.

The fuse for these explosions had been lit early in their careers. Gladstone had begun life on the sour right of the Tory Party. Macaulay had called him the 'rising hope of the stern and unbending Tories'. But his views, though extreme, were thoughtful and not unfeeling; they were born of a strong and uncompromising Evangelicalism. His first book, which he published in 1838, was called *The State in its Relations with the Church*, and made a strong case for the authority of the Church of England – a fact which Disraeli had delightfully exposed later in Gladstone's career when Peel's Government proposed extra funding for the Irish Catholic College at Maynooth. As the years went on Gladstone's disapproval of Disraeli deepened into detestation. Politics brought the two men into unavoidable contact and increasingly they lined up on opposite sides. Gladstone became more liberal and indeed radical as he got older; Disraeli, as we have seen, steadily abandoned his youthful radicalism to become the chief champion of the landed interest.

Gladstone's private life was also of a different character to that of Disraeli. We have seen how Disraeli pitched himself to Mary Anne with a melodramatic statement of his own emotional and financial needs. Around the same time Gladstone was awkwardly courting a girl called Catherine Glynne, whom he later married. He initially proposed to Catherine by letter, in a vast sentence which is not only devoid of romantic emotion but is also unintelligible: 'I seek much in a wife in gifts better than those of our human pride, and am also sensible that she can find little in me: sensible that, were you to treat this note as the offspring of utter presumption, I must not be surprised: sensible that the lot I invite you to share, even if it be not attended, as I trust it is not, with peculiar disadvantages of an outward kind, is one, I do not say unequal to your deserts, for that were saying little, but liable at best to changes and perplexities and pains which, for myself, I contemplate without apprehension, but to which it is perhaps selfishness in the main, with the sense of inward dependence counteracting an opposite sense of my too real unworthiness, which would make me contribute to expose another – and that other!'*

But there were also larger considerations. Gladstone supposed that he was sent to do God's will on earth. He examined every decision made against that awesome test. Gladstone felt that Disraeli believed in nothing, and that his decisions were based on an unscrupulous nihilism, without foundation in Christian belief, or indeed any beliefs at all. Later he coined the phrase 'Beaconsfieldism' to define what he saw as the lack of any moral content in his rival. But at this point in the 1850s he was still casting around to find some

* On one minor point the two men did agree. As a youth Disraeli had visited York Minster and was impressed by the size of the cathedral. 'Westminster Abbey is a toy to it,' he had written. Gladstone, when he read this description many years later, ticked the passage in agreement.

way of expressing his frustration. Thus in February 1857 he referred to 'motives which I could neither describe nor conquer' which prevented him from working with Disraeli, and looking back in later years he admitted that 'a strong sentiment of revulsion for Disraeli personally, a sentiment quite distinct from that of dislike was alone sufficient to deter me absolutely from a merely personal and separate reunion'.

Disraeli, for his part, thought Gladstone was a hypocrite who could summon up reserves of bogus indignation to further his political purposes. He did not credit Gladstone with any genuine feeling. He was merely a self-righteous, but more negligible, reincarnation of Robert Peel. More specifically, Disraeli thought Gladstone was a prig. One choice nugget of evidence strongly supports Disraeli's verdict. At Hawarden where Gladstone lived there is a library which contains many of his own books. One such book is an early edition of Froude's life of Disraeli. On page 204 there is the following description of Gladstone: 'The purity of his life, the loftiness of his principles, his well-known because slightly ostentatious piety commended him generally to the national confidence.' Most of us, when reading such a passage about ourselves, would have felt a warm sense of pride; perhaps we might have lingered a little longer over these particular words. But Gladstone, in a typically portentous display, decided to mark this passage out for future readers with a small but neatly formed tick in the margin, so that others might know he approved.

Gladstone was not anti-Semitic, but it is hard to read his criticisms of Disraeli without assuming that anti-Semitic prejudice played some part in his thinking. That prejudice did not extend to Mary Anne, for whom Gladstone felt sympathy and respect; it was her misfortune to be married to a scoundrel. Gladstone's dislike of Disraeli was near the surface of his emotions and from time to time vented forth in passionate indignation. It was contrary to Disraeli's character to retaliate in kind. He channelled his anger instead into an epigram; an enemy was best dealt with in a cutting phrase. Thus on one occasion he described Gladstone as 'intoxicated with the exuberance of his own verbosity'. And on another: 'He has not a single redeeming defect.'

We have seen how it fell to Gladstone to respond to Disraeli's death in 1881. It is fascinating to imagine how Disraeli would have reacted if the roles had been reversed. Disraeli would have thought long and hard about his handling of the necessary tribute, while dismissing it to others as a matter of no importance at all. He would probably have tried in a solemn voice to mimic Gladstone's eloquence and the way in which he had moved the House of Commons. He would have stopped short of parody, but only just. Only the closest of his friends, such as Monty Corry, Bulwer-Lytton, or Lord Stanley, would have spotted beneath the suave and melancholy tone the bitter fun with which he carried out what was actually an amusing charade.

After Derby's administration fell in 1852 Lord Aberdeen was asked to form a government. He achieved this by creating Disraeli's predicted coalition of Peelites and Whigs. Gladstone was appointed as Disraeli's successor as Chancellor of the Exchequer, and in one of the twists that came to dominate their careers, Gladstone realised that the Chancellor's robe which had belonged to William Pitt had gone missing. He wrote to Disraeli asking for it back. Disraeli ignored the request and instead asked for money for the furniture he had provided for the Chancellor's residence in Downing Street. Gladstone refused to pay, making a complicated point about a new reimbursement process. In the end, neither man gave ground; the Chancellor's robe remains at Hughenden to this day.

The final irony of Disraeli's Chancellorship lay in the calendar. Disraeli had been compelled to introduce his 1852 Budget, which in effect covered two financial years, in the middle of a financial year. The result was that the estimates he had been presented with were some way off the mark. If he had been able to produce a Budget as normal in the spring of the following year he would have benefited from a much larger and less contentious surplus. As it was, this larger surplus, and all of the political credit, fell into his successor's lap.

FRIENDS AND FOES

The fifteen years which followed Disraeli's first stint as Chancellor of the Exchequer were a dreary grind of gloom and frustration. As general elections came and went in the 1850s and early 1860s, no Conservative majority materialised. Disraeli was able to take some comfort from the fact that he was now a national celebrity; from 1853 he was flattered by a new waxwork in Madame Tussaud's and in that same year a shilling edition of his novels sold more than 300,000 copies. But this was scant consolation for the drudgery of Opposition. Having tasted the delights of a Ministerial position, experiencing the frills and trappings of power, Disraeli knew that the pleasure he sought could only be achieved by a sustained and remarkable career in government. So he persevered in his fatiguing quest for political allies.

Meanwhile events were crowding in all around him. Although in these years Britain was enjoying a period of steady growth and prosperity, an era of instability was breaking out overseas. The Crimean War, the Indian Mutiny, a new war in China, Italian Unification, Prussian aggression and the American Civil War all took place with Disraeli on the Opposition benches, unable to move the international scene. From a novelist's point of view he enjoyed the spectacle. He wrote whimsically to Mrs Brydges Williams: 'It is a privilege to live in this age of rapid and brilliant events. What an error to consider it an utilitarian age! It is one of infinite romance. Thrones tumble down and are offered, like a fairy tale, and the most powerful people in the world, male & female, a few years back, were adventurers, exiles and demireps.' But, himself an adventurer, he yearned for the chance to be more closely involved.

Disraeli's chief ally at this time was Lord Derby, but this was not a sturdy partnership on which to build. The correspondence for these years when they were jointly running the Conservative Party sometimes ceased altogether; according to Blake, only one letter survives for the whole of 1856. As Disraeli struggled to find ways of gaining momentum for the Conservatives he tried to lobby, persuade or compel Derby into accepting a large and bewildering number of new projects and initiatives which might give the Party more seats. These efforts did little to improve their relationship, but succeeded in giving the Conservatives the impression of restless energy.

Sometimes these manoeuvres were on administrative matters. For example, in 1853 Disraeli instigated a significant restructuring of the Conservative Party organisation and made his own solicitor, Philip Rose, the Party's chief organising agent. There were also attempts to win more support from the newspapers. Disraeli took great care to cultivate relations with the various editors. After a notable speech he was known to pay visits to John Delane, the editor of *The Times*, in order to secure more favourable coverage. But this did not solve the main deficiency, namely the overwhelming hostility of much of the London press to the Conservatives. So together with Derby's son, Edward Stanley, Disraeli took matters into his own hands and wrote to various Tory patrons canvassing for funds for a new publishing venture.

'The state of the Press,' Disraeli wrote on 9 March 1853, 'as regards the Tory party, has become so intolerable that we think of making a great effort to terminate a condition of affairs, which exercises a very bad influence on our preparations.' Remembering a former attempt to achieve a similar fix, Disraeli elaborated: 'We require something which will produce as striking, and as rapid, an effect on opinion, as the Anti-Jacobin when it was started by Mr Canning.' The publication which Disraeli and Stanley eventually created was a new magazine called *The Press*, published weekly on Saturdays. In the event it proved a greater success than either *The Anti-Jacobin* (which had folded after less than a year) or Disraeli's previous publishing efforts with *The Representative* newspaper (which had ended in John Murray's partial bankruptcy). But it failed to remedy the main problem, which had deeper roots than a hostile and partisan media.

There were three dominant political issues in this period: religion, foreign policy and plans for a future Reform Bill. Disraeli had flexible views on all of these issues, so he took each one as a way of repositioning the Party. Religion was for Disraeli the most difficult as, however hard he tried, he simply could not outflank Gladstone as either a credible defender of the Church of England or an effective voice of dissent. But he did his best, pressing Protestant buttons one moment and trying to win Roman Catholic votes the next. His finest moment came in 1864 when, during a debate on Darwinism at the Sheldonian Theatre in Oxford, he dismissed the entire concept of evolution in one capricious phrase: 'Is Man an Ape or an Angel? My Lord, I am on the side of the Angels.'

Disraeli found the ground more fertile when it came to political reform. After one election bloodbath in 1857 he wrote buoyantly to Derby: 'Our party is now a corpse, but it appears to me that, in the present perplexed state of affairs, a Conservative public pledged to Parliamentary Reform, a bold and decided course might not only put us on our legs, but greatly help the country and serve the State.' Disraeli had already dabbled in this territory as a supporter of reform in the 1830s; the subject appealed more to his love of the dramatic than any deep commitment to democracy. But in any case, there was only a limited appetite for another instalment of electoral reform in the 1850s, and it was unlikely a new Reform Bill would be carried, particularly by a half-hearted Conservative minority.

Foreign policy was trickier. Here Palmerston reigned supreme. Nevertheless Disraeli was not short of ideas and he did his best to topple him. In the late 1840s he began to sketch out new imperial policies. First came a proposal for imperial Protection. As Disraeli put it in a campaign speech, 'they had heard much of the Customs Union of Germany ... why should not England have her Imperial Union, the produce of every clime coming in for free?' A little later Disraeli had the idea of creating a number of new colonial constituencies which would send MPs to Westminster. Burke had suggested a similar scheme at the time of the American War of Independence, and later in the nineteenth century the Round Table movement would actively champion this policy. But this was a mere pipe dream in the 1850s, and in any case Derby did not agree with Disraeli. He thought that the new MPs were more likely to be Radical than Conservative and would do little to help the Party.

Disraeli's time at the Treasury in 1852 somewhat tempered these imperial ideas. His letters from this period contain occasional grumbles about the cost of defending the colonies; at one point he described them as 'millstones round our necks'. But this was out of character. His instinctive views owed far more to his imagination as a novelist than any cool reappraisal of British diplomacy. Throughout his career he relished the notion of a world divided into great empires, which were themselves controlled by the magical skill of high financiers and secret societies. As he put it in one letter to Mrs Brydges

Williams in 1863: 'For the last three months it has been a struggle between the secret societies and the European millionaires. Rothschild hitherto has won ...'

This was of course a far cry from reality but, typically, Disraeli combined the surreal with the real, and displayed a strong scepticism towards the occasional outbursts of public outrage which drove foreign policy in these years. In particular he took a surprisingly calm and rational attitude towards the series of wars and revolutions that occurred during the 1850s and 1860s. For example, Disraeli largely resisted the passionate outbreak of patriotism during the Crimean War. After Sebastopol fell in 1855 he pressed hard for an early peace. Similarly, when reports of the Indian Mutiny reached Britain in 1857 he was a strong voice of moderation. In several letters he indicated that he did not believe the atrocity stories which were published in *The Times*. On one occasion he wrote to Lady Londonderry: 'The details of all these stories are suspicious. Details are a feature of the Myth. The accounts are too graphic; I hate the word. Who can have seen these things? Who heard them? The rows of ladies standing with their babes in their arms to be massacred ... One lady says to a miscreant: "I do not ask you to spare my life, but give some water to my child." The child is instantly tossed in the air and caught upon a bayonet!' In the same letter he compared the public thirst for vengeance to the War of Jenkins's Ear.*

These efforts were not always politically helpful; it was difficult to outflank populist policies at the polls. For example, in 1857 Disraeli launched a stern critique of Palmerston,

---

* Jenkins, a mutilated sailor, had appeared before a Committee of the House in the 1730s without his ear, having been recently captured by Spanish pirates. The Commons promptly waged war on the barbarous Spanish, but it later emerged that Jenkins may have lost his ear at the pillory.

condemning his warmongering in China and the East. He ended his attack by challenging Palmerston to test his policies in a general election. 'I should like to see the programme of the proud leader of the Liberal party – "No Reform! New Taxes! Canton blazing! Persia invaded!"' A general election duly followed – in which Palmerston laid waste the Conservatives.

These manoeuvres did not impress Lord Derby. Indeed, a number were made without his consent. On several occasions Derby criticised what he called Disraeli's 'fanciful alliances' and he was particularly irritated with Disraeli's Crimean peace policy. He sent Sir William Jolliffe, the Whip, to Hughenden in protest, to which Disraeli replied that it was 'impossible for a party to exist without a policy, and still less for an opposition to be of the same policy as the Government to which it is opposed'. Several times the relationship between Disraeli and Derby broke down. Professor Hawkins, who has assiduously elevated Lord Derby's political career, points out that on at least four occasions strong winds blew the partnership off-track. One of the worst was in 1854. Disraeli wrote in exasperation to his long-time friend and epistler, Lady Londonderry, that Derby was spending more time horse-racing than leading his party: 'As for our Chief we never see him. His House is always closed, he subscribes to nothing tho' his fortune is very large; and expects nevertheless everything to be done. I have never yet been fairly backed in my life. All the great persons I have known ... have been unequal to the grand game.'

The following year, things grew worse. The Aberdeen coalition collapsed over its handling of the Crimean War. The Queen invited Derby to form a government. But Derby dithered, saying that no government could stand without Palmerston. The Queen, who disliked Palmerston, tried almost every alternative before at last inviting Palmerston to become Prime Minister. Disraeli again erupted, and once again Lady Londonderry was the recipient: 'our chief has again bolted! This is the third time that in the course of six years, during which I have had the lead of the Opposition in the House of Commons, I have stormed the Treasury Benches ... You cannot, therefore, be surprised that I am a little wearied of these barren victories, which like Alma, Inkerman, and Balaclava, may be glorious, but are certainly nothing more.'

The truth was that these were two very different men with different temperaments and attitudes. Their social backgrounds also created a deep divide. Disraeli was not invited to Knowsley until the end of 1853, and when he got there he bored Derby by talking incessantly about politics. Six years later, Mary Anne was invited to accompany Disraeli to Knowsley, but the visit was a disaster as Derby poked fun at her during dinner. The two men also had different political ideas. When he was bidding for the leadership of the Party in the Commons, Disraeli had written to Derby that the task of the Conservative leader was 'to uphold the aristocratic settlement of the country'. But of the two, it was Derby who took this task more seriously. Indeed he saw his role in these years as a stately block on democracy. He ended up leading the Conservative Party for longer than any other, for a total of twenty-two years, during which time he became the first Prime Minister to hold office three times. But he was a Stanley and he did not regard these milestones as worthy of celebration. His object, as his son noted, was simply to prevent change: 'The Captain', as his underlings called him, 'does not care for office but wishes to keep things as they are and impede "Progress". This being the case, it is no use to talk to him about not having a majority in the House of Commons.' This did not necessarily mean opposing everything carried out by the Whig Government; indeed, so long as Palmerston continued in office, there was a reassuring lack of domestic policy which appealed to Lord Derby. Rather, he believed in decisive but occasional interventions on important matters which would not disrupt Party unity.

Disraeli did not share such stately principles. He had few views on policy which could not be manipulated to suit the situation. 'Criticise, but suggest nothing' was how he summed up his attitude to Opposition; and, more than any Party leader before and many since, Disraeli fundamentally believed that the only viable tactic of Opposition was to oppose everything the Government did. In the end, something would stick. But the trouble with this tactic was that it could do more harm than good. As Derby tried to explain during the row over Crimean policy, 'we cannot with honour, or even with regard to party interests, constitute ourselves a peace Opposition, merely because we have a war Ministry'. But Disraeli could not be dissuaded. Just as his natural talent was to criticise not commend, so his natural instinct in politics was to oppose, even if it meant converting potential friends into grumpy foes.

There was however an important side story to this political partnership: the deep and fruitful relationship which Disraeli formed with Derby's son, Lord Stanley, in these years. Although the heir to the earldom and politically a Tory, he was in other respects quite unlike his father. Physically he was dumpy and unimpressive. Indeed, he looked exactly what he was not: a round face, weak chin and protruding belly made him appear more like a modestly prosperous shopkeeper than one of the richest men in the kingdom. His appearance mirrored his sober views. He enjoyed science and detailed matters of engineering and technology. Politically he was to the left of his party and was one of the strongest voices against Protection and for a new Reform Bill. But he combined these attitudes with a deep aristocratic pessimism. For example, he told Disraeli one evening that 'science disqualified one for public life: the whole thing seemed so small (speaking of our globe) that it required a great deal of effort to treat affairs seriously'.

Disraeli was quick to recruit the young Stanley as a pliable ally. The age gap between them was considerable – Stanley was twenty-two when he became an MP in 1848 – but this did not inhibit a close intimacy. For example, in July 1852 Disraeli wrote to him: 'We must consult together; the ship requires fine steering,' and in August Disraeli addressed him in the same terms as his old Young England followers: 'My Dear Comrade'. As a link to Lord Derby Stanley proved of limited value, as his father held him in low regard; but as a political ally and intellectual companion he was invaluable. He soon became a regular visitor to Hughenden and in 1857 Disraeli wrote that Stanley's friendship was 'one of my chief sources of interest in existence'.

While Parliament was sitting the two men often dined together at Bellamy's chop house, where they indulged in large and sweeping conversations about the state of the world. On one occasion Disraeli suggested that it was a privilege to live in such an age of dramatic events. The electric telegraph, railroads and new discoveries of gold were reshaping the planet. But Stanley was not swayed. He said that it was not a particularly exciting time to be alive. The invention of printing, the compass and the discovery of the New World had all been as significant as anything currently happening. Indeed previous eras were probably more remarkable; for example, had not mail carriages been as influential as railroads? What about the age of American and French revolutions? What about the Thirty Years War? The point was that 'everybody at every time thought the age <u>critical</u>'. What was happening was interesting, but no more.

On another occasion the two discussed Thucydides. Disraeli recorded the conversation later: 'Stanley said he could never understand what was meant by Thucydides being looked upon as a great philosophical historian: philosophy of history and statesmanship and all that. Saw no signs of it. Read him with admiration as a matchless master of narrative. I agree with Stanley. I think the history of the Sicilian expedition has never been approached.' Disraeli was also very interested in Stanley's views on how families joined the aristocracy. Stanley told Disraeli that the first 200 years were key: 'If a family could maintain itself for 200 years, it became so numerous & diffused, that it was difficult, certainly in these times, that it should be extinguished.'

In these ways and others, the two men formed a deep bond and connection. Their letters and Stanley's diaries provide a treasure trove of glittering information about the politics of these years. Yet occasionally a warning note creeps in. For example, Disraeli complained that the Stanleys lacked imagination: 'The Stanleys had no imagination – but Ld Derby, if he had a passion, had one for Shakespeare and when he was quite alone with his family, especially at Knowsley, used to read aloud every night. When we were discussing any grave point, especially on affairs, & Stanley saw nothing but difficulties, & I evinced my impatience he used to say "I know what you are going to say, I know what you are going to say." He meant that he had no imagination – and sometimes when I said so he would reply "I knew you would say that".' Stanley also had doubts about Disraeli. These were of a more alarming variety. 'I admire his perseverance not less than his talent; but how can I reconcile his open ridicule, in private, of all religions, with his preaching of a new church-and-state agitation? Or how can I help seeing that glory and power, rather than the public good, have been his objects?' At the time, the lonely demands of Opposition papered over these problems; under more exacting circumstances in government in later years, the gulf between them would tell.

Throughout this period, politics consumed every ounce of Disraeli's creativity. Literature he had indeed abandoned for politics. As he wrote to Lady Londonderry in September 1857, 'I have lost all zest for fiction, & have for many years.' Instead he was driven by a boundless appetite for intrigue and took delight in small political victories. These days we are used to complaining about the increasing dominance of a southern, metropolitan elite in our political system. In the nineteenth century the bias went the other way. Several times Disraeli complained that northern families such as the Peels, the Stanleys, the Gladstones and the Grahams dominated the political arena. But he consoled himself with the knowledge that his own rise had helped to balance the scales. As he declared in an election address, 'Now let the men of the North who thought that they were to govern England – let them bring a political pedigree equal to that of the county of Buckingham.'

In these ways and others, Disraeli took great delight in the daily twists and turns of life in Parliament. As Stanley observed, politics formed 'his chief, almost his sole pleasure'. But, pleasurable or not, the grind was exhausting. Several times Disraeli was worn out by the slog. In May 1853, just a few months after he had become Chancellor, he suggested to Stanley that he might give up politics: 'He talked of retiring from affairs, of writing an epic poem, and a life of Christ from the national point of view.' His letters from these years dwindled in numbers: only around half as many survive for the years of 1853, '54, '55 and '56 as there had been in 1852. He put himself under added strain by making a number of over-excited, and false, prophecies. Disraeli had a wild record of implausible predictions, and in these years he pushed this to an extreme. Thus in 1854 he said that Palmerston was 'utterly exhausted', and at the best 'ginger beer and not champagne' – but the vintage years of Palmerston still lay ahead. On 2 February 1857 Disraeli claimed that 'by this day fortnight we shall be in office' – they were in Opposition for another year. And like many in the 1860s, Disraeli thought the American Civil War would end in the triumph of the Southern planter aristocracy; the result instead was victory for Northern democracy.

More serious was Disraeli's continuing unpopularity with fellow Conservatives. His persistent politicking cast a cloud over his credibility, and he was surprisingly bad at building backbench relationships. In 1855 and 1856 he suffered a particular dip in his reputation, about which Derby wrote to Malmesbury: 'As to Disraeli's unpopularity, I see it and regret it, and especially regret that he does not see more the party in private, but they could not do without him even if there was anyone ready and able to take his place.' Stanley also spotted that Disraeli was isolated within the Party. He noted that he 'has not been successful in forming and retaining personal friendships. By none of his colleagues in office and opposition is he personally beloved.'

Nor was Disraeli beloved by those in other parties. He made only two notable recruits in these years. One was Stafford Northcote, a Peelite, who had jointly authored the famous Northcote-Trevelyan report on the Civil Service. Disraeli spotted his potential and pushed him forward as a rising Tory star. The other was Disraeli's old literary companion, Bulwer-Lytton. Bulwer had been a Whig MP between 1831 and 1841, but he was also a strong Protectionist and in 1852 Disraeli negotiated for him to stand as a Tory for Hertfordshire. Six years later he was invited to serve in Derby's second minority Government as Colonial Secretary. The presence of another well-known novelist and minor celebrity added an extra layer of romance to Derby's Government. But by this stage Bulwer was deaf and also a hypochondriac. He perplexed Derby and Disraeli by repeatedly threatening to resign on account of his supposed impending demise. Disraeli handled these histrionics calmly. On New Year's Day 1859 he wrote to Derby explaining that Bulwer 'expects to die before Easter, but if so I have promised him a public funeral'. In the event, Bulwer-Lytton survived Easter and lived another fourteen years. He eventually died in Torquay in 1873 after the explosion of an abscess in his ear.

As before, Disraeli found it easier to form relationships with men much younger than himself. These were the years of Lord Henry Lennox, to whom Disraeli wrote: 'I can only tell you that I love you.' During the early 1850s the two men exchanged a steady stream of letters. For example in July 1852 Disraeli wrote: 'I am glad you are dull in my absence. I also feel lonely.' In August: 'I think very often of my young companion, and miss him sadly, for his presence to me is always a charm, and often a consolation.' And in September: 'even a line is pleasant from those we love'. Disraeli did his best for Lennox, giving him a junior job at the Treasury and later the role of First Commissioner of Works, but as the years rolled on Disraeli tired of him and the two men drifted apart.

To a significant extent Lennox was supplanted from 1856 onwards by a negative creature called Ralph Earle. Disraeli seems to have met Earle, who was a junior Foreign Office official, during a trip to Paris in 1856. Soon afterwards Earle began furnishing Disraeli with secret pieces of information which he might use against Palmerston. It was a squalid arrangement, and it brought little political benefit. But Earle was a man on the make. Like a character from one of Disraeli's early novels, he saw a quick path to power by hitching himself to Disraeli. He was prepared to sacrifice all bounds of propriety if it provided a way of making a name for himself. He became Disraeli's Private Secretary and later a Conservative MP, but in the end he lost Disraeli's confidence and slipped from the scene.

Eventually, in the mid-1860s, Disraeli found a more suitable aide-de-camp. The story goes that he discovered Montagu Corry during a visit to Raby Castle. Corry, who had a reputation as an entertainer, was persuaded by a group of ladies to sing a comic song. Disraeli happened to witness the scene and, rather than dismiss the man as a social gadfly, promptly appointed Corry as his Private Secretary. It was a masterstroke. Corry proved entirely capable and trustworthy. He remained in the position from 1866 through until Disraeli's death. A Spy cartoon from Disraeli's later years shows the elderly politician being supported by a bearded and upright Corry. This captures the spirit of the relationship. Without in any way appearing improper or over-the-top, Disraeli came to depend on Corry absolutely.

While politics proved disappointing for Disraeli in this period, his private life made notable strides forward. In particular, two total strangers rescued his finances. The first, as we have seen, was Mrs. Brydges Williams. Her promise of a large share of her estate was rewarded by Disraeli with a flow of colourful letters and a series of autumnal visits to Torquay. In 1859 she asked Disraeli for assistance in having her coat of arms authorised by the College of Arms. She also requested that she be buried with Disraeli. But otherwise she asked for nothing, and received little in return. The result was a remarkable friendship. Surprisingly little is known about her, although one black and white sketch has survived showing a large, flat-faced, heavily dressed old woman towing two bulldogs round Torquay. She died on 11 November 1863, leaving Disraeli a large legacy of around £30,000. Philip Rose, entrepreneurially, suggested making her legacy public in the hope of attracting other similarly lucrative, lonely, letter-hungry widows. But there was only ever one Mrs Brydges Williams.

The other stranger who helped Disraeli was Andrew Montagu, a Yorkshire landowner and strong Tory. In the winter of 1862–3 he contacted the Conservative Party asking what he could do to help; the answer came back that the best thing would be to buy up Disraeli's debts, which were at that moment running at a high rate of interest. This he promptly did in return for a mortgage on Hughenden. The arrangement saved Disraeli some £4,000 in interest payments each year. After Disraeli's second period in office in 1858–9 he was given an annual pension of £2,000. This meant that, together with Montagu's loan, Mrs Williams's promised inheritance and the stream of income his wife received each year, Disraeli for the first time in his adult life was on a firm financial footing. By now, in his mid-fifties, he was no longer broke.

There was one major blow in these years. On 19 December 1859 Sarah Disraeli passed away, having recently complained of a pain and swelling in her bowels. Disraeli was devastated, his grief perhaps tinged with guilt that despite a regular flow of letters she had gradually been replaced in his life by his wife. Later Disraeli paid tribute to Sarah in literature, taking her as the model for Myra in *Endymion* – the sister who drives forward her brother's political career. But for the rest of his life Disraeli felt a deep emptiness that his sister was not alive to witness his achievements. When Disraeli later became Prime Minister, Sir Philip Rose mentioned how happy his sister would have been; Disraeli simply replied: 'Ah! poor Sa, poor Sa; we've lost our audience, we've lost our audience.' She was laid to rest at Willesden Lane cemetery.

There remains one foe whom Disraeli converted to friendship in these years. In 1851 the Queen still despised Disraeli. She blamed him for the hounding of her beloved Peel. Indeed she made these feelings clear to Lord Derby when she invited him to form a government in that year. 'I do not approve of Mr Disraeli. I do not approve of his conduct to Sir Robert Peel.' Derby defended his colleague, using terms which were well chosen to appeal to the Queen: 'Madam, Mr Disraeli has had to make his position, and men who make their position will say and do things which are not necessary to be said or done by those for whom positions are provided.' The Queen accepted this explanation, but added cautiously: 'Remember that you make yourself responsible for him.'

A year later Disraeli was Chancellor of the Exchequer and Leader of the Commons. It was at this point that he began to lay the flattery on with a trowel. As he stood down after the defeat of his Budget, he informed the Queen that it was only Her Majesty's gracious sympathy which had sustained him during the unequal contest. It is not clear whether the Queen was convinced by this flummery, but Disraeli made real headway with her husband. Just before the Government collapsed in December Disraeli had helped persuade the Commons to vote a grant of £150,000 towards a series of cultural projects Prince Albert was planning in South Kensington. He also wrote the Prince a preposterous letter on leaving office: 'I shall ever remember, with interest and admiration, the princely mind in the princely person.'

One of the great riddles about Disraeli is that people could never be sure whether he was being sincere or sarcastic. But when it came to royalty, he was a willing participant in his own theatre. He had a genuinely romantic notion of monarchy, inspired by his novels and his father's support for the Cavaliers. Several times he made a case for a larger public role for the monarchy. Thus in 1847 he said during a Poor Law debate, 'I have always believed that the power of the Crown has diminished, is diminishing, and ought to be increased.' Ten years later he pressed for a closer link between the Queen and her possessions in India after the Mutiny. And after Prince Albert's death he said on several occasions that if he had survived Britain would willingly have become an absolute monarchy within a few years. The tongue was only half in cheek.

It was indeed the untimely death of the Prince in 1861 that proved the turning point in Disraeli's relationship with the Queen. He and Mary Anne had been invited to Windsor in 1861 and their occasional meetings and conversations were now warm and cordial. But where Disraeli surpassed himself was in the warm, extravagant and glowing tribute he paid the Prince after his death later that year. A flow of grateful letters followed between the broken Queen and Disraeli; in Parliament he spoke and voted in favour of increasing the Albert Memorial subscription fund by £50,000. Two years later, in 1863, Disraeli was invited to attend the Prince of Wales's wedding. At some point in the service he used his spyglass to ogle the Queen. He was caught in the act by Her Majesty, but there was no embarrassment. Indeed she probably rather enjoyed the attention. As Melbourne and Peel had found before him, so Disraeli discovered that the Queen dealt almost entirely in emotions and personalities. He had found a way of appealing to these emotions through immaculate courtly manners which verged on a parody. There was still much work to do, and in the Queen's eyes he remained an exotic conundrum, but he was fast becoming a trusted adviser and indeed a favourite.

In February 1858 Palmerston, by now Prime Minister, got into another scrape. The French Emperor Napoleon III had almost been killed by a bomb thrown by an Italian named Orsini. The Emperor survived, but it turned out that Orsini's bomb had been made in a Birmingham factory. Palmerston introduced a new law against foreign conspiracies in Britain; Parliament erupted at this un-Palmerstonian submission to French demands; Palmerston was defeated and forced to resign.

As before, the Queen sent for Lord Derby. As before, Derby cobbled together a minority Ministry. As before,

Disraeli became Chancellor of the Exchequer. And as before, the new Government was not destined for a long life – in this case, a little over a year. In that time the Derby Government became notable for doing three things: legalising a compromise on Jewish Emancipation which allowed Lionel de Rothschild finally to take his seat in Parliament; passing the Government of India Act which ended the rule of the East India Company; and bringing in a new Reform Bill in 1859, which made little progress in Parliament but reinforced the idea that the Conservative Party might not be uniformly opposed to a further change in the franchise – even if it meant creating what Bright called the 'fancy franchises' which gave extra votes to educated and thrifty members of the middle classes while denying it to others.

Meanwhile, for Disraeli as Chancellor this was an opportunity to gain some economic credibility. His efforts were steadier and less dramatic than in 1852. Although the Government collapsed before the new Budget could be brought forward, Disraeli had nonetheless learned his lesson, observing that 'a good management of the finances is the only thing which will get the country with us'. There were no flighty attempts to distinguish between earned and unearned income, and when Derby again proposed extra funds to build new ironclad ships in order to preserve British naval superiority, Disraeli resisted strongly.

More significantly, the years 1858 and 1859 were the occasion of Disraeli's last two great implausible efforts to recruit new allies. The political wheel was turning fast. The Peelites were disappearing from Parliament or falling into the ranks of the Whigs. But the prime Peelite, namely William Gladstone, was still at this point technically a Tory. So Disraeli laid one final siege.

On 25 May 1858 Disraeli wrote to Gladstone urging to him to join the Cabinet. The difficulty was as much personal as political. So Disraeli took the matter head-on: 'Our mutual relations have formed the great difficulty in accomplishing a result which I have always anxiously desired.' He gave a succinct account of his past willingness to make personal sacrifices in order to secure a stronger government. 'Thus you see, for more than eight years, instead of thrusting myself into the foremost place, I have been, at all times, actively prepared to make every sacrifice of self for the public good, which I have ever thought identical with your accepting office in a Conservative Government.'

Up to this point, Gladstone would have read the letter politely; indeed he perhaps might have felt a degree of respect, to his surprise. But sustaining this display was too great a struggle for Disraeli. In his next sentence he let loose the scorn which he had hitherto managed to suppress: 'Don't you think the time has come when you might deign to be magnanimous?' Disraeli concluded his pitch by reflecting on the uncertainty of politics: 'I may be removed from the scene, or I may wish to be removed from the scene. Every man performs his office and there is a Power greater than ourselves that disposes of all this.'

This was not his normal idiom and Gladstone would have detected the mockery. He replied coldly: 'You consider that the relations between yourself and me have proved the main difficulty in the way of certain arrangements. Will you allow me to assure you that I have never in my life taken a decision which turned upon them?' Inevitably, Gladstone ended his letter by rising to Disraeli's fly: 'I state these points fearlessly and without reserve, for you have yourself well reminded me that there is a Power beyond us that disposes of what we are and do, and I find the limits of choice in public life to be very narrow.' So that was that. Gladstone refused to join the Government, but he did agree to be sent on a mission to the Ionian Islands, where he tried to persuade them of the advantages of constitutional government.

Meanwhile the hunt for allies went on. This time the quarry was even grander, namely the formidable lone stag of the wood. Disraeli had throughout his career cultivated a relationship with Lord Palmerston. It is likely each respected the other as a fellow buccaneer. Back in 1852, Disraeli had written to Palmerston that 'there are few things nearer my heart than political cooperation with yourself'. Disraeli's notebooks are scattered with nuggets and observations on the great man, for example that he was one of three men who 'rouged', and the suggestion, put to him by the 2nd Duke of Wellington, that Palmerston managed his numerous romantic affairs with 'Hush Money'. But his main interest was in Palmerston's handling of foreign policy. Although Disraeli had often joined the chorus attacking the boisterous exuberance of Palmerston, in his heart Disraeli accepted the underlying premise, namely that Britain depended for her authority on prestige, and that the prime duty of Her Majesty's Ministers was therefore to maintain, deploy and if possible increase that prestige.

Disraeli's approach to Palmerston in May 1859 was well planned. He humoured both of the old man's concerns that he should have a commanding role in foreign policy, and that any future Reform Bill should have no meaningful content. Disraeli opened loftily: 'I address you in our ancient confidence. Consider well the views I am taking the liberty of placing before you.' On foreign affairs, Palmerston would be the 'entire master of the situation. The foreign policy of every Government of which you are a member must be yours.' And as regards domestic policy, a Reform Bill would be as empty as Palmerston wished. Disraeli skirted around the question of the premiership, which was of course crucial. He had not cleared his approach with Lord Derby, but he was bold enough to say that Derby retained the leadership only as a point of honour in the absence of a suitable successor. The ice was thin here and it was perhaps fortunate that Palmerston politely declined.

Disraeli kept one final idea up his sleeve. He was faced with the prospect of a vote of no confidence supported by both wings of the Liberal Party. At Willis's Rooms on 6 June 1859, Palmerston and Lord John Russell had patched up their differences and worked out a plan to defeat the Government. The two men symbolised their reconciliation when Palmerston gleefully helped his younger colleague up onto the platform to the accompaniment of loud cheers. Faced with this new Liberal alliance, Derby's Government could not survive. So Disraeli proposed to Derby that they should both resign in favour of Stanley. 'There is only one man who at this moment, with our influence, could combine the whole of the Conservative party, and would immediately obtain a considerable section of those opposite. It is Stanley.' This idea followed its predecessors into oblivion. Derby and Stanley were not on cosy terms and it is highly unlikely that Derby would have agreed to stand down in favour of his son. So Palmerston formed a new Government. Gladstone again became Chancellor of the Exchequer and joined the Liberal Party. Disraeli and Derby returned to the Opposition benches where they had spent most of the previous twelve years.

Over the next six years Derby and Disraeli began to give up. By now Derby was getting old and becoming less interested. He spent large amounts of time translating the *Iliad*. Disraeli was also ageing and slowing. Years of ceaseless manoeuvring were at last taking their toll on him. He suffered from gout and often felt tired. In 1860 he started to sketch out a series of reminiscences and aphorisms; he seems to have had the idea of producing the political equivalent of his father's *Curiosities of Literature*. In 1863, according to Professor Hawkins, Disraeli only voted in eight out of 188 divisions in the Commons. The following year he voted in seventeen out of 156. A photo of Disraeli which survives from the 1860s shows him looking weary and ill, leaning on some books and carrying a walking stick, his black hair having receded into one unruly curl. He was no longer the sprightly novelist or slashing politician he had once been.

In 1864 the Prussian invasion of Schleswig-Holstein appeared briefly to threaten Palmerston's Government. Disraeli bestirred himself and put down a motion of censure. He complained that Palmerston's policies were damaging British prestige. 'Within twelve months we have been twice repulsed at St Petersburg. Twice have we supplicated in vain at Paris. We have menaced Austria, and Austria has allowed our menaces to pass her like the idle wind. We have threatened Prussia, and Prussia has defied us. Our objurgations have rattled over the head of the German Diet, and the German Diet has treated them with contempt.' But Palmerston survived and indeed won the subsequent general election in the summer of 1865. It seemed as though he would go on for ever. After eighteen years of nearly continuous Opposition, Derby and Disraeli had made almost no progress.

It was therefore in a spirit of deep despondency that Disraeli wrote to Derby from Hughenden that August. 'I am quite aware that I have had an opportunity in life to which I have not been adequate ... I look upon my career in the House of Commons, so far as office is concerned, to have concluded.' Lamely, he suggested that the time had come to retire. 'This course involves really no sacrifice on my part. The leadership of hopeless opposition is a gloomy affair, and there is little distinction when your course is not associated with the possibility of real power.' Derby sent a warm reply, explaining that he greatly valued Disraeli's support and that neither man should give up their positions. But as they surveyed the scene that summer in 1865, the prospect of power must have appeared more distant than ever. There seemed no escape from Opposition.

Disraeli in these years had picked up a new and dangerous critic. In April 1860 a young Robert Cecil MP, the son of Lord Salisbury, wrote a highly hostile article about Disraeli in the *Quarterly Review*. Cecil's argument was twofold: first, Disraeli had failed to lead his Party to victory as Peel had done; and second, that in intriguing for office he had abandoned every Conservative principle. His sole notable achievements were destructive: by his 'various ... flexible ... shameless' manoeuvrings, he had simply made every other government an impossibility.

Cecil wrote this and other critical articles anonymously, but his authorship was widely known. Meanwhile other Tories were making similar noises in private. In 1852 Henry Lennox's father, the Duke of Richmond, had complained bitterly about Disraeli's abandonment of Protection: 'I can see they are, damn them, at the old game of throwing over their principles.' Later in the 1850s Henry Drummond, a hardened Tory, complained to the Whips that 'Lord Derby and Mr Disraeli have led the Conservative Party to adopt every measure they opposed as Radical ten years ago. They have made the party the tool of their own ambition.'

Time certainly was ticking and the Party's patience was wearing thin. But, for the time being, three things saved Disraeli. First, he was indispensable and there was no alternative leader in the Commons. Second, and as a result of this, Lord Derby continued to stand by Disraeli as his deputy, which made Disraeli's position impregnable. And third, unlike Peel, Disraeli was almost immune to slights on his personal honour. He therefore found it easier to try and charm his opponents. At one point he went to stay at Lord Salisbury's Hatfield estate and happened to bump into Robert Cecil in the garden. Rather than greet him stiffly and coldly, as Peel would have done, Disraeli warmly embraced his opponent and told him how good it was to see him. In these and other ways, Disraeli was able to sustain an almost theatrical display of disregard for others' opinions. It was exceptionally difficult to wound him.

Nonetheless, the poor political record, the repeated general election defeats and the long and fruitless years in Opposition cannot be ignored. If, as many observed, Disraeli was such a talented parliamentary performer, why was he so unsuccessful at overhauling the Whigs?

Gladstone came close to the answer when he said that Disraeli was simultaneously Lord Derby's necessity and his curse. By this he meant that in the day-to-day dogfights of parliamentary warfare, Disraeli was the Tories' sharpest weapon – but the collateral damage he created destroyed all his gains. In particular, he drove as many into the ranks of his enemies as he recruited as reliable allies. Thus in 1853, after Aberdeen had formed his coalition Government, Derby noted ruefully that 'personal feeling has had much to do with this step and that the course pursued is mainly to be attributed to the jealousy and hatred (the word is not too strong) felt by the Peelite party in the House of Commons towards Disraeli'.

This was a considerable handicap. Indeed, it is why at some universities tongue-in-cheek exam questions are set asking whether Disraeli was the founder of the modern Liberal Party. But what was the alternative? How could Disraeli have behaved and acted differently in order to puncture the long period of Whig ascendancy? The answer, as Disraeli knew, was not to abandon the attempt to change his party. Protection was not only an economic failure; it was a poor

vote-winner too. Disraeli had no choice but to change the
Party's position and 'throw over its principles'. It was the
way he went about it that provoked outrage.

More than any other nineteenth-century politician, perhaps apart from Canning, Disraeli called politics a 'game'.
Occasionally it was the 'High Game'; at other times it was a
'Grand Game'. But it was always a game, in which pieces were
moved about to try and outflank the enemy. It had no moral
content. Today we are used to such language. A generation
of political journalists have made the vocabulary of tactics,
strategy, positioning and repositioning part and parcel of
modern politics. Of course, there is nothing wrong with
this. All successful political parties need a robust campaign
strategy. But what Disraeli attempted was too brazen and
extreme. For example, he had vigorously backed a Reform
Bill in 1858; yet the following year he confidently advised
Lord Palmerston that such a Bill might be politically empty.
Likewise, when he met Bright in 1857 he strongly implied
that the Manchester School of Free Trade politicians could
abandon their principles if given Ministerial positions. This
is why Bright later claimed that Disraeli would have been a
statesman if his abilities had been directed by any ennobling
principle or idea.

In these ways, and countless others, Disraeli did himself
great damage. Worse still, he flew in the face of an intangible
but all-powerful mid-Victorian moral code. These were the
years of high and heavy morality, when most believed that
Britain was ordained by Providence to pioneer a new spirit
of development and economic progress. The zeitgeist was
reflected in any number of sturdy, respectable politicians.
Even Palmerston, although absurdly casual in his private life,
spoke the language of Providential justice, sympathy for the
oppressed, and eternal standards of liberty when defending
British interests overseas. This was a language which Disraeli

never could master. His efforts to do so always sounded like a parody. It would take something dramatic to change the game and gain momentum for himself and his party; and Disraeli was running out of time.

TORY DEMOCRACY

We do not know how Disraeli heard about Palmerston's ab-
dominal problem, but by the summer of 1865 he regarded
it as a weighty political fact. On 3 September 1865 he dispatched a bulletin to Lord Derby: 'his bladder complaint,
tho' in itself not fatal, deprives him of his usual exercise, and
of sleep which was his <u>forte</u> and carried him through everything'. Palmerston was the oldest Prime Minister in history,
but his jaunty manner and romantic exploits gave the impression that he might defy the ageing process. Now old age
was catching up with him. In October he caught a chill which
drove down his defences. He died on the morning of 18 October, two days short of his eighty-first birthday.

The death transformed politics. Although Disraeli joined
when necessary for Party purposes in attacking his rum-
bustious foreign policy, he was at heart a keen admirer of
Palmerston and later made a touching parliamentary tribute in which he singled out the old man's enduring taste for
fame.* Privately however he was greatly encouraged by the

---

*In his notebooks, Disraeli made a record of Palmerston's last joke: 'Lord
Granville had a dairy farm near London: 100 cows, & they all died ... early
in October, Lord Granville married, a very young lady indeed, "sweet
seventeen", he himself being upwards of 50 ... When told, Palmerston
said "So, having lost his cows, Granville has taken a heifer."'

development. Stanley, who visited Disraeli in these weeks, found him 'in good health and excellent spirits. It seemed as if the prospect of renewed political life had excited him afresh, and that he had thrown off the lethargy which had been growing upon him for the last year.' The tectonic plates had indeed shifted. For the Whigs, Palmerston's death raised worrying questions about the Party's future, prompting Sir Charles Wood to lament: 'Our quiet days are over; no more peace for us.'

There had been general agreement on two facts about Lord Palmerston. It was most unlikely that he would be defeated in a general election. Disraeli had done his best to shake Palmerston's popularity, but in vain. The second fact was that so long as he lived it was impossible to imagine that a second Reform Bill of substance would succeed. He had therefore been the despair of Russell, Gladstone, Bright and that whole band of instinctive reformers, each of whom had a favourite plan up their sleeve. But to every sensible, old-fashioned Whig, he was a sound vote-winner and a welcome reassurance that the roof of the Constitution would not fall in. They were safe so long as 'Pam' was Prime Minister, resisting the Radicals, fighting the foreigner, leaning on a fence and chewing a straw in every cartoon.

Now this great pillar of resistance had been swept away. In its place, the ageing but erratic Lord John Russell became Prime Minister once again, eager to chalk one final measure to his name. Years before he had been one of the authors of the Great Reform Bill. Afterwards however he seemed worn out by the effort and made clear there would be no early move to democracy. He thus earned for himself the label 'Finality Jack' – but he then spent much of the ensuing decades defying his nickname by fidgeting about with fresh figures and new schedules of the electorate. These activities had exasperated his colleagues, but now he could give them free rein.

Russell found a keen ally in these efforts in the Chancellor of the Exchequer, Gladstone. A year before, Gladstone had made a famous utterance in which he suggested that every responsible citizen should come within the pale of the Constitution. The two men began to turn their minds to how this constitutional manoeuvre might be completed.

There were strong arguments in favour of a new Reform Bill. This was partly because the Great Reform Act of 1832 had defied the doom-mongers and the naysayers. In spite of the Duke of Wellington's predictions, the Queen remained on her throne; gentlemen continued to play their part in politics; and no guillotines had appeared on Tower Hill. The Houses of Commons and Lords had continued much as before the Act, which had given the vote to £10 householders in the boroughs and to £50 tenants in the counties. Whereas before 1832 one in seven men in England and Wales had the vote, after 1832 the number was one in five. This was far short of democracy, but it had provided a strong measure of stability for thirty years.

The main issue in 1866 was that the 1832 Act had opened a door which could not easily be shut again. Once you had created a rule for the franchise which applied across the country, sweeping away the haphazard muddle of centuries, there was no logical reason why you should not repeat the endeavour and again change the qualification. A figure was simply a mathematical definition, not a heavenly decree. The issue had become not the sacredness of some political principle but a matter of numbers and movable boundaries. These could all be changed at will.

The difficulty for Russell and Gladstone was that the will within their own party was weak. True, the new Reform League was applying considerable pressure outside Parliament. There was also a strong appetite among Radical MPs for a bold new Bill. But the Liberals who had been elected in

1865 were Palmerstonian Liberals – obstinate, evasive and in most domestic matters soundly conservative. This posed a considerable problem for Russell and Gladstone. As the new session approached, the Government Whips warned the Prime Minister that a new Reform Bill would be met by a rebellion in Parliament.

For Disraeli there was no issue of principle here, just infinite room for manoeuvre. He had first stood for Parliament in 1832 and indeed fought the last by-election under the pre-reform system. But he had no particular nostalgia for the old regime. The instinct of the Party was of course against enlarging the franchise, but what if a scheme could be devised which actually benefited the Tories or, if that could not be proven, at least confounded the Liberals and their noisy champion, Gladstone? For Disraeli what was intolerable was the assumption which for the Liberals was self-evident: he could not accept that because they had passed the Great Reform Act, the Liberal Party held a grip on all future attempts to enlarge the franchise.

There was one certainty in Disraeli's mind: the Party needed an unmistakable triumph under his leadership. Twenty years had passed since Peel had been Prime Minister with a Conservative majority. The backbenchers were becoming frustrated. There was talk about replacing Derby and Disraeli with Stanley, while a powerful band of diehards were gathering around Lord Bath and Peel's brother, General Peel. A Tory Reform Bill, carried against Liberal opposition, might shake the ground under Gladstone's feet and provide the necessary victory. The odds were against it but, skilfully managed, the Party might perform with the necessary discipline. In 1866 the time was not yet ripe, but Disraeli began to master the details of election law and voting statistics in a way he had never attempted with the finances of the nation when he was Chancellor of the Exchequer.

On 12 March 1866 Gladstone brought the new Reform Bill before Parliament. Its proposals were not earth-shaking. The Bill proposed that the borough franchise would be lowered from £10 to £7 per annum; in the counties, the vote would be given to those occupying property worth £14 a year instead of £50. There were also a number of 'fancy franchises' which gave votes to those who had held bank savings worth more than £50 for two years. All told, the Bill would enfranchise some 400,000 new votes.

This measured, inoffensive, eminently reasonable Bill was designed to please everyone. Unfortunately it pleased no one at all. The Radicals wanted a larger extension of the franchise and quibbled about many of the details. The conservative Whigs thought it went too far. The result was a highly hostile reception in which, true to form, the Liberal Party split again. A powerful minority formed what was called the Cave of Adullam after the figure in the Old Testament who provided a place of refuge for all manner of discontented folk. The leader of the Cave was Robert Lowe, a highly articulate, half-blind albino. Intelligent but inflexible, he had been put off democracy when he was struck on the head during a riot at the Kidderminster election in 1857. Thereafter he specialised in powerful denunciations of the working classes as strikingly stupid, drunken, irresponsible and venal. He thus inflicted considerable damage on the cause he was defending, namely resolute opposition to the Reform Bill.

On the other side of the argument John Bright made the outstanding speeches. It was indeed he who first compared the Bill's opponents to the Cave of Adullam, and over the following few weeks he mounted a fierce campaign to extend the franchise. He was disappointed that the new franchise would still be highly restrictive, but he made clear that this was a move in the right direction and signalled that the long stalemate on this subject had at last dissipated.

Meanwhile the leaders of the two main parties adopted different tactics. It was around this time that Disraeli remarked to one ally that 'it was a great advantage to a leader of the House of Commons that he should be, not unable, but unwilling to speak'. In the weeks that followed Disraeli put this technique into practice, restricting himself to short volleys and harassing interruptions, and steering clear of detailed statements of his own philosophy. Gladstone on the other hand talked too much and did so in an extravagant manner, making bold and alarming statements about Christian equality and the rights of man. This gave the impression of an unhinged demagogue, hell-bent on full-scale democracy. He therefore alienated even those among his supporters who wanted to achieve a balanced but final settlement.

Over the following weeks the Liberal Bill faced a battering of hostile amendments. It scraped through the Second Reading by five votes. Many Liberals were worried about the redistribution proposals which would follow the Reform Bill. In an effort to reassure them, the Government published its plans. This made matters worse. The Adullamites by now were in close talks with the Tory Party. On 18 June it was agreed that the Liberal Adullamite Lord Dunkellin would launch another attack on the Government. At issue was the seemingly technical question of whether a borough voter should be registered to the relief of the poor. The Tories and Adullamites argued that whether an individual was registered to pay local poor relief rates was a good test of the civic responsibility needed to qualify for the franchise. Lord Dunkellin therefore tabled an amendment calling for the franchise to be linked to personal payment of rates. This provided the necessary issue of principle around which many Liberals, Whigs and Tories could agree. The Government was beaten by 315 votes to 304.

It seemed certain that Russell would resign, but who would take his place? A fresh struggle was about to unfold. Disraeli knew from bitter experience how difficult it could be to persuade Lord Derby to accept the Queen's Commission. The acute disappointment of 1855 was never far from his mind. But now there was an added complication. The Adullamites, encouraged by their victory, were aiming at a higher prize. True, they were few in numbers, but they were fully conscious of their status as key cogs in the balance of power. They therefore required a decisive say in choosing the new government and selecting the new Prime Minister. They singled out the Whig Lord Clarendon as the likely leader of a new anti-reform administration.

When Derby heard what the Adullamites were planning he immediately consulted Disraeli, who fired off a despairing tirade. There was only one course compatible with Derby's honour and the reputation of the Party. He must at once let it be known that he fully intended to form a government with himself as Prime Minister. 'The question is not Adullamite; it is national. You must take the Government; the honor of your house and the necessity of the country alike require it.' Faced with this language, Lord Derby had little choice but to accept the Queen's summons. He called a meeting of senior Conservatives who, with the exception of the errant Lord Bath, agreed that he should accept the premiership and first of all try to form a government with the Liberal dissidents. If they refused he should proceed to form a purely Conservative administration.

So it was decided, and so it came to pass. The Adullamites refused to serve in a Tory government, so Derby formed his third administration without them. Disraeli returned as Chancellor of the Exchequer and ensured that a number of his own supporters were rewarded with attractive posts. Sir Stafford Northcote joined the Cabinet as President of

the Board of Trade, while Lord Stanley became Foreign Secretary. A junior job was found for Ralph Earle, Disraeli's
fellow intriguer, as Secretary of the Poor Law Board. Lord
John Manners resumed the position he had held during
the previous two Derby administrations, as First Commissioner of Works. Meanwhile Robert Cecil, who had written
hostile articles about Disraeli in 1860, joined the Cabinet as
Secretary of State for India under his new title of Viscount
Cranborne.

These were the men, but what of the central measure,
namely the future of the Reform Bill? The Tories had voted
against Gladstone's Bill, but now faced pressure to produce
a definite policy of their own. *Punch* magazine captured the
confusion in a cartoon: a working man asks Lord Derby and
Disraeli what they intend to do for him. Lord Derby remarks:
'Ah, if only he were a racehorse,' and Disraeli adds, 'or an
Asian mystery'. But by now reform was no laughing matter.
Bright had taken his campaign beyond Parliament and was
addressing mass meetings up and down the country. These
meetings and those held by the powerful Reform League
were on the whole orderly but reached a climax at the end
of July with three days of rioting in London. On 23 July a
crowd broke through the railings into Hyde Park, which the
Home Secretary, Spencer Walpole, had ordered be closed.
Many were injured in the mayhem and one police constable
later died from his wounds. Walpole broke down under
pressure and later resigned his office. But the violence gave
Disraeli an idea. On 29 July he wrote to Derby suggesting
they resuscitate Gladstone's Bill with £6 and £20 ratings for
borough and county seats. 'You could carry this in the present House, and rapidly. It would prevent all agitation in the
recess; it would cut the ground entirely from under Gladstone: it would smash the Bath Cabal, for there would be no
dangerous question ahead. Think of this.'

Derby was indeed thinking, but he was determined to make up his own mind. Years before he had been a Whig member of the Government that passed the Great Reform Bill. Although now a staunch Conservative, he could see the conservative case for limited reform of the franchise. But he was a Derby, the scion of a great dynasty, and his hand would not be forced by a group of drunken hooligans. As his son, Lord Stanley, had observed, much of the trouble in Hyde Park had come from a group with no strong political views whatsoever but a keen interest in causing mayhem. What was required was a calm and sensible settlement of reform, passed by Parliament in spite of, not because of, the uproar. Derby was anxious above all to restore the authority of Parliament. He saw that this depended on Parliament's ability to settle the question of reform. He took his time in reaching this conclusion, but on 16 September he wrote to Disraeli: 'I am coming reluctantly to the conclusion that we must act on the matter.' In the weeks that followed, the initiative rested with Derby. His correspondence contradicts the idea that it had been Disraeli who pushed hard for early legislation, and only needed time to re-educate his party into the new way of thinking. Derby was determined to keep the matter in his own hands. He did not envisage an immediate Bill but rather a set of resolutions, agreed by Parliament, which would serve as a leisurely prelude to legislation.

Derby gained strong support from the Queen. On 19 September he travelled to Balmoral, where he discovered that the Queen had reached the same conclusion as he for opposite reasons. The Queen in these years was the torment of her supporters and a nightmare to successive Private Secretaries. She veered from the merely erratic to the unhinged, refusing to attend to various official duties and setting tongues wagging by insisting on being accompanied by a somewhat random Highlander called John Brown. The result was that she became deeply unpopular and indeed was booed on her way to the opening of the 1867 Parliament. Increasingly she grew concerned for her own safety and she was genuinely alarmed for the security of the throne. Reform in her opinion was therefore urgently needed to stave off revolution and anarchy. Over the following weeks she made these views known to her Prime Minister. As Derby reported to Disraeli in October, 'we cannot escape doing something'; the Queen wanted the matter settled 'by us'.

Through the autumn of 1866 Derby and Disraeli followed the Queen's wishes and began to frame resolutions to present at the next session of Parliament the following year. Occasionally the Queen pushed her interest in the matter to a degree which even Disraeli could not tolerate. Disraeli's usual method of handling his Sovereign was to treat her wishes with courtly deference, but he could not sanction her suggestion that she might mediate with the Liberals. 'The royal project of gracious interposition with our rivals is a mere phantom,' he told Stafford Northcote. 'It pleases the vanity of a Court deprived of substantial power.' This vanity of course was something which Disraeli had done his best to stimulate.

Besides, Disraeli by this point had lost his initial enthusiasm for a rapid Reform Bill. He was focusing his attention instead on preparing a Budget for the following spring. His mauling at Gladstone's hands in 1852 still haunted him and he was determined to produce a Budget which gave him a reputation for financial prudence. He therefore waged a determined campaign to curb spending and waste by the Admiralty. As before, so once again, he grumbled about the Navy and the high cost of keeping the colonies. In October he wrote to Derby: 'leave the Canadians to defend themselves; recall the African squadron; give up the settlements on the west coast of Africa and we shall make a saving which will at the same time enable us to build ships and have a good budget'. In the end he found more conventional methods of making savings, but he came under pressure from the Tory squires to make those cuts to the Malt Tax which he had failed to deliver in the 1850s.

On 8 November Derby and Disraeli pushed their draft resolutions through Cabinet. Their colleagues showed scant enthusiasm, but the draft was loosely drawn and there seemed plenty of scope for delay. But as the new session approached, Derby had a more promising idea. He discussed it first over dinner with Stanley and then wrote to Disraeli on 22 December, using typical sporting vocabulary: 'of all possible hares to start I do not know a better one than the extension to household suffrage coupled with plurality of voting'. Household suffrage appealed to Derby because it offered both decisiveness and simplicity. Instead of scurrying about drawing temporary lines in the sand based on property values which would then need to be changed over and over again, why not simply give the vote to every householder who personally paid their rates? This would mean a big expansion of the franchise, but it might at least provide a lasting settlement. Besides, the large increase in the electorate might be outweighed by giving wealthier or better-educated individuals an extra vote. These 'fancy franchises' were therefore seen as a handy device for limiting democracy while maximising the Tory vote.

Parliament was due to meet at the start of February 1867. A vague reference to reform was included in the Queen's Speech. Meanwhile Derby and Disraeli introduced the idea of household suffrage to Cabinet. They immediately ran up against the considerable obstacle of General Peel. Eleven years younger than his brother, the fallen Prime Minister, Peel was a genial and popular member of the Cabinet – strong in views, successful at the races, and well liked by the Queen.* He was however dead against Derby's policy. Both Derby and Disraeli did their best to persuade him, but by early February were forced to admit defeat. 'You will find him very placable,' Disraeli wrote to Derby on 7 February, 'except on the phrase "household suffrage", when his eyes light up with insanity.'

The debate on the resolutions opened on 11 February. Disraeli spoke at great length about the history of Reform Bills since 1832, taking their repeated failure as evidence that the only way forward would be to agree resolutions before proceeding to a full Bill. 'Do not let the House suppose that we are asking them to go into Committee and allow us to propose Resolutions because we are angling for a policy,' he said. 'We are not angling for a policy. We have distinct principles which will guide us, and which we wish the House to sanction. But there are several subjects ... upon which it would be desirable that the opinion of the House should be given; and on these subjects we should defer to the opinion of the House.' It was not a great speech and Bright later remarked that Disraeli had taken two hours to say nothing. The general impression was that the Government was floundering. As the debate went on Disraeli found himself increasingly boxed in and by 14 February he was talking openly about bringing forward an early Reform Bill which would set out a firm policy.

Meanwhile, behind the scenes, the split in the Cabinet was hardening. Cranborne refused to tolerate anything beyond a £5 rated borough franchise and there were further objections

---

*In a twist, General Peel owned the horse that came second in the 1844 Derby. He had therefore been the chief beneficiary of Lord George Bentinck's campaign to prove that the winner had been a four-year-old running in a three-year-old race. Two years later, Bentinck used the same skills of tenacity and single-mindedness to destroy his brother, Robert Peel.

from Lord Carnarvon and General Peel. Indeed Peel now tried to resign. On Sunday 17 February Disraeli travelled to Osborne where he reported the problems to his Sovereign. She at once offered to write to the General. This offer was hastily accepted and, under royal pressure, Peel agreed to rescind his objections. On 19 February Derby and Disraeli once again brought up the idea of household suffrage in Cabinet. Derby pulled out all the stops, saying that the Queen now believed the security of her throne depended on the measure. After further discussion, the Cabinet agreed to proceed with household suffrage based on personal payment of rates, but Disraeli was commissioned to produce detailed statistics showing the effect of household suffrage in the borough seats. A final discussion was scheduled for Saturday 23 February.

The Cabinet assembled at three o'clock on the Saturday afternoon. Derby set the tone by briskly announcing that he was due at Windsor that evening and would be catching the 6.15 train. Discussion therefore turned to the statistics which Disraeli had produced with the help of a man called Dudley Baxter, a partner in Philip Rose's law firm. Cranborne was concerned that the estimates were some way off the mark, but he agreed along with the rest of the Cabinet to put the plan for household suffrage and dual voting before Parliament on Monday. With his colleagues united, Derby set off for Windsor Castle, where he told the Queen that everything was in order. The Cabinet retired for the weekend.

But Cranborne was still not convinced. He was a lifelong devout Anglican and a strong Christian feeling underpinned his thinking. That weekend however he broke with the Ten Commandments and spent Sunday hard at work, unpicking Baxter's statistics. By nightfall he had worked himself up into an intellectual frenzy at what he by now believed to be a brazen act of duplicity by Disraeli. He visited Lord Carnarvon to share his findings. Carnarvon, whose intelligence was matched only by his unpredictability, and whom Disraeli later referred to as 'Twitters', was equally alarmed at what now appeared to be a radical and dangerous proposal. He proceeded to wake General Peel, and they all agreed that they would not tolerate the policy. Cranborne wrote to Derby demanding an immediate Cabinet meeting making clear that they would not support the plan which the previous day they had agreed.

Derby read Cranborne's letter over breakfast the next day, at 6.45 a.m. He hastily forwarded the letter to Disraeli at Grosvenor Gate. The situation was extraordinary. Derby was due to set out the new policy at a Party meeting in Downing Street at 2.30 p.m.; Disraeli was then expected to introduce the plan to Parliament at 4.30; but now there seemed to be no policy at all. Disraeli was still in bed when Derby's message arrived at Grosvenor Gate, but the Prime Minister's words would have shaken off any lingering sleep. 'The enclosed, just received, is utter ruin,' wrote Lord Derby. 'What on earth are we to do?'

An emergency Cabinet was summoned for 12.30 p.m. at Derby's house on St James's Square. All sides by now were enraged. Derby in particular was furious and Disraeli had gone deathly pale. Cranborne made matters worse by arriving late. By 2 p.m. the Cabinet had still not agreed on a new policy – but the backbenchers were beginning to arrive in Downing Street. With ten minutes left, Stanley tried to salvage the situation by suggesting a compromise of a £6 rating franchise for boroughs without dual voting and a £20 rating franchise for the counties. No one was particularly impressed with this measure, but equally no one could think of an acceptable alternative. This became known as the 'Ten Minutes Bill'. It would live only a little longer than the time it took to conceive.

Meanwhile Derby rushed back to Downing Street to tell

the backbenchers about the new policy. Disraeli skipped lunch to prepare his Commons speech. 'The ship floats, that is all,' he reported to Mary Anne as he set off for the House. He spoke for around an hour that afternoon, but made no attempt to remove the impression that the new franchise had simply been plucked at random from the sky. As soon as he finished he came under heavy fire from all sides. Robert Lowe summed up the Government's message as 'say what you please, but for God's sake leave us our places'. This impression of unprincipled manoeuvring was toxic to Disraeli and the following day he beat a hasty retreat.

The Government was now on a knife edge. They had no policy and no agreed direction on reform. It was merely a matter of time before the Opposition grew tired of the confusion and united to throw out the Government. But over at the Carlton Club something curious was happening. On the evening after Disraeli's speech, a group of grumpy Tories had gathered in the smoking room. There was nothing unusual about this, except that the topic of their grumbles on this particular night was strange, indeed unique. They complained at length how the Government was failing them – not by being too radical, but rather by being too conservative. The time had come for a bold and decisive policy. They were wearied of the endless shilly-shallying. Why not bring an end to the issue and defy Gladstone and his supporters by proposing household suffrage? The group put their thoughts down in a letter to Disraeli. By Wednesday a large proportion of the Party agreed. At a backbench meeting on Thursday a sizeable majority of Tory MPs formally agreed to back a policy of household suffrage.

The smoking-room revolution breathed new life into the Government. Now Derby and Disraeli could appeal over the heads of Cranborne, Peel and Carnarvon by invoking the will of the Parliamentary Party in favour of household suffrage.

Moreover, as Disraeli later admitted, it was much easier for the Government to present a policy which did not look as though it actually emanated from the Government itself. Separately, that same week the Liberal Adullamites were shaking their heads and grudgingly revising their own position. They too were wearied of the whole subject and wanted above everything to get it resolved. There was a strong feeling that the matter could not be settled until a definite resting point for the franchise had been found. This was impossible so long as the franchise was linked to a specific arbitrary rental value. As the Tories had, so the Adullamites agreed that household suffrage matched by suitable checks was the only credible policy. The news of this about-turn soon filtered through to Derby and Disraeli.

The following day Disraeli happened to meet John Bright while walking through the parliamentary lobby. For many years they had enjoyed a warm and genial acquaintance, even though Bright thought that Disraeli was an engaging charlatan who believed in nothing. They spent some time talking through the situation, and Disraeli made his views on reform plain to his old adversary. The meeting ended with a burst of sentimental affection, as Disraeli reached forward and said: 'Well, whatever happens, we shall always be friends.'

On Saturday 2 March the Cabinet met again. Derby and Disraeli urged a return to the original policy, namely household suffrage with plural voting in order to balance the democratising effect. The meeting lasted an hour and at the end Derby went round each member of the Cabinet in turn to ask if they agreed. Peel and Carnarvon took their cue from Cranborne, who refused to agree to the proposals. Otherwise the Cabinet displayed surprising unity. As the rebels left the room Derby called after them that this was the end of the Tory Party, to which Disraeli wryly added, 'poor Tory Party'. Peel then lamely cried, 'I will waive my objections if you will,' but Cranborne was off and the rebels followed him.

The resignations were announced in Parliament on Monday, 4 March. At the same time, Disraeli made it clear that a new and full measure of reform would be brought forward within a fortnight based on the Cabinet's original scheme of rated residential suffrage. The Government was reconfigured, with several of Disraeli's friends receiving new positions. Stafford Northcote replaced Viscount Cranborne as Secretary of State for India; the Duke of Buckingham took over as Colonial Secretary; and Sir John Pakington took on Peel's role as Secretary of State for War. The Dukes of Marlborough and Richmond, along with Monty Corry's father, Henry Lowry-Corry, joined the Cabinet for the first time.

Meanwhile Gathorne Hardy, the President of the Poor Law Board, was becoming a key figure in Government. In May he would replace the weeping Walpole as Home Secretary. Hardy was important to Disraeli in part because he was known to be relatively cautious about reform, but also because he was a fast-rising star in Parliament and offered vital support in the daily fire fights with Gladstone. He and Disraeli therefore began to consult together, although Hardy was not entirely taken in. On 7 March he noted in his diary: 'I had more talk with Disraeli, whose fault is that he is always looking for what will suit others, rather than what is sound in itself...'

A full plan for the new Reform Bill was agreed by Cabinet the following week. It was decided that all male borough residents who personally paid poor rates would receive the vote, while second votes would also go to those who paid more than twenty shillings per year in direct taxes and had been resident in the constituency for at least two years. This combined the idea of linking voting rights to civic duty with an added extra check against what was called the 'residuum' of irresponsible and loutish individuals. Disraeli however already saw that dual voting would cause problems in Parliament and he began to argue against the idea in Cabinet.

But at this moment Disraeli suddenly became caught up in a new battle of a peculiar kind. Baxter, the researcher who had produced an initial draft of the Reform Bill, was disgruntled that Derby and Disraeli had consulted a civil servant called Thring to improve and correct the drafting. Thring had made some stern criticisms of Baxter's handiwork; now the two men were not speaking. By 14 March Thring vs Baxter had become a matter of great political import; the Bill was due to be presented the following week, but there was no new draft to consider. Derby wrote to Disraeli insisting that he pick one or other of the apparatchiks; Disraeli, perhaps wisely, plumped for Thring, who agreed to work through the night so that a draft would be ready for the weekend. He completed his work with the support of two secretaries by early Friday evening; the Bill was printed overnight ahead of one final Cabinet meeting scheduled for Saturday.

Meanwhile Derby and Disraeli introduced an innovation. On Friday they called together the Parliamentary Party and briefed the backbenchers on what would be in the new Bill. This novel institution has in recent years become standard practice for smart Prime Ministers looking to maintain strong relations with their Members of Parliament, but it was a new development in the nineteenth century. Gathering together the grumpy with the enthused helped to instil a sense of trust and unity. Over the next few weeks this technique paid dividends, helping Derby to avoid the fate which had befallen Robert Peel. Although Cranborne continued to snipe from the sidelines, the majority of the Party stood fast behind Disraeli and gave him much-needed support in Parliament. In fact, it was the backbenchers, though often mocked, who in their frustration had provided the Government with a policy.

Disraeli introduced the new Bill on Monday 18 March. He got straight to the point. 'I would, in the first place, call the attention of the House to that part of it which is perhaps the most important ... I allude to the franchise, and especially that which should prevail in towns.' Many in the Commons were perplexed and confused by the baffling array of voting statistics to which they had been subjected in previous reform debates. Disraeli cut through this noise by pitching his scheme not on the basis of voter numbers but rather as a simple new idea. In 1832 the franchise had been founded on the principle of property value. All those whose houses were valued at £10 or more qualified for the borough franchise. Subsequent Reform Bills had all accepted this principle and merely sought to change the value of property at which an individual could vote. These Bills had all failed, however, and for good reason – after all, why was one particular property value more acceptable than the next? Disraeli's new Bill was therefore founded on a new and more lasting principle, right for the country and in tune with the times: the borough franchise should no longer be based on property value, but rather on rating. All those who paid local poor relief rates provided the necessary guarantee of regularity of life and trustworthiness of conduct. They should therefore qualify for the franchise. This sounded sensible and was also simple to comprehend. As Disraeli explained, 'if you are going to invest men with the exercise of public rights, let that great trust be accompanied with the exercise of public duty'. It was a strong performance and it set the tone for the debate. As Gladstone later reflected, by speaking in such simple terms about household suffrage Disraeli bowled over the Opposition by sheer force of phrase. Here was a proposal which everyone could understand and which seemed to be based on a solid principle. Of course, it went a great deal further than many had wished, but at last the path to a final settlement seemed clear.

Nevertheless, over the next few days Gladstone sought to derail the Government. Indeed he worked himself up into a state of choleric outrage. He disliked the casual disregard for key details in the Bill, but mainly he was gravely alarmed that Disraeli was now claiming to be the champion of reform. He and his followers launched a strong onslaught, and for several days the survival of the Bill was not clear. On 24 March Disraeli reflected fatalistically to Lord Derby: 'It is very trying, and no doubt we shall, both of us, always remember the year 1867.'

Disraeli responded to Gladstone's criticisms on 26 March. He remarked that listening to Gladstone speak had made him concerned for his own safety. 'Not that I much care for that kind of thing, but really his manner is sometimes so very alarming that one might almost feel thankful that Gentlemen in this House who sit on opposite sides of this table are divided by a tolerably broad piece of furniture.' One by one he dismissed his opponent's objections. The only issue on which he gave way was on the matter of dual voting, which Disraeli now struck from the scheme. He ended his speech with a strong call for co-operation in concluding the measure. 'Pass this Bill, and then change the Ministry if you like.'

It was a mature and highly intelligent performance. He joked, but did not trivialise. He argued, but did so clearly and without invective. He made a great effort to explain what the Government was trying do. Above all, he sounded reasonable and appeared to be sincere. This is why everyone afterwards agreed that the speech changed the debate and gave momentum to the Conservatives. The Bill passed its Second Reading without division. As Derby told him afterwards, 'you have won our game for us'.

This was indeed a moment of triumph, but the game was far from won. On 4 April, Disraeli as Chancellor was due to make his financial statement. He knew from painful experience that this could destroy the Government. Time was tight and he was under great pressure. He therefore kept his speech short and spoke for forty-five minutes, a blink of the eye by Victorian standards and the shortest Budget speech in history. He had done his sums and, based on the projections, total Government spending for the following year would be around £68.1 million; total revenue would be a little over £69.3 million. This left a surplus of £1.2 million. The Tory squires were still pressing for relief from the Malt Tax but he disappointed them by using the money to pay down part of the National Debt. It was a remarkable transformation by a man who fifteen years earlier had suggested borrowing money in order to balance the books. Disraeli was rewarded by a cordial display of support from Gladstone, who ended his own speech by awarding high marks to his adversary: 'I think the right hon. Gentleman deserves credit for having resisted the temptations to which he must have been subjected; and I believe the course he has taken a wise one, and one well adapted to the promotion of the national wealth.'

There was only one minor setback in these weeks. Ralph Earle had some time ago fallen from Disraeli's favour. He no longer had access to the Chancellor's inner counsels. A junior job in Government was meant to have compensated him for this change of status, but he was bitter and now turned savagely on Disraeli. Perhaps mindful of how Disraeli had once made a name for himself, he selected the new Reform Bill as his moment for a powerful rebellion. He resigned his office and railed against the proposals. Disraeli was somewhat shocked at the development and admitted privately that he felt ashamed at his 'want of discrimination' in employing Earle originally. But Earle was a negligible Parliamentarian and his revolt attracted no following. He later left Parliament and started a new career as a financier in the Middle East.

Disraeli was now in total command of the situation. Derby had again fallen ill, worn out by his efforts to achieve Cabinet unity, and through April he was frequently absent from Cabinet meetings, leaving Disraeli to steer the Bill. The battleground was now the House of Commons and here Disraeli was on top form. The Government was still in a minority of around eighty, and was therefore vulnerable to any wrecking amendments. But Disraeli was in possession of a potentially lethal unexploded weapon, namely the power to ask the Queen to dissolve Parliament and call a general election. No one, least of all the Liberal MPs, wanted this. It was one thing to oppose Disraeli's Bill within the comfort of Parliament; quite another to return to one's constituency and explain to disgruntled supporters why the matter had still not been settled. This gave considerable scope for manoeuvre to Disraeli. For the next twelve weeks he had one sole driving purpose: to outwit Gladstone by carrying the Bill.

In the Commons Disraeli was from now on all smiles and sunshine. He listened carefully and politely, accepting amendments, with or without consulting Cabinet colleagues. Secretly he was in touch with his old travelling companion, James Clay, who as a dissolute young man had sailed round the Mediterranean with Disraeli in the 1830s, but these days was a leading Radical Member of Parliament and one of the world's foremost authorities on whist. Clay wanted to see the Reform Bill carried by Parliament and his approach was to try and open the door as far as possible through a series of radical amendments which did not unduly damage the Government. The result was that over the following weeks the numbers enfranchised by the Bill grew wildly as Disraeli accepted a wide range of radical changes tabled by Clay's friends. One by one, the fancy franchises tumbled down, the residential qualifications were reduced from two years to one year, £10 lodgers received the vote; and the county franchise was further lowered from £15 to £12 in annual rent. The net effect of these and other changes would be a threefold increase in the number enfranchised.

There was one exception to this rule. Disraeli was prepared to accept every amendment, except those which emanated from Gladstone. The whole purpose of his policy was to prove he could defeat Gladstone on his own territory. Now at last it seemed that such a victory was in sight. But everyone knew that Gladstone was planning a decisive intervention and Disraeli was on watch for the moment when Gladstone would try to scupper his scheme. That moment arrived in early April.

On 5 April, the day after Gladstone had congratulated Disraeli on his sober financial statement, he instructed his party to defeat the Reform Bill by backing his proposed amendment to replace household suffrage with a £5 franchise in the boroughs. The Liberal MPs disliked being told what to do in this high-handed manner; fifty of them decided while having a cup of tea in the House of Commons to rebel against Gladstone's scheme. Gladstone however was desperate to halt Disraeli and he tabled his amendment on 9 April. This was the moment which Disraeli had been waiting for. He instantly changed gear. He wrote a letter to his supporters which he leaked to *The Times* making clear that the Reform Bill would be dropped if Gladstone's amendment was carried. This served to focus Liberal minds. In Parliament on the night of 12 April Disraeli spoke forcefully against his tormentor. Gladstone, he explained, was a 'candidate for power'. He had 'had his innings'. He was showing himself to be a narrow partisan who sought to use reform for his own political gain. Disraeli was in effect attacking Gladstone on the same grounds as Gladstone had attacked him throughout the previous ten years. This was risky territory, but it worked admirably. The division was taken late that evening; the Government won by a majority of twenty-one votes.

This was the crowning moment for Disraeli. Gladstone himself admitted that he and his followers had been smashed that evening and he beat a hasty retreat, declining to play a leading part during the remaining passage of the Bill. But for Disraeli the success was almost complete. He was now seen as both indispensable and undisputed as Derby's deputy and indeed as the future leader of the Conservative Party. There were celebrations that night at the Carlton Club. When Disraeli called in he was received as a conquering hero, and Sir Matthew Ridley proposed a fine toast: 'Here's to the man who rode the race, took the time, kept the time and did the trick.' The Members urged Disraeli to stay for supper, but he was anxious to return home where Mary Anne was waiting. At last, late that evening Disraeli reached Grosvenor Gate. A pie from Fortnum & Mason and a bottle of champagne had already been prepared by his faithful wife. Disraeli rarely failed when a deft compliment was needed, but that night he excelled himself: 'Why, my dear, you are more like a mistress than a wife.'

The following day Parliament adjourned for the Easter recess. Around the country there was a sense of awe and bafflement at Disraeli's performances. His success had been like an elaborate conjuring trick, in which a star performer had pulled off a great feat of human wizardry in defiance of convention. No one had ever seen anything like it. Monty Corry reported the views of his aunt's carpenter, who said that he had heard 'that Mr Disraeli had laid Mr Gladstone on his back', and thought that 'you really knocked the godly man down'. Praise also came in from Germany from the former Saxon Minister in London, Count Vitzthum: 'If I understand right your present position, you are the Oedipus who solved the Sphinx's riddle ... At the eve of such a crisis, what are

ten-pounders and lodgers? The great point was to settle and
to subdue the internal agitation.'

In these ways and others, that Easter was a pleasant one
for Disraeli. As he wrote to Stanley on 22 April: 'we ought
to carry our Reform now in a canter, if all I hear be true'.
But one key question was not settled. In his speech introducing the Reform Bill, Disraeli had spoken at some length
about what was known as the 'compounder household'.
These were men who did not pay poor rates directly, but
rather compounded their contributions as part of their rents.
Under Disraeli's scheme, these individuals would not receive
the vote, although he had made it clear that every effort
should be made to encourage them to pay their rates personally, thereby qualifying for the vote. This however was not
deemed sufficient by many Liberals and when Parliament
returned after the recess it became the focus of much discussion. This was no narrow technical matter, as it concerned
almost half a million potential new votes.

On 17 May an obscure Liberal backbencher called
Grosvenor Hodgkinson tabled an amendment which attempted to solve the problem by making compounding
illegal. Henceforth all occupiers were to be responsible for
paying their rates personally. This would in effect mean
that every male householder in England and Wales would
have the vote. No one seriously thought that the amendment
would be carried, so most MPs retired for dinner. Disraeli
was left alone on the front bench and it was here, at 9 p.m.,
in an almost empty House with fewer than fifty Tories present, that he announced that the Government would accept
Hodgkinson's proposal. When the news reached Gladstone
he hurtled back to the Chamber to cause trouble. But he was
too late. At a stroke, and without consulting any of his colleagues, Disraeli had added almost half a million men to the
electorate.

There is some evidence that even Disraeli thought he had gone too far that evening. He wrote a long letter to Gathorne Hardy, explaining why he had acted so unilaterally. When he heard the amendment, he explained, he 'felt that the critical moment had arrived, and when ... we might take a step which would destroy the present agitation and extinguish Gladstone and Co.'. But Hardy expressed his approval and by now Disraeli's hold over the Party was complete.

From then on it was plain sailing. The Committee and Report stages of the Bill were complete by the middle of the summer. The Bill passed its Third Reading in the Commons without division on 15 July. In the Lords, Lord Derby stirred himself to make one last great speech. He was by now so weak that he could not move his right arm, but when he rose on 22 July he spoke defiantly. Three times he had formed a minority Government. Twice he had suffered defeat and frustration. But this time he had decided that this would be no stopgap administration. The country required a decisive answer to the reform question; that is what this Government had endeavoured to provide. There was some murmuring among a number of Peers and a number of amendments were tabled. But on the whole the Lords obeyed his instructions. Within days the Bill was carried into law.

The Representation of the People Act received Royal Assent on 15 August 1867. In its final form, the Bill had given the vote to all male householders in boroughs who had been resident for a year; to men in the counties who paid annual rates to the value of £12; to lodgers in boroughs who paid an annual rent of £10; and to free- and leaseholders in counties with land valued at £5 a year. It was followed in 1868 by separate Irish and Scottish Acts. The total effect of these measures was almost to double the size of the electorate, from around 1.3 million to 2.5 million. A redistribution Bill was also put forward by the Government. This was highly biased in favour of the Conservatives, providing twenty-five new seats for the largely Tory counties against fifteen new borough seats. The Liberals managed to revise some of the changes later, but the pinnacle of Disraeli's achievement had already been reached. It had taken Derby and Disraeli twenty years to get a major Conservative Act on the statute books. For the first time since they had been running the Party, they were winning.

Historians have bestirred themselves in search of metaphors to describe Disraeli's success in passing the Second Reform Bill. Perhaps the prize goes to Robert Blake, who described the way Disraeli led the Conservative Party as a 'moonlight steeplechase. In negotiating their fences few of them saw where they were going, nor much cared so long as they got there first.' This was indeed a racecourse beset by obscure difficulties. Momentum was everything. Although there was much detailed study of electoral statistics in Parliament, in the end these voting numbers meant nothing at all. Nobody really could tell which way a £10 lodger would vote, whether a £12 county franchise was more appropriate than a £15 franchise, or whether an individual who paid his rates was in every instance going to be more responsible than someone who was thrifty enough to store up regular bank savings. The thing that mattered, indeed the only thing that counted, was to get a Bill passed which provided some way of settling the question and breathing life into the Conservative Party. In this way the Act was, as several MPs and later Lord Derby explained, a leap in the dark, but a step in the right direction for the Conservatives.

We have deliberately set out in detail the manoeuvres and tactical successes which secured the Bill's passage. In doing so, we may have reduced the reader to exhaustion or incomprehension. These were indeed the emotions through which the Tory backbenchers lived during those anxious nights in the Commons. They followed Disraeli without fully understanding the significance of what was happening. Few grasped the meaning of every manoeuvre or the implications of each tabled amendment. Sir Robert Peel twenty years earlier had carried the repeal of the Corn Laws because enough MPs trusted that he was doing the right thing. Disraeli relied on a different quality, that of the magician. The Commons in the end gave him the victory he wanted because, however baffled and bemused they were by the details of the Bill, his cleverness persuaded them to follow his lead. They followed the magician up hill and down dale, and came to trust not so much his integrity as his cleverness and determination.

Once the Bill had been passed, the mythmakers in both parties got to work. Later that year, Gladstone visited Scotland and made a speech in which he argued somewhat disingenuously that the Reform Act marked the final triumph of the Liberal Party; now the Conservatives were doing their bidding and following Liberal principles. This ignored the obvious point that Gladstone had done his best to defeat Disraeli's Bill. Meanwhile that autumn Disraeli also visited Scotland. It was the first time he had travelled north of the Border since his visit to Walter Scott and John Lockhart on behalf of *The Representative*. He spoke at a Tory banquet in Edinburgh, selecting as his theme the relationship between conservatism and change. Cranborne had recently written another article in the *Quarterly Review* called 'The Conservative Surrender' attacking Disraeli's policies. Disraeli dismissed the article but stopped short of damning the author. 'I should say that article was written by a very clever man who has made a very great mistake.' The point, as Disraeli explained, was that being Conservative did not mean avoiding change. The key test was whether any specific reform was in tune with the character and ancient spirit of the people. It had

taken him time to 'educate' the Party on this point – 'I had
to prepare the mind of Parliament and the country on this
question of Reform' – but at length the nation had come
round to his way of thinking. The result was his balanced
and conservative measure of reform. He illustrated his argument in a famous passage: 'In a progressive country change
is constant; and the great question is not whether you should
resist change which is inevitable, but whether that change
should be carried out in deference to the manners, the customs, the laws and the traditions of a people, or whether it
should be carried out in deference to abstract principles, and
arbitrary and general doctrines. The one is a national system;
the other, to give it an epithet, a noble epithet – which it may
perhaps deserve – is a philosophic system.'

A few days later Disraeli addressed a Conservative working men's meeting and elaborated on this argument. He said
that the Tory Party were the natural champions of the poor.
'I have always believed that the interests of the labouring
classes are among the most Conservative in the country,'
he said. This was the same language that Peel had used in
a speech at Glasgow thirty years before. But over the next
few years it became part of a much larger philosophy of Tory
Democracy in which the Conservatives set themselves up as
the only party which looked out for the interests of the country as a whole.

In the decades which followed, the idea of Tory Democracy took on a life of its own. In his biography of Disraeli
written in the early twentieth century, the Earl of Cromer attributed a strong line of enlightened consistency to Disraeli.
Disraeli, he explained, had seen that 'the tide of democracy
was rising and that both the aristocracies were wholly out of
sympathy with democratic ideas. He rightly judged that they
could not or would not combine ... The remedy that at once
suggested itself to his powerful and subtle brain was that the

aristocracy with which he was connected should outbid its rivals in the democratic market ... Hence the genesis of the Tory Democracy ... An alliance was therefore to be made between the House of Lords and the people ... Disraeli's general conception of democratising the Tory Party eventually led to the enactment of the Reform Act of 1867...' Others since then have picked up on this line of thinking, including the present Prime Minister. When asked in 2007 about his favourite political quotation, David Cameron selected Disraeli's speech in Edinburgh and the idea that the Conservative Party should be 'the party of change but change that goes along with the customs and manners and traditions and sentiments of the people rather than change according to some grand plan'.

But was Disraeli in his heart a Tory Democrat? So far as we can tell he never used the phrase; he preferred to flirt with phrases about the aristocratic fundamentals of British society. Indeed, as we have seen, after he had passed the Bill he set about using the redistribution proposals to protect Tory rural constituencies from the new working-class voters in borough seats. This was hardly the action of a man who trusted in the inherent wisdom of mass democracy. Throughout these months his behaviour was driven by a desperate need to deliver a major parliamentary victory. Another defeat and his time at the top would almost certainly have been over; but by passing the Bill his name was on everyone's lips.

Arguably, we should rephrase the question. It did not really matter whether Disraeli was a deep convert to democracy. The point is that he was not afraid. He was confident that he could handle a change in the electorate and was prepared to cope with the fallout. Given his views on the inevitability of change it is impossible to imagine Disraeli resisting the different proposals which later transformed Britain into a working democracy. In his heart he would have lamented the passing of the old system, but when necessary he would have stirred himself to make a convincing argument. One can indeed relish the task of writing Disraeli's speech in favour of giving the vote to women. It would certainly have been a cracker.

Perhaps the last word should go to Disraeli himself. In a passage from *Sybil*, written twenty years earlier, he recounted the story of Pitt's reform plans at the end of the eighteenth century. 'Was he sincere, is often asked by those who neither seek to discover the causes, nor are capable of calculating the effects of public transactions. Sincere! Why he was struggling for his existence!' Disraeli in 1867 was also struggling for existence; in the event he not only survived, but excelled.

There was in 1867 one step yet to take. Derby was suffering from a disabling form of gout. In February 1868 he was warned that he would only recover if he allowed himself total rest. He was reluctant to leave office but agreed with the advice and told the Queen. After a brief delay, Derby relinquished the reins and Disraeli was summoned to form a government. He kissed the Queen's hand as Prime Minister on 27 February 1868.

Afterwards Disraeli and Derby reflected on their long and arduous partnership in a courteous exchange of letters. Derby congratulated Disraeli on reaching the milestone. Disraeli told Derby that he would always consider himself Derby's deputy and wrote that 'your wishes will always be commands to me'. The Queen meanwhile penned an extravagant letter to one of her daughters: 'Mr Disraeli is Prime Minister! A proud thing for a Man "risen from the people" to have obtained! And I must say – really most loyally; it is his real talent, his good temper and the way in wh. he managed the Reform Bill last year – wh. have brought this about ...'

It was indeed a remarkable moment and Disraeli decided to celebrate. Mary Anne got to work in organising a great party. She deemed the rooms in Number 10 grim and unattractive, so Stanley gladly offered the big reception rooms at the new Foreign Office, which was still not quite complete. The police put up a giant poster advising the guests where they could pick up their carriages, and Mary Anne busied herself in sending many hundreds of invitations.

In the end the appointed evening was a mild disappointment. Outside there was rain and sleet and the next day Mary Anne received many hundreds of regrets and apologies; some were sick, others lacked courage to brace the pouring rain. But inside the rooms there was beauty and splendour. Disraeli escorted the Princess of Wales, then in her full beauty, while Mary Anne looked after the Prince. Gladstone also made an appearance and spoke courteously to those with whom he came into contact.

Disraeli himself was not in the best of spirits. Already Gladstone was stirring himself and plotting his revenge on the Government. New political problems were flooding in, and people were forgetting about Disraeli's great success in passing the Reform Bill. But at some point that evening, as he wandered round the room and sipped champagne, Disraeli must have reflected over his last forty years. He would have looked back with a mixture of puzzlement and pride. Pride, because as a Jew and an admitted adventurer he had forced his way, as he told someone that evening, to the top of the greasy pole. It had been uphill all the way. But puzzlement, because he was now sixty-three years of age: at last he was famous, but had fame come too late?

Already he knew that the road was still uphill and no rest was in sight. He knew the full weight of passionate indignation which his chief opponent could hurl against him. Gladstone had been his detractor for the best part of twenty years; where would he find the strength to withstand him in the future? How could he hold his position at the top of the greasy pole? Was this to be the highpoint of his career? We do not know to which gods Disraeli prayed, but on that night of success he needed their help.

PROGRESSIVE CONSERVATIVE

Disraeli never liked the Irish and never visited Ireland. He spent much of his early career denouncing their seditiousness, and once wrote that their fair ideal of human happiness was an alternation of clannish broils and coarse idolatry. On one occasion he claimed that Daniel O'Connell was a more dangerous enemy than Napoleon; on another, he compared Bulwer-Lytton's Irish wife to a hod of mortar and a potato. But in March 1868 the Irish exacted their revenge on their tormentor. A violent new crisis spilled over into England: the Prime Minister was called on to redress a multitude of Irish grievances; but he was beaten to it by Ireland's new self-appointed defender, Gladstone.

Ireland had never recovered from the potato famine. Repealing the Corn Laws had done little to alleviate the suffering. Around a million Irish peasants had died from disease and starvation in the 1840s and 1850s, and a million more had quit the country for the USA. It had taken some time for the full horror of the famine to seep into the national consciousness, but by the 1860s a new violent strand of Irish terrorism had surfaced, spearheaded by the Fenian Brotherhood. In December 1867 twelve people were killed when a bomb exploded outside Clerkenwell Prison in an attempt to rescue members of the Brotherhood. Three months earlier a police constable had been killed in Manchester during another rescue attempt. The Tories and Liberals had both taken a hard line in response to these atrocities, but it was fast becoming clear that a new policy of conciliation was needed. It fell to the new Prime Minister to take the lead.

The difficulty was that Disraeli was ill-equipped to supply such leadership. When he had been making his name as a flamboyant backbencher in the 1840s he had made one thoughtful speech about Ireland, describing the Irish Question as 'a starving population, an absentee aristocracy, and an alien church, and in addition the weakest executive in the world'. But these arguments hit the buffers when Disraeli opposed Peel's attempts to bring forward reform and provide an increased grant to the Roman Catholic College of Maynooth. In his heart, Disraeli could not shake off the idea that Irish Catholicism was somehow murky and suspicious – not so much a popular religion as a dangerous threat to be contained. He therefore found it difficult to summon up the compassion which might inspire a new programme of reform. But in 1868, leading the country, Disraeli had to do something significant to restore order in Ireland. He flailed around in search of an answer, before settling on the idea of establishing a new Roman Catholic University.

Disraeli had no experience of higher education and even less of Irish Catholicism. But he found a wily tutor in the form of Cardinal Manning, the Catholic Archbishop of Westminster. Manning encouraged Disraeli in his researches and helped to float his policy with the Catholic hierarchy. For a while it looked as though progress might be possible and a new institution established. But abruptly on 16 March Manning cut all ties with Disraeli and the policy reached a dead end. The reason for this rupture was that Gladstone had launched himself dramatically back onto the scene.

The previous winter, Lord John Russell had stepped down as leader of the Liberal Party. Gladstone had at last come into his inheritance. The Liberals had endured a disappointing few years since Palmerston's death, suffering defeat and arguing with each other. In particular, many Liberals felt disgruntled at the manner in which Gladstone had handled the Reform Bills. He therefore needed a decisive performance to unite the Party under his leadership. Somewhat surprisingly in light of his stout Evangelicalism, Gladstone decided that the way to do this was to attack the Anglican Church of Ireland.

On 16 March 1868 Gladstone set out his new policy for Ireland. In feverish language, he announced to the world that the solution to Ireland's problems was to disestablish the Irish Church. Disraeli's Government had comprehensively 'failed to realise in any degree the solemn fact that we have reached a crisis in the affairs and in the state of Ireland'. The appropriate response was dramatic but simple: the Irish Church 'as a State Church, must cease to exist'. This was an extraordinary about-turn for a man who had once been the chief advocate of state religion. But it gave Gladstone a firm grip over his own party and united the various wings of Whigs, Liberals and Radicals.

Disraeli seems to have been drunk when he responded to Gladstone's policy. He was seen to drink from a glass of dark-coloured liquid as he rose to speak. Unfortunately, the alcohol failed to fire his imagination and his speech was a mess, in which he meandered through a baffling argument about a new Catholic conspiracy. 'They have their hand on the Realm of England,' he tried to explain. In reply, Gladstone showed a lightning strike of wit to point out that his opponent's speech had been 'delivered under the influence ... of a heated imagination', and he was subsequently rewarded with a series of parliamentary victories. The brief sunny period in which Disraeli had been basking was now at an end. When Mary Anne gave her party at the Foreign

Office later that month, observers noted that the Prime Minister seemed to be in a deep melancholy.

On 1 May the Government were heavily defeated in the Commons. For a time it looked as though Disraeli would have to resign. He managed to cling on over the summer, relying on the need to complete the passage of the outstanding Scottish and Irish Reform Bills. But his grasp on power was slipping away. A general election was planned for the end of November, but in reality Gladstone was already in control.

In the meantime, Disraeli diverted himself with a dramatic episode of foreign policy. The King of Abyssinia had taken several British missionaries hostage. An expeditionary force under Sir Robert Napier was dispatched from India to come to their aid. The campaign was successful and all hostages were rescued, but at a staggering expense. Parliament had originally voted £2 million for the expedition but the final sum soared to four times that figure. There was outrage in the House of Commons, but Disraeli ignored such trifling objections. 'Money is not to be considered in such matters; success alone is to be thought of.'

Meanwhile Ireland remained the central battleground of politics. Disraeli deployed the arguments he had worked up in his novel *Tancred* during the run-up to the election, and spent his time arguing for a new kind of romantic theocracy. In April he baffled the House of Commons by declaring that 'an intelligent age will never discard the divine right of government. If government is not divine, it is nothing.' This was incomprehensible to most listeners, but Disraeli was warming to his theme. Around the same time, he wrote to a vicar who had complained about his Irish policies: 'as I hold that the dissolution of the union between Church and State will cause permanently a greater revolution in this country than foreign conquest, I shall use my utmost energies to defeat these fatal machinations'. Then, in his autumn election address,

Disraeli enlarged on these ideas for the benefit of the wider public: 'the connection of religion with the exercise of political authority is one of the main safeguards of the civilisation of man,' he explained.

Such utterances tended to perplex rather than persuade the voters. The question of course was not whether the established Church should cease to exist in England, but rather whether it should continue to operate with state support in Ireland. To the extent that the voting public actually cared, there was a general feeling that something needed to be done for Ireland. Gladstone, it seemed, had the energy and appetite to settle the question decisively.

Immediately before polling began in November 1868, Disraeli had to handle another matter which would shape the future of the established Church. On 27 October, Charles Longley, the Archbishop of Canterbury, died. The task fell to Disraeli of advising the Queen on his successor. Quick on the draw, Victoria wrote to him strongly supporting the claims of the Bishop of London, Archibald Tait. Disraeli disagreed on the grounds that Tait's religious views were obscure and inconsistent, and politically he was a Liberal. But in the correspondence that followed, Disraeli gradually yielded and the Queen won this particular encounter.

In general, the 1868 election showed that Disraeli had exaggerated the popular enthusiasm for a strongly Protestant House of Commons. When the voting was over, the Conservatives had been trounced: the Liberals won 384 seats compared to 271 for the Tories – the worst result for the Conservatives for over ten years.

Disraeli was not inclined to linger in office. The established convention for a defeated Prime Minister was to wait until Parliament met before offering his resignation. But Disraeli immediately sent word to the Queen that he was prepared to resign before the new session began. When the news reached

Gladstone that he was to become Prime Minister he was hard at work felling a tree on his estate at Hawarden. The story goes that after receiving the telegram he took a pause from his slaughter to remark to the bearer: 'My mission is to pacify Ireland.' He then continued to hack away at the tree.

Disraeli had one final request to make of the Queen. As an outgoing Prime Minister, he was entitled to a peerage. This, however, would have required him to quit the Commons, which he had no intention of doing any earlier than physically necessary. He therefore wrote to the Queen and asked her to transfer the honour to Mary Anne. This caused a small flutter at Court and even the Queen found the request embarrassing. But in the end her devotion to Disraeli won through and the honour was granted; Mary Anne became the Viscountess Beaconsfield. It was a fitting tribute for years of ceaseless devotion to Disraeli. Naturally, Mary Anne was over the moon at her new elevated status. The letter 'B' was chiselled into wardrobes and embroidered into her furniture. She subsequently signed all her letters to Disraeli 'Your Devoted Beaconsfield'.

The months which followed were a bleak time for Disraeli. The defeat of 1868 hit him hard. The leadership of the Tory Party was once again in question; there were influential voices arguing behind Disraeli's back that Lord Stanley would be a more effective Party leader. Gladstone, now in secure control of the Commons, launched a radical reforming programme. Disraeli did not attempt to mount a counterattack. Instead he left the battlefield. He once declared that when he wanted to read a novel he would write one. He now acted on that advice.

The result was *Lothair*, which was published in May 1870. It was a big success with the public, bringing in some £6,000 by the end of 1876; but it fell foul of the critics, who felt that it was foolish, indeed unworthy of a man who had been

Prime Minister and might be Prime Minister again. Nonetheless it remains the most readable of Disraeli's novels, in part because it carries no message at all. It has a well-constructed plot which this time does not peter out. Read as a whole, the novel provides a witty and well-drawn portrait of mid-Victorian society. But Disraeli makes no attempt to conceal the hollowness at its core.

Lothair is yet another story of an ambitious young man in search of a philosophy. But, unlike the majority of Disraeli's heroes, the young protagonist is looking for a truth which will satisfy his religious as well as political needs. Just as Paris had to choose between three goddesses, so Lothair has to select one of three beautiful ladies: the first a firm Catholic, the second a convinced if not wholly convincing Anglican, and the third a determined and passionate Italian nationalist.

Lothair, captivated by the fervour of the nationalist, fights at her side against the Pope alongside Garibaldi. He is wounded and falls into the hands of the Papal armies. He regains consciousness to find his wounds being tended in a hospital run by Catholic nuns. In a monstrous sleight of hand, the nuns try to persuade Lothair that all the time he had been fighting on their side against the nationalists. Lothair wavers, but eventually breaks free and returns to marry the slightly insipid Anglican lady.

Lothair is similar to earlier novels in that almost everyone is titled. There are several splendid mansions, many abundant parties, the women are all beautiful and the food and drink is outstanding. It is characteristic of Disraeli's prose style that his priests tend to 'glide' from one room to another in the palaces and churches which they inhabit. They are led by Cardinal Grandison, a portrait of the duplicitous Cardinal Manning. In a masterly exchange, the Cardinal comes close to persuading Lothair that his own recollection of the recent battle must be less credible than the majesty and wisdom of the Holy Church. Yet Lothair emerges, shaken but intact, from these intrigues and finds a fishing boat to take him by way of Malta back to London, where he proclaims the truth of his experiences.

The most vehement critic of *Lothair* was a Professor of History named Goldwin Smith. He resented particularly the author's description of himself in *Lothair* as being 'like sedentary men of extreme opinions ... a social parasite'. The Professor thundered across the Atlantic from Cornell University in an elaborate denunciation of the novel: 'while sheltering yourself under the literary form of a work of fiction, you seek to traduce with impunity the social character of a political opponent ... your expressions can touch no man's honour; they are the stingless insults of a coward.' The Professor may have forgotten, but Disraeli certainly remembered that many years earlier Smith had written an anonymous denunciation of Disraeli in the *Morning Chronicle*.

Disraeli also received a number of critical letters from Irish Catholics, and there was a general feeling in educated classes that he had somehow sullied himself by writing such a work. But these criticisms gave him no concern. He would have paid more attention to the letter from a lady in Seaford: 'I am a poor governess whose opinion is hardly worth the paper on which I write.' She had thoroughly enjoyed *Lothair* and told Disraeli that 'from the beginning to the end there is not one hateful character'. The general public largely agreed with this verdict. A steamship was named *Lothair* and Lord Rothschild won the Cesarewitch with a filly named after the heroine, Corisande. Refreshed and enriched by this experience, Disraeli returned to the serious business of politics.

In political terms, these years were leisurely rather than dramatic for Disraeli. He liked to bask in the knowledge that he had been Prime Minister, and regarded that as a notable achievement in itself. His long-serving supervisor, Lord

Derby, finally died in October 1869, and his son, Lord Stanley, inherited the title to become the 15th Earl of Derby. This reinforced Stanley's claims to lead the Party, but he did nothing to push this argument himself. Instead he continued to visit Hughenden, where he tried to stir Disraeli into action. These efforts came to nothing. As Stanley noted in his diary: 'He admitted to me that though still willing to exert himself for the benefit of the party if necessary, his interest in it was diminished, he had obtained his object, and if he never held office again, he should not feel that his life had been a failure.'*

Disraeli's detachment drove disenchantment within the Party. The backbenchers grumbled and the frontbenchers began to make sharp comments and arch their eyebrows. Disraeli was well aware of these mutterings; he had after all an uninterrupted record of election defeats. There was however a thought-line underpinning his idleness; the doctrine of the pendulum was becoming established in British politics.

Disraeli knew that Gladstone was an irresistible force for the time being. The public greatly respected his moral fervour. Relentless opposition would do little to halt Liberal progress, but Disraeli believed that, given a little time, the public would grow tired of Gladstone's ceaseless legislating. The constant meddling would become maddening. All that was required was for the Tories to stay calm and bide their time in Opposition. 'I think on our part there should be the utmost reserve and quietness,' he told Derby. Unfortunately not everyone in the Party agreed.

Matters came to a head early in 1872. On 1 February many of the big beasts of the Party assembled at Burghley, the seat of Lord Exeter. Northcote, Hardy, Marlborough, Pakington, Cairns and Manners were all present – but Derby and

*Henceforth Stanley will be referred to as Lord Derby.

Disraeli were not there. The discussion was long and cathar-
tic. Gerard Noel, the Chief Whip, reported the mood of the
backbenchers. Apparently there was a feeling that Disraeli
ought to be relieved of the leadership. He was lazy and past
his peak. Many MPs felt that Lord Derby might be a more
assiduous leader; in an election, his name alone would help
to swing forty or fifty seats. Cairns also raised the prospect
of a change of leadership and of letting Disraeli know of
the strong feelings against him. As the discussion drew to a
close, only Stafford Northcote and Lord John Manners spoke
strongly in Disraeli's defence. The meeting concluded with a
general feeling that Disraeli's time as leader had come to an
end.

There was just one thing missing: no one could bring
themselves to inform Disraeli. It was a meeting with many
minutes but no action points. A few weeks later the political climate turned suddenly. On 27 February a service of
thanksgiving was held at St Paul's to celebrate the Prince of
Wales's recovery from typhoid. The public were relieved,
not so much because the Prince was loved and respected,
but rather because he was a familiar figure on the national
scene, particularly since his mother had plunged herself into
determined widowhood. As the Queen and her son drove
through the City for the service they were greeted by cheering crowds on all sides. It marked a surge of loyalty at the
end of a period of dangerous unpopularity for the Queen and
the monarchy generally. It may also have heralded a shift in
political loyalties.

Both Gladstone and Disraeli attended the service, but
there was a notable difference in the reception which the two
men received from the public. The crowd watched Gladstone
walk down the steps in grumpy silence; there were even a
few hoots and jeers. But Disraeli was rewarded with enthusiastic cheering as he left, and this continued as he made his

way home through Regent Street. Later that day Disraeli looked in at the Carlton Club. Another member engaged him in conversation, but it was noticed that Disraeli was gazing past him in deep pensiveness. 'His face was as of one who looks into another world,' the former Tory MP Sir William Fraser noted. 'He seemed more like a statue than a human being.' Later Sir William met the man whom Disraeli had been ignoring and informed him portentously: 'I will tell you what he was thinking about: he was thinking that he will be Prime Minister again.'

The story, though it may be fanciful, illustrates a truth. Today we are used to an almost scientific mode of political forecasting. The regularity of opinion polls means that there is rarely a policy or politician about which or whom we do not have some evidence of what the public are feeling. But in the 1870s there was no such facility. The contestants had to struggle against one another in the darkness, aiming their blows with only the vaguest understanding as to whether they were landing anywhere near the target. In such a world, the political class fell back on haphazard guesswork, informed by a chance encounter with a stationmaster or carriage driver who happened to scrutinise the opinions of any given constituency. Faced with such limitations, the sound of a large crowd booing Gladstone and cheering Disraeli was as close as anyone could get to measuring the national mood.

From this moment on Disraeli was in the ascendant. The pendulum had begun to operate in favour of the Conservatives. As Disraeli had predicted to the new Lord Derby the previous year, 'it is well that ... the reign of priggism should terminate. It has done its work, and in its generation very well, but there is another spirit abroad now, and it is time that there should be.' A string of by-election results in these years reinforced this verdict, as did Disraeli's successful election as Lord Rector of Glasgow University ahead of

John Ruskin in 1871. He saw that he had now to build on the momentum and extend the Conservative lead across the country. The 1867 Reform Act had enfranchised almost a million new voters who were now busily being registered in their constituencies. Winning their vote meant pioneering a new kind of politics and a new kind of campaigning. Disraeli stirred himself to change the message and galvanise the Party machine.

After the defeat of 1868, Disraeli had launched a sweeping review of the Party organisation. A key part of this was the appointment of a former MP named John Gorst. A Lancastrian by background and a mathematician by training, Gorst now combined these two influences to assemble a campaign infrastructure which could win support from the newly enlarged national electorate. In 1870 he established the new Conservative Central Office and began to build a new army of Conservative Associations and activists. The main focus of his attention was the new National Union of Conservative and Constitutional Associations.

Such was the machine, but the message needed changing as well. A key part of Gorst's plan was for Disraeli to make a speaking tour of the north-west of England. Disraeli had never built up a reputation as a national speaker, but he now saw the advantage of such an expedition. He agreed to make two substantial speeches, first at the Free Trade Hall in Manchester, and then to the National Union of Conservative Associations at the Crystal Palace in London. Taken together, these two speeches put forward the claim which Disraeli had first made in the 1830s, and which later became his most powerful legacy to the Conservative Party: the idea that the Tory Party was the truly national party of England.

The first of the two speeches was given on 3 April. Some 6,000 people crammed into Manchester Free Trade Hall to hear Disraeli speak. He sustained himself with copious amounts of alcohol and drank two bottles of white brandy over the course of his three-hour speech. This time, the alcohol seemed to enhance Disraeli's arguments and the general view was that the speech was an enormous success.

Disraeli was of course first and foremost a politician. It is therefore not surprising that the bulk of this speech and his later speech at the Crystal Palace should have been an onslaught against Gladstone's Government. At Manchester he was in fine fettle and his denunciation of the Ministry as a 'range of exhausted volcanoes' has been quoted many times since. But two other features of these speeches were novelties. The first novelty was the emphasis Disraeli placed on social improvement. This meant rather more than exhorting the aristocracy to improve their behaviour, as Disraeli had done in his Young England novels and previous speeches. Now there was a clear pointer towards specific policies; in particular, on public health. Disraeli declared that the 'first consideration of a minister should be the health of the people' and he made an obscure Latin joke to reinforce this argument: 'Sanitas, Sanitatum, Omnia Sanitas'. As always, it was not entirely clear what this might mean in practice, and the Liberals mocked the way he talked about public drainage as a 'policy of sewage'. But Disraeli had given as clear an indication as he ever did as to what a future Conservative government might do in office. It was up to others to flesh out the details.

The other novelty about these speeches was imperial. Here the change was startling indeed. The Chancellor of the Exchequer who had been scathing about the cost of defending Canada became the Leader of the Opposition who urged the duty of reconstructing the colonies as much as possible. He called for closer links with those peoples who might become 'the source of incalculable strength and happiness to this land'. Empire remained a somewhat cloudy concept for Disraeli. It was based overwhelmingly on the view, borrowed from Palmerston, that national prestige was a tangible asset. To this Disraeli added the skeleton of future imperial policies, including the idea of a new Imperial Assembly and a tariff union which might help consolidate the colonies. It was vague stuff, but it caught the mood of an increasingly noisy and self-assertive country.

In these ways and others Disraeli and the Conservatives were on the march in 1872. Disraeli's leadership of the Party was once again secured. 'It is all well and good,' he noted after his speech at the Crystal Palace. 'I feel my position assured.' But as the year wore on a dark spot began to blacken the horizon. Mary Anne had travelled with Disraeli to Manchester, but she had collapsed soon afterwards. A few weeks later she had to leave Buckingham Palace when she almost collapsed again during a reception. Gossips had noticed how frail she looked at the famous Foreign Office party, and there were whispers that her health was failing. By the end of summer, there could no longer be any doubt on the matter. Mary Anne's health was deteriorating and she would not see out the end of the year.

It was an inevitable tragedy. Mary Anne was twelve years older than Disraeli and she had been suffering from cancer of the stomach for several years. In November 1867 both she and Disraeli had been confined to their sickbeds, she with the early stages of cancer, he with an attack of gout. For several days they scribbled messages to each other from their bedrooms. 'Grosvenor Gate has become a hospital,' Disraeli wrote lovingly, 'but a hospital with you is worth a palace with anybody else.' As time went on her sickness became more regular. The experience of seeing his wife die broke Disraeli. 'To witness this gradual death of one who has shared so long and so completely my life entirely unmans me,' he told Corry. To Rose he confided: 'I am totally unable to meet the catastrophe.'

Mary Anne was an odd and in some ways ridiculous woman. Her conversation could be artless and indiscreet. But Disraeli did not seem to mind. For thirty-three years Mary Anne had sustained and supported him in ways we can only glimpse today. For example, in their letters there is much detailed discussion of clothing. Thus on one occasion Disraeli wrote: 'My dearest, please send me a pair of boots for my feet are quite damp in these varnished ones.' On another in the late 1850s: 'My dearest wife I have not got my right clothes. Give James breeches, drawers, silk stockings and shoes. This is the only time you have tripped since our marriage – and therefore I punish you by sending only one kiss.' Disraeli, who was unscrupulous in so many of his dealings, nonetheless felt bound to Mary Anne by a compelling tie of gratitude. She had devoted herself, and her wealth, to him and he had shown himself entirely true to his vows. It is true that recent biographies have suggested that in the late 1850s and early 1860s Disraeli's affections may have wandered elsewhere and that he had a liaison with a family friend named Lady Dorothy Nevill. But the evidence for this is slight and unconvincing. The overwhelming impression remains that of all the relationships in Disraeli's life, this was the most straightforward. He loved and was loved, and the thought of losing her was a torment to him.

As the parliamentary session dragged on over the summer, Disraeli and Mary Anne were confined to Grosvenor Gate in London. For entertainment, they took long carriage rides through hitherto undiscovered suburbs in Middlesex and Surrey – expeditions which Disraeli reported in vivid notes for the Queen. 'What miles of villas! And of all sorts of architecture! What beautiful churches ... One day we came upon a real feudal castle, with a donjon keep high in the air. It turned out to be the new City prison in Camden Road, but it deserves a visit; I mean externally.' Eventually that autumn they were released from London and embarked on what Disraeli called their 'Hegira from Grosvenor Gate'. A final house party was held at Hughenden at the end of November. For one last time, Mary Anne entertained old friends. But at the start of December she again fell ill, this time with pneumonia. A local priest called to inquire after her spiritual health, but Mary Anne could not turn her attention to the thought of the life hereafter. 'You know, Dizzy is my J.C,' she said. She died on Sunday 15 December, while sitting upright in her chair.

The funeral took place at Hughenden Church five days later. It was a frightful day, beset by wet and howling weather. After the ceremony Disraeli stood bareheaded for some ten minutes in the pouring rain, alone and motionless, staring down at the grave.

Mary Anne's death created numerous practical difficulties for Disraeli, not least the loss of Grosvenor Gate, which was returned to her family, as well as the end of her annual income of £5,000. Andrew Montagu helped Disraeli cope with the financial setback by lowering the interest rate on his loan. But the bigger problem was the loss of the London home. Early in the new year Disraeli was obliged to move into Edwards's Hotel, just off Hanover Square, in order to be on hand for the new parliamentary session. The rooms were comfortable, but his life was increasingly one of solitude. As he put it, 'hotel life in an evening is a cave of despair'.

It was against this gloomy background that Disraeli embarked on one last love affair. Many years before, Mary Anne had written a note to Disraeli recommending him in the event of her death to seek out a new female companion, 'as attached to you as your own devoted Mary Anne'. Lonely and hotel-bound at the start of 1873, Disraeli now followed his dead wife's advice.

There was no shortage of willing candidates. Disraeli was already under watch from a number of lonely ladies and it was not long before he received his first approach. The Countess of Cardigan was on the lookout for a new husband. Her last one had led the Charge of the Light Brigade. The leader of the Conservative Party seemed like a logical successor. So she wrote to Disraeli proposing marriage. To her surprise, he declined. This rejection was not taken kindly and the Countess went about town spreading rumours about Disraeli and telling people that he had bad breath.

If Disraeli came off the worse from this first encounter, he enjoyed more success with two elderly sisters, Lady Bradford and Lady Chesterfield. The story is bizarre. Anne, the widowed Countess of Chesterfield, was seventeen years older than Disraeli, while her sister Selina was in her sixties and still happily married to Lord Bradford. Both were grandmothers by the time Disraeli decided to pursue them in 1873, but this only added to their attractiveness in his eyes. On the whole he preferred Selina to her older sister, but when it became clear that Selina had no intention of abandoning her husband, he switched his attentions and proposed marriage to Anne so that he might see more of her sister. She turned him down but the affectionate correspondence continued, and he became a regular guest at their homes.

It was the start of a curious connection, the main outcome of which was an enormous collection of letters from Disraeli to the sisters between 1873 and his death. In all some eleven hundred letters remain from Disraeli to Selina, and another five hundred from Disraeli to Anne. As one would expect, Disraeli wrote to the sisters in all moods, from devotion to despair. The letters race along from one gossipy anecdote to the next. Disraeli was quick to record the comments of eminent ladies and the latest witticisms of intelligent lords. But they hardly delve deep into the substance of politics. Indeed, this was their point. As Disraeli's political fortunes improved and he prepared to become Prime Minister again, these letters provided a congenial tonic to the pressures and frustrations of office. At times the tonic took up more time than the duties of his post. For example, in late 1874 he told Selina: 'When you have the government of a country on your shoulders, to <u>love</u> a person, and to be <u>in love</u> with a person makes all the difference ... I have devised schemes for seeing, or writing to, you in the midst of stately councils, and the thought and memory of you, instead of being an obstacle, has been to me an inspiration.' Such admissions may seem alarming to the puritanical, but for Disraeli they were a necessary outlet for his lifelong need to be loved. As he put it in a letter to Selina: 'I live for Power and the Affections.'

Affections he now had, but in 1873 power was still out of his grasp. Then, in March, Gladstone's Government suddenly collapsed. Like Disraeli, Gladstone had tried to tackle the thorny problem of Irish universities. Like Disraeli, Gladstone believed the key was to try and place Catholic and Anglican education on a more equal footing. But, just as Disraeli had found in 1868, when it came to putting these principles into practice Gladstone found powerful forces arrayed against him. His Bill to extend the remit of Trinity College, Dublin into a wider, non-denominational institution was defeated by three votes in the House of Commons. As was his way when thwarted in his mission, Gladstone resigned.

The stage was set for a fourth minority Conservative administration. The only glitch was that the main player refused to perform. Disraeli declined the Queen's invitation to form a new government and, in a state of apoplectic fury, Gladstone was obliged to return to office. When attacked by the Liberals in Parliament, the Tories countered by claiming that the prospect they faced was not power but powerlessness. After thirty years in the political wilderness they had learned the lessons of defeat and frustration; now they were winning and had momentum. All they had to do was hold their nerve and await the next general election, which would surely give them the elusive majority.

In the meantime, they continued to pillory their opponents. Disraeli's attack on the 'incessant and harassing legislation' of the Liberal Party caught the mood of the nation; the public felt increasingly exhausted by Gladstone's high moral tone. There was no doubt that Gladstone had been a strong reforming Prime Minister but, as happens, his reforms had offended rather more than they had pleased, particularly as he treated his critics as devoid of morality. For the rest of the year, Disraeli harassed the Government at every opportunity. One speech in March 1873 in particular gives a vivid impression of the arguments he used against Gladstone: 'You have despoiled Churches. You have threatened every corporation and endowment in the country. You have examined into everybody's affairs. You have criticized every profession and vexed every trade. No one is certain of his property, and nobody knows what duties he may have to perform tomorrow.'

In this manner, Disraeli stirred himself ahead of the forthcoming election. After a summer and autumn of solitude at Hughenden he returned to London in preparation for the new parliamentary session. It was certain that Gladstone would call a general election in 1874, but most felt he would leave it as late as possible. But out of the blue, in the newspapers on 24 January 1874, Gladstone announced that Parliament would be dissolved immediately and a general election held within weeks.

As was often the case when significant political developments took place, Disraeli was in bed when the news reached him. He read Gladstone's announcement at Edwards's Hotel and immediately summoned his senior lieutenants to work on a response. He wrote hard through the weekend to get his address into the Monday newspapers and pinned his campaign

cry on three themes: the social welfare of the people; the
security of British imperial interests; and an end to the ceaseless interfering of recent years. It was a strong, clear and
compelling message, more plausible than Gladstone's pledge
to abolish Income Tax.

The polling began on 1 February. It soon became clear that
Gorst had done his work well. The campaign machine swung
into action, and for the first time the election was managed
as a single national contest rather than a series of haphazard
local encounters. The Conservatives had more money and
more candidates than ever before. When the polls closed a
few weeks later, the Conservatives had achieved their first
majority since the time of Sir Robert Peel. Some 350 Conservatives were elected, against 245 Liberals and fifty-seven
supporters of Irish Home Rule.

It was a stirring victory, made sweeter by Gladstone's rage.
He blamed the defeat on the money the Tories had received
from the brewing industry in protest against his Licensing
Act. 'We have been borne down in a torrent of gin and beer,'
he declaimed. But the truth was much simpler. The country
was fed up with Gladstone. As was his wont when things
went against him, Gladstone later resigned the leadership of
the Liberal Party, returning to the backbenches and leaving
Lord Hartington to pick up the pieces.

And so it was that Disraeli formed a new government with
the country behind him. At last he had the majority he had
craved. Everything he had sought since a teenager now lay
open before him – fame, yes, but also the opportunity for
great action. Many years before he had said, 'I am only truly
great in action.' Now true greatness lay within his grasp.

Yet there was something missing. Today we might call
it a plan. There was no detailed manifesto, no blueprint of
policies, no agenda for reform ready to be unveiled in 1874 –
only the sentiment implied by his speeches of a responsible

and sober-minded government, committed to improving the living standards of the people and protecting British interests. Some observers had already spotted the omission. Two years earlier *Punch* had published a marvellous cartoon around the time of Disraeli's Crystal Palace speech; a deputation arrives to inquire about the Conservative leader's programme for government; Disraeli replies to his companion: 'Ah yes, quite so. Tell them, my good Abercorn, with my compliments, that we propose to rely on the Sublime Instincts of an Ancient People.'

To rely on the Sublime Instincts of an Ancient People. It was the purest distillation of Disraeli's agenda for government. But while the people's instincts may have been sublime, their patience was limited. Sooner or later they would expect to see some kind of policy from the new Government. But, for once, Disraeli seemed short of ideas.

The secret here is that there was no secret. To *be* Prime Minister had always been Disraeli's ambition. When it came to the point, he relished the trappings and privileges of office for their own sake. Nor did he despise the social obligations of his position. Soon after he became Prime Minister, he started to host a number of grand dinner parties at which he celebrated being at the top of the greasy pole again. If necessary, he could always summon a clever phrase which might illustrate a vision or adorn an argument. But that was the bulk of it. He dismissed as humbug the idea that a Prime Minister should do anything, let alone concern himself with the details of policy or the drudgery of departmental work. This was lesser men's labour and Disraeli had toiled hard over many years to be in a position where he no longer had to weary himself with such obligations.

There was also another consideration. In *Coningsby*, Disraeli had written that when men are young they want experience, and when they have experience they lack energy.

This phrase now became prophetic for Disraeli's own life. Increasingly, he was unwell and unable to carry out political functions. His ailments included asthma, bronchitis and gout, which by now also affected his eye. He walked with a stick and wore velvet slippers during debates in the Commons. A first trip to Ireland for the winter of 1874–5 was cancelled owing to ill health. Already a pattern had been set whereby Disraeli would sit in silence during meals and dinner parties, making no attempt to speak to those around him.* The truth, as he himself admitted, was that 'power has come to me too late. There were days when on waking I felt I could move dynasties and governments, but that has passed away.'

Disraeli no longer needed to prove himself a master of parliamentary detail. His performances in 1867 with the Second Reform Bill had shown exceptional skill in the arts of parliamentary manoeuvre. The man who had juggled with Hodgkinson's amendment, outwitted Gladstone and steered the Bill through the Commons had no need for further exertion in this field. All this meant that once the Cabinet had been formed on 18 February, something close to a crisis occurred. It was one thing to avoid the hyperactivity of Gladstone, quite another to do nothing at all. Indeed, the act of assembling a government in itself had been wearisome for Disraeli. Throughout his life he had been in favour of small Cabinets. The one he formed in 1874 was among the smallest of the century. Six MPs and six Lords gave a balance to the overall complexion, and the members were a mix of old names and new. Lord Derby returned as Foreign Secretary,

---

*Such behaviour is not unique among past Prime Ministers. One of us, while working for Ted Heath in the 1970s, had the job of encouraging him to be a more engaging dinner host. On one occasion a note was sent reminding the Prime Minister that he must speak to both influential ladies who sat beside him at the table. A few moments later the note came back with a line from the Prime Minister. It simply said: 'I have'.

while Stafford Northcote became Chancellor of the Exchequer and Gathorne Hardy Secretary of State for War. Disraeli's old friend Lord John Manners returned to government, this time as Postmaster General, and the Duke of Richmond became Lord President of the Council. Malmesbury agreed to serve as Lord Privy Seal and George Ward Hunt became the First Lord of the Admiralty. Lord Cairns became Lord Chancellor and Lord Carnarvon, who had resigned from Derby's Government in revolt against the Second Reform Act, now agreed to serve under Disraeli as Secretary of State for the Colonies, perhaps guided by the influence of his mother-in-law, Lady Chesterfield.

The two most surprising appointments were the return of Viscount Cranborne – now the 3rd Marquess of Salisbury – and the arrival of Richard Cross. Disraeli worked hard to persuade Lord Salisbury to join his Cabinet. Salisbury had remained bitter against what he believed to be Disraeli's duplicity over the Reform Bill. Disraeli mustered all possible forms of persuasion in asking him to serve, pointing out that this was a decisive moment in the history of the Conservative Party, and if he failed to take it he would drift into fruitless opposition. His title apart, Salisbury in 1874 was not unlike Disraeli in the 1840s – able, resentful and liable to turn his talents to destructive purposes if he chose such a path. But when it came to the point, Salisbury yielded to the advice of his friends and flattery of the Prime Minister, agreeing to become Indian Secretary once again.

Meanwhile Disraeli found himself short of a Home Secretary. There were several possible candidates, but Disraeli chose Richard Cross, whom he hardly knew, and who had never served in government. Cross was a Lancashire lawyer who had been an MP off and on since the 1850s. His appointment owed much to the guiding hand of Lord Derby, who was impressed by Cross's commitment to social reform.

Together with the new Financial Secretary, one W.H. Smith, Cross added an air of middle-class sensibility to the Government. His role was to turn Disraeli's rhetoric on poverty into actual reforms.

We do not know if Cross ever read any of Disraeli's novels. By doing so, he could have spared himself the moment of dismay that occurred soon after he joined the Cabinet. Disraeli, as we know, dealt in his novels overwhelmingly in lofty principles and the pursuit of vague truths. He showed no interest in policy-making or the administrative tasks which government required. When it came to a conclusion, or a call for a new kind of politics, the plots collapsed and the sentences descended into banality. As it was in fiction, so now happened in real life, as Disraeli's Cabinet met to prepare the Queen's Speech. Cross later made a record of this meeting in his memoirs. 'When the Cabinet came to discuss the Queen's Speech I was, I confess, disappointed at the lack of originality shown by the Prime Minister. From all his speeches, I had quite expected that his mind was full of legislative schemes; but this did not prove to be the case. On the contrary, he had to rely on the various suggestions of his colleagues, and as they themselves had only just come into office, there was some difficulty in framing the Queen's Speech.'

In other governments, and for other Prime Ministers, this might have become a serious problem. But this was not like other governments, and Disraeli was not like other Prime Ministers. He was known by his colleagues as the Chief – and this Chief took his orders from a superior power. All his life, Disraeli believed in bountiful and reawakened monarchy. His task now was to bring about such a regeneration. When, on taking office, he saw the Queen he told her, somewhat rashly, that whatever she wished should be done, 'whatever the difficulties might be'. He now set himself to deliver on this promise.

The Queen for her part was simply delighted to be treated with proper deference for a change. Five and a half years of Gladstone as Prime Minister had confirmed her feelings of deep hostility towards him. 'So very arrogant, tyrannical and obstinate with no knowledge of the world or human nature,' was how she described him, 'all this, and much want of regard towards my feelings.' But there was also another element. The Queen in old age retained the same girlish preoccupation with being the centre of attention as she had shown as a nineteen-year-old with Lord Melbourne. She may have been the Queen, but she would always be a princess. A part of her wished to be fawned over and flattered extravagantly. As she complained at one point, 'People are apt to forget that the Queen is a <u>woman</u> – who has far more on her hands and far more to try mind and body than is good for anyone of her sex and age.'

This is where Disraeli came into his element. He had already grown to understand the mixture of boredom, sadness and frustration which shaped the Queen's daily life. He did everything in his power to play to her emotions and inject greater colour into her routine. By this stage, the Queen and Disraeli were sending each other regular exchanges of flowers. Now Disraeli added a new dimension to his flattery; he called the Queen, even in letters to her directly, the 'Faerie Queen', 'Queen Titania', 'the kindest of mistresses'. Naturally this served him well. The Queen was overjoyed at the lavish attention. After a while, she invited Disraeli to address her in the second person and allowed him to sit in her company, a unique mark of favour among her subjects.

The Queen also began to rekindle her interest in politics and public life. In particular she began to make her views on religion and, later, foreign policy known. On religion, the Queen herself had few strong doctrinal opinions; she liked her sermons short and her priests straightforward. She was not interested in detailed and laborious theological exchange. But alongside these views she entertained a strong hostility to Popish practices and disliked the influence of the Catholic Church on the Church of England. Such practices were linked in her mind to foreign and seditious behaviour.

So when in 1874 the Archbishop of Canterbury, Archibald Tait, brought forward a Private Member's Bill to regulate the litany and root out Roman Catholic influences, Queen Victoria urged Disraeli to give the Bill Government support. Disraeli wavered, sensing that to interfere in this way would divide his Cabinet and isolate many within his own party, although he already had a record of supporting the Low Church against High Anglicans in his clerical appointments. Eventually he came out fighting as Gladstone decided to oppose the Bill. Gladstone attacked the Public Worship Bill as a 'Bill to put down Ritualism', but found to his horror that this phrase failed to have the desired impact and indeed helped to secure support from among the Low Church party. Disraeli repeated the taunt in his own speech on the subject and in the end the Bill was passed without opposition in August 1874, with no serious damage done to the Government.

It was a rocky start for the new Government but, by chance rather than by design, the following year turned into a short golden era for the Conservatives. Thanks in no small part to Gladstone's retreat from the Opposition front bench, the Government brought forward a long list of social reforms which became the basis of much wide-ranging legislation. Here, it seemed, was the promise of *Sybil* applied to domestic politics.

It would be churlish to claim that Disraeli played no part in these policies. His first Government had already pointed the way on social reform, for example by overseeing the abolition of public executions, and by setting up a Royal Commission on Sanitary Laws. Disraeli himself had sent a signal for further activity on social issues in his 1872 speeches, and as long ago as his 1851 election address in Buckinghamshire he had been talking about the 'principles of Conservative Progress' by which Tory governments would seek to improve the lot of the poor.

But the bulk of the legwork in the 1875 session, and indeed throughout the next five years, was carried out not by Disraeli but by Richard Cross under Lord Derby's influence. The pattern tended to be that Cross would work up a proposal with Lord Derby; he would then bring the measure to Cabinet, where a significant number would raise their objections, before Disraeli would intercede and issue his beneficent consent. Thereafter the policy would proceed through Cabinet as they worked out the details, during the discussions of which Disraeli would fall asleep.

If the commitment to the cause was hardly compelling, the scale of the legislation was undoubtedly impressive. In the 1875 session alone the Government carried a Public Health Act, two pieces of trade union legislation, an act to protect Friendly Society funds, the Artisans Dwellings Act, the Agricultural Holdings Act and a Sale of Food and Drugs Act. Of all this legislation only the Agricultural Holdings Act was driven by Disraeli personally.

These Bills can be cast into three categories – health, housing and industrial relations. They were underpinned by a policy of fiscal prudence and thrift at the Treasury, where Northcote set up a new sinking fund to cut the National Debt. On the surface at least, the subjects of these reforms were similar to those Gladstone had tackled in his Government. They also belonged to the same spirit of progressive improvement which fitted the mood of the age. What was new, however, was that they were brought forward by a Conservative administration – and how far that administration had travelled from the Victorian political orthodoxy of laissez-faire.

Housing came first, and the Artisans Dwellings Act gave local authorities the power to replace slums with adequate housing. From now on, public authorities were empowered to amend or remove existing buildings owned by private landlords on grounds of health and later overcrowding. This Act was complemented by another, the Agricultural Holdings Act, which compensated rural tenants for improvements they had made to their properties. These measures did not in themselves solve the squalor which afflicted large swathes of Britain, but they were regarded as a significant attempt to address the grievances of poor tenants across the country.

The second, and most surprising, category of new legislation covered public health. Disraeli in his speeches had spoken about air, light and water as the basic staples of a healthy life, and the new Government set itself to make improvements on all three of these fronts. The Public Health Act of 1875 did not contain much that was new, but rather consolidated a great deal of existing legislation on living conditions. In particular, local authorities were obliged by the Act to maintain sewers and ensure a supply of fresh water to local residents. Street lighting and rubbish collections were also required of local authorities in an effort to improve the quality of life in Britain's grey and overcrowded cities.

In many ways, however, the most successful pieces of legislation passed in this period were two measures of reform related to trade unions – the Employers and Workmen Act and the Conspiracy and Protection of Property Act. The first transformed relations between employee and employer by rewriting the legal code that made workers liable to criminal proceedings in case of breach of contract, while their employers would only face civil action. Henceforth, all breaches of contract would be subject to civil courts. The second Bill put trade unions onto a stronger and fairer legal footing, by overturning the doctrine of conspiracy which had hitherto covered the ordinary actions of trade unions. In effect, the measure legalised peaceful trade union picketing. This was indeed a major development, as Disraeli himself observed in his letters. 'We have settled the long and vexatious contest between Capital and Labour,' he claimed. Be that as it may, this Act was one of the measures which Disraeli slept through when it was discussed in Cabinet.

There were other Acts too in these years and later, including the Merchant Shipping Act, the Rivers Pollution Act, an Education Act and two Factory Acts of 1874 and 1878. Taken together, they gave rise to Lord Blake's suggestion that the measures passed by Disraeli's Government 'constitute the biggest instalment of social reform passed by any one government in the nineteenth century'. In many respects the measures were strikingly interventionist and imposed significant new obligations on businesses and local authorities. But they did not signal a lurch to socialism. Most stopped short of compelling public authorities to act in any given situation, merely giving such bodies the power to take action where appropriate and where funds allowed.

The word Disraeli liked to use to describe this was 'permissive' legislation. He claimed this was the 'characteristic of a free people'. Characteristic it may have been, but it also had drawbacks. For example, Blake records that six years after the Artisans Dwellings Act only ten of the eighty-seven English and Welsh towns to which it applied had implemented its provisions. And Professor Vincent points out that while the Merchant Shipping Act required a Plimsoll line to be painted on the sides of commercial shipping, it allowed the owners to decide where to draw the line. It was not until many years later that the position of the line was fixed in law.

But for Disraeli the message mattered more than the meat. To him, it was not a significant problem that local rate payers would baulk at large spending by local authorities to build better housing, or indeed that shipowners might draw their Plimsoll line around the main deck if they desired. His methods were more mysterious than that. Taken together, these reforms showed that the Conservatives were the only true progressive force in the country. As he predicted to Lady Chesterfield, the legislation 'will gain and retain for the Conservatives the lasting affection of the working classes'.

When it came to the general election of 1880, Disraeli made no mention of these measures in his election address. He left it to others to mould the myth which he had begun. And across all parties, the MPs were already hard at work. For example in 1879, Alexander Macdonald, a Scottish miner and Radical MP, told his constituents in Stafford that the 'Conservative Party have done more for the working classes in five years than the Liberals have in fifty'. Much later John Gorst, who by this point had split with the Conservative Party, wrote a famous letter to *The Times* in 1907. 'The principle of Tory Democracy is that all government exists for the good of the governed ... It is democratic because the welfare of the people is its supreme end; it is Tory because the institutions of the country are the means by which the end is to be attained.'*

Conservative methods, progressive ends – such has been the cry of countless Conservatives down the years. Baldwin was the first to point repeatedly and in detail to Disraeli's social legislation. More recently, David Cameron gave speech after speech in Opposition making clear that traditional

---

* As for Richard Cross, he returned as Home Secretary in the 1880s but it seems that thereafter his career underwent something of a decline. Derby notes in his diaries that during one speech in the Commons, Cross was so drunk that he had be pulled down by his friends. He lived until he was ninety, dying in 1914, and for many years served as a Director of the Great Central Railway. It is said that he used to mutter during board meetings, 'Where is the money to come from?'

Tory methods of decentralisation and local empowerment held the key to a fairer and stronger society. Often he and his colleagues would invoke Disraeli in their defence. Ahead of the Party Conference in 2008 David Willetts wrote an article holding up Disraeli as the standard-bearer for modern Conservatives. Of course, every so often the means are forgotten and it is simply Disraeli's progressive vision that is remembered. For instance, Lord Birkenhead claimed early in the twentieth century that 'if providence could have made Disraeli a dictator in the early 1830s there would have been no social problem today'. But, one way or another, validly or invalidly, Disraeli is the name mentioned more than any other today as the first compassionate Conservative leader who fought hard to improve the lives of the poor.

Disraeli himself would of course be delighted by this legacy – delighted, and perhaps also a little surprised. But in the end it does not really matter how interested he was in the social measures which were passed while he was Prime Minister. His aim was to show that such policies were not the exclusive preserve of Gladstone and the Liberal Party. His words had breathed life into the idea which Peel had set out laboriously many years previously in the Tamworth Manifesto, about the importance of making necessary and considered reforms in order to preserve the power of the landed aristocracy. Peel may have believed more strongly in the principle, but it was Disraeli who translated it into the marketplace of mass politics. Without Peel, the Party might not have survived the Great Reform Act. Without Disraeli – or to be more precise, without the words and images conjured by Disraeli – it would not have become the dominant force in twentieth-century politics.

All this lay far in the future. Disraeli in 1876 was running out of steam. Quietly, and without warning or fanfare, it was announced in August that Disraeli would be quitting the

Commons and taking his wife's title as Lord Beaconsfield in
the House of Lords.* The news was received with unparalleled sadness on all sides of the House. One of the best letters
Disraeli received came from Sir William Hart Dyke. After
naming at some length the colleagues who were distressed
by the development, he told Disraeli: 'All the real chivalry
and delight of party politics, seem to have departed; nothing
remains but routine...' Another letter came from Viscount
Barrington. 'My individual interest in the House of Commons
is from this day gone, and nothing will remain but duty – a
very poor substitute indeed.' Lord John Manners, Disraeli's
Young England old friend, told his leader: 'I cannot bear to
think of the future; the change will be so mournful, the conditions of service in our House so altered.' And Lord George
Hamilton wrote: 'I am not the only Under Secretary who ...
will feel that he is in a different place now that you are not
in it.'

But perhaps the most telling letter came from an opponent.
Sir William Harcourt wrote: 'Henceforth the game will be
like a chessboard when the queen is gone – a petty struggle
of pawns ... To the imagination of the younger generation
your life will always have a special fascination. For them you
have enlarged the horizon of the possibilities of the future.'

It was an outpouring of emotion unlike that which accompanied any other elevation. What was the clue to Disraeli's
success? Partly, of course, it was his peculiar concern for
diction which characterised his speeches. When he spoke,
there were always four syllables in 'Parl-i-a-ment' and three
syllables in 'bus-i-ness'. There was also a purely theatrical
element to his rhetoric. Before any great attack or cutting
phrase about an opponent, Disraeli would extract a pure
white handkerchief and hold it in front of him, like a signal

---

*Though for clarity we shall continue to call him Disraeli.

for blood sport to begin. But mainly it was simply Disraeli's use of imagination that created such a powerful effect. Through his range of vocabulary, his armoury of arguments, his romantic, indeed fictionalised imagery of English life, he had injected imagination into an industrial age. He brought politics to life and his like would not be seen again.

As for Disraeli himself, he too felt a deep sadness at leaving the Commons. It had been both office and home for the best part of four decades. The Lords would never match the drama of a debate in the Commons. He knew that he was in a way being put out to graze. When he was asked by a friend how he felt at the transition, he said: 'I am dead – dead, but in Elysian fields.' In this seraphic setting, the final, thrilling and implausible chapter of Disraeli's life and career was about to begin.

PEACE WITH HONOUR

Disraeli was seventy-one and ailing. His letters from these years are filled with references to aches, ailments and physical impairments. On one occasion he explained to Corry that he had been laid up for three weeks 'with much pain, all the result of a too hurried descent from the railway carriage'. On another, he complained that asthma 'destroys my nights, and makes me consequently shattered by day'. In 1877 Disraeli hired a doctor called Joseph Kidd who prescribed a range of homeopathic remedies to soothe his patient. He also began to take ten-minute breaks during his evening meals, pausing between courses to read snatches of his favourite novels. But none of these measures could remedy the central affliction, namely that Disraeli's powers of perseverance were wearing thin.

Disraeli had not retreated from the dazzling array of ideas he had assembled as a young man. But they remained where they had always been, in his imagination. Two years as Prime Minister had been enough to make clear that there would be no return to an age of chivalry. The alliance he had hoped for between the people and good-looking young peers would not materialise. Despite Disraeli's utterances to the contrary, the Queen remained a dumpy Hanoverian monarch and not the harbinger of a benign despotism. There was, however, one area of politics where it might just be possible to sprinkle some magic and do something spectacular. That field was foreign affairs.

For Disraeli, foreign policy was real politics. It was played out on the big stage, with a huge audience for the talented performer. There was no need here to worry about the dull details of legislation. The fate and reputation of nations was at stake. Later Disraeli made no attempt to conceal his priorities when writing *Endymion*: 'Look at Lord Roehampton – he is the man. He does not care a rush whether the revenue increases or declines. He is thinking of real politics: foreign affairs: maintaining our power in Europe.'

Disraeli had no detailed experience of diplomacy and scant handle on European geography. He spoke no languages and rarely travelled abroad. But foreign affairs appealed to the deep recesses of his heart and spirit. 'There is no gambling like politics,' he told Lady Bradford, 'but when you have to deal only with Emperors and High Chancellors, and Empires are on the main, the excitement, I suppose a little increases ...' The very process of diplomacy was congenial to Disraeli. He thoroughly enjoyed the flutter of a court, the robes of a cardinal, the subtlety of a diplomatic conversation and the splendour of a dynastic banquet. It followed that as Prime Minister he wished to dominate the foreign policy of his Government, to ensure that it was vigorous, even dramatic, and to play a vivid personal part in carrying it out.

Vigorous it would certainly be, but to what purpose? Lord Palmerston and George Canning were the natural role models for Disraeli. All his life Disraeli had admired the boldness that Palmerston had shown in his prime during the 1830s. He also marvelled at the swagger with which Canning had handled foreign policy during and after the Napoleonic Wars. Like Canning, Disraeli was determined not to allow a bunch of Continental monarchies to dominate European diplomacy.

Like Palmerston, Disraeli believed that diplomacy should be accompanied by deafening noise.

But there was a difficulty. Disraeli did not agree with Canning and Palmerston about the way the world was going. Both these men had believed in and admired the growth of nationalism as a driving force in Europe and America. By contrast, Disraeli almost alone refused to meet the Italian nationalist Garibaldi when he was lionised in London in 1864. For Disraeli, Garibaldi was a noisy upstart; the Austro-Hungarian Empire was a more interesting and worthwhile entity than any contrived Italian state. Disraeli, the novelist turned politician, believed in a world of empires, sustained and manipulated by the skill of bankers, priests, beautiful women and secret societies.

Increasingly, Disraeli spoke of Britain as an imperial country. When he used the phrase, for example in the famous Crystal Palace speech, he was thinking only partly of the colonies scattered across the globe, though he played with imprecise suggestions of an imperial tariff and a representative council based in London. His main preoccupation was with Britain as an Asiatic power. When referring to Oriental states he meant, of course, British rule over India, but as the years passed he became equally preoccupied with Britain's unique relationship with the decaying Ottoman Empire.

The key to success in this world of empires was the protection and accumulation of prestige. To Disraeli, prestige was a solid asset. It conferred authority; it provided security; indeed it was the true currency of international relations. A country which enjoyed high prestige would prevail in any contest where otherwise the scales were balanced. Moreover, the process of acquiring prestige was most enjoyable: the skilful manoeuvre, the march of an army, the sudden arrival of the British fleet – this was what politics should be about.

In short, Disraeli carried into foreign policy as much of

the paraphernalia of a novelist as proved portable. He had already begun to show his hand in the first two years of his Government. The most stunning example was the purchase of Suez Canal Company shares. In November 1875 the Sultan of the Ottoman Empire had gone bankrupt. One of the ripple effects was that his client, the Khedive of Egypt, also ran out of money. The Khedive therefore opened negotiations with two French syndicates for the sale of his 44 per cent holding in the Suez Canal Company. The French already held most of the shares in the company, and the sale of the remainder might have posed a risk to the considerable British shipping interests which used the Canal. When Disraeli heard the news he moved fast to table a rival British bid. Parliament was not sitting, so he could not raise money through the usual channels. The only option was a private loan. Monty Corry waited outside during the crucial Cabinet meeting. At length the door opened and Disraeli gave his lieutenant the sign. Corry hurried round to Lionel de Rothschild's headquarters and said that the Prime Minister wanted £4 million.

'When?' asked the Baron, who was eating a muscatel grape at that moment.
'Tomorrow.'
'What is your security?'
'The British Government.'
'You shall have it.'

The coup had all the elements close to Disraeli's heart: the hurried Cabinet meeting, the enigmatic financier, the con-founding of the French, the flattering of the Queen ('It is just settled: you have it, Madam'). True, the Rothschilds charged a steep rate of interest. True, the Khedive's shares were mort-gaged and had no voting rights until 1895. True, the French had not been confounded, but (recognising the help they had recently had from Britain against Germany) the French Government refused to back the private French offer once they had been told it would be opposed by Britain. True, as Blake points out, Disraeli seemed to confuse control of the shares with control of the Canal itself. But as an act of prestige the purchase was powerful and successful; in the long run it also proved a decent commercial investment.

The second instalment of Disraeli's new doctrine had been the Royal Titles Bill early in 1876. Titles were a subject of boundless fascination for Disraeli; his novels are filled with sultans, grand viziers, doges and dowager duchesses. But to Disraeli the most relevant titles were those which were held by the Queen of England. Since Peel's time, the idea had been circulating that the Queen should be crowned Empress of India. Now Disraeli took up the scheme. 'It is only by the amplification of titles that you can often touch and satisfy the imagination of nations; and that is an element which Governments must not despise,' he argued, and quite naturally his royal mistress agreed. There were also powerful personal considerations at stake. The Queen's daughter was married to the son of the German Emperor. This meant that once old William died she would become Empress of Germany and take precedence over her mother, which obviously would not be right. To this Disraeli added the argument, of questionable credibility, that the change would show Russia that Britain was determined to cling on to India. The Bill provoked great controversy in Parliament, with Gladstone particularly noisy in Opposition. It also prompted a new battle with Robert Lowe, formerly of the Cave. Lowe inveighed strongly against both the Queen and Disraeli, but he pushed his attack too far when he claimed that Victoria had applied unconstitutional pressure on the Prime Minister to bring forward the Bill, and he was obliged to retract the claim. In the end the Bill passed through the Commons, and there were immense celebrations in India, culminating in a Great Durbar which lasted fourteen days.

In these ways and others, Disraeli set the tone for what was to follow in the second half of his Government. There was nothing collective about his idea of foreign policy. It required not a daring Cabinet but a single daring leader, namely himself. A Foreign Secretary was needed for the dull, humdrum purposes of sending dispatches and meeting ambassadors. He might scout new opportunities for enhancing prestige. But there was no question of his becoming a fellow architect of policy. For all these reasons, and sheer force of long friendship, Disraeli had selected the 15th Earl of Derby for this pedestrian role.

Derby, as we have seen, had been Disraeli's most stalwart supporter for three decades. He had stood by Disraeli through the weary slog of Opposition. Together, they had dragged the Party back from Protectionism. Together, they had pushed through the Second Reform Bill. When the back benchers had suggested that Derby should replace Disraeli as leader, Derby had refused to participate in their proposals. The two men had spent much time together, talking and dining in Bellamy's alone, grumbling about the idleness of Derby's father and arguing about the bleak future course of the world.

Disraeli knew that Derby was loyal, hard-working, conscientious and low in ambition. These were the qualities needed in a field of policy where the dash and imaginative courage would be provided by himself. He counted on Derby to stand by him in Cabinet and implement his proposals. But this analysis had a flaw. As we have seen, Disraeli thought that Derby had no imagination, and this defect started to show itself in the warning shots of frustration that began to appear in Derby's diaries during these years.

Increasingly the two men disagreed about foreign policy.

Disraeli believed in a policy of tireless activity. Prestige was everything. The agents of Britain should be everywhere – her ambassadors, like her fleets, always looking for opportunities to assert themselves and advance the Queen's reputation. Derby saw no point and some danger in all this. For him Britain was Britain, solid and respected for her solidity in an unstable world. Britain should wherever possible be a spectator not an actor in the European controversies. He did not mind being called an isolationist: 'to me it appears that when isolated we have generally been most successful'. And on another occasion: 'If foreigners can settle their affairs without us, why should we intervene?'

Of particular note are Derby's comments on the Suez Canal shares. In his diary for 29 November 1875 he jotted: 'so far as I can make out, the purchase is universally popular. I might say even more, it seems to have created a feeling of something like enthusiasm far in excess of the real importance of the transaction. It is a complete political success: yet the very fact of its being so causes me some uneasiness: for it shows the intense desire for action abroad which pervades the public mind, the impatience created by long diplomatic inactivity, and the strength of feeling which might under certain circumstances take the form of a cry for War.' He went on to grumble that if a few years back a Minister had suggested that the British Government should buy shares in a foreign company, the proposal would have been thought absurd, and the Minister ruined.

In truth what separated the two men was not intellect and opinion, but temperament and upbringing. Derby was not stupid or lazy, but he was held back from memorable achievement by natural pessimism. By nature he was a worrier. He worried about money, of which he had plenty, and about his health, which was generally good. He worried about the Conservative Party and about the future of Britain. On these wider matters, after worrying, he usually concluded that there was not much to be done.

Despite his own ancestry, Derby was an unstinting admirer of the bourgeoisie. Indeed, he possessed most of the solid progressive virtues which that class embodied. He once remarked after meeting a group of northern businessmen that he knew no class in English life to equal them. He admired John Stuart Mill, and was a friend of Charles Darwin. He was a sceptic in religion, sometimes going to church as a social duty, but impatient of doctrinal argument. Derby wanted the Conservative Party to base itself firmly on centre ground and worried, rightly, that Disraeli privately despised the middle class.

Yet ancestral attitudes lurked in the background. Derby still owned 57,000 acres in Lancashire as well as 11,000 elsewhere. He valued his position there, and in particular his popularity in Liverpool. As head of one of the most ancient families of England he was connected by marriage with another, having married Mary, widow of the second Marquess of Salisbury and stepmother of the present Lord Salisbury. Derby was devoted to her, and she to politics; they had no children. This background shaped the way he thought and expressed himself. For example, he liked living in the south because 'the peasantry of Western Surrey are better looking and better mannered than those I meet with elsewhere'. His criticism of a Russian envoy was easily summarised. 'In one word, he is not a gentleman.' Another of his strongest prejudices had an aristocratic base. As a Stanley he felt no particular reverence for a Hanoverian Queen who spent her time in bizarre places like Balmoral and was served by men like John Brown. He pitied rather than envied Disraeli for his attendance on Victoria, whom he found self-centred and dangerously unbalanced.

Derby lacked that thrust of personal ambition which

propels most politicians. He once explained why he continued as a politician in terms which deserve a record for
lack of enthusiasm. Resignation would mean 'loss of a kind
of employment which habit has made not uncongenial and
which, if sometimes disagreeable, keeps off mere vacancy
and weariness'. Derby was a Minister because he worried
that otherwise he would be bored.

This is not the stuff of magnetic leadership. Derby felt no
need to prove himself. He was no arriviste; from the moment
of his birth he had arrived. These characteristics played across
to his handling of foreign affairs. Derby was neither lazy nor
prejudiced. He worked diligently at his Foreign Office boxes.
But idleness and inaction are not the same thing. When
Derby supported inaction, as he usually did, this would be
the result of hard study and clear thought. Lady Gwendolen
Cecil, a biased critic, summed him up well in her biography
of her father Lord Salisbury: 'He was a master of the arts by
which initiative in others is obstructed and definite conclusions are postponed; how to ignore inconvenient suggestions
without combating them, and the use of silence in avoiding
consideration of unarrived emergencies. Lord Salisbury used
to declare that contending with him in council was like fighting a feather bed – and yet the obstruction was never that of
stupidity or incomprehension.'

Derby had already given an example of his invincible dislike of adventure during his brief period as Foreign Secretary
in 1867–8. A dispute between France and Prussia over the
future of the Grand Duchy of Luxembourg escalated into
serious talk of war. Stanley (as he was then) allowed himself to be persuaded into holding a conference in London
to resolve the matter. The conference succeeded, but only
because the powers including Britain agreed to guarantee
the neutrality of the independent Grand Duchy of Luxembourg. This was a necessary commitment but, having given

the guarantee, Stanley immediately explained it away. He and his father, the Prime Minister, told a puzzled Parliament that the guarantee was collective and could only come into effect if all the signatories agreed to abide by it. Since only France or Prussia could conceivably threaten Luxembourg the guarantee was thus meaningless. It would become invalid the moment it was needed. History would have been very different if in 1914 Britain had evaded by the same device her commitment to Belgium when the country was invaded by the Kaiser's army.

Back at the Foreign Office in 1874, Derby returned to these principles. By this point France had suffered a crushing defeat at the hands of Prussia, and Prussia had grown into a united Germany. A formidable new player was dominating the European scene, namely Otto von Bismarck, the German Chancellor. His policy was to keep France isolated through an alliance with Austria and Russia, known as the League of the Three Emperors, or *Dreikaiserbund*. But Derby saw no reason to match Bismarck's restless and ingenious energy. He argued against an active European policy, which would only lead Britain into fresh entanglements overseas.

By a paradox in 1875, one of Bismarck's mistakes seemed to confirm Derby's analysis. For once Bismarck placed one card too many on the house of cards he was building at the time. He banned the export of horses from Germany and started a press campaign hinting at a German pre-emptive strike against France. This seems to have been an attempt to bully France into giving up her rearmament programme, but it misfired. The result was uproar. The press began to write of 'The War in Sight' and even the old German Emperor William was shaken. Britain and Russia joined in urging restraint on Bismarck, who gave the appearance of backing away from a war which he had never in fact intended. Derby drew the obvious lesson: if a mild move of traditional diplomacy had achieved this striking success against the mighty new Germany, what need for a more active policy?

The following spring, Bismarck made a secret approach to Britain through Odo Russell, the British Ambassador in Berlin. He seemed to hint at intimate cooperation on various matters, in particular with regard to the Ottoman Empire. This offer was highly attractive to Disraeli, but Derby remained cool and defused the idea. He sent a polite inquiry as to what exactly Bismarck was suggesting; there was a delay; the idea petered out. But now, for almost the first time in his career, Disraeli asked doubting questions of Lord Derby: 'It appears to me, that we are hardly taking as much advantage as we might of Bismarck's ... overture to us. Odo writes, as if it were something that had happened in a dream.'

These then were the men in charge of foreign policy in the summer of 1876. They were different characters, but their partnership seemed strong and, despite their private differences, likely to survive. They had formed a strong alliance on domestic matters, with Disraeli making great speeches and Derby and Cross producing new policies. Even on foreign policy there were few visible signs of the tension which would tear them apart later. That their partnership did collapse after so many years, amid such acrimony, was another example of the collateral damage caused by the decline of the Ottoman Empire in these years.

The Ottoman Empire was always declining. Indeed, its disintegration is one of the dominant themes of nineteenth-century history. By the mid-1870s its problems had become the main topic of European diplomacy, and yet it still covered vast and heterogeneous zones, including Turkey, Palestine, Arabia, Egypt and the Balkan nations. At irregular intervals another province flaked away into an untidy and insecure independence. The residue remained under the rule of Constantinople. The issue of how to handle this decline became known as the Eastern Question. That vague phrase contained a multitude of hatreds and ambitions. It baffled successive Prime Ministers down the years. At moments of crisis, the Sultan and his advisers were prolific in promises of improved government for their subjects. All these promises proved futile. The moment had passed when the Ottoman Empire could cure itself of corruption and abuse of power. The whole prospect was of uninterrupted gloom.

The Eastern Question was a painful dilemma for many, but for Disraeli an excitement. Memories of his own visit to Palestine as a young man mingled with his fascination as a Jew and novelist with the kaleidoscope of Eastern faiths and mysteries. Moreover, in this drama Britain could dominate the big stage, using her fleet to apply pressure on Russia or Turkey through the Dardanelles. One way or another, Disraeli was determined to play the part with the utmost boldness. As he told Lady Bradford, 'I really believe "the Eastern Question" that has haunted Europe for a century ... will fall to my lot to encounter – dare I say settle.'

This was trickier than it seemed. The previous summer the Eastern Question had creaked into crisis; the Slavs in Bosnia-Herzegovina had risen in rebellion against Ottoman Rule. The Sultan's bankruptcy followed in the autumn, and in 1876 further uprisings broke out in Serbia and Montenegro. These events in themselves need not have created a wider European confrontation. But this crisis was of a different calibre to those of previous years.

Traditionally, in circumstances such as these, the great powers of Europe would make their priority the preservation of the Ottoman Empire; this was seen as vital to the overall balance of power. But since 1871 there had been no balance in Europe – or, to be more precise, the balance had been re-defined. Now a new, powerful Germany stood at Europe's centre and the once-mighty France lay weak and isolated.

This left the League of the Three Emperors, namely Russia, Austria and Germany, free to pursue their own favoured policies.

Bismarck for his part had little interest in the Eastern Question, but looked forward to partition of the Turkish Empire. He saw that allowing Britain to take Egypt would stoke up a useful Anglo-French quarrel. The other two powers, which bordered the Turkish Empire, were more closely concerned with Turkey's future. Russia felt a strong natural sympathy with the Balkan rebels on grounds of race and religion; she also saw that the crisis in Constantinople gave an opportunity to extend her power west into Europe and south into Central Asia. Austria on the other hand, herself ruling over a Slav population in Slovenia as well as millions of Czechs and Hungarians, was by definition a multinational entity, and objected strongly to the idea that the Balkans might disintegrate into a group of noisy national states. But avarice swam alongside her insecurity, and the wily, ambitious Foreign Minister, Count Andrássy, saw that the revolting Balkan nations might without difficulty be swallowed into the Austro-Hungarian Empire.

Disraeli, never a nationalist except as regards Britain herself, felt no sympathy for the insurgents but a lurking attraction for the fading empire. But he too saw that Turkey's condition was fatal. On 6 September 1875 he had written to Lady Bradford: 'When I entered political life there were three Great Powers in danger – the Grand Signior of the Ottomans, the Pope of Rome, and the Lord Mayor of London. The last will survive a long time; but the fall of France has destroyed the Pope, and will, ultimately, drive the Turk from Europe.' Faced with this prospect, Disraeli focused his attention on securing vital British interests – but what precisely those vital interests were seemed unclear.

One of the great clichés of Victorian politics was that

'Constantinople was the key to India'. The idea was that the decline of Turkey threatened Britain's whole imperial position, because control of Constantinople would give Russia a clear run at the Suez Canal, which was the route used to transport British troops and equipment to India. But the flaw in this assessment was basic geography. In reality Port Said, at the head of the Canal, is nearly a thousand miles by sea from Constantinople and much further overland. The notion that if Russia took Constantinople it could make a quick march on the Canal was a fantasy. In truth, the real nightmare was not Russia advancing into Turkey, but Russian troops moving south through Central Asia, towards India through Afghanistan. But maps did not feature in Disraeli's reckoning. He swallowed the idea that the safety of Constantinople held the key. If Turkey fell and Russia entered its capital, there would in his mind be no alternative but Anglo-Russian war.

In early 1876 this prospect seemed distant. Throughout the spring the Great Powers shuttled about, trying to agree reforms which would restore calm in the Ottoman Empire. A note proposing various changes was duly sent by the Powers but produced no clear improvement. A second note, prepared by Bismarck in May 1876, proposed further reforms and ended with a paragraph at the end hinting at coercion by the Great Powers if the Turks rejected them. This time Disraeli refused to fall in. His gout was bad. He was cross because the Foreign Office were slow in sending him details of the Memorandum; when he made inquiries it emerged that the Resident Clerk of the Foreign Office had gone out for a walk, and so was not actually in residence at that time. Worse still, the plan had been put together by the *Dreikaiserbund* before Britain had been consulted. This was intolerable. 'England has been treated as though we were Montenegro or Bosnia,' he told the Russian Ambassador. Derby agreed and the Cabinet unanimously rejected the plan. The Queen and some qualified observers thought this might be a mistake. The British rejection confirmed most Turks in their view that they could rely on British support whatever they did; in this way it cemented, not softened, the obstinate Turkish mood.

In the event, however, the Berlin Memorandum came to nothing. Within days the Sultan had been deposed and a new administration came into being under his nephew, Murad V. It appeared as though the new government was favourable to reform, so the Memorandum was withdrawn. Disraeli rejoiced at the idea that the northern powers had been outwitted: 'I look upon the tripartite confederacy to be at an end. It was an unnatural state of affairs and never would have occurred had England maintained, of late years, her just position in public affairs.'

But nothing was settled. Rumours began to trickle through that a rising of Christians in Bulgaria had been suppressed by the Turks with extreme cruelty. On 23 June these rumours swelled from a trickle to a torrent when the *Daily News* reported that some 25,000 men, women and children had been massacred by a Turkish paramilitary force of 'bashi-bazouk' soldiers. In Britain public opinion reacted with outrage, and the Eastern Crisis erupted into a political controversy.

In Parliament, the Liberal Opposition began to harass the Government over its own response to the atrocities, and Disraeli made a hash of his defence. All his life Disraeli demonstrated a congenital inability to display sympathy. The emotions he himself concealed never surfaced in public displays of sentimentality. Indeed, he regarded such feeling in others as hypocrisy and a device to discredit his Government. He therefore found it impossible to share the sense of alarm felt across the country. When confronted in Parliament with accusations of torture, he turned them away casually: 'Oriental people ... seldom, I believe, resort to torture, but generally terminate their connection with culprits in a more expeditious manner.'

Within days Disraeli became aware that a British consul, Mr Reade, had sent a dispatch from the spot giving cautious support to the accusations. Disraeli now turned strongly on his Foreign Secretary. 'I must again complain of the management of your office,' he wrote to Derby. 'It is impossible to represent the F.O. in the House of Commons in these critical times without sufficient information.' A new and murky element now entered the equation. The reports of the consuls came through the British Ambassador in Constantinople, Sir Henry Elliot, who was strongly pro-Turkish. One way or another, these reports were watered down and hid damaging evidence about the atrocities. This tendentious editing was the responsibility of the Permanent Under Secretary, Lord Tenterden, a particular bête noire of Disraeli's. As time wore on Disraeli became more and more frustrated with what he saw as the sluggishness of the Foreign Office. Indeed 'Tenterdenism' became his chosen byword for the pedantry of officialdom in general. But on the central issue of evidence about the atrocities, even when more fully informed, Disraeli did not alter his position. Two weeks later he horrified Parliament by describing further evidence of atrocities as 'coffee house babble brought by an anonymous Bulgarian to a Consul'.

As July turned into August, Disraeli struggled to assert his authority in Parliament. On Friday 11 August he gave his last speech in the House of Commons before his elevation to the Lords. He ended with a line that became a common refrain in his speeches on foreign policy during the crisis: 'those who suppose that England ever would uphold, or at this moment particularly is upholding, Turkey from blind superstition and from a want of sympathy with the highest aspirations of humanity are deceived. What our duty is at this critical moment is to maintain the Empire of England.'

All accounts agree that the heat was unbearable that
summer. After the recess, Disraeli briefly visited the Queen at
Osborne before spending a week's holiday with Lady Bradford and her husband at their home in Castle Bromwich. He
arrived back at Hughenden on 22 August, where he resumed
a disciplined focus on work. One letter to Corry dated 13 September 1876 gives a jovial impression of his routine: 'I rise at
seven, when my post arrives: very heavy: at 11, second post
– & all the papers which I must look at – at ½ pst one messages ... from 7 to eleven it is high pressure = no time even
for anything but sandwich ... and yet you – even you – cd
little help me. The things must be done with my own hand
& that hand is wearied. The only things I recoil from are the
cyphered texts: which come in pages = but even at these, I
have become adroit: almost as good as the fellow at the F.O.'

In his letter to Corry, Disraeli went on to defend his Eastern policy. 'All I have felt throughout this storm is that if
we appear to have "modified" our policy, we are lost: we
become contemptible, & the Cabinet quarrels among themselves.' But by this stage, an old antagonist had taken centre
stage. On 6 September Disraeli had received in the post a free
copy of a new pamphlet by Gladstone. *The Bulgarian Hor-
rors and the Question of the East* had been written in three
days while Gladstone was laid up with lumbago. It proved
to be a sensational success, selling 40,000 copies in the first
week of publication. Gladstone, never happier than when on
a crusade, for several weeks carried all before him. His latest
period of self-imposed political exile was at an end.

But Gladstone nearly overplayed his hand. He had
rounded off his tirade by calling for what amounted to ethnic
cleansing towards Turkey. 'Let the Turks now carry away
their abuses in the only possible way, namely by carrying
off themselves,' and in a separate section he called Turkish people 'one great anti-human specimen of humanity'.

Understandably, Disraeli was incensed that Gladstone had avoided the criticism he himself had been subjected to for his casual comments that summer. To Corry he complained: 'What a man is Gladstone! What a scoundrel! He publishes a pamphlet urging the expulsion on ethnological grounds of the Turks from Europe; an inferior & debased race – and then, becoming alive almost immediately to his folly, he writes a letter to the Times, saying he did not mean that the Turkish race shd be expelled, only the Turkish Ministers. That he meant the expulsion of some Ministers, I have little doubt, only I think they were not Turks.'

But Disraeli should have kept these frustrations to himself. In a speech a week later in Aylesbury he told his audience that Gladstone's conduct 'may, I think, fairly be described as worse than any of those Bulgarian atrocities which now occupy attention'. At the same time, he tried to blame Serbia's behaviour on the manoeuvres of European secret societies. None of this did Disraeli any favours, and as the weeks rolled on he found himself firmly on the wrong side of the prevailing mood in the country.

That autumn, Disraeli bombarded his Foreign Secretary with a series of mutually contradictory policies in which Britain was always in the lead, sometimes in an alliance with Austria, sometimes taking charge of Constantinople on her own. But as the autumn advanced, the popular mood began to change. In Turkey the new Sultan was deposed at the end of August and replaced by his half-brother, Abdul Hamid II. The Russians were not content to sit back and wait for the new government to restore stability. A powerful war party became prominent in St Petersburg, urging intervention against Turkey as a way of reversing Russia's defeat during the Crimean War. This changed the nature of the debate. Now, instead of a wail of humanitarian horror about Turkish atrocities, a noisy body of British opinion voiced alarm at

Russian behaviour. It was not so much that the same citizens who had bought Gladstone's pamphlet now stood behind Disraeli; then as now, different voices were vocal at different times. But the wheel was quickly turning, and it was the menace of Russian aggrandisement rather than the cruelty of Ottoman rule that captured the public mood.

This change saved Disraeli from his own mistakes. The Conservatives held on to the Buckingham seat in the by-election following Disraeli's elevation to the Lords. Increasingly, Derby and Disraeli found themselves on opposite sides of this argument. Hitherto they had largely shared the same opinion about the atrocities. In his letter to Corry, Disraeli had singled out Derby for praise following his contributions in Cabinet, saying he spoke 'wisely & manfully, all his natural clearness & cleverness & with pluck', and two weeks later he warmly welcomed Derby's 'repugnance to enthusiasm, and his clear, callous, common sense'. On 30 September he told Derby directly: 'You have shown some of the highest qualities of public life, and I believe the great mass of the nation believe in you.' But from now on the two men began to diverge over how to handle the Russian threat. In October Derby, for the first time in his career, foresaw 'the probability or at least the chance of a breach between us: not that as yet we have differed materially in regard to anything that has been done, but that our points of view and objects are different. To the Premier the main thing is to please and surprise the public by bold strokes and unexpected moves; he would rather run serious national risks than hear his policy called feeble or commonplace; to me the first object is to keep England out of trouble, so long as it can be done consistently with honour and good faith. We have agreed in resisting the agitation got up by Gladstone: but if war with Russia becomes popular, as it may, we are not unlikely to be on different sides.'

On 9 November Disraeli gave the annual speech at the Lord Mayor's Banquet. He spoke in strident tones. 'Peace is especially an English policy. She is not an aggressive Power, for there is nothing which she desires. She covets no cities and no provinces ... But although the policy of England is peace, there is no country so well prepared for war as our own. If she enters into conflict in a righteous cause ... if the contest is one which concerns her liberty, her independence, or her empire, her resources, I feel are inexhaustible ... She enters into a campaign which she will not terminate till right is done.' The feeling that a confrontation with Russia was inevitable became more pronounced when news arrived that the Russian army corps had been mobilised.

While others began to panic, Disraeli was thoroughly enjoying himself. On 15 November he visited Ingestre Hall to stay with the Earl of Shrewsbury, where Lady Bradford was temporarily a guest. On arrival, he wrote to Corry that Russia had neither 'clearness of vision' nor 'firmness of purpose' to achieve its purpose, but was instead 'blustering with indefinite schemes'. He was not concerned by the possibility of war, but was very interested in the young man he had met at the railway station. 'It was lucky I was not asleep when the train arrived which I was $\frac{1}{4}$ of an hour before. A tall, handsome young man with a white wand, saluted me, & said his father regretted he cd not come &c. &c. I thought it might be the Mayor's son ... but it was Ingestre, who was only 16 the day before yesterday. I never saw a finer young fellow, with more finished manners & sweet simplicity.'

From now on Disraeli talked often in Cabinet about the need for bold measures, in particular about sending the fleet up to Constantinople through the Dardanelles. These proposals were blocked by Cabinet. Meanwhile plans developed for a European conference to stave off intervention by Russia. Disraeli and Derby agreed that the Secretary of State for India,

Lord Salisbury, should go and represent Britain at this conference in Constantinople. Salisbury was not keen ('an awful
nuisance – not at all in my line – involving sea-sickness,
much French and failure'), but grudgingly accepted the commission. In an effort to make the trip seem more worthwhile,
the Prince of Wales suggested that Salisbury might meet the
masters of policy-making in Paris, Berlin, Vienna and Rome
on his way to Constantinople. Disraeli strongly endorsed this
suggestion, and in his letter to Salisbury added a personal
hint of unmistakable significance. 'Also, personally for yourself, I wish it. This is a momentous period in your life and
career. If all goes well you will have achieved a European
reputation and position which will immensely assist and
strengthen your future course. You should personally know
the men who are governing the world.'

Disraeli was not a man to write carelessly on such a matter.
As Derby had seen, so Disraeli now saw that the time might
come when he would need a new Foreign Secretary. Salisbury, quick, clever, though still something of a threat to
Disraeli, would make an excellent candidate in support of
a more active foreign policy. But Disraeli had misjudged his
man. Once Salisbury had arrived at the conference he fell
in with the subtle Russian negotiator Count Ignatyev, who
played on Salisbury's Christian sympathies for the suffering Slavs. In frustration, Disraeli wrote to Derby: 'Sal. seems
most prejudiced and not to be aware that his principal object
in being sent to Const. is to keep the Russians out of Turkey,
not to create an ideal existence for the Turkish Xtians.' Meanwhile Salisbury's scathing comments to Derby showed none
of the Prime Minister's lurking sympathy for Turkey. He
wrote on Boxing Day that he could not shake Turkey's belief
that Britain would in the end help them however badly they
behaved; 'an army of European advisers made up of fanatics,
oddities and all the declared scoundrels of Europe, who hope

to feed on war ... Convincing the Turks is about as easy as making a donkey canter.'

As it became clear that the Constantinople conference would not resolve anything, the discussions in Cabinet became increasingly unhappy and confused. Among Disraeli's papers, a document survives containing his speaking notes for the Cabinet meeting on 22 December 1876. 'Policy to be recommended in event of Turkey proving obstinate at Conference. Principle – not to coerce the Porte or to Sanction coercion by others – but to use every means of friendly influence and persuasion. Russian system – always to induce England to join in coercion of the Porte.'*

He went on to remind his colleagues of 'Mr Canning's experience & its consequences' during the 1820s and pointed out the different effect on England from that on other powers of suspension of diplomatic relations with the Sultan. The final bullet point of his speaking notes said simply: 'What we should do'. On this point the Cabinet could find no agreement. In Constantinople there was small progress when the pro-Turkish Ambassador, Sir Henry Elliot, withdrew from his position and became Ambassador in Vienna; by a fluke his replacement, the antiquarian Henry Layard, also happened to be Sara Austen's nephew. But still the Turks refused to conciliate their suffering subjects or grant autonomy for the revolting provinces. As a result the Russian Tsar, Alexander II, hesitated on the edge of war against Turkey.

Disraeli pressed at meeting after meeting for action to forestall the Russians. His suggestions varied but basically he wanted to send a land force to occupy the Dardanelles, backed by the fleet. In a letter to Derby on 9 February 1877 he laid bare his belief in action for action's sake. 'You must

---

*The Porte was the name given collectively to the Sultan and his government.

pardon the roughness of this communication, but I am in the gout which is fatal to finished composition and penmanship. The position of affairs is that critical and requires decision ... I don't fancy the country will stand laissez-faire but they will back us, I believe, in whatever we do, provided we are doing.'

The Prime Minister remained on good terms with his Foreign Secretary. In January 1877 he asked Derby to introduce him to the House of Lords. He phrased the request with some cunning: 'What do you think of introducing me to the House of Lords? I know it would bore you, and I always try to save you from being bored, but one has a feeling that it would be the proper thing.' Derby replied the same day: 'I should have felt sorry ... if you had applied to anyone but me ... Considering we have pulled together for nearly 30 years I think that office of friendship is mine by right, and I accept it with real pleasure.'

That part of the British public which had denounced Turkish atrocities in 1876 fell silent in 1877. Gladstone's second pamphlet on the atrocities, *Lessons in Massacre*, published in January, was a flop. There was again a noisy agitation but this time against the Russians, not Turkey. This fury was strongly shared by the Queen who, as 1876 rolled into 1877, became a determined player in the tragicomedy. Disraeli assured others that he was doing his best to attempt to restrain her, but his flattery often had the opposite effect. 'Oh if the Queen were a man,' she wrote at one point, 'she would like to go and give those horrid Russians, whose word one cannot trust, such a beating.' The Queen had initially been horrified by the reports of Bulgarian atrocities, but on 21 March 1877 she wrote to Disraeli: 'This mawkish sentimentality for people who hardly deserve the name of real Christians, as if they were more God's creatures and our fellow-creatures than every other nation abroad, and forgetting the great interests of this great country – is really incomprehensible. Only say if the Queen can do anything ...'

Increasingly, the political controversy became bitter and divisive. Both Derby and Disraeli believed that a strong class element was at play, with the upper and lower classes in favour of standing firm against Russia, while the middle classes urged neutrality. Indeed, as time went on Derby used this argument on Disraeli, saying that the middle classes would never forgive a government which wasted tens of millions on a war with Russia. But Disraeli was not impressed by such reasoning, noting that 'fortunately the middle classes did not now govern'.

Meanwhile diplomacy continued to fail. Everything hinged on the position of Austria. So long as Austria favoured a diplomatic solution she acted as a block on Russian ambitions. But unbeknownst to Disraeli, the wily Andrássy had already been squared by the Russians. By a secret convention signed by Russia and Austria, the Russians promised Andrássy that Austria would be allowed to occupy Bosnia-Herzegovina if she remained neutral in a Russo-Turkish war. A final, futile attempt to find a diplomatic solution occurred a few weeks later when the Russian Envoy, Count Ignatyev, visited England. But his protestations of goodwill failed to convince. Finally, after months of manoeuvring, on 24 April 1877 Russia declared war on Turkey.

Three days earlier another prolonged discussion in Cabinet ended with Derby and most of his colleagues blocking a decision on any pre-emptive military or naval action to secure Constantinople. Derby took the unheroic view that if war broke out, 'the first thing to do was to ascertain the views of the other Powers'. Now a clear split appeared in Cabinet. Salisbury and the Colonial Secretary Carnarvon were even more emphatic than Derby against helping Turkey. Disraeli meanwhile began to toy with the idea of war. Derby saw himself as keeping the balance inside Cabinet; this was becoming more difficult as feeling 'out-of-doors' became more anti-Russian each day.

The day after Russia declared war, the Cabinet held yet another discussion. Again, no conclusions were reached. Derby analysed Disraeli's attitude, which he found 'bouncing and excited ... his state of mind makes me uneasy: he evidently thinks that for England to look on at a war, without interfering even for a limited time, is a humiliating position: and of the injury to finance and industry which would be caused by taking an active part he either does not care to think, or considers that such sacrifices are a less evil than playing a secondary part. In this view of things he has the Court with him, the army and navy of course, and a section of the public but that section though noisy is small.' Derby added that he was coming into 'a sort of antagonism to the Premier, with whom I have hitherto acted in the closest union'. In order to block the Prime Minister's policies, Derby began to deploy a new tactic in Cabinet discussions which Lord Carnarvon described as 'wet-blanketing'.

Through the summer of 1877 the crisis showed faint signs of easing. The lynchpin was the security of Constantinople. In May the Cabinet summoned up enough unity for Derby to send a warning to Russia that Britain had vital interests which would be put at risk by military action that threatened the Gulf, Egypt, the Suez Canal straits or Constantinople: 'Her Majesty's Government are not prepared to witness with indifference that passing into other hands than those of its present possessors of a capital holding so peculiar and commanding a position.' But this was as far as they would go.

As the months passed, war between Britain and Russia grew more likely. But, contrary to the expectation of the British military authorities and just about everyone else, in July the Turks themselves held up the Russian advance. In

Britain lingering concerns about Turkish atrocities in Bulgaria were finally brushed aside by the fame of the Turkish General Osman Pasha, who for five months gallantly defended the fortress of Plevna against the attacks of the Grand Duke Nicholas. But this could only be a temporary pause. Although both warring countries were administratively weak and quickly exhausted, clear-sighted observers knew that eventually the Russians would resume their campaign.

Faced with this prospect, Disraeli tried to seize control of the agenda. On 15 August he proposed to Cabinet that a message should be sent to the Russians saying that Britain would not remain neutral in the event of a second Russian campaign in the New Year. But the numbers in Cabinet held against him. Disraeli, unable to defeat Derby by frontal argument, turned on the diplomats. On 13 September he wrote approving several appointments, but adding, 'I wish we could get rid of the whole lot. They seem to me quite useless. It is difficult to control events, but none of them try to. I think Odo Russell the worst of all. He contents himself with reporting all Bismarck's cynical bravado which he evidently listens to in an ecstasy of sycophantic wonder.' This splendid barrage of letters, written in Disraeli's sprawling hand on small sheets of notepaper thickly lined with mourning black in memory of Mary Anne, should rank in any anthology of prime-ministerial exhortation.

In October, Disraeli went to Brighton to improve his health and recover his energy. He used the time to reflect more widely on foreign policy. He worried that the European power which was profiting most from the Eastern Crisis was Germany. There seemed to be no limits to Bismarck's skulduggery. On 20 October he wrote to Corry: 'For my own part, I believe Bismarck is contemplating the partition of France, & if Spain, instead of 15 mil of population, had 30 ... so that she cd send 500,000 armed men into the field, I believe Germany,

Italy & Spain – & perhaps Belgium let in for a slice – could do it. I don't think B wishes to destroy an Empire, but he wishes to deprive us of all our influence. An Empire without influence wd not be of long duration. Yours, B.'

By now, the mood of the country was febrile. The Queen, encouraged by Disraeli, turned strongly against both Russia and Lord Derby. She was enraged that British warnings to Russia against any occupation of Constantinople were diluted and made useless as they passed through the Foreign Office: 'she <u>urged strongly</u> ... the <u>importance</u> of the CZAR knowing that we <u>will not let him have Constantinople!</u> ... It maddens the Queen to feel that all our efforts are being destroyed by the Ministers who ought to carry them out. The Queen must say that she can't stand it!' The Queen wrote against a background of growing public enthusiasm for a showdown with the Russians. At one banquet Disraeli was heckled by a patriotic lady: 'What are you waiting for, Lord Beaconsfield?' He responded: 'At this moment for the potatoes, madam.' Meanwhile a new word entered the English language in a music hall song: 'We don't want to fight, but by jingo if we do, we've got the ships, we've got the men, we've got the money too.'

But a wide body of opinion maintained a quite different view. It was from this point that Gladstone's most bitter hatred of Disraeli can be dated. His own suspicions had been aroused when someone recommended that he read *Tancred*. This book, with its elaborate tales of Eastern mysteries, and the advice given to the Queen by the duplicitous Fakredeen that she should move her capital from London to Delhi, confirmed Gladstone in his opinion that deeper forces were driving Disraeli's behaviour. 'I have a strong suspicion that Dizzy's crypto-Judaism has had to do with this policy,' he had told the Duke of Argyll. 'The Jews of the East *bitterly* hate the Christians; who have not always used them well.'

Others sank into outright anti-Semitism. The *Church Times* called Disraeli the 'Jew Premier' and Robert Browning produced his own take on the popular poem: 'I don't want to fight; But, by Jingo, if I do, The man whose head I'd like to punch is Beaconsfield the Jew.'

None of this distracted the Prime Minister. He prided himself on the thick sheet of expressionless armour which he used in the face of such taunts. Meanwhile he continued to chip away at the caution and evasiveness of his Cabinet. Through the autumn, he kept up a friendly relationship with his Foreign Secretary. Despite the strains, Derby admired Disraeli's speech at the Mansion House on 9 November for its caution and tact. 'Ill or well his pluck never fails, and he had his reward in an enthusiastic audience.' But in private conversation Disraeli was constantly shifting his ground. In truth Disraeli, though anxious to keep Derby, could not conceal his unchanged appetite for a different and much bolder policy. By 27 November Derby was again doubting whether the two of them could get through the winter together.

The real question was whether the Prime Minister could find a way of breaking the firm majority which Derby could still muster in the Cabinet for peace and caution. Firmly aligned on Derby's side were Salisbury and Carnarvon, plus the Chancellor of the Exchequer, Stafford Northcote. This group was also supported by Lord Cairns, Richard Cross and the new First Lord of the Admiralty, W.H. Smith, who had joined the Cabinet following the death of Ward Hunt earlier that year. Disraeli had a small band of supporters urging for a more active policy, in particular Lord John Manners and Gathorne Hardy. But he could not act as he, the Queen and much of the press wished so long as the Cabinet continued to hold against him, and while Derby controlled the formal machinery of decision-taking.

On 14 December Disraeli launched his next offensive in

Cabinet. He urged that Parliament be recalled as soon as possible; that a large extra sum should be voted for the Army
and Navy, and that Britain should peremptorily put herself
forward to mediate between the Turks and Russians. Derby's
counter-arguments were now weaker because of events on
the ground. On 9 December Plevna had fallen and the Russian army had resumed its long march, crawling ineptly but
irresistibly in thick snow through the mountains towards
Constantinople. Derby had to fall back on the judgement derived from his conversations with the Russian Ambassador
in London, Count Shuvalov, that the Tsar had no intention
of permanently occupying the city or the straits – unless provoked by British action. Even so, and despite a formidable
speech by Disraeli to Cabinet on 17 December, Derby managed to draw the teeth of the Prime Minister's proposal. At
a further meeting the following day, the Cabinet agreed on
a set of compromise proposals, including that Parliament
should meet on 17 January. They then parted for the holiday, uneasy but still in one piece.

In achieving this success, Derby had summoned the middle-class Ministers as reinforcements. 'We can hardly make a
change of proceeding without consulting such men as Cross
and Northcote – who will have to bear the chief burden of
defending [in the Commons] whatever we do.' Meanwhile,
Disraeli had called in a higher authority on his side. On Saturday 15 December, by chance the anniversary of Mary Anne's
death, the Queen had travelled to Hughenden to take lunch
with Disraeli. Together with Princess Beatrice, the Queen
before departing planted two trees on the south lawn. This
public mark of support was all the more powerful and telling
as it was the first time the Queen had visited the home of a
serving Prime Minister since the time of her beloved Peel.

Over Christmas, Disraeli and Derby brooded in their re-
spective country houses. Disraeli knew that, given time,

the Cabinet would come round to a more assertive position; the key pivot was the view of Salisbury. As we have seen, Salisbury had initially disappointed the Prime Minister, who thought he had been duped by the Russians at Constantinople. In his own mind Salisbury had long ago rejected as out of date the traditional British policy of helping Turkey, to which Disraeli still clung. In September 1876 Salisbury had written to Disraeli: 'it is clear enough that the traditional Palmerstonian policy is at an end. We have not the power even if we have the will to give back any of the revolted districts to the discretionary government of the Porte.' But by the end of 1877 there was no longer any question about restoring Turkey's possessions. The British interest now lay in tough diplomacy and in holding back the Russian advance.

This analysis played on Salisbury's mind as he began to revise his own position over the winter. Sensing this shift, Derby wrote to Salisbury on 23 December, a long and frank letter – in effect, a final appeal to those prejudices which he supposed that as British aristocrats the two men shared. Derby had worked closely with Disraeli as a political friend for many years, but this crisis had opened up the feeling that somehow Disraeli was different. After analysing the background he wrote of Disraeli: 'He believes thoroughly in "prestige" – as all foreigners do, and would think it (quite sincerely) in the interests of the country to spend 200 millions on a war if the result was to make foreign states think more highly of us as a military power. These ideas are intelligible but they are not mine or yours, and their being sincerely held does not make them less dangerous.'

But Derby's appeal came too late. Salisbury was already on the move in the opposite direction. It is hard to believe that personal ambition played no part in that move; indeed soon after Derby's letter, Salisbury had received a private communication from the Prime Minister himself. Once again,

Disraeli threw a hint that before long he would hold a new
position if he made the right decision. 'You and I must go together into the depth of the affair,' Disraeli urged his Indian
Secretary, 'and settle what we are prepared to do.'

The crunch came in the New Year. Lord Carnarvon
made an unwise speech to a deputation of South African
merchants, saying that nobody in the country was 'insane
enough' to desire a repetition of the Crimean War. Disraeli
made the most of this mistake, ticking Carnarvon off in front
of the Cabinet and suggesting that he might like to consider
his position. But others in the Cabinet came to Carnarvon's
defence and encouraged him to remain in his post, including
Salisbury. The Cabinet thus clung together and so Disraeli
returned to the central issue, namely the need for bold measures against Russia.

An undated speaking note gives a vivid impression of the
arguments Disraeli used around this time. 'We are on the eve
of great events: you are called upon in yr generation to solve
that mighty difficulty which perplexed your forefathers, and
which diplomacy for $\frac{1}{2}$ a century has attempted to avert or
procrastinate: The Eastern Question is not the concern of a
few million subjects of the Porte, the descendants of conquered tribes. This is the subterfuge of diplomacy, playing
with the amiable but too often thoughtless sympathies of humanity. The veil is rent – the Eastern Question is the partition
of the Empire of the Ottomans ... The impending wars may
be intermittent but they will be long, & when the states of
the world assemble round the council table to desire peace,
rest assured, that some powers will be absent who now speak
with authority.'

Unfortunately for Disraeli, these arguments did not work.
On 12 January 1878 he was again defeated in Cabinet. Derby,
Carnarvon and Salisbury resisted a proposal for an expe-
dition to seize Gallipoli and hold it as a guarantee for the

security of the Dardanelles. Meanwhile, in the Lords Disraeli had begun to lay the ground for a new policy. In another speaking note he turned the humanitarian argument on its head, arguing that the real atrocities were not those carried out by the Turks in Bulgaria, but those committed by the invading Russians against Turkey. 'What should – and does, I hope – absorb our attention most is the vast, the unspeakable, mass of human suffering brought on by this invasion. I do not merely speak, my Lords, of the wounds and death and lingering sickness inseparable from armed strife – but of the desolated provinces – the ruined homes – the thousands of hapless persons – Christian & non Christian – driven hither and thither by the red wave of war. Some of the fairest regions of Europe have been transformed by this campaign – however lofty its objects – into Golgothas – and if all that we can desire, in our most hopeful moments for the amelioration of Bulgaria could be realised I fear its cost wd have to be set already at a price in human bloodshed too dreadful to contemplate.'

Battle resumed in Cabinet in three crucial meetings on 21, 22 and 23 January. At the last of these meetings, Disraeli told the Cabinet that their reputation would be ruined if they did not at once agree to send ironclad ships through the Dardanelles to Constantinople and ask Parliament for an emergency grant of £6 million. Salisbury had by now turned full circle and became fierce in supporting Disraeli. Derby and Carnarvon, overruled at last, both resigned from the Cabinet. But the next day the situation changed. A telegram arrived from Henry Layard in Constantinople advising the Government that Turkey and Russia had agreed to open peace negotiations, and that the terms should be settled at a congress attended by all the Great European Powers. This removed the need for Britain to send the fleet to Constantinople, and the following day the naval order was countermanded.

It turned out that Layard's telegram was a mistake, and the Russians had no intention of negotiating collectively. But by this point the fleet had returned to its original holding position, and it seemed farcical for it to be moved for a third time. All this meant that there was no longer any reason for Derby to resign and, under pressure from the Conservative Whips who were alarmed at a wider disintegration of the Government, Disraeli agreed that he should be urged to remain in Cabinet. After a day of thought, Derby rescinded his decision. 'I am a check on the Prime Minister, and though I do not put much faith on them I have the assurances of several of my colleagues that they will support me in resisting a war-policy.'

But his position was now fatally undermined. Colleagues who had supported him flaked away despite their assurances. Disraeli increasingly took foreign policy into his own hands. By this time the Prime Minister had his own particular confidant in St Petersburg, the British military attaché Colonel Frederick Wellesley. Professor Vincent describes the Colonel as 'a classic Victorian scoundrel ... a young rogue, a Disraelian young man'. The previous summer he had been accused by Salisbury of corruption, and two years later he ruined his career by capturing a lady called Kate Vaughan, who was not only a dancer and actress but the mistress of a member of White's Club. In 1878 however Wellesley was still well connected at Court and with the Prime Minister. Rumours originating with the Colonel suggested that the Russians were kept intimately informed of Cabinet discussions, either by Derby or his wife in their conversations with Shuvalov. There was even a juicy rumour that Shuvalov and Lady Derby were sleeping together. The Ambassador was certainly a friend of the Derbys, and Derby often spoke frankly to him as a known supporter of the peace party in St Petersburg. But Disraeli and other Ministers regularly chatted to foreign diplomats about politics. No one was more naturally communicative than Disraeli. Indeed Derby complained in his diary and to Disraeli of leaks from the Cabinet, which he would hardly have done if he were the main culprit. But the Queen and those sympathetic to her increasingly looked on the Derbys as halfway to being traitors. Disraeli did nothing to counter this view. By now he had abandoned the effort to keep on board the Foreign Secretary who had consistently and successfully blocked his ambition for an adventurous foreign policy.

Events now closed in on Derby. The Russian army hovered on the outskirts of Constantinople, waiting for the Tsar to give the order to take the city. The British fleet dropped anchor off Constantinople on 15 February. A few days before, Derby saw Disraeli and discussed the situation. For weeks they had been avoiding one another, using Stafford Northcote as an intermediary. But now, face to face, the Prime Minister set out his views. In his diary Derby recorded that Disraeli was 'excited and inclined to swagger, saying war was unavoidable; it would last three years; it would be a glorious and successful war for England ... I dissented but said little; being in truth disgusted with his reckless way of talking.'

The final straw came in March. On 3 March the Turks signed with Russia the Treaty of San Stefano, which gave the Russians and their friends sweeping gains in the Balkans and Central Asia. Of particular concern was a new and large independent state of Bulgaria which would be vulnerable to Russian pressure. This was intolerable to Disraeli. He demanded that the treaty be decided at a Great Power conference, but Russia ignored this request. On 27 March the Cabinet agreed to mobilise the army reserves and move a sizeable number of troops from India to the Mediterranean. There was also talk of seizing a suitable Turkish territory to use as a permanent British *place d'armes*. This changed the game. The Russians backed down as the troops moved from India to Malta and agreed to discuss the peace treaty at a new European Congress. But Derby had reached the end of the road. He received no support from any colleague in Cabinet when arguing against the new policy and handed in his resignation, which this time he did not rescind. The following day he made a short resignation statement in Parliament, to which Disraeli replied cordially and with dignity. So ended the longest and most productive partnership of Disraeli's political career.

Disraeli had already marked out a replacement. Once he had appointed Salisbury as Derby's successor, Disraeli was content to delegate the detail. He decided to trust his new Foreign Secretary in spite of their past problems and quarrels. More than that, he gave Salisbury almost a free rein in resolving in advance by secret diplomacy the main issues which would make or break the European Congress.

Within hours of taking office, Salisbury had set out his new policy in sweeping and magisterial tones. On 1 April a circular dispatch was sent out to all British diplomatic positions. This did not go into detail about the objectionable Treaty of San Stefano which the Russians had imposed on Turkey, but concentrated on its general effect. This was 'to depress almost to the point of entire subjection, the political independence of the Government of Constantinople'. It was unacceptable to Britain that Turkey 'should be so closely pressed by the political force of a greatly superior power that its independent actions, and even existence, is almost impossible'. Britain would only join in a congress which was able to examine the Treaty of San Stefano as a whole to remedy this defect.

The next few weeks were crucial. If Disraeli had been in sole charge he would have relied on fleet movements and defiant public speeches designed to catch the anti-Russian mood, in all probability provoking war. If Derby had been in charge he would have allowed matters to develop at their own pace, relying on Bismarck to restrain the Russians and anyway not persuaded that they intended Britain any serious harm. By contrast Salisbury embarked on a highly energetic diplomatic enterprise, designed to check the Russians without war. He acted with the benevolent understanding of Bismarck, who had already established himself as the chief arbiter of European affairs but was content to stand aside from an active role in this particular episode. The great Chancellor was suffering painfully from shingles, and he was happy to see the Russians blocked in the Balkans so long as this was done without infuriating the Tsar, and without a war in which Germany might have to take sides.

Within a month, Salisbury reached in private three interlocking agreements with the three governments most closely involved. With the Russian Ambassador Shuvalov he agreed a complicated rearrangement of boundaries in the Balkans. The new pro-Russian state of Bulgaria would not as in the Treaty of San Stefano stretch south beyond the Carpathian mountain range. A province south of the mountains would remain under Turkish sovereignty. In return the Russians would be allowed to keep their conquests in Central Asia, notably the fortresses of Kars and Batum.

The two outstanding questions were the attitudes of Austria and Turkey. The negotiations with Austria were not difficult. Andrássy was granted his wish to occupy Bosnia-Herzegovina, but his other schemes for reordering the Balkans came to nothing. More difficult was the attitude of the Sultan in Constantinople. The Sultan lived in an atmosphere of confused conspiracies, fearing for his throne and his life. On one matter he was clear: he was desperately short of money, and needed £4 million urgently so that he could include meat in his soldiers' rations. With Disraeli's consent,

Salisbury managed some of his most pressing concerns by offering a British guarantee of Turkish security. He also rescued for the Sultan a slice of southern Bulgaria which he was no longer particularly interested in. But Salisbury now turned from protector to predator, and joined in the hunt for spoils by demanding a *place d'armes* for Britain in the Mediterranean from which it could carry out its promised protection of Turkey. The Sultan was given only forty-eight hours to consider this proposed secret convention; the deadline expired on the day of the Queen's birthday party in the new Foreign Office building. News of Turkish acceptance arrived just in time.

At a crucial moment a badly paid copyist at the Foreign Office leaked the draft Anglo-Russian agreement to the *Globe* newspaper before all the other pieces on the board were in place. Salisbury denied the report, which was largely accurate. By nature given to frankness, even to indiscretion, he nevertheless would have thought it pedantic to allow literal truth to put his enterprise in danger.

The way was now clear for the carefully planned European Congress. In a bow to Bismarck's dominance of European diplomacy, Berlin was selected as the preferred location. The next question was who should represent Britain. There was no precedent for a Prime Minister to attend such a conference, and the Queen was worried about the health of her favourite. But Disraeli was not one to be held back by such things. He set out on 8 June and travelled at a leisurely rate, dining with the King of the Belgians in Brussels on the way. He arrived in Berlin at 8 p.m. on 11 June, taking residence in the Kaiserhof Hotel.

In his heart, Disraeli must have realised that this would be the climax of his career. He was now constantly ill and hobbled about on the arm of Monty Corry. But he was determined to enjoy his first and last international conference.

Disraeli, the classless but class-conscious novelist, relished the company of chancellors, princes and European plenipotentiaries who formed the conference delegates. He played to the full his part in the pageant of balls and banquets which made up the conference routine. 'Der alte Jude, das ist der Mann,' was how Bismarck described Disraeli during the congress, and Disraeli thoroughly earned the accolade. After fifteen years of relative inaction, Britain was back at the heart of European diplomacy. It was the theatre Disraeli had yearned for throughout his long and turbulent career.

But Disraeli's role at the congress, though stylish, fell short of masterful. He never grasped the details of negotiations, and Salisbury wrote of 'the Chief': 'he is not really false; but has such a perfect disregard for facts that it is almost impossible for him to run true'. Disraeli also found Bismarck's way of speaking incomprehensible, prompting Salisbury to complain again: 'Disraeli has the dimmest idea of what is going on – understands everything crossways – and imagines a perpetual conspiracy.' Of particular concern to the Foreign Secretary was Disraeli's grasp of geography: 'Lord Beaconsfield can't negotiate; he has never seen a map of Asia Minor.'

There was also a more practical problem. Then, as now, French was the official language of diplomacy – but Disraeli was a master of no language but his own. As a way out of this difficulty, the British Ambassador in Berlin, Odo Russell, suggested that instead of stumbling his way through in broken French, Disraeli might like to address the congress in English; after all, or so he said, the delegates were agog to hear the famous novelist speak in his mother tongue. Disraeli found himself persuaded by this idea, and the moment passed without disaster.

Faced with these and other limitations, the bulk of the work at the conference fell to Salisbury. There were a number of important questions at stake: the name of the new province in southern Bulgaria (Disraeli was keen that it should not share its larger neighbour's name to avoid pressure for unification); the Sultan's military rights in this new province; and the right of Russia to fortify the Central Asian port of Batum. On the first two issues Salisbury was successful and resisted Russian demands, but he was obliged to compromise on the Russian role at Batum and the Russians turned it into a formidable naval fortress within a few years.

The masterstroke from Disraeli's point of view was the announcement to the world of Britain's new *place d'armes* in the Mediterranean. This had been the subject of much deliberation before the congress. Where should it be? Mitylene, Lemnus, Acre and Crete had all been suggested; all four had supporters and critics. Some had poor harbours; Crete had too many Greeks. In the end the lot had fallen on Cyprus. Disraeli attempted to coin a new cliché in explaining this choice to the Queen: 'Cyprus is the key to Western Asia', he claimed. The agreement with Turkey to cede this possession had been agreed earlier in the summer, but had been kept secret until almost the end of the Berlin Congress. When at last it was unveiled, there was a great sensation at this latest conjuring turn from the master performer. In Parliament the Liberals were sceptical about this new possession, with Lord Granville claiming, wrongly, that Cyprus was further from the Dardanelles than Malta, which Britain already possessed. But none of this detracted from the central impression created by Disraeli of the Cyprus Convention, which was that it was an unparalleled success.

The Treaty of Berlin was signed on 13 July. Disraeli returned home the following day, arriving in London on 16 July. Charing Cross Station had been decked out with flowers to greet his arrival, the whole foliage amounting to some 10,000 plants. Large crowds also gathered, many of whom had been recruited for the purpose by Disraeli's old friend

Lord Henry Lennox. Disraeli left the train on Salisbury's arm and the two men drove in an open barouche to Downing Street. On arrival the Prime Minister read a letter of congratulations from the Queen and told the cheering crowds through the windows: 'Lord Salisbury and I have brought you back peace, but peace with honour.'

It was the high watermark of Disraeli's career. In political terms the Government were on a high tide, and for a few weeks Disraeli was regarded as a national hero. The Queen offered him a dukedom and a barony for his nephew, all of which he declined; but he agreed to receive the Order of the Garter along with Salisbury. The whole nation seemed to hum the jingo tune. Not even Gladstone's onslaughts could dampen the mood. Indeed, when Gladstone's attacks were put to him, Disraeli responded with one of his most famous counter-attacks: 'a sophistical rhetorician inebriated with the exuberance of his own verbosity'.

There are two ways to look at the Congress of Berlin. On the one hand, the Ottoman Empire survived for another forty years without causing a new European war. On the other, the Ottoman Empire crumbled within forty years, helping to cause the First World War. Either way, there was no doubt that the Ottoman Empire had been gravely weakened by the Eastern Crisis. Henceforth it survived on sufferance alone. Within seven years a new, big Bulgaria had come into existence, despite British protests; but this proved to be a far more effective barrier on Russian ambitions than the Ottoman Empire had ever been.

The direct impact of the congress on Britain itself is debatable. It is true that the alliance between Russia, Austria and Germany had been breached. This made the European scene more fluid and gave Britain a stronger voice in Continental diplomacy. But in terms of territorial gains and imperial strategy, the outcome for Britain was negative. Disraeli had checked Russian ambition but not reversed it. Disraeli's own reputation helped to defuse the criticism of the 'jingoes', who were indignant that Russia had been able to avoid total humiliation in Asia and had held on to Kars and Batum. A more valid criticism was passed by the historian A.J.P. Taylor almost a hundred years later in this pithy epitaph on the congress: 'Great Britain won a bloodless victory with a music hall song, a navy of museum pieces and no land forces at all, except the 7,000 troops sent demonstratively to Malta ... The resounding achievement of 1878 weakened the effectiveness of British policy in the long run; for it led the British public to believe that they could play a great role without expense or exertion – without reforming their navy, without creating an army, without finding an ally.'

None of this dented Disraeli's enthusiasm. Once again, the mythmaker worked his magic. Britain had baffled Russia through her policy of daring, and in doing so she had expanded her empire. 'Her Majesty has fleets and armies which are second to none,' he told the House of Lords. 'England must have seen with pride the Mediterranean covered with her ships ... But it is not on our fleets and armies, however necessary they may be for the maintenance of our material strength, that I alone or mainly depend in that enterprise on which this country is about to enter. It is on what I most highly value – the consciousness that in the Eastern nations there is confidence in this country, and that while they know we can enforce our policy, at the same time, they know that our Empire is an Empire of liberty, of truth, and of justice.'

On 6 August Disraeli and Salisbury received a mass deputation from almost a thousand Conservative Associations at the Foreign Office, each one stopping to shake Disraeli's hand. Three days earlier Disraeli had received the Freedom of the City of London. But one of the most remarkable tributes was paid by Cardinal Newman in a private letter. 'As to Disraeli's firework, I confess I am much dazzled with it ... It is a grand idea, that of hugging from love the Turk to death, instead of the Russian bear ... And then it opens such a view of England, great in the deeds of their forefathers, shewing that they are not degenerate sons, but rising with the occasion ... And then it is so laughably clever a move, in a grave diplomatic congress – and then it opens such wonderful views of the future – that I am overcome by it.'

THE ASSIDUOUS MUMMY

Taken together, the Congress of Berlin and the Cyprus Convention made a great confection of myth and achievement. The question now was what to do next. On 10 August the Cabinet met to consider their options. One idea was to hold an early general election. There were obvious political arguments in favour of an appeal to the electorate, but for once Disraeli put partisan concerns to one side. Parliament had been elected in 1874; this meant that, under the law at that time, it still had some two and a half years left to run. There was no constitutional case for holding an election before the end of this allotted period. Even for Disraeli, the idea of dissolving Parliament at this particular moment in 1878 seemed too opportunistic. Better to carry on and build on the momentum which was now with the Conservatives.

We do not know whether Disraeli later regretted this decision. But it was undoubtedly a mistake. From the summer of 1878 onwards, Disraeli and the Government were weakened, held back and ultimately destroyed by a series of setbacks across domestic and foreign politics, many of which were beyond their control. Within two years the cheering crowds of Charing Cross Station had faded to a warm but distant memory as a noisy and unhappy electorate took their revenge on Disraeli's Government.

One of the ironies of our history is the way that many Prime

Ministers are brought down by those same areas of policy on which they had once built their reputations. Thus Anthony Eden, who had forged a career based on skilful diplomacy, was broken as Prime Minister by the Suez Crisis. Similarly Gordon Brown, who for a decade dominated the economy, was unhorsed by this very subject when he at last made it to Number 10. As it was for these men, so it proved for Disraeli who, beginning in 1878, came under siege on those very subjects where he had made his name, namely imperial policy and the defence of agricultural interests.

Imperial problems came first and were, at least initially, a hangover from the Eastern Crisis. Earlier in the summer of 1878, the Russians had sent a military delegation to Kabul in response to the movement of British troops from India to the Mediterranean. This seemingly innocuous move was viewed with great hostility by the British administration in India. For two years the British had been attempting to secure their own Military Delegation in Afghanistan, but they had repeatedly been rebuffed by the Ameer. Now, with Russia seemingly poised on India's doorstep, there was pandemonium among the British officials in India.

The prime promoter of pandemonium was the British Viceroy himself. Disraeli had selected for this delicate position the son of his old literary companion, Bulwer-Lytton. Robert Lytton had inherited from his father an erratic temperament and a degree of poetic skill. Disraeli warmly admired these talents; indeed they were the main reason for his appointment. As he explained for the benefit of Lord Salisbury: 'Had it been a routine age, we might have made, what might be called, a more prudent selection, but we foresaw what might occur and indeed saw what was occurring; we wanted a man of ambition, imagination, some vanity and much will – and we have got him.' But there was a price to pay.

The key issue for Indian administrators was the security of

the northern frontier. Afghanistan had been a long-standing problem for successive viceroys and there was a strong temptation to carry British influence into that country as a barrier against Russia. Disraeli himself was by instinct a strong supporter of a forward policy, explaining at one point that 'I have always been opposed to and deplored, "masterly inactivity".' He was therefore inclined to favour moves to extend British influence into Afghanistan. Consequently, when Lytton was appointed in 1876 his specific brief was to persuade the Ameer to receive a British delegation in his capital city.

For two years Lytton faithfully followed these instructions. But each application ended without success. Lytton was therefore understandably frustrated when he received news that the Ameer had welcomed a rival Russian delegation at Kabul. He immediately pressed for its dismissal – but back in Britain, the Cabinet took a more leisurely approach. The Secretary of State for India at this point was Gathorne Hardy, by now Lord Cranbrook, who had lost all interest in politics and spent the summer deerstalking in Scotland. On 19 August the Foreign Office sent a dispatch to St Petersburg protesting at the Russian mission, but Lytton did not hear of this missive for almost a month. Meanwhile Lytton had taken matters into his own hands and was planning to send a British delegation up the Khyber Pass to Kabul. When the Cabinet heard of this agenda, a firm order was sent to delay the mission and also to take a different route, through Kandahar. But Lytton pressed on and on 21 September the delegation set off up the Khyber Pass.

What happened next bordered on farce. The British mission never made it into Afghanistan. Far from restoring British prestige, they were humiliated at the border and forced to return to India. This snub changed the game. Regardless of their own views, Disraeli and the Government now had no choice but to come to the aid of their unruly Viceroy; the preservation of prestige was at stake. In October Parliament was recalled and an ultimatum was sent to the Ameer, demanding that he accept a permanent British military mission in Afghanistan. When no reply was forthcoming, a full invasion began on 21 November.

Within weeks the Afghans had been crushed by British forces and the Ameer had fled his throne. He was replaced by his son, who agreed to accept a British mission at Kabul. Prestige had been restored, but the whole situation had been a great nuisance for Disraeli: 'When V-Roys and Comms-in-Chief disobey orders, they ought to be sure of their success in their mutiny,' he complained to Cranbrook.

As the year came to a close, Disraeli returned to Hughenden where he spent Christmas alone with his servants. On 27 December he wrote to Lady Bradford: 'I have now been here a week tomorrow and have not spoken to anyone.' He returned to London on Monday 10 February, hoping that this peacefulness might continue during the new session of Parliament. It did not. Parliament was due to open on 13 February, but two days beforehand news broke of an unprecedented imperial catastrophe, this time in South Africa. On 22 January a British force of 1,200 soldiers had been slaughtered in their camp at Isandlwana by 20,000 Zulu warriors.

The news hit Disraeli like a bolt from clear sky. For several days he was prostrate and unable to do anything meaningful beyond writing lamely to the Queen: 'It will change everything, reduce our Continental influence, and embarrass our finances.' The general feeling amongst the public was that the disaster at Isandlwana was as serious as the Indian Mutiny, and its impact on the national psyche was almost as significant. But in truth the tragedy was predictable and should have been predicted, for South African policy had been under heavy strain throughout the previous year.

When Disraeli had come to power in 1874, the situation in South Africa had been unhappy but straightforward. A number of settler communities jostled for authority; British settlers and Boers struggled to find an accommodation with the native populations. The real difficulty was in the Transvaal, where clashes between Zulus and Boers threatened to spill out across South Africa. It was for this reason that the Colonial Secretary, Lord Carnarvon, embarked on a policy of confederation across South Africa and annexation of the Boer republic of Transvaal as a way of restoring order to South Africa in general.

To prepare the way, Lord Carnarvon had sent out his friend, the historian J.A. Froude, to examine the scope for confederation. At the time Disraeli had accepted the case for confederation as a way of restoring stability to South Africa, but he showed no real interest in the subject and was increasingly irritated by the trouble the policy seemed to create. On 13 May 1878 Monty Corry reported: 'Ld. B. is extremely dissatisfied with all that has taken, or is taking, place at the Cape. The troubles commenced by Lord Carnarvon, who, he says, lived mainly in a coterie of editors of Liberal papers who praised him and drank his claret, sending Mr Froude – a desultory and theoretical litterateur who wrote more rot on the reign of Elizabeth than Gibbon required for all the Decline and Fall – to reform the Cape, which ended naturally in a Kaffir War ...'

But by this time the annexation of the Transvaal had been completed with the grudging support of the Boers, while Carnarvon had resigned as Colonial Secretary over the Eastern Crisis. Policy-making was now in the hands of his successor Sir Michael Hicks Beach, along with the Governor of Cape Colony, Sir Henry Bartle Frere. These two men now found that in taking control of the Transvaal they had in effect inherited the Boer war with the native Zulu population. Frere himself was a highly respected and experienced imperial administrator, with an impressive record in India to his name. But he was ruthlessly ambitious and believed the only way to bring about long-term stability was for the Zulus, under their leader, Cetawayo, to abandon their warlike culture and submit to British rule. He therefore began to press hard for a showdown with the Zulus and the situation became volatile.

The flaw in South African policy throughout these years was the absence of the telegram. There was no cable to the Cape, which meant that any urgent information was delayed as telegraphs were sent by steamer from the Cape Verde Islands, a journey which took sixteen days. This made it almost impossible for the Cabinet in London to restrain Frere, or even to understand his intentions. As the autumn of 1878 wore on, Frere continually ignored or wilfully misinterpreted instructions not to escalate the situation as he sought to lay the foundations for his policy of confederation.

Sensing danger, and following an appeal by Frere for extra support in South Africa, the Cabinet agreed to send reinforcements in November 1878, but with the clear proviso that these should be used for defensive purposes only. But on 11 December Frere again defied his instructions and submitted an ultimatum to Cetawayo demanding that the Zulu population abandon their practice of prohibiting marriage by males before they had shed blood in battle. This insistence on 'washing the spears' lay at the heart of a Zulu system based on success in war. News of this ultimatum did not reach London until the deadline had almost expired on 9 January. By this time it was too late. The Cabinet, fresh from one conflict in Afghanistan, now found themselves embroiled in another imperial war.

The report of the disaster at Isandlwana, which arrived in London early in February, was the first news from the campaign. Once Disraeli had recovered his calm, the Cabinet

found themselves in an invidious position. To remove Frere
in the middle of the conflict risked throwing the situation
into even greater confusion; but to keep him in his post implied granting approval of what he had done. The Cabinet
therefore reached the unhappy conclusion that they should
send a public reprimand to South Africa, but allow Frere to
stay in his position. In Parliament the Liberals had great joy
in dismantling this decision. Sir William Harcourt read out
an imaginary note sent by the Colonial Secretary to the Governor: 'My dear Sir Bartle Frere; I cannot think you are right.
Indeed I think you are very wrong; but after all, I feel you
know a great deal better than I do. I hope you won't do what
you are going to do; but if you do, I hope it will turn out
well.'

Almost as bad as Frere's diplomacy was the wayward
performance of Lord Chelmsford, who commanded the British forces in the Cape. For months he manoeuvred listlessly
against the Zulus, and in the end Disraeli sent Sir Garnet
Wolseley to take control of the whole situation as High Commissioner for South Africa and Commander-in-Chief. Shortly
after Wolseley arrived Chelmsford crushed the Zulu army at
Ulundi, but this did little to assuage Disraeli. Indeed, the performance of Chelmsford provoked one of Disraeli's few rows
with the Queen. The view of some, including the Queen, was
that Chelmsford's success at Ulundi had evened out the disaster at Isandlwana; he should therefore be granted a lavish
and laudatory reception on his return. But Disraeli saw things
quite differently, as he explained, with unusual firmness,
to the Queen: 'Lord Beaconsfield charges Lord Chelmsford
with having invaded Zululand "avec un Coeur léger," with
no adequate knowledge of the country he was attacking,
and no precaution or preparation. A dreadful disaster occurred in consequence, and then Lord Chelmsford became
panic-struck; appealed to yr. Majesty's Govt frantically for

reinforcements, and found himself at the head of 20,000 of yr Majesty's troops, in order to reduce a country not larger than Yorkshire.' Disraeli resisted pressure from the Queen to invite Chelmsford to Hughenden, restricting his contact with the Commander to a formal interview in Downing Street.

Before the Zulu War was completed, there was a fresh disaster in South Africa which caused particular distress to the Queen. Accompanying the British forces in South Africa was the son of the deposed French Emperor, Napoleon III. The Prince Imperial had been trained at the Military Academy at Woolwich and, with the intervention of the Queen, was granted permission to travel to South Africa as an observer with the British Army, despite the concerns of Disraeli and Salisbury. Once there, the inevitable disaster occurred. On 1 June the Prince and a scouting party were ambushed by Zulus; the scouting party fled, but when they returned they found that the Prince had been killed. The Queen was badly shaken and demanded an inquest; among Disraeli's papers there remain the detailed accounts of how the soldiers who had been accompanying the Prince had abandoned their royal charge at the crucial moment and only realised he was missing after their escape, riding back to discover the royal body with eighteen assegai wounds. The whole episode cast a baleful light on the war effort, but Disraeli's sense of humour did not fail. When he received news of the latest disaster, he is supposed to have noted: 'a very remarkable people the Zulus: they defeat our generals, they convert our bishops, they have settled the fate of a great European dynasty'.*

The wars in South Africa and Afghanistan had a corrosive effect on the Government's reputation. But they were also costly in a more literal way. On 24 July 1879 Disraeli wrote

---

*John Colenso, the Bishop of Natal, had been accused of heresy as a result of his defence of polygamy and his criticisms of Anglican orthodoxies.

to the Queen about the ruinous impact of the various military campaigns on the public finances. 'We may be said to have carried on four wars, for our movements in the Levant entailed a war expenditure, and we have done it all at a cost of 11 or 12 millions. A moiety of this has been supplied by taxation, and it would seem to me, that the other moiety might be left to posterity.' The problem Disraeli faced was that at the same time as the Government became embroiled in various military campaigns, the economy had begun to fail. Unemployment had grown from under 5 per cent in 1877 to over 11 per cent in 1879, and this coincided with a run of bankruptcies. In October 1878 the City of Glasgow Bank had failed, draining confidence from the economy. All this placed Disraeli in a difficult position, with no immediate way of paying for the wars except for raising taxation or increasing borrowing. The Chancellor, Stafford Northcote, was strongly opposed to the latter course of action, but Disraeli refused to sanction the idea that taxes might be raised in the run-up to an election. He therefore returned to his old policies of deficit spending and raiding the sinking fund. The result was that in 1879–80 alone, the Government ran a deficit of over £3 million. This put Disraeli on a collision course with Gladstone, but it avoided piling extra pressure on an increasingly unhappy electorate.

There was however one area of the economy which no amount of political chicanery could alleviate. For four years in a row, the harvest in England and Ireland had failed. Whereas previous harvest failures had resulted in an increase in wheat prices, in the late 1870s there was no countervailing effect. With the opening-up of the cornfields of the USA and the fall in the cost of international freight in a world of steam and rail, bulk imports of cheap grain flowed into the country. This was great news for consumers, but a disaster for British agriculture, as the price of wheat per quarter sank by over ten shillings within two years. Around Europe tariffs were raised to help the agricultural interest, and agitation in England now resumed for a return to the Corn Laws which Peel had destroyed in the 1840s.

The stage was set for Disraeli to complete the work he had started in 1846. Surely this was his moment to stand up and bring back Protection. Across the country, landowners looked to the Prime Minister to revive the Corn Laws or, at the very least, to implement some kind of reciprocal measures with other trading nations. After all, had Disraeli not been the chief defender of Protection in the 1840s? But of course, he did no such thing. Disraeli knew that cheap bread now trumped the agricultural interest, particularly since the Second Reform Act had enfranchised a million more voters, many of them in urban constituencies. On 28 March and 29 April 1879 he came under heavy fire in the House of Lords for refusing to take action, and took refuge in vague words about the changing circumstances. He dismissed with some difficulty what he called 'rusty phrases of mine forty years ago' and resisted the notion that this was the moment to bring back Protection. Just as Peel had experienced in 1846, so now the agricultural classes turned on Disraeli. A new Protectionist party called the Farmers' Alliance was founded and began to campaign against him.

All this was bad, but what happened next seemed much worse. On 6 September 1879, just when Disraeli thought he had come through the worst of his difficulties, news arrived that the entire British Mission in Afghanistan had been massacred in Kabul, including the Resident Envoy, Sir Louis Cavagnari. The response was firm and swift: a new invasion took place which crushed all resistance. Thenceforth the agreed policy was to divide but not conquer, as the British took command of the Southern Hills of Afghanistan but made no attempt to rule the nation as a whole, which they left to feuding warlords. It was a more satisfactory situation from the point of view of Indian security, but the episode was a devastating blow to the reputation of the Government and its imperial policies.

The disaster also brought Gladstone, frail but furious, back into the fray. Gladstone, as we have seen, had spent much of Disraeli's Government in self-imposed exile. He had returned during the Bulgarian Atrocities, although Hartington and Granville had remained in nominal control of the Liberal Opposition. But this did not restrain Gladstone and in the autumn of 1879 he decided to embark on a noisy and dramatic new campaign against Disraeli. Disraeli's foreign adventures had convinced Gladstone that the Prime Minister and his Government must be destroyed. Indeed, in one speech Gladstone cheerfully admitted that was his sole purpose, 'day and night, week by week, month by month'. What Gladstone needed however was a suitable platform for his oratory. He found this in late November 1879 when he put himself forward as the Liberal candidate for Midlothian. For two weeks at the end of November and the first week of December Gladstone vented his spleen to a sizeable section of the Scottish population. The sheer energy of the man was incredible. Aided by a young Lord Rosebery, who put to good use American campaign techniques which he had witnessed during a Democrat Convention in New York, Gladstone spoke at mass meeting after mass meeting, telling vast crowds of people that the Government was immoral and committing atrocities. 'Remember that the sanctity of life in the hill villages of Afghanistan, among the winter snows, is as inviolable in the eye of Almighty God as can be your own,' he declaimed.

Disraeli pretended not to notice these performances and took refuge in Hughenden for the final weeks of 1879. For the remainder of the year he ran the country almost entirely alone from Buckinghamshire, once again spending Christmas by himself with his servants. There is no evidence to suggest that he found this an ordeal. Several years earlier he had written to Lady Bradford: 'I never was a great admirer of a merrie Xmas, even when a boy. I always hated factitious merriment, in the form of unnecessary guzzlement, and those awful inventions, round games, worse even than forfeits, if that be possible!' His main entertainment this particular Christmas was a brief visit by the Prince of Wales on 12 January. Disraeli had been somewhat concerned by this prospect, as he admitted to the Queen: 'A Prince, who really has seen everything, and knows everybody, is a guest one might despair of interesting and amusing even for a passing hour...' But in the event the party was viewed as a great success and a welcome break from the mounting political woes.

As Disraeli returned to London early in 1880, his attention turned to the general election. The key question was when it might be. There were two choices, either in the spring or the autumn, and the temptation was to continue as long as possible before going to the country. But a string of by-election results changed his reckoning. In February Conservative candidates won key elections in both Liverpool and Southwark, suggesting that support for the Government was still strong across the country. The general view was that the election would be close, but that the Conservatives would pull through. On 6 March therefore the Cabinet agreed to dissolve Parliament immediately and two days later the dissolution was made public. Disraeli's appeal to the country appeared the following morning in the form of an open letter to the Lord Lieutenant of Ireland, the Duke of Marlborough.

The letter itself is a curious document – curious, because so underwhelming. Rather than focus on the early success of his Government, or the usefulness of Cross's domestic policies, Disraeli selected as his sole driving concern the danger

that Ireland might try to cut ties with Great Britain. It is true
that problems in Ireland, never far from the surface, had
again come to dominate the House of Commons. A new and
powerful lobby of Irish MPs under the leadership of Charles
Parnell had begun to manipulate parliamentary rules and
conventions in order to obstruct legislation. The bad harvest
that had been affecting England had also caused widespread
misery in Ireland. Disraeli had tried to address Ireland's
problems and the previous year the Government had at last
passed an Irish University Act which broadened the basis
of higher education. But to most voters in Britain, facing
growing problems in the economy and rising unemployment, these Irish issues were a distraction. Disraeli's letter
was an attempt to scare the electorate, but it failed. In an
upright, pedantic, late-Victorian way the critics complained
about grammatical mistakes in Disraeli's letter. But the main
flaw was not so much the odd faulty phrase in the letter as
the focus of the whole. Only occasionally did Disraeli's political acumen show through – for example when he called the
Liberal approach to the Colonies a 'policy of decomposition'.
But read as a whole, the letter seemed irrelevant, exaggerated
and oddly slow.

This feeling of half-heartedness coloured the whole of the
Conservative campaign. The convention of the time was that
Peers could not give speeches during an election; this meant
that half the Cabinet could in effect play no part in the campaign. Without Disraeli, Salisbury, Cairns or Cranbrook it
was left to Cross, W.H. Smith and Stafford Northcote to lead
the Conservative effort. But none of these men could match
the virtuous oratory of Gladstone and his followers; across
the country the Conservatives were outgunned by their
opponents. Indeed, in Melton Mowbray Lord John Manners
came under physical siege as he was pelted with eggshells
filled with tar gas.

Meanwhile, Disraeli suffered a damaging personal and political blow immediately before the dissolution when Lord Derby announced that he would be leaving the Conservatives and joining the Liberal Party. This meant not only the final rupture in their relationship, but also the loss of many Lancastrian votes.

The main Conservative weakness in 1880 was largely of the Party's own making. The good work which Gorst had done in 1870 had not been sustained in Government and the organisation of the national Party was a mess. By contrast, the Liberals had built up a formidable campaign machinery and it was this which Gladstone used with such success as he resumed his crusade around the country and in Midlothian itself. As before, so again, he attacked the Tories as shamelessly immoral but now also expanded his campaign cry to assault almost every area of policy. One speech from April 1880 gives a vivid impression of the almost demonic manner in which he ran his campaign:

> At home the Ministers have neglected legislation, aggravated the public distress ... augmented the public expenditure and taxation ... plunged the finances, which were handed over to them in a state of singular prosperity, into a series of deficits unexampled in modern times ... Abroad they have strained, if they have not endangered, the prerogative by gross misuse, have weakened the Empire by needless wars, unprofitable extensions, and unwise engagements, and have dishonoured it in the eyes of Europe by filching the island of Cyprus from the Porte ... they have aggrandized Russia, lured Turkey on to her dismemberment ... replaced the Christian population of Macedonia under a debasing yoke, and loaded India with the cost and danger of a prolonged and unjustifiable war ... As to domestic legislation for the future, it is in the election address of the Prime Minister a perfect blank. No prospect is

opened to us of effectual alterations in the land laws, of better securities for occupiers, of the reform and extension of local government throughout the three kingdoms, of a more equal distribution of political franchise, or of progress in questions deeply affecting our social and moral condition. It seems, then, that, as in the past, so in the future, you will look with more confidence to the Liberal party for the work of domestic improvement.

Disraeli had no way of responding to Gladstone, and as a Peer was unable to take part in the campaign. He therefore accepted an invitation from Lord Salisbury to stay at Hatfield House until the election was over. Salisbury himself was in France with his wife on holiday, but he left instructions that Disraeli should be afforded every luxury, and for the next few weeks Disraeli was able to reflect in tranquillity on the campaign. On Salisbury's instructions, Disraeli was kept supplied with a particularly fine 1870 Grand Château Margaux – a pleasure denied to the other guests.

It was clear almost immediately that the Conservatives had been defeated. The first results filtered through on 31 March and showed a loss of fifteen seats in sixty-nine constituencies. Within three days the Conservatives had lost fifty seats and all hopes of a Conservative majority were dashed. But the worst was still to come, as the results from the counties showed big losses in Conservative strongholds, where the squires and farmers who had once lined up behind Disraeli took their revenge on the Government. The final scorecard showed an almost total reverse from the success of 1874, as the Liberals won 353 seats, the Tories 238 and Home Rulers sixty-one. As the results came in Gladstone reflected on the task before him: 'It seemed as if the arm of the Lord had bared itself for work that He has made His own.'

No one was angrier than the Queen. In particular, she

despaired at the prospect of having Gladstone as her Prime Minister again. 'She will sooner <u>abdicate</u> than send for or have any <u>communication</u> with <u>that half mad firebrand</u> who wd soon ruin everything & be a <u>Dictator</u>. Others but herself <u>may submit</u> to his democratic rule but <u>not the Queen</u>.'

For Disraeli, however, there was a deeper dimension to Gladstone's victory. Over the next thirty years the number of agricultural labourers would fall by a third. Agriculture, while remaining the biggest employer in the country, would no longer be the dominant industry. This created a large and unfixable crack in the idea that Britain was at heart a landed aristocracy. Indeed there is a heavy helping of irony in the way that Disraeli, who had fought for the landed classes in the 1840s, was himself brought down in part by the efforts of those same families in 1880. It was not so much that the cupboard of ideas which Disraeli had been filling since the 1820s was now smashed and redundant; rather that he lacked the physical and mental energy to repair the damage. It was the beginning of the end of Disraeli's dream.

Disraeli on the whole took the news of defeat with great calmness, even though it came as a surprise. After the election he returned to Downing Street, where he busied himself with the work of winding up the Government. He told Lady Bradford that this task was as hard as forming a government had been, 'without any of the excitement. My room is full of beggars, mournful or indignant and my desk is covered with letters like a snowstorm. It is the last and least glorious exercise of power and will be followed which is the only compensation by utter neglect and isolation.'

Throughout his life Disraeli had taken great interest in questions of patronage. In a perverse way he thoroughly enjoyed this final exercise of power, skilfully selecting the right awards for the deserving and smoothing out difficulties as they arose. 'Discomforted, defeated, and if not disgraced, prostrate, by a singular anomaly and irony of fate I pass my life now in exercising supreme power – making Peers, creating Baronets and showering places and pensions on a rapacious crew.' But not all applicants were rapacious. Among those rewarded for their service, Cross and Northcote were granted the Order of the Bath and Cranbrook was awarded the Order of the Star of India. Robert Lytton received an earldom for his efforts as Viceroy. Meanwhile, Lord John Manners, the only man to have served with Disraeli in all Conservative Cabinets since 1852, was also granted the Order of the Bath.

Once again the Queen offered Disraeli a title of his choosing and a barony for his nephew, Coningsby Disraeli. But Disraeli declined this offer and turned his attention to securing an honour for his Private Secretary. Corry was by now in his forties and had sunk his own aspirations into supporting Disraeli's career. For years he had steadfastly sustained the Prime Minister, and Disraeli was determined to grant him that same reward which Mary Anne had received in 1868, namely a peerage. Disraeli showed great resourcefulness in bringing this about, tracking down a wealthy aunt of Corry's who stood to leave an income of £5,000 to Corry as well as the deeds to Rowton Castle in Shropshire. He then wrote to the Queen claiming, somewhat disingenuously, that Corry had already received this property as well as an annual income of £10,000. 'Is it not possible that your Majesty might make him Baron Rowton of Rowton Castle in the county of Shropshire?' The Queen agreed and despite Gladstone comparing the honour to the decision by Caligula to make his horse a Roman Senator, the elevation was on the whole well received.*

Meanwhile Disraeli advised the Queen on his successor.

---

* Comparisons with Caligula have since become a cliché; Gladstone was one of the first to use the phrase.

Gladstone, despite his oratory, was still in theory operating under the leadership of Hartington and Granville. There was therefore a constitutional impropriety in asking Gladstone to form a government before the official leaders of the Liberal Party had been offered the chance to do so first. The Queen happily went along with this suggestion, but when summoned Hartington made it clear that no Liberal government could stand without Gladstone, and Gladstone would not be prepared to accept anything other than the first post. After a further exchange of letters with Disraeli the Queen summoned Gladstone, who calmly accepted her commission to form a new government.

Disraeli held his last Cabinet on 21 April and left Downing Street four days later. He stayed at Hatfield before holding his farewell audience with the Queen. By Saturday 1 May he was back at Hughenden where, apart from occasional trips to London and three more visits to the Queen, he remained for the rest of 1880.

It was here, among the birds and trees of Hughenden, that Disraeli completed his last novel, *Endymion*. Although there had been years in which Disraeli had produced nothing, he had by no means given up the novelist's trade. He had begun this new work early in the 1870s, not long after completing *Lothair*, but he had been unable to finish the story while in government. Now, free at last from the grind of papers, dispatches, official correspondence and Cabinet meetings, Disraeli completed the book in four months.

Endymion is a good-tempered novel about mid-nineteenth-century politics. It is not so much the story of a particular political crisis, but rather an account of what was for Disraeli the most exciting part of politics: the ascent. The main character is Endymion Ferrars, the son of a politician who fell on bad times and had to retire from public life. The novel describes the gradual recovery of Endymion from this inherited

mishap and his rise up the political ladder. It begins in the
time of Canning's premiership and ends with that of Lord
Aberdeen. But these Premiers and their governments are less
important to the novel than the women who sustained them
and promoted their careers.

The fault of the novel is that Endymion himself is an
empty character, to whom things happen. There is nothing
to be said against Endymion, but little in his favour. He is
simply wafted upwards by the efforts of others. The most
notable of these is his twin sister, Myra. In order to advance
Endymion's career she marries Lord Roehampton, a vivid
portrait of Palmerston, and is thus propelled into the field
of foreign affairs. Undaunted by Lord Roehampton's demise,
Myra moves on to marry Prince Florestan, alias Louis Napoleon of France. In this capacity she pays with her husband a
state visit to England from which she escapes for a few hours
in order to visit her brother (by now a prominent Whig in the
Cabinet) at the house in which they were brought up as children. The novel ends as brother and sister embrace among
their childhood memories.

As usual with Disraeli, the plot verges on the preposterous
and wanders off into wider musings about the meaning of life
and the role of politics. It is an old man's book, full of advice
to the young. For example, the aspiring politician should
build up a close relationship with his Private Secretary. As
regards dress, 'in youth, a little fancy is rather expected, but
if political life be your object, it should be avoided at least
after one and twenty'. 'I cannot send you out looking like
Lord Byron if you mean to be a Canning or a Pitt.' There is
also plenty to eat and drink in the novel. 'The dinner was a
banquet – a choice bouquet before every guest, turtle and
venison and piles of whitebait and pineapples of prodigious
size and bunches of grapes that had gained prizes. The champagne seemed to flow in fountains and was only interrupted

that the guests might quaff Burgundy or Tokay.' And among the superlatives are several famous phrases: 'an insular country subject to fogs and with a powerful middle class, requires grave statesmen'. Only one character is treated with absolute scorn and that is St Barbe, a portrait of Thackeray, who manages to be both a peevish critic and a snob.

Endymion was on the whole well received by the public. The Queen could not understand why Disraeli had chosen a Whig as the novel's hero, while the Archbishop of Canterbury finished the book 'with a painful feeling that the writer considers all political life as mere play and gambling'. But Disraeli received praise from both Salisbury and also his former friend Lord Derby, and the book generally sold very well.

For Disraeli this commercial success was particularly important. The negotiations with publishers had been handled by Monty Corry, by now elevated as Lord Rowton. One afternoon in the House of Lords he had passed Disraeli a note with the news that Longmans had offered no less than £10,000 as an advance. This was a magnificent sum in those days, believed to be the highest ever paid for a work of fiction. There is some evidence that Disraeli felt a pang of conscience that his publishers the Longmans might be well out of pocket by this transaction, but in a letter to Rowton Mr Longman set his fears at rest. 'The matter [of the advance] rests entirely with Lord Beaconsfield and I am content to let it do so. Indeed it is but equitable and right that he should endeavour to receive what he, not without practical evidence, considers the value of a work of fiction from his pen; he has done me the honour of giving me the first offer of this valuable property.' In April the following year, Longman was able to report that sales of the book had exceeded 8,000 copies and that the debt had been erased.

As soon as Disraeli had finished *Endymion* he began a new

novel which unfortunately he never completed. He would probably have christened it 'Falconet', which is the name of the principal character. Unlike the leading characters in Disraeli's other novels, Falconet is a sententious young man with no redeeming qualities except a natural eloquence. This eloquence gains him a strong position in Parliament, as Disraeli explains: 'He was essentially a prig and among prigs there is a freemasonry which never fails. All the prigs spoke of him as the coming man.' It is not difficult to work out who Falconet was meant to represent. Disraeli by this time was implacable against Gladstone, whom in his letters he now described as the AV (arch villain).

It is tempting to speculate how Falconet's career would have evolved had Disraeli completed the book. Would he have changed his ways and become a human being? It hardly seems probable but of course the unexpected is commonplace in Disraeli's novels. Or would he have collapsed in the disgrace which Disraeli obviously thought he deserved? But speculation is vain. Whatever his intentions, Disraeli was too ill to complete them and all we have are nine remarkable chapters and the fragment of a tenth.

Disraeli in these months could have given up politics. There was no reason for him to continue as leader of the Party. Gladstone had a large and commanding majority, and no election seemed likely for five or six years, by which time Disraeli would be in his eighties. Yet Disraeli showed no inclination to return to the back benches, nor were his Party keen to see their star performer leave the stage. Indeed Disraeli, who no longer had a house in London and had been borrowing rooms belonging to the Rothschilds during his brief visits to Parliament, took out a six-year lease on 19 Curzon Street at the start of the new year. All the evidence therefore suggests that Disraeli did not think his prime-ministerial career had finished.

During these months Disraeli was particularly important to the leader of the Conservatives in the House of Commons, Stafford Northcote, who found himself having to deal with an unruly group of Tory MPs known as the Fourth Party. These men, who included Randolph Churchill, Drummond Wolff, Arthur Balfour and Gorst, chafed at what they saw as the indecisiveness of Stafford Northcote and pressed for more aggressive Opposition. But Disraeli urged them not to push their rebellion to an extreme, and told Wolff when he visited London in August 1880: 'I fully appreciate your feelings and those of your friends, but you must stick to Northcote. He represents the respectability of the party. I wholly sympathise with you all, because I was never respectable myself . . .'

Disraeli meanwhile maintained a mournful watch on the direction of the country. He strongly rejected the absoluteness of Gladstone's politics, condemning his policy of 'perpetual and complete reversal of all that has occurred'. But he found he could do little to shake Gladstone's grip on the country, and his most notable political success was a speech early in 1881 on Afghanistan in which he at last took revenge on Lord Derby: 'I do not know that there is anything that would excite enthusiasm in him except when he contemplates the surrender of some national possession.'

In truth, Disraeli's life was now a shadow of his old existence. He spent most of his time alone. As he explained to Lady Bradford, this meant that he felt increasingly detached from the political process: 'It is no easy thing to step out of the profound solitude in which I live – often not speaking to a human being the whole day – and walk into the House of Lords and make a speech on a failing Empire.' But by this point it was not just the Empire that was failing, but also Disraeli's body and health.

Disraeli was always sensitive to the weather and in 1880 he had enjoyed at Hughenden the pleasures of a mild English autumn. He wrote to the Queen: 'we have and have had for some days the climate of Cannes or Nice or the Riviera, cloudless skies, westerly breezes and almost scorching suns, so that at noon I can sit on the southern terrace for a couple of hours and feel like Egypt. But alas the sun sets at 4!' The good weather did not last, and on 31 December Disraeli left his beloved Hughenden for the last time. Though suffering from the biting east wind, he continued a relentless round of social commitments in London, moving still, in Lytton Strachey's famous phrase, like 'an assiduous mummy, from dinner party to dinner party'. On 15 March 1881 he gave a fine speech in the Lords, supporting a Vote of Condolence to the Queen following the assassination of the Russian Tsar. The Tsar had once been Disraeli's opponent, but he now called him 'the most beneficent prince that ever filled the throne of Russia'. Three days later he put a short question to Lord Granville on the timings of Britain's withdrawal from Kandahar. They would be his last words on that stage.

For two years, Disraeli had been complaining of 'a confused brain and exhausted body'. Now both body and mind gave way. The weather that spring was unusually severe and at the end of March Disraeli caught a chill which became bronchitis. 'I am blind and deaf. I only live for climate and I never get it,' he complained. From then on the road was steadily downhill. The doctors were at first hopeful, but their hopes were not shared by their patient. Disraeli told his old friend Philip Rose, 'I shall never survive this attack. I feel it is quite impossible ... I feel this is the last of it.'

So it proved. For three weeks Disraeli was faithfully attended by Dr Kidd, his valet Baum, plus a number of other doctors and expert professionals, all of whom scurried about in vain, trying to repair the former Prime Minister's health. Meanwhile, Monty Corry hurried back from Algiers where he had been looking after an ailing sister. Disraeli in these days slipped in and out of consciousness, but he had taken his wit with him into the sickroom. When he was told that the Queen was anxious to visit him, he dismissed the suggestion with wry perceptiveness: 'No it is better not. She would only ask me to take a message to Albert.'

The 17th of April was Easter Day, when Disraeli normally took Holy Communion. The doctors refused to tell him the date, believing that this would warn him that his condition was hopeless. Two days later, Disraeli died peacefully at half past four in the morning. His last recorded words were: 'I had rather live but I am not afraid to die.'

Philip Rose gave one account of Disraeli's final moments: 'He passed away without suffering, calmly as if in sleep, at 4.30 in the presence of Lord Rowton, Lord Barrington, myself, and the physicians. We kissed his fine noble forehead ... I never saw anything more fine and impressive than his peaceful and tranquil expression, and his appearance is one of the greatest dignity and repose.'

Monty Corry's account was more profound. 'The last day and hours were distressing from his laboured breathing,' he told Lady Bradford, 'but the last minutes and moments were very quiet and evidently quite painless. The very end was strikingly dignified and fine, and as I looked on his dear face, just at the moment when his spirit left him, I thought that I had never seen him look so triumphant and full of victory.'

EPILOGUE

Britain mourned the death of Disraeli with all the customary display of Victorian grief. This mourning was not on the epic scale accorded to Sir Robert Peel or the Duke of Wellington. But the nation knew it had lost a strange and remarkable individual. Bells were pealed in towns across Britain. On public buildings, flags were flown at half mast. In newspapers and journals, touching tributes were paid to the man who 'made England feared all across the world'. The Queen herself was bereft and for some days inconsolable. 'I can scarcely see for my fast falling tears,' she told Monty Corry, 'never had I so kind and devoted a Minister and very few such devoted friends.'

In these ways and others, Disraeli's death was marked by great anguish and ritual. But more remarkable was what happened next. We began our book with the story of Disraeli's funeral. Almost as soon as Disraeli had been laid to rest, his reputation underwent a transfiguration. With amazing speed, the controversies which had surrounded his career disappeared from the nation's memory. The myth became mightier than the man. Primroses were worn on the anniversary of Disraeli's death. The 19th of April became a day of national remembrance, observed throughout the Edwardian era. After the Great War, Disraeli's life became the focus of films in Hollywood. As the American film-maker Nunnally

Johnson put it: 'All actors want to play Disraeli, except fat ones. It's such a showy part – half Satan, half Don Juan, man of so many talents, he could write novels, flatter a Queen, dig the Suez Canal. Present her with India. You can't beat that, it's better than Wyatt Earp.'

Why did this happen and what was the justification? In Britain it was partly a matter of demand and supply. The Conservative Party needed a hero; better candidates than Disraeli were hard to find. Lord Derby had been ineffective; Robert Peel was divisive; Disraeli's successor as leader, Stafford Northcote, was known as The Goat. This left only Disraeli out of the ranks of recent leaders as a plausible Party symbol, and he was duly elevated from skilful politician to the pantheon of Conservative Great Men.

But there was also something else driving this agenda. To write about Disraeli is to embark on a treasure hunt; the clues are the epigrams with which he built his career. Part of the reason why Disraeli seemed so attractive to his successors was that his quotations offered answers to the great questions of politics. Thus 'Peace with Honour' caught the mood of a stately, self-satisfied late-Victorian nation. 'Imperium et Libertas' was a fine cry for all those who championed Empire. Tory Democracy – which Disraeli never actually said – was a sign that the Tories were in favour of mass democracy. Later, in the grim world of the Great Depression, 'Two Nations' became a powerful, unifying idea of national togetherness. 'Progressive Conservative' has become the watchword of every Tory leader down the years looking for a way of explaining why the Party must change. Through these words and countless others, Disraeli took on a new life in twentieth- and twenty-first-century politics. But when it comes to understanding the man himself, more often than not, these phrases lead us down a false trail. The purpose of this book has been to strip away the posthumous glamour and to bring alive the true genius of Disraeli. The result is a man in some ways more remarkable than the mythical Disraeli, driven by a relentless thirst for excitement and a taste for extravagant ideas.

Disraeli's whole life was indeed a prolonged search for excitement, fuelled by the conviction that he was an extraordinary man. He could not be content with quiet, solid achievement; he needed to see his fame blazed abroad. Somewhere could be found the switch which would illuminate the path to glory. For individuals, as for nations, prestige in his book was the only measurement that counted.

Obviously, fame could not be found in the solicitors' office where his father had secured him a place at the start of his career. Nor was it enough to enter the literary profession. Money was essential, and in the 1820s the quick route to financial success was through speculation in South American mining shares. But for Disraeli the result of this speculation was not wealth but crippling debts. Only at the very end of his life, after the windfalls from Mrs Brydges Williams, *Lothair* and *Endymion*, did Disraeli find himself on a sound financial footing. His final will was proved at £84,000 and his family were at last able to repay the mortgage on Hughenden to Andrew Montagu.

To debts were added an inherited difficulty, namely Disraeli's Jewish race and religion. We do not know what Disraeli felt when he was baptised a Christian while a teenager, but it was a necessary precursor to a political career. Even so, the slurs to which he was subjected as a politician always focused on his supposed foreignness. 'The Jew Premier', 'wizard', 'conjuror', 'Dizzy' all gave the impression of a man who was somehow different from the rest of society – and not for the better.

As a barrier against this abuse, Disraeli developed an elaborate defence mechanism. He did not deny that he was different; rather, he revelled in it. Initially this took the form of an extreme dandyism, by which he dressed and spoke as if he were an Oriental, and indulged in excessive drinking and extravagant foods. But later he moved in the opposite direction, wearing dark clothes and setting his face in an almost static expression, his sallow features showing no emotion as cutting comments flowed out of his mouth. He reflected on this transformation in a letter to the Queen at the very end of his career: 'Men of action, when eminently successful in early life, are generally boastful and full of themselves ... if Lord Beaconsfield, with many other imperfections, has escaped these two imputations, it is, probably, only due to the immense advantage, which he has enjoyed, of having been vilified and decried for upwards of forty years, and which has taught him self-control, patience, and some circumspection ...'

Early in his life, Disraeli developed strange views about religion. Like others in Victorian times, Disraeli believed that religion lay at the heart of human existence. Unlike others, he held this to be true despite the fact that he was not a strong believer himself. Instead he believed powerfully in the social utility of religion. This was the glue that held a nation together and gave it a coherent purpose. In terms of Disraeli's own faith, we are left these comments from his last novel:

'Sensible men are all of the same religion.'
'And pray what is that?'
'Sensible men never tell.'

So spoke Waldershare in *Endymion*; and with this riddle we must be content.

On one related point Disraeli is more emphatic. He argued that Jews deserved respect, not because they were equal in importance to Christians, but because they were superior. As he wrote in *Tancred*: 'The greatest of legislators; the greatest of administrators; and the greatest of reformers; what race, extinct or living, can produce three such men as these?' This belief in the superiority of the Semitic race was linked in Disraeli's mind to the need for a spiritual renewal led by the Church of England, which he thought was the only Jewish institution remaining.

In this manner Disraeli painted a picture of an outsider from society. It is a paradox that Victoria came to regard Disraeli as her favourite Prime Minister when in his own life his behaviour and values ran against the mood of Victorian Britain and indeed Victoria herself. He would have been more at home in the previous century. He disliked the middle classes and despised middle-class values. Disraeli had nothing in common with the dull, mechanical spirit of liberal progress which was the main feature of the Victorian age. When the French statesman François Guizot told Disraeli that his being the leader of the Tory Party was 'the greatest triumph that liberalism has ever achieved', Disraeli must have been incensed by the tribute. His success had nothing to do with liberalism; his was the triumph of exceptionalism.

This was reflected in Disraeli's personal life and relationships, which were bizarre even by the standards of the times. Disraeli did not enjoy the company of equals. His closest relationships were with younger men and older women. There was nothing straightforward about his feelings. What he craved was not reciprocal love or intellectual fulfilment, but rather emotional support and political encouragement. Thus Sara Austen, Clara Bolton and Henrietta Sykes all fell by the wayside when they ran out of patience or outlived their usefulness to Disraeli. Only Mary Anne survived where these women had failed, because she sank her soul into supporting and sustaining her husband's genius.

Disraeli was a selfish man, but he had one strong redeeming

virtue. Self-possessed in many ways, nonetheless he was grateful to those individuals who helped him at various stages of his career. As we have seen, not only did Disraeli reward his wife and Monty Corry with peerages, but he also secured an important clerical post at Ripon Cathedral for the son of his father's friend Sharon Turner, who had showed an interest in Disraeli's own upbringing.

Indeed, gratitude is the theme of one of the most remarkable stories about Disraeli's career. Late in his time as Prime Minister, Disraeli invited the young 6th Duke of Portland to Hughenden. The Duke, who was a twenty-two-year-old officer in the Coldstream Guards, had recently inherited his title and was now the most senior surviving member of the Bentinck family, who had been instrumental in establishing Disraeli's career. The Duke travelled to High Wycombe by train in the company of Monty Corry. The three men ate dinner alone, Disraeli wearing his Blue Sash of the Garter which he had received from the Queen. Throughout the meal the Prime Minister was almost silent, until the pudding, when he suddenly rose to his feet and gave a short speech. He told the young man that he had decided to recommend a peerage for his stepmother Mrs Cavendish-Bentinck, adding by way of explanation: 'I come from a race which never forgives an injury, nor forgets a benefit.' The Duke began to utter his thanks to the Prime Minister, but was halted as Disraeli left the room. The peerage was duly gazetted in the Resignation Honours of 1880.

The key question that Disraeli wrestled with in his early years was over a choice of career. What should it be? His early novels were an attempt to help answer this question, and having written them he realised that real fame could only be found in politics. 'I am only truly great in action,' he noted and Parliament was the theatre where great action took place. He therefore plunged into a series of bruising election campaigns before finally being elected as an MP for Maidstone in 1837.

On entering politics, Disraeli did not abandon literature. On the contrary, he remained faithful to his cupboard of finely polished literary ideas. These ideas were largely preposterous, based on three extravagant themes: a chivalric alliance between the working classes and aristocratic England; a Cavalier promise of a reawakened English monarchy; and a personal belief in national prestige as the only valid basis of foreign policy in a world of empires, priests, beautiful palaces and secret societies. As the years wore on, these ideas were beaten to the dust by the realities of mid-Victorian Britain and by Disraeli's own ambition to clamber up the greasy pole. By the time he became Prime Minister with a full working majority, they had faded to a dream.

From time to time Disraeli did try to bring about a new feudalism. For a while the Young England movement seemed like an attractive scheme. But in real life, men such as George Smythe and Alexander Baillie-Cochrane were not suited to the hard work of government. It tended to be men such as Richard Cross, W.H. Smith and the 15th Earl of Derby who understood the self-help spirit of Victorian Britain. Lord John Manners, the other survivor of Young England, never rose above the rank of Postmaster General. For aristocratic company, Disraeli had to be content with the elderly ladies with whom he claimed to be in love, or young men such as Lord Henry Lennox.

By the time Disraeli left office, it was not just the background of men in government that was changing. Following a period of agricultural distress, the whole landed interest was in decline. Disraeli had made his name by attacking Peel's decision to repeal the Corn Laws, but now in government he made no attempt to reverse this decision. Protection was dead and the importance of cheap bread to urban classes across Britain meant that no politician could make their priority the defence of the landed settlement.

As for the monarchy, Disraeli took great pleasure in flattering Victoria. Indeed, Disraeli laid it on thick, pretending that this erratic Hanoverian monarch was Queen Titania or the Faerie Queen. Victoria, though shrewd in many respects, was particularly vulnerable to this treatment, which appealed to her loneliness. She summed up the main difference between Disraeli and Gladstone in enchanting terms: 'after sitting next to Mr Gladstone, I thought he was the cleverest man in England. But after sitting next to Mr Disraeli, I thought I was the cleverest woman in England.' It is significant that Disraeli was less successful with her eldest son Bertie. In general, the Prince of Wales shared Disraeli's political views and certainly supported his strong foreign policy. Nevertheless every now and then, for example over the handling of his visit to India, the Prince of Wales came across an aspect of Disraeli which was less than straightforward. The Prime Minister had led the Queen to believe that the idea of this visit had been discussed and approved in Cabinet, whereas it was very much a project of his own devising, connected of course with the aim of making the Queen Empress of India. But none of Disraeli's words or actions had a dramatic effect on the power of the British monarchy. Indeed, in his royal encounters Disraeli liked to pick and choose which of the Queen's opinions were useful to him. As he explained to Lord Esher, with the Queen he followed a simple set of rules: 'I never deny; I never contradict; I sometimes forget.'

Only in foreign affairs did Disraeli come close to living out his fantasy. When it came to promoting prestige, he was ceaselessly vigilant and for a brief period he sustained the idea that Britain's policies of boldness and daring had maintained peace in Europe and defied the Russian Bear. But even here the illusion gave way, as Beaconsfieldism was dashed to

pieces by Afghan atrocities and Zulu spears. Had he lived,
Disraeli would have taken some comfort from the disasters
which befell Gladstone in later years, when in a famous
display of hypocrisy he outdid Disraeli by bombarding Alex-
andria following a breakdown of order in Egypt. But even
this would have been scant consolation for the battering to
which Disraeli's policies had been subjected. All in all, his
imperial achievements were spectacular rather than substantial or lasting.

If all this is a fair judgement, how should we value Disraeli's contribution to our history? Certainly, we must put
to one side much of the hagiography which still hangs over
him. He was not a One Nation Conservative – and this was
not simply because he never used the phrase. He rejected
the concept in its entirety. The whole point about the phrase
'two nations' was that they represented two different ways
of life and thought which could not be reconciled. Nor was
Disraeli a Tory Democrat. He manoeuvred his party with immaculate skill into a position where it put forward and passed
a Second Reform Act, but he was no ardent convert to democracy himself. The Bill was in large part a way of rescuing his
own career. Above all, in his heart Disraeli was very far from
progressive. His starting point was backward-looking; he
wanted to revive but improve the old ways of doing things.

By swallowing these myths, subsequent leaders of all
parties have, to borrow Vernon Bogdanor's telling phrase,
perhaps been 'dominated more by Disraeli's ghost than by
the man'. And yet when we strip away the paint of present-
day politics, the portrait that remains of Disraeli is far from
unimpressive. His contribution to British politics was vast,
transformative and special – and it was chiefly built around
two notable gifts.

The first gift concerned the integrity of political parties.
Disraeli believed that partisan politics were an essential

ingredient of stable politics. 'We should always remember that if we were not partisans we should not be Ministers,' he said at one point. And on another he explained: 'I say you can have no parliamentary government if you have no party government.' At the time, this was a new and radical concept; political parties were only beginning to take shape and the idea that a politician had duties not just to the nation and to his constituents, but also to a political organisation took many years fully to come to fruition. At the time it helped transform the nature of parliamentary democracy, equipping it for an era of mass politics in which votes were no longer based on factional and highly localised interests, but on wider arguments about the national interest as a whole.

Of course, the difficulty with this concept was that inevitably there would be antagonisms between Party and national interests. Indeed, this is one of the most frequent complaints against the continued power of sizeable political parties in our parliamentary system today. But at the time these arguments were still evolving, and they formed the main battleground between Disraeli and Peel in 1846. When was it right to sacrifice the Party in the name of the national interest? In his heart Disraeli agreed with Peel that the Corn Laws were not in the national interest; indeed he later became one of the leading voices urging Lord Derby to abandon Protection. His argument against Peel was that he failed to carry his Party with him. Peel had chosen to bring forward Repeal in spite of the pledges given by many Conservative MPs. As Disraeli put it in one debate in January 1846, by repealing the Corn Laws regardless of his colleagues' positions, Peel was in effect saying, 'I will rule without respect of party, though I rose by party; and I care not for your judgment, for I look to posterity.'

This was not how Disraeli approached things during the 1850s and 1860s when he was leading the Party himself. He knew that the Tory squires needed to change direction; but rather than ram this change down their throats as Peel had done, he chose to persuade and cajole his colleagues into moving to more sensible positions. This was indeed precisely how Disraeli approached parliamentary reform. As with repealing the Corn Laws, so extending the franchise provoked deep hostility among many Tories. When Disraeli took up the cause in the 1860s, a number of his Cabinet colleagues resisted, and three resigned. They believed that Disraeli was selling them down the river, and they were not in politics to deceive. But the difference between 1867 and 1846 was that the Conservative Party was now led by a tactician whose skill and manoeuvre verged on the magical. Disraeli did not simply outwit his opponents. He also persuaded the vast majority of his supporters that this was actually a direction in which they wanted to go. The picture painted by Walter Bagehot in his essays of Disraeli guiding the Conservative Party as the mahout guides the elephant – light in strength, but knowing all the Party's habits and ways – is a fitting tribute to Disraeli's political skill.

After passing the Second Reform Act, Disraeli talked arrogantly about 'educating' his party on the franchise; in fact the only lesson they had learned concerned the success that comes from leaping ahead of the game. The result of this 'education' was that, to Disraeli's great credit, the Conservative Party has maintained a general flexibility which has served it well through to this day. Crises are there to be countered; opportunities to be taken with whatever tools come to hand. The key, then as now, is to maintain a Conservative approach which is open to reform and progress; the idea had been Peel's, but it took Disraeli's wit to carry it out.

The point about wit takes us to Disraeli's second gift to politics. This gift was essentially literary. This does not mean that his novels are all-important. Far from it: they are not great works. Disraeli's contribution was literary in another way. He was never happier than when tossing ideas into the air and watching them fall to the earth.

Time and again, Disraeli used his imagination to make politics interesting. His most powerful strength was the creative energy with which he transformed Victorian politics. The public were fascinated by his speeches in the Commons. As Lord Curzon later put it: 'the jewelled phrase, the exquisite epigram, the stinging sneer. He was like a conjuror on a platform, whose audience with open mouth awaited the next trick.'

The result was that half a century before mass democracy, Disraeli made Parliament popular. He did this not by dint of legislative achievement, but simply by using his imagination to say brilliant, witty, and memorable things. Oscar Wilde wrote that Disraeli after his death would not be spoken of on Parnassus, but he would be quoted in Piccadilly. This has indeed become the way we remember Disraeli today. He was the phrasemaker.

An interesting piece of evidence gives an insight into the way he achieved this feat. One day news reached him that Bismarck had been explaining that, unlike Disraeli, he could never write a work of fiction; 'all the creative power that he had, he gave to politics'. Disraeli was taken by this admission and wrote to Lady Bradford: 'What Bismarck says as to writing fiction is perfectly true. I have told you the same thing. I never cd. do two things at the same time; at least 2 wh. required the creative power.'

The point is that Disraeli was always a novelist, even when writing no novels at all. His creativity changed the nature of Victorian politics. But it was not just creativity which counted. Courage was also necessary. Mary Anne once explained that 'Dizzy has the most wonderful moral courage, but no physical courage. When he has his shower bath, I always have to pull the string.' By moral courage Mary Anne did not mean that Disraeli always tried to do the right thing; he certainly did not. But what he did do was make courageous and remarkable decisions in Parliament. He was not afraid to make dramatic and unusual arguments; and he never spoke unless he had something clever or interesting to say.

Forti nihil difficile – to the brave nothing is difficult. This was Disraeli's motto and it can be seen carved into the wooden chimney piece in the dining room at Hughenden. Indeed, courage and bravery have since been etched into that house's history in a more dramatic way. Disraeli would have been thrilled had he lived to witness the scenes in the scullery at Hughenden during the 1940s when secret bombing raids were planned against Germany. Skill, secrecy, ruthlessness, daring – this was a project after Disraeli's own heart.

If Disraeli were alive today he would despair at the lack of courage and bravery among our political classes. These days we are subjected to parliamentary performances that border on banal. Hour after hour, politicians in Parliament and in the media operate at the bottom of their abilities, churning out featureless, indeed often thoughtless, phrases without the courage to take a real argument to an interviewer or an opponent. The result is that we are driven to accept, even applaud, the platitudinous exchange of abuse as the essence of politics. Wit has almost disappeared from our political discourse. Indeed, this is partly why our leaders so often resort to the quotation book in order to borrow their wit from Disraeli.

The contrast between past and present is depressing but instructive. We do not believe that Members of Parliament today are less intelligent than their predecessors in the 1860s and 1870s. On the contrary, the average level of education and native intelligence among our legislators is almost certainly higher now than then. It is easy to forget the dead weight of mediocrity which then peopled the benches of the House of Commons on both sides. Many Members of Parliament never spoke at all; others spoke to no particular purpose. Many were content with their lot as backbenchers and the prestige which it gave them; the level of ambition is certainly greater now than then, being more widely spread.

But the ambitious backbencher today faces a barrier which is hard to surmount. He or she finds themself confronted with the general dislike and distrust of those whose votes they seek. There are different ways of tackling this difficulty. Some Members of Parliament busy themselves in their constituencies and make a name for themselves through local campaigns. They have their reward; it is common to find people who join in the general contempt for the political class while retaining an admiration for their own Member of Parliament. There are others who achieve the decisive advance by the intensity of their convictions. In our lifetimes the clearest example of this was Enoch Powell, who by the force of his intellect compelled the attention and admiration of his audience.

Yet all these techniques merely skirt around the main problem. In truth, it is boredom rather than cynicism which most accurately explains the present disillusionment with politics. We are strong in analysis, weak in imagination. Not lacking in strong feeling, but missing genuine eloquence and integrity which can persuade us by lifting our spirits. Above all, people have lost confidence in politicians because politicians have lost confidence in themselves. They bustle about, renouncing power at every opportunity, eagerly shifting decision-making down to expert bodies or local government. All this may be virtuous, but it ducks the main difficulty – that politicians are too timid to say interesting things.

Of course, we are not calling for countless clones of Disraeli. Not all can – or should – try to soar to the heights that he did. Imagination can show itself in many ways. One of us, when in politics, supplied far fewer phrases than Disraeli to the *Oxford Dictionary of Quotations*. Indeed, his most famous quotation is currently subject to a paternity test: did D. Hurd or G. Howe first say that 'Britain punches above its weight in the world?' But to quibble over this distracts from the main point. What matters, and is missing today, is that politicians should show genuine independence of thought when they debate. They should stir themselves to find imaginative ways of making an argument, not simply repeat the lines to take. At the moment, too often, too few try to do this – adding to the widespread impression that politicians are all the same.

There are of course notable exceptions, and at present, it is the most prominent exception who proves the rule. According to most accepted wisdom on modern politics, Boris Johnson should have been ruined years ago. He has been accused of all kinds of conventional wickedness, including being unfaithful and insulting the people of Liverpool. And yet his reputation has soared past these difficulties. This is in large part because he is entertaining and makes good use of his education in his rhetoric. Of course, there is a question of control. While Disraeli tried to keep his comedy in check and did not let his wit gallop away with him, Boris allows himself to be consumed by his own jokes. This makes it difficult when he wants to make a serious point. But, one way or another, Boris has nonetheless done today what Disraeli did in the nineteenth century, namely raise the level of interest in politics up several pegs.

We must not push this parallel too far. In some ways it was easier for Disraeli to capture people's imagination in the nineteenth century. Political rivalries loomed larger in nineteenth-century politics than they do today. This was an age without footballers or film stars. Kings and queens, though once at the top of the tree, were by the nineteenth century less noteworthy than in previous centuries. This left a gap for politicians that no longer exists, to use the strength of their lungs and their wits to capture and hold an audience. Yet our aspirations should be the same today. This does not mean politicians should try to compete with celebrities; nothing good can come of that. Rather, they should be bold enough to make good use of the platform and position which they have earned by their election. They should use their standing to campaign and speak out, making genuinely thoughtful and imaginative speeches about the future of our country and the purpose of politics.

This in the end was Disraeli's great achievement. He may not have reformed the nature of British society. He may not have transformed our standing overseas. But he did make politics interesting and engaging, including for those with no vote. As one contemporary observed, 'I never listened to a speech of yours without thinking, this word, this sentence, will be remembered a hundred years hence.' This was indeed the true magnetism of Disraeli. It is the reason why successive generations of politicians are drawn to him. If we look in his career for solid achievement we shall be disappointed. But if we want something to raise our game, Disraeli is the man.

SOURCES AND FURTHER READING

The two outstanding lives of Disraeli remain Robert Blake's *Disraeli* (London: Eyre and Spottiswoode, 1966) and William Monypenny and George Buckle's *The Life of Benjamin Disraeli, Earl of Beaconsfield* (London: Murray, 1910–20). Of these two works, Blake is on balance a better book but Monypenny and Buckle a more useful source. Their six volumes include over several thousand pages a large quantity of Disraeli's private notes and letters, the full collection of which can be found in the Hughenden Papers in the Special Collections at the Bodleian Library, Oxford.

In researching this book, we have also been particularly encouraged by John Vincent's *Disraeli* (Oxford: OUP, 1990) and the work carried out by Jane Ridley in her *The Young Disraeli, 1804–1846* (London: Sinclair-Stevenson, 1995), both of which take a fresh look at Disraeli and explode some of the myths which surround his career.

In recent years, the study of Disraeli has been transformed by the publication of eight meticulous volumes of his letters by a team of scholars at Queen's University, Canada. The Senior Editor of the *Benjamin Disraeli Letters* series is Mel Wiebe and the letters are published by the University of Toronto Press. Many of the letters quoted here are drawn from this source.

As with our previous works on Sir Robert Peel and British

Foreign Secretaries, we have sought to add to the canon of published sources by embarking on fresh fishing trips in search of new material. We spent many pleasant hours in the relocated Special Collections Reading Room at Oxford University where we focused on those boxes of letters which have attracted less attention from other scholars. In particular, we were delighted to discover details of Disraeli's reading habits during the 1850s and 1860s from his bookshop invoices. We also enjoyed reading the long lists of names and anecdotes from Disraeli's commonplace books, his Cabinet and speech notes during the Eastern Crisis, and the hotchpotch of notes regarding conversations with Stanley and others during the 1850s and 1860s. These latter notes have been published in *Disraeli's Reminiscences*, ed. Helen M. Swartz and Marvin Swartz (London: Hamish Hamilton, 1975), and are an invaluable guide to Disraeli's life and thinking at this time. At Gladstone's Library at Hawarden in Flintshire we found several dozen intriguing annotations in Gladstone's own hand on contemporary books about Disraeli. Many of these markings are published in this biography for the first time.

Disraeli's novels are now largely forgotten but we enjoyed rediscovering them as part of our research. We have given an account of the most important books in this biography but have spared our readers the more trivial works. These latter include *England and France, or a Cure for the Ministerial Gallomania* (1832), *The Rise of Iskander* (1833), *Ixion in Heaven* (1832/3), *The Infernal Marriage* (1834), *The Revolutionary Epick* (1834), and *The Tragedy of Count Alarcos* (1839).

As part of the myth-making which surrounds Disraeli's career, a number of phrases have been attributed to him which were in fact not his own. Disraeli never said 'there are three kinds of lies: Lies, Damn Lies, and Statistics'; the phrase may have been invented by Mark Twain. Nor did Disraeli ever talk about 'One Nation'. This phrase was coined by Stanley Baldwin. With many of the official parliamentary reports now available online, it has been easier to avoid such errors by reading Disraeli's many parliamentary speeches first hand. We are extremely grateful to the House of Commons and House of Lords Libraries for their work in building this resource.

What follows is a list of sources for quotations and key events in this book. Some readers may find this format ungainly, but we thought it preferable to provide full references at the end of the book rather than to interrupt the reader with numbers and footnotes during the main text. Where appropriate, we have also highlighted interesting areas for further reading.

Introduction

For details of Disraeli's quotations, see the 2009 *Oxford Dictionary of Quotations* (Oxford: OUP, 2009). Disraeli also has a strong showing in other quotation books. For example, in the *Concise Oxford Dictionary of Quotations* (2011) there are thirty-seven quotes from Disraeli, thirty-six from Churchill, seven by Gladstone and none by Robert Peel. In the *New Penguin Dictionary of Quotations* (2006) there are sixty-three quotations by Disraeli compared to sixty-one by Churchill, sixteen by Gladstone and, again, none by Peel.

David Gelernter's article, 'The Inventor of Modern Conservatism', appeared in the 7 February 2005 issue of the *Weekly Standard*, vol. 10, no. 20. For an account of Disraeli's reputation as the greatest Leader of the Opposition see Vincent, *Disraeli*, p. 6.

Ed Miliband's speech to the 2012 Labour Conference can be found on the Labour Party website, while the responses from David Cameron and William Hague are available on the Conservative Party site. John Prescott's thoughts on Disraeli can be seen in an interview with Andrew Neil for the BBC: http://www.bbc.co.uk/news/uk-politics-19817520

Chapter I: The Funeral

Two of the best accounts of Disraeli's funeral can be found in Monypenny and Buckle, *Disraeli*, vol. VI, and Richard Aldous, *The Lion and the Unicorn: Gladstone vs Disraeli* (London: Hutchinson, 2006). The origins and growth of the Primrose League have been ably chronicled by Alistair Cooke in *A Gift from the Churchills: The Primrose League, 1883–2004* (London: Carlton Club, 2010). Gladstone's response to receiving news of Disraeli's death by telegram can be found in Herbert Gladstone, *After Thirty Years* (London: Macmillan, 1928), p. 55. Lord Salisbury's tribute to Disraeli in the House of Lords can be found in Hansard, House of Lords Debates, 9 May 1881, Vol. 261, col. 7; Gladstone's tribute is in Hansard, House of Commons Debates, 9 May 1881, vol. 261, cols 38–58. We also owe thanks to John Jeffries for highlighting the 1994 poll of Conservative MPs.

'As he lived so he died...': Stanley Weintraub, *Disraeli* (London: Hamish Hamilton, 1993), p. 659; 'Where is your Christianity...': Hansard, House of Commons Debates, 16 December 1847, vol. 95, col. 1325; 'not to the bees, but to the wasps...': quoted by Margaret Thatcher in her 1968 Conservative Political Centre (CPC) Lecture, 'What's wrong with politics?', available on the Margaret Thatcher Foundation website; 'No man rose...': J.A. Froude, *Lord Beaconsfield* (London: Sampson, Low, Marston, Searle and Rivington, 1890), p. 260; 'he has been so long associated...': Andrew Roberts, *Salisbury: Victorian Titan* (London: Weidenfeld and Nicolson, 1999), p. 254; 'Some bright bands of primroses...'; 'He likes the primroses so much better...': Monypenny and Buckle, *Disraeli*, vol. VI, p. 629; 'The purpose of my letter...': Cooke, *The Primrose League*, pp. 11–12; 'The glorious lily...': Cooke, *The Primrose League*, p. 9; 'I declare on my honour and faith...': Cooke, *The Primrose League*, pp. 24–5; 'Children of the Empire...': Cooke, *The Primrose League*, p. 66; 'I want to see the spirit of service...': Alistair Cooke, *A Party of Change: A Brief History of the Conservative Party* (London: Conservative Party, 2008), p. 18; 'We were fighting the battle of the factory hand...': Philip Williamson, *Stanley Baldwin* (Cambridge: CUP, 1999), pp. 179–80; 'if Providence could have made Disraeli a dictator...': See William John Wilkins, *Tory Democracy* (New York: Columbia University, 1925), p. 55; 'the constellation of acts...': Simon Heffer, *Enoch Powell* (London: Phoenix Giant, 1999), p. 164; 'It is curious how each generation...': D.R. Thorpe, *Supermac: The Life of Harold Macmillan* (London: Pimlico, 2011), p. 245; 'I am quite sure that all those...': Stanley Baldwin, speech at Birmingham Town Hall, 6 October 1933; 'Disraeli's style was too ornate...': Margaret Thatcher, *The Path to Power* (London: HarperCollins, 1995), p. 118; 'My opponent at Beaconsfield...': Tony Blair to Michael Foot, July 1982, available at: http://www.telegraph.co.uk/news/uknews/1521418/The-full-text-of-Tony-Blairs-letter-to-Michael-Foot-written-in-July-1982.html; 'There is no shame...': Michael Portillo, *The Sunday Times*, 13 May 2007; 'My favourite political quote...': Dylan Jones, *Cameron on Cameron* (London: Fourth Estate, 2010); 'the idea of social responsibility...': David Cameron, 'Responsible Capitalism', 19 January 2012; Ed Miliband, 'Speech on Banking', 3 February 2012; 'Disraeli was one of the few...': Ian Gilmour, *Inside Right* (London: Hutchinson, 1977), p. 86; 'The sun has been taken...': B.R. Jerman, *The Young Disraeli* (Princeton: Princeton University Press, 1960), p. 15.

Chapter II: Christian and Jew

The letters between Isaac D'Israeli and the Rabbis can be found in the Isaac D'Israeli Papers at the Bodleian, in file 246/1. Extracts from some of these letters appear in Monypenny and Buckle, but we have not seen printed elsewhere the final battle with the elders in October 1821 when Isaac realised that they still had in their keeping his sons' birth certificates. This exchange can be found between folios 18 and 24 of the file. Disraeli's bookshop accounts are also in the Hughenden Papers, in file 19/5. The name of Disraeli's bookshop was Bain and his shop was located at no. 1 Haymarket.

Blake records Disraeli's baptiser as the Reverend J. Thimbleby, but the Clergy of the Church of England Database suggests that J. Thimbleby was in fact one Thomas Thimbleby. For further details see: http://www.theclergydatabase.org.uk/jsp/persons/index.jsp

'Nature had disqualified him...': Monypenny and Buckle, *Disraeli*, vol. I, p. 9; 'against commerce which was the corruption of man': Monypenny and Buckle, *Disraeli*, vol. I, p. 10; 'D'Israeli the elder lived through...': Monypenny and Buckle, *Disraeli*, vol. I, p. 16; 'Instead of joyousness and frank hilarity...': Benjamin Disraeli, *Tancred* (Teddington: The Echo Library, 2007), p. 275; for a clear account of the restrictions on Jews in early-nineteenth-century England see Adam Kirsch, *Benjamin Disraeli* (New York: Schocken Books, 2008), pp. 6–7; 'infinite multiplicity of customs...': Isaac D'Israeli, *The Genius of Judaism* (London: Edward Moxon, 1833), p. 263; 'For the first time in my life...': Benjamin Disraeli, *Contarini Fleming* (London: M. Walter Dunne, 1905), p. 29; 'Nothing was thought of...': Monypenny and Buckle, *Disraeli*, vol. I, pp. 24–5; 'I was not bred among my race...': *Disraeli Letters*, vol. VI, no. 2493; 'Throughout his life...': Blake, *Disraeli*, p. 50; 'Allah is Great': Blake, *Disraeli*, p. 80; 'Pallid and mad, he swift upsprang...': Benjamin Disraeli, *Alroy* (Teddington: The Echo Library, 2007), p. 12; 'The Jews are humanly speaking...': Vincent, *Disraeli*, p. 28; 'Look at the old clothes man...': *Punch, or the London Charivari*, 1847, p. 145; 'What w'd be the position of the Hebrew race in universal History...'; 'Anthropomorphism: a great cry against it by the Philosophes...': Hughenden Papers, 26/2, Book I, no. 6; 'the country, he said, had ample...': Kirsch, *Disraeli*, pp. 90–91; 'the general influence of race...'; 'the decay of a race...': Blake, *Disraeli*, pp. 194, 204; 'All is race there is no other truth': Disraeli, *Tancred*, p. 104; 'Lord and Master of the money market...': Benjamin Disraeli, *Coningsby, or The New Generation* (London: Longmans, Green, and Co., 1881), pp. 213, 250; 'In days when...': Kirsch, *Disraeli*, p. 133; 'The connexion of religion...': Monypenny and Buckle, *Disraeli*, vol. V, p. 88; 'Man is made to adore and obey': Disraeli, *Coningsby*, p. 240; 'a main remedial agency...': *Disraeli Letters*, vol. VIII, p. xii; Blake, *Disraeli*, p. 201; Disraeli, *Tancred*, pp. 214, 36; 'I do not believe I ever was fish': Disraeli, *Tancred*, p. 77; 'instead of believing...': *Disraeli Letters*, vol. VIII, p. 381; 'Though calling himself a Christian...': Froude, *Beaconsfield*, p. 84.

Chapter III: Doer or Dreamer?

For Disraeli's letters during his 1824 summer holiday see *Disraeli Letters*, vol. I, 1815–1834. The account of Disraeli's Maiden Speech with Gladstone's annotations can be found at Gladstone's Library in Hawarden in Froude's *Beaconsfield*, pp. 71–3.

'I am one of those...': Ridley, *Young Disraeli*, p. 64; 'Fame, although not posthumous fame...': Disraeli, *Contarini Fleming*, p. 195; 'I have heard my father say...': Blake, *Disraeli*, pp. 18–19; 'To be a great lawyer...': Benjamin Disraeli, *Vivian Grey* (London: Routledge, Warne and Routledge, 1859), p. 18; the description of Disraeli as an 'obliging and useful' solicitors' clerk, and the reference to 'ruffles and red clocks' can both be found in a letter sent by Mr Maples's son to Disraeli's executors in February 1889 in the Hughenden Papers, Dep Hughenden 10, Fol.7; Disraeli's tribute to his legal career – 'It gave me great facility...' – can be found in Monypenny and Buckle, *Disraeli*, vol. I, pp. 32–3. 'York Minster baffles all conception...': Sam Smiles, *Memoir of John Murray*, vol. II, copy at Gladstone's Library, Hawarden; 'sensible clever young fellow...': Blake, *Disraeli*, p. 29; 'immense organ...': Blake, *Disraeli*, p. 28; 'I have no doubt...': Monypenny and Buckle, *Disraeli*, vol. I, pp. 64–6; 'When I was quite a youth...': Hughenden Papers, 26/2, Book I; 'a sprig of the Rod of Aaron': Ridley, *Young Disraeli*, pp. 36–9; 'Vivian, you are a juggler': Disraeli, *Vivian Grey*, p. 121; 'a branch of study...': Disraeli, *Vivian Grey*, p. 19; 'written by boys...': Monypenny and Buckle, *Disraeli*, vol. I, p. 85; for details of Lucien Wolf's research into the speed of Disraeli's writing see Vincent, *Disraeli*, p. 58; 'I would like very much to know what was the amount that Macaulay made...': Hughenden Papers, 26/2, Book I; 'the secret history of my feelings...': Kirsch, *Disraeli*, p. 77; 'a new number of the great critical journal...': Disraeli, *Contarini Fleming*, pp.

230–32; 'The Spanish women...': Vincent, *Disraeli*, p. 64; 'What does Ben know...': Blake, *Disraeli*, p. 57; for further details on *Venetia* see Blake, p. 146; 'the glory has been the glory...': Anthony Trollope, *An Autobiography* (London: University of California Press, 1947), p. 216; Blake, *Disraeli*, p. 54; 'for while you were expressing...': John R. Murray, *Spoutings & Writings: Some Incidental Pieces* (Yeadon: Smith Settle, 2010), p. 71; 'the football of all the dinner-tables...': Sam Smiles, *A Publisher and his Friends: Memoir and Correspondence of John Murray*; 'devoured by an ambition...': Blake, *Disraeli*, p. 55; 'humbly requested him...': Blake, *Disraeli*, p. 63; 'Live then for me': *Disraeli Letters*, vol. I, 114; 'If the Reform Bill passes...': Weintraub, *Disraeli*, pp. 111–12; 'I was never more confident...': Froude, *Beaconsfield*, p. 50; Ridley, *Young Disraeli*, p. 112; 'Let us not forget...': Blake, *Disraeli*, p. 93; 'In your chivalry alone...': Benjamin Disraeli, *Letters of Runnymede* (London: John Macrone, 1836), Letter V to Sir Robert Peel, 26 January 1836; 'a vile creature...': for this speech, and a full account of the row with O'Connell, see Monypenny and Buckle, *Disraeli*, vol. I, pp. 285–93, and Blake, *Disraeli*, pp. 125–6; 'gratified and surprised...': Blake, *Disraeli*, p. 130; 'lurches wildly...': Vincent, *Disraeli*, p. 24; 'This innocent monarch...': Disraeli, *Vindication of the English Constitution* (London: Saunders and Otley, 1835), p. 32; 'whole and important districts...': Disraeli, *Vindication*, p. 128; 'It is this great principle...': Disraeli, *Vindication*, p. 163; 'cold, inanimate...': Disraeli, *Letters of Runnymede*; 'The two greatest stimulants...': Disraeli, *Tancred*, p. 145; 'There is not a party...': William Kuhn, *The Politics of Pleasure: A Portrait of Benjamin Disraeli* (London: Free Press, 2006), p. 171; 'There is no calling...': Hughenden Papers, Dep Hughenden 10, Fol. 60, 19 May 1832; 'Peel has asked me to dine...'; 'I trust there is no danger...': Blake, *Disraeli*, p. 134; 'I get duller...': Ridley, *Young Disraeli*, p. 345; 'devoid of constructive genius': Walter Bagehot, 'Mr Disraeli', from *The Economist*, 2 July 1859, *Bagehot's Historical Essays*, ed. Norman St John Stevas (New York: Anchor Books, 1965), 'Disraeli'; 'We govern men with words': Vincent, *Disraeli*, p. 46; 'No people relish...': Ridley, *Young Disraeli*, p. 122; 'He has not been at your schools...': Benjamin Disraeli, *Sybil, or The Two Nations* (Oxford: OUP, 1956), p. 136; 'Very few will venture on Latin...': Hughenden Papers, 26/2, Book I, no.19; 'It is the fashion now...'; 'The Utilitarians in Politics...': Ridley, *Young Disraeli*, p. 139; 'Power is neither the sword...': Disraeli, *Tancred*, p. 201.

Chapter IV: Men and Women

Disraeli's notebooks are in the Hughenden Papers. The Commonplace Book in file 30/1 contains his long lists of eunuchs and adventurers. It seems that Disraeli lifted his list of heroes, impotent or averse to women, from vol. IV of Pierre Bayle's famous seventeenth-century *Historical and Critical Dictionary*.

The idea that Disraeli saw himself as a Grand Vizier to the Empress Victoria has been explored in more detail by Isaiah Berlin in his superb essay, 'Benjamin Disraeli, Karl Marx and the Search for Identity', as published in *Against the Current: Essays in the History of Ideas*, ed. Henry Hardy (New York: Viking Books, 1980).

'You will not make love...': Weintraub, *Disraeli*, pp. 170–1; on Disraeli's appearance at the Taunton election, see Ridley, *Young Disraeli*, p. 158; 'The life of this people...': *Disraeli Letters*, vol. I, no. 107; 'to govern men...': Monypenny and Buckle, *Disraeli*, vol. I, pp. 154–5; 'harbor of refuge...': *Disraeli Letters*, vol. VII, xxii; 'There was a boy...': Disraeli, *Contarini Fleming*, pp. 31–2; 'I can only tell you that I love you': Blake, *Disraeli*, p. 327; 'There is nothing in life like female friendship...': Blake, *Disraeli*, p. 378; 'Talk to women...': Disraeli, *Contarini Fleming*, p. 140; 'I have not gained much in conversation...': Blake, *Disraeli*, p. 83; 'she is so thoroughly a daughter of Erin...': Blake, *Disraeli*, p. 156; 'I thought you had tamed...': Kuhn, *Politics of Pleasure*, p. 263; 'all my friends who married for love...': *Disraeli Letters*, vol. III, no. 276 (in an earlier edition of Disraeli's letters at Hawarden, Gladstone has put a tick beside this passage); 'It is the night Dearest...': Blake, *Disraeli*, p. 99; 'There is no love but love at first sight...': Benjamin Disraeli, *Henrietta Temple: A Love Story* (Leipzig: Bernhard Tauchnitz, 1859), pp. 70–71; 'I cannot bear that your amusement should spring...': Blake, *Disraeli*, p. 136; 'I will not be drawn off and on...': Blake, *Disraeli*, p. 127; 'Do you think any misery can occur...': Blake, *Disraeli*, p. 100; 'Madam cried and wrung her hands': Blake, *Disraeli*, p. 103; 'How long will these feelings last?...': Blake, *Disraeli*, p. 104; 'after, but not before': *Disraeli's Reminiscences*, ed. Helen M. Swartz and Marvin Swartz; 'Lyndhurst arrived...': Blake, *Disraeli*, p. 118; 'often the only adventure of life': Disraeli, Commonplace Book, Hughenden Papers, 30/1; 'He looked upon marriage...': Disraeli, *Vivian Grey*, p. 51; 'Oh anything rather...': Blake, *Disraeli*, p. 80; 'ungloved': Kirsch, *Disraeli*, p. 105; details of the row between Disraeli and Mary Anne can be found in Blake, *Disraeli*, pp. 157–8; this list is published in Monypenny and Buckle, *Disraeli*, vol. II, p. 68; 'George, there is one word...': Blake, *Disraeli*, p. 158; 'Though I have many people who call themselves my friends...': Kuhn, *Politics of Pleasure*, p. 288; 'rosy coloured tribute of Torbay': *Disraeli Letters*, vol. VIII, 3515; 'Lord M thought 9 hours not too much...': Hurd, *Peel*, p. 208; 'a <u>very bad</u> dream': Hurd, *Peel*, p. 368; 'that dreadful Disraeli': Hurd, *Peel*, p. 368; 'elaborate, malignant, mischievous': Monypenny and

Buckle, *Disraeli*, vol. III, pp. 353–4; 'mild and graceful...': Monypenny and Buckle, *Disraeli*, vol. IV, p. 125; 'Mr Disraeli (alias Dizzy)...': Kuhn, *Politics of Pleasure*, p. 276; 'She declares...': Blake, *Disraeli*, p. 492; 'The Prince is the only person...': Blake, *Disraeli*, p. 431; 'with a trowel': Blake, *Disraeli*, p. 491; 'To-day Lord Beaconsfield ought fitly...': Monypenny and Buckle, *Disraeli*, vol. VI, p. 430.

Chapter V: The Two Nations

The letters between Disraeli and Peel are in the Hughenden Papers, File 139/3. The early outline of the Two Nations idea can be found in Disraeli's 1842 Commonplace Book, also in the Hughenden Papers, on fol. 23. Disraeli's two accounts of Peel's last days are in his notebook in File 26/2 of the Hughenden Papers, nos 21 and 22. The Croker story is in the same file, no. 23. A detailed account of Disraeli's destruction of Peel can be found in our previous work, *Robert Peel: A Biography* (London: Weidenfeld and Nicolson, 2007). We have drawn on this for our account of the Condition of England, in the portrait of Lord George Bentinck, and in the parliamentary drama over the repeal of the Corn Laws.

'a perpetual vortex of agitation...': Hurd, *Peel*, pp. 174–5; on the Condition of England see Hurd, *Peel*, p. 3; 'In making the government strong...': Hansard, House of Commons Debates, 8 February 1841, vol. 56, cols 375–451; 'I entirely agree with you that an union...': Monypenny and Buckle, *Disraeli*, vol. II, pp. 88–9; an account of the first dinner with Peel can be found in Froude, *Beaconsfield*, p. 50; Gladstone's support for Disraeli's claim that Peel cheered his maiden speech can be found in the copy of Froude at Hawarden; 'it appears to me both solemn and tawdry...': *Disraeli Letters*, vol. II, January 1837; the offer to draft a manifesto came in a letter to Peel on 2 February 1838 – see *Disraeli Letters*, vol. III, no. 738; 'I am not going to trouble you...': Hughenden Papers, File 139/3; 'Literature he has abandoned for politics...': Monypenny and Buckle, *Disraeli*, vol. II, pp. 118–19; for a description of the Young England disciples see Blake, *Disraeli*, pp. 169–72; 'Bold, acute, and voluble...': Disraeli, *Coningsby*, p. 10; 'There is some portion...': Disraeli, *Coningsby*, p. 418; 'A sound Conservative government...': Disraeli, *Coningsby*, p. 103; 'I am sorry...': Disraeli, *Coningsby*, pp. 407–8; 'I be a reg'lar born Christian...': Disraeli, *Sybil*, p. 170; 'We are asked sometimes what we want...': Walter Sichel, Introduction to Disraeli, *Sybil* (Oxford: OUP, 1956), p. vii; 'Two nations...': Disraeli, *Sybil*, p. 67; 'to secure the social welfare...': Disraeli, *Sybil*, p. 278; 'profoundly and despairingly anti-democratic...': Ridley, *Young Disraeli*, p. 302; 'The Five Great Forces': Hughenden Papers, 1842 Commonplace

Book, fol. 23; 'The Duke and Duchess of Bellamont...': Disraeli, *Tancred*, p. 340; 'I was quite unaware until Friday night...': Hughenden Papers, File 139; 'great Parliamentary middleman': Hansard, House of Commons Debates, 11 April 1845, vol. 79, fol. 565; 'caught the Whigs bathing and walked away with their clothes': Hansard, House of Commons Debates, 28 February 1845, vol. 78, col. 155; 'When I was establishing a reputation by attacking Peel...': Hughenden Papers, 26/2, no. 13; 'You set to work to change the basis...': Froude, *Beaconsfield*, p. 161; 'He always traces the steam engine...': Hansard, House of Commons Debates, 11 April 1845, vol. 79, fol. 558; 'We have the country with us': Hughenden Papers, 26/2, no. 7; 'Peel always 'pût' a question...': Hughenden Papers, 26/2, no. 45; 'With his supercilious expression...': Monypenny and Buckle, *Disraeli*, vol. II, p. 315; 'Now I think it is a false famine...': Hurd, *Peel*, p. 338; 'Let men stand...': Hurd, *Peel*, p. 333; 'on general subjects...': Robert Stewart, *The Politics of Protection: Lord Derby and the Protectionist Party, 1841–1852* (Cambridge: CUP, 1971); King of the Turf...: Hurd, *Peel*, p. 355; 'When I examine the career...': Hansard, House of Commons Debates, 15 May 1846, vol. 86, col. 675; 'I have a strong belief...': Hansard, House of Commons Debates, 15 May 1846, vol. 86, col. 706; '...I can assure the House...': Hansard, House of Commons Debates, 15 May 1846, vol. 86, cols 708–9; 'the Manners, the Somersets, the Bentincks, the Lowthers and the Lennoxes...': Benjamin Disraeli, *Lord George Bentinck: A Political Biography* (London: Archibald Constable and Co., 1905), p. 195; 'like a subaltern...': Blake, *Disraeli*, p. 247; 'watchful eye and strong arm of England': Douglas Hurd and Edward Young, *Choose Your Weapons: The British Foreign Secretary – 200 Years of Argument, Success and Failure* (London: Orion, 2010), pp. 95–6; 'Next morning, Peel was dead, or as good!': Hughenden Papers, 26/2; 'Search my speeches through...': Ian St John, *Disraeli and the Art of Victorian Politics* (London: Anthem Press, 2005), p. 28; 'was more the result of winning over the bourgeoisie...': Blake, *Disraeli*, p. 211; 'the apathy of the party...': Kirsch, *Disraeli*, p. 169; 'there is a very general feeling...': Hurd, *Peel*, pp. 262–9; 'If Sir Charles had such cases before him...': Hurd, *Peel*, pp. 268–9; 'his frigid efficiency...': Hurd, *Peel*, p. 266; 'The aristocracy of England...': Disraeli, *Lord George Bentinck*; 'Lord Derby (the Premier) set up a welfare state...': Vincent, *Disraeli*, p. 53; 'he never could...': Disraeli, *Lord George Bentinck*, p. 208; 'It was rather embarrassing...': Hughenden Papers, 26/2, no. 23.

Chapter VI: The Greasy Pole

The history of this period during the late 1840s and 1850s has been greatly enhanced by the recent publication of Angus Hawkins's two-volume life of Lord Derby, *The Forgotten Prime Minister: The 14th Earl of Derby*, Volumes 1–2, (Oxford: OUP, 2011). Together with the publication of Disraeli's letters from this period by the University of Toronto Press, we now have a much fuller picture of what many regard as Disraeli's wasted years.

Gods and Giants: this metaphor can be found in Trollope's novel *Framley Parsonage* (London: Smith, Elder and Co., 1861); 'Where is your Christianity...?': Hansard, House of Commons Debates, 16 December 1847, vol. 95, col. 1325; 'I cannot, for one...': Hansard, House of Commons Debates, 16 December 1847, vol. 95, col. 1330; details of how Disraeli was able to purchase Hughenden Manor can be found in Monypenny and Buckle, *Disraeli*, vol. III, pp. 147–53; 'Mama at last confesses...': Monypenny and Buckle, *Disraeli*, vol. III, p. 142; 'Papa thinks...': Monypenny and Buckle, *Disraeli*, vol. III, p. 70; 'My father lived...': Hughenden Papers, 26/2, Book I, no. 2; for details of Isaac D'Israeli's estate and library see Weintraub, *Disraeli*, pp. 279–8; on Tita see Blake, *Disraeli*, pp. 255–6; 'the greatest loss...': Monypenny and Buckle, *Disraeli*, vol. III, pp. 112–13; 'This he declared...': Monypenny and Buckle, *Disraeli*, vol. III, pp. 151–2; 'Dear Lady of Hughenden...': *Disraeli Letters*, vol. V, no. 1774; 'I find great amusement...': Monypenny and Buckle, *Disraeli*, vol. III, pp. 158–9; 'Old Lord Londonderry...': Hughenden Papers, 26/2, Book I; 'No chance of that in our time...': Blake, *Disraeli*, p. 114; 'no one but Disraeli...': Weintraub, *Disraeli*, p. 285; Beresford on Disraeli: see St John, *Disraeli*, p. 65; 'I have been warned...': Monypenny and Buckle, *Disraeli*, vol. III, pp. 120–21; 'can be no doubt...': Monypenny and Buckle, *Disraeli*, vol. III, p. 86; 'I have never seen...': Monypenny and Buckle, *Disraeli*, vol. III, p. 126; 'I am doing you bare justice...': Monypenny and Buckle, *Disraeli*, vol. III, pp. 122–3; 'I am gratified...': Monypenny and Buckle, *Disraeli*, vol. III, p. 125; 'Sièyes, Roger Ducos, and Napoleon Bonaparte': Monypenny and Buckle, *Disraeli*, vol. III, p. 139; 'After much struggling...': Monypenny and Buckle, *Disraeli*, vol. III, p. 140; 'Not in this hall...': *Disraeli Letters*, vol. IV, pp. 297–8, n. 1; 'He made no parade...': *Disraeli, Derby and the Conservative Party: Journals and Memoirs of Edward Henry, Lord Stanley 1849–1869*, ed. John Vincent (Hassocks, Sussex, 1978), pp. 23–4; 'where Disraeli proposed...': Hawkins, *The Forgotten Prime Minister*, p. 26; 'One thing was established...': Blake, *Disraeli*, p. 305; 'a very sorry Cabinet': Hawkins, *The Forgotten Prime Minister*, p. 16, and Monypenny and Buckle, *Disraeli*, vol. III, p. 346, n. 2; 'The Great Unknown': Hawkins, *The Forgotten Prime Minister*, p. 16; 'You know as much as Mr Canning...': Blake, *Disraeli*, p. 311; 'more than ever...': from the *Illustrated London News*, 8 May 1852, as cited in Hawkins, *The Forgotten Prime Minister*,

p. 27; 'I called thee to curse...': Hawkins, *The Forgotten Prime Minister*, p. 25; 'the <u>Protectionists</u> themselves...': Hawkins, *The Forgotten Prime Minister*, p. 26; 'already stinketh': Hawkins, *The Forgotten Prime Minister*, p. 25; 'The spirit of the age...': Monypenny and Buckle, *Disraeli*, vol. III, p. 369; 'I despise you...': Hawkins, *The Forgotten Prime Minister*, p. 38; 'We built an opposition...': Hawkins, *The Forgotten Prime Minister*, p. 39; 'is now established...': Hawkins, *The Forgotten Prime Minister*, pp. 47–8; an excellent account of Disraeli's Budget, and government spending during these years, can be found in Blake, *Disraeli*, pp. 329–49; 'My budget greatly expands...': *Disraeli Letters*, vol. VI, no. 2360; 'Great will be your glory...': *Disraeli Letters*, vol. VI, p. 111, n. 3; 'I... must deeply regret...': *Disraeli Letters*, vol. VI, no. 2453; 'Put a good face on it...': Monypenny and Buckle, *Disraeli*, vol. III, p. 426; 'I could have said...': Blake, *Disraeli*, p. 338; 'the least conservative...': Blake, *Disraeli*, p. 339; on Bright's meeting with Disraeli see Bill Cash, *John Bright: Statesman, Orator, Agitator* (London: I.B. Tauris and Co., 2012), pp. 64–65 and Monypenny and Buckle, *Disraeli*, vol. III, p. 439; 'I was not born...': for this quotation and the full text of Disraeli's speech that evening, together with Gladstone's reply, see Hansard, House of Commons Debates, 16 December 1852, vol. 123, cols 1570–698; 'Gladstone's look...': Aldous, *Lion and the Unicorn*, pp. 70–71; 'now we are properly smashed...': Hawkins, *The Forgotten Prime Minister*, p. 57; for an account of Lady Derby's party see Hawkins, *The Forgotten Prime Minister*, p. 50; 'artist who wishes...': Blake, *Disraeli*, pp. 345–6; 'I seek much in a wife...': Aldous, *Lion and the Unicorn*, p. 28; 'Westminster Abbey is a toy to it': see Sam Smiles, *Memoir of John Murray*, vol. II, copy at Gladstone's Library, Hawarden; 'motives which I could neither describe nor conquer': John Morley, *The Life of William Ewart Gladstone*, 3 vols (London: Macmillan, 1903), ch. VIII, p. 561; 'a strong sentiment of revulsion...': St John, *Disraeli*, p. 48; 'The purity of his life...': Froude, *Beaconsfield*, p. 204.

Chapter VII: Friends and Foes

For details of Disraeli's literary successes and the waxwork in Madame Tussaud's see Kuhn, *Politics of Pleasure*, p. 246; 'It is a privilege...': *Disraeli Letters*, vol. VIII, no. 3750; for details of the shortage of letters see Blake, *Disraeli*, p. 365; 'The state of the Press...': *Disraeli Letters*, vol. VI, no. 2502; 'Is Man an Ape or an Angel?...': Froude, *Beaconsfield*, p. 176; 'Our party is now a corpse...': Monypenny and Buckle, *Disraeli*, vol. IV, p. 79; 'they had heard much...?': Monypenny and Buckle, *Disraeli*, vol. III, p. 24; 'millstones round our necks': Blake, *Disraeli*, p. 760; 'For the last three months...': Monypenny and Buckle, *Disraeli*, vol. IV, p. 339; 'The details of all these stories...': *Disraeli Letters*, vol. VII, no. 2964; 'I should like to see the programme...': Douglas Hurd, *The Arrow War: An Anglo-Chinese Confusion 1856–60* (London: Collins, 1967), p. 69; 'impossible for a party to exist...': Monypenny and Buckle, *Disraeli*, vol. IV, p. 20; 'As for our Chief...': Blake, *Disraeli*, p. 360; 'our chief has again bolted!...': Blake, *Disraeli*, p. 363; 'to uphold the aristocratic settlement...': Blake, *Disraeli*, p. 266; 'The Captain...': Blake, *Disraeli*, p. 354; 'Criticise, but suggest nothing': Weintraub, *Disraeli*, p. 403; 'we cannot with honour...': Blake, *Disraeli*, p. 364; 'science disqualified one...': Hughenden Papers, 26/3, no. 64; 'We must consult...': *Disraeli Letters*, vol. VI, no. 2336; 'My Dear Comrade': *Disraeli Letters*, vol. VI, no. 2371; 'one of my chief sources...': *Disraeli Letters*, vol. VI, no. 2894; 'everybody at every time...': Hughenden Papers, 26/2, nos 6, 29, 59, 70; 'I admire his perseverance...': *Journals of Lord Stanley 1849–1869*, p. 179; 'I have lost all zest...': *Disraeli Letters*, vol. VII, no. 2964; 'Now let the men...': Blake, *Disraeli*, p. 257; 'his chief...': *Journals of Lord Stanley 1849–1869*, p. 31; 'He talked of retiring...': Aldous, *The Lion and the Unicorn*, p. 83; 'utterly exhausted...': Aldous, *The Lion and the Unicorn*, p. 83; 'by this day fortnight...': *Journals of Lord Stanley 1849–1869*, p. 148; 'As to Disraeli's unpopularity...': Blake, *Disraeli*, p. 368; 'has not been successful...': *Journals of Lord Stanley 1849–1869*, p. 33; 'expects to die...': Monypenny and Buckle, *Disraeli*, vol. IV, p. 192; 'I can only tell you...': *Disraeli Letters*, vol. VI, no. 2382; 'I am glad...': *Disraeli Letters*, vol. VI, no. 2335; 'I think very often...': *Disraeli Letters*, vol. VI, no. 2346; 'even a line...': *Disraeli Letters*, vol. VI, no. 2398; the Spy cartoon is 'Power & Place', from *Vanity Fair*, 16 December 1879; for a reprint of a photograph of the caricature of Mrs Brydges Williams see Monypenny and Buckle, *Disraeli*, vol. III; for full details of Montagu's loan see Blake, *Disraeli*, p. 424; 'Ah! poor Sa...': Monypenny and Buckle, *Disraeli*, vol. I, p. 180; 'I do not approve...': Weintraub, *Disraeli*, p. 303; 'I shall ever remember...': *Disraeli Letters*, vol. VI, no. 2468; 'I have always believed...': Monypenny and Buckle, *Disraeli*, vol. III, p. 18; for an example of Disraeli's views on Britain becoming an absolute monarchy see *Disraeli Letters*, vol. VIII, p. 165, fn. 6; for details of the Prince of Wales's wedding see Kuhn, *Politics of Pleasure*, pp. 289–90; 'a good management...': *Disraeli Letters*, vol. VII, no. 3213; 'Our mutual relations...': *Disraeli Letters*, vol. VII, no. 3128; 'You consider that...': Monypenny and Buckle, *Disraeli*, vol. IV, p. 158; 'there are few things nearer my heart than political cooperation...': *Disraeli Letters*, vol. VI, no. 2445; 'Hush Money': See Hughenden Papers, 26/2; 'I address you in our ancient confidence...': *Disraeli Letters*, vol. VII, no. 3343; 'There is only one man...': Monypenny and Buckle, *Disraeli*, vol. IV, p. 259; for details of Disraeli's withdrawal from Westminster see Hawkins, *The Forgotten Prime Minister*, p. 268; 'Within twelve months...': Hurd and Young, *Choose Your Weapons*, p. 113; 'I am quite aware...': Monypenny and Buckle, *Disraeli*, vol. IV, pp. 416–17; 'various... flexible... shameless': Monypenny and Buckle, *Disraeli*, vol. IV, p. 286; 'I can see they are...': Monypenny and Buckle, *Disraeli*, vol. III, p. 422; 'Lord Derby and Mr Disraeli...': Blake, *Disraeli*, p. 408; 'personal feeling...': Monypenny and Buckle, *Disraeli*, vol. III, p. 475.

Chapter VIII: Tory Democracy

The definitive account of the Second Reform Act remains Maurice Cowling's *1867: Disraeli, Gladstone, and Revolution; The Passing of the Second Reform Bill* (Cambridge: CUP, 1967). Angus Hawkins's biography of Lord Derby has helped highlight the key driving role which the Prime Minister played during the Bill's genesis. A clear account of the Bill and its impact can be found in Ian St John, *Disraeli and the Art of Victorian Politics*, while the detailed work in Monypenny and Buckle is also an invaluable guide. There is, however, no substitute for reading the long, detailed speeches in the House of Commons first-hand. These can now be found online at http://hansard.millbanksystems.com/

Reading these speeches chronologically illustrates the way events toppled over into one another during the Bill's passing. For example, many historians have ignored or downplayed Disraeli's responsibilities as Chancellor of the Exchequer which occupied his attention during the passing of the Bill. Few have pointed out that the day after Disraeli had delivered his Budget speech, Gladstone began to plot his main onslaught on the Reform Bill. In these ways and others, issues and events crowded in all around him; Disraeli's skill was in propelling the Reform Bill onwards while holding other pressing problems at bay.

'his bladder complaint...': Cowling, *Passing of the Second Reform Bill*, p. 80; 'Lord Granville had a dairy farm...': Hughenden Papers, 26/2; 'in good health...': Hawkins, *The Forgotten Prime Minister*, p. 50; 'Our quiet days...': Hawkins, *The Forgotten Prime Minister*, p. 50; for an authoritative guide to the Great Reform Act see M. Brock, *The Great Reform Act* (London: Hutchinson and Co., 1973); 'it was a great advantage...': Monypenny and Buckle, *Disraeli*, vol. IV, p. 432; 'The question is not Adullamite...': Monypenny and Buckle, *Disraeli*, vol. IV, p. 440; this cartoon of Disraeli and Derby appeared in *Punch* on 7 July 1866; 'You could carry this...': Monypenny and Buckle, *Disraeli*, vol. IV, p. 453; 'I am coming reluctantly...':

Monypenny and Buckle, *Disraeli*, vol. IV, p. 453; 'we cannot escape...': Hawkins, *The Forgotten Prime Minister*, pp. 320–21; 'The royal project...': Monypenny and Buckle, *Disraeli*, vol. IV, pp. 456–7; 'leave the Canadians...': Blake, *Disraeli*, p. 455; 'of all possible hares...': Monypenny and Buckle, *Disraeli*, vol. IV, p. 484; 'You will find him very placable...': Blake, *Disraeli*, p. 456; 'Do not let the House suppose...': Hansard, House of Commons, 11 February 1867, vol. 185, cols 214–49; 'The enclosed, just received...': Hawkins, *The Forgotten Prime Minister*, p. 337; 'say what you please...': Hansard, House of Commons, 25 February 1867, vol. 185, col. 959; 'Well, whatever happens...': Monypenny and Buckle, *Disraeli*, vol. IV, p. 510; 'poor Tory Party...': Hawkins, *The Forgotten Prime Minister*, p. 341; 'I will waive...': Monypenny and Buckle, *Disraeli*, vol. IV, p. 511; 'I had more talk...': Monypenny and Buckle, *Disraeli*, vol. IV, p. 516; 'I would, in the first place...': Hansard, House of Commons, 18 March 1867, vol. 186, cols 6–94; 'It is very trying...': Monypenny and Buckle, *Disraeli*, vol. IV, p. 522; 'Not that I much care...': Hansard, House of Commons, 26 March 1867, vol. 186, cols 569–665; 'you have won...': Monypenny and Buckle, *Disraeli*, vol. IV, p. 527; 'I think the right hon. Gentleman deserves credit...': Hansard, House of Commons, 4 April 1867, vol. 186, cols 1110–59; 'want of discrimination...': Monypenny and Buckle, *Disraeli*, vol. IV, pp. 528–9; for details of Clay's writings on Whist see Blake, *Disraeli*, p. 62; 'candidate for power...': Hansard, House of Commons, 12 April 1867, vol. 186, cols 1599–703; 'Here's to the man...': Blake, *Disraeli*, p. 467; 'Why, my dear...': this story is told by Thomas Kebbel in *Lord Beaconsfield and Other Tory Memories* (New York: M. Kennerley, 1907), p. 40; 'that Mr Disraeli had laid...': Monypenny and Buckle, *Disraeli*, vol. IV, p. 534; 'If I understand...': Monypenny and Buckle, *Disraeli*, vol. IV, p. 535; 'we ought to carry...': Monypenny and Buckle, *Disraeli*, vol. IV, p. 535; 'felt that the critical moment...': Monypenny and Buckle, *Disraeli*, vol. IV, p. 540; for details of the Act see St John, *Disraeli*, p. 83; 'moonlight steeplechase...': Blake, *Disraeli*, p. 477; the phrase 'leap in the dark' is generally associated with Lord Derby, but records from Hansard reveal that the phrase was in general usage as a description of the Reform Bill throughout its passage and long before Lord Derby used it on 6 August 1867. For example, Baillie-Cochrane used the phrase to describe the Reform Bill on 20 May (see Hansard, House of Commons, 20 May 1867, vol. 187, col. 808), and a month later Bernal Osborne repeated the epithet (see Hansard, House of Commons, 20 June 1867, vol. 188, col. 204); 'I should say...': for extended extracts of Disraeli's famous speech in Scotland see Monypenny and Buckle, *Disraeli*, vol. IV, pp. 555–7; 'I have always believed...': St John, *Disraeli*, p. 114; 'the tide of democracy...': Evelyn Cromer, *Political*

& *Literary Essays*, vol. 2 (London: Macmillan and Co., 1914), p. 65; 'Was he sincere...': Disraeli, *Sybil*, p. 19; 'your wishes...': Monypenny and Buckle, *Disraeli*, vol. IV, p. 590; 'Mr Disraeli is Prime Minister...': Blake, *Disraeli*, p. 487; the full file of invitations and regrets for Mary Anne's famous party is preserved in the Hughenden Papers.

Chapter IX: Progressive Conservative

For Disraeli's views on O'Connell see Blake, *Disraeli*, p. 131; 'a starving population...': Hansard, House of Commons, 16 February 1844, vol. 72, col. 1016; 'failed to realise...': Hansard, House of Commons, 16 March 1868, vol. 190, col. 1741; 'as a State Church...': Hansard, House of Commons, 16 March 1868, vol. 190, col. 1764; for details of Disraeli's alleged drunkenness and Gladstone's response to his speech, see Aldous, *The Lion and the Unicorn*, p. 193; 'They have their hand...': Hansard, House of Commons, 3 April 1868, vol. 191, cols 837–946; 'Money is not to be considered...': Disraeli made this comment later, in a letter to Lady Bradford in 1874 looking back on the Abyssinian campaign. See Monypenny and Buckle, *Disraeli*, vol. V, p. 45; 'an intelligent age...': Hansard, House of Commons, 3 April 1868, vol. 191, col. 918; 'as I hold that the dissolution...': Monypenny and Buckle, *Disraeli*, vol. V, p. 25; 'the connection of religion...': Monypenny and Buckle, *Disraeli*, vol. V, p. 88; 'My mission is to pacify Ireland': Aldous, *The Lion and the Unicorn*, p. 202; 'Your Devoted Beaconsfield': Aldous, *The Lion and the Unicorn*, p. 201; 'like sedentary men...': Benjamin Disraeli, *Lothair* (Stroud: Nonsuch Publishing, 2007), p. 99; 'sheltering yourself...': Monypenny and Buckle, *Disraeli*, vol. V, p. 166; 'I am a poor governess...': Hughenden Papers, Correspondence on *Lothair*; 'He admitted to me...': *Journals of Lord Stanley 1849–1869*, p. 347; 'I think on our part...': St John, *Disraeli and the Art of Victorian Politics*, p. 131; 'His face was as of one...': Aldous, *The Lion and the Unicorn*, pp. 218–19; 'it is well that...': Monypenny and Buckle, *Disraeli*, vol. V, p. 132; 'range of exhausted volcanoes': Blake, *Disraeli*, p. 523; 'first consideration...': St John, *Disraeli and the Art of Victorian Politics*, p. 136; 'policy of sewage': Blake, *Disraeli*, p. 524; 'the source of incalculable strength...': St John, *Disraeli and the Art of Victorian Politics*, p. 137; 'It is all well and good...': Aldous, *The Lion and the Unicorn*, p. 224; 'Grosvenor Gate has become a hospital': Weintraub, *Disraeli*, p. 458; 'To witness this gradual death...': Aldous, *The Lion and the Unicorn*, p. 225; 'I am totally unable...': Aldous, *The Lion and the Unicorn*, p. 225; 'My dearest...': *Disraeli Letters*, vol. VII, no. 3136; 'My dearest wife I have not got my right clothes...': *Disraeli Letters*, vol. VII, no. 3283; 'What miles of villas...': Monypenny and Buckle, *Disraeli*, vol. V, p. 225; 'Hegira from Grosvenor Gate': Weintraub, *Disraeli*, p. 507; 'You know, Dizzy is my J.C.': Aldous, *The Lion and the Unicorn*, p. 225; 'hotel life in an evening...': Blake, *Disraeli*, p. 527; 'as attached to you...': Weintraub, *Disraeli*, p. 512; 'When you have the government of a country on your shoulders...': Monypenny and Buckle, *Disraeli*, vol. V, p. 249; 'I live for Power and the Affections': Weintraub, *Disraeli*, p. 529; on Disraeli's refusal to form a government see Weintraub, *Disraeli*, p. 511; 'incessant and harassing legislation': Monypenny and Buckle, *Disraeli*, vol. V, p. 275; 'You have despoiled Churches...': Hansard, House of Commons, 11 March 1873, vol. 214, col. 1827; 'We have been borne down in a torrent of gin and beer': Morley, *Gladstone*, p. 495; 'I am only truly great in action': St John, *Disraeli and the Art of Victorian Politics*, p. 209; this *Punch* cartoon was published on 6 July 1872; 'power has come to me too late...': St John, *Disraeli and the Art of Victorian Politics*, p. 145; 'When the Cabinet came...': Sarah Bradford, *Disraeli* (London: Weidenfeld and Nicolson, 1982), p. 313; 'whatever the difficulties might be': Monypenny and Buckle, *Disraeli*, vol. V, p. 286; 'So very arrogant...': Aldous, *The Lion and the Unicorn*, pp. 244–5; 'principles of Conservative Progress': Blake, *Disraeli*, p. 319; for a detailed account of Disraeli's Government's domestic policies see Monypenny and Buckle, *Disraeli*, vol. V, ch. X, and Blake, *Disraeli*, pp. 552–6; 'We have settled...': St John, *Disraeli and the Art of Victorian Politics*, p. 149; on the Plimsoll Line see Vincent, *Disraeli*, p. 11; 'will gain and retain...': Blake, *Disraeli*, p. 555; 'Conservative Party have done more...': Monypenny and Buckle, *Disraeli*, vol. V, p. 369; 'The principle of Tory Democracy...': Monypenny and Buckle, *Disraeli*, vol. V, p. 369; on Richard Cross's tipsy speech see *The Diaries of Edward Henry Stanley, 15th Earl of Derby Between 1878 and 1893: A Selection* (Oxford: Leopard's Head Press, 2003), 22/6/85; on Cross's murmurings during Board meetings of the Great Central Railway, see George Dow, *Great Central*, vol. II (London: Ian Allan, 1971), p. 28; David Willetts's article can be found on the *Guardian* website, at http://www.guardian.co.uk/commentisfree/2008/sep/30/conservatives.toryconference; 'if providence could have made Disraeli a dictator...': Wilkins, *Tory Democracy*, p. 55; 'All the real chivalry...': Monypenny and Buckle, *Disraeli*, vol. V, p. 497; 'My individual interest...': Monypenny and Buckle, *Disraeli*, vol. V, p. 497; 'I cannot bear...': Monypenny and Buckle, *Disraeli*, vol. V, p. 497; 'I am not the only Under Secretary...': Monypenny and Buckle, *Disraeli*, vol. V, p. 498; 'Henceforth the game...': Monypenny and Buckle, *Disraeli*, vol. V, p. 498; for accounts of Disraeli's speaking style see Monypenny and Buckle, *Disraeli*, vol. V, p. 504 and Blake, *Disraeli*, p. 567; 'I am dead...': Monypenny and Buckle, *Disraeli*, vol. V, p. 522

Chapter X: Peace with Honour

An earlier version of this chapter was published in our previous book, *Choose Your Weapons*. In researching these critical years, we were inspired by the running commentary provided by the 15th Earl of Derby's diary. This diary only came to light when rescued by workmen at Knowsley, and in a masterpiece of skilful and intelligent editing Professor Vincent has brought the 15th Earl back to the centre of the stage.

We are grateful for the assistance we received when we first decided to tackle this subject from the staff of Liverpool's Record Office, who opened up for us a range of letters between Derby and Disraeli from 1874 to 1878. We have also included in this chapter a number of key speech drafts and side notes prepared by Disraeli during the crisis which we discovered among the Hughenden Papers. The letter in which Disraeli describes the 'tall, handsome young man ... with finished manners and sweet simplicity' whom he met at Stafford train station can be found in the Hughenden Papers, in file 69/1, dated 15 November 1876.

In addition to these published sources and archives, R.W. Seton-Watson's *Disraeli, Gladstone and the Eastern Question: A Study in Diplomacy and Politics* (London: Macmillan, 1935) remains a compelling guide to the drama, as does A.J.P. Taylor's *Struggle for Mastery in Europe: 1848–1918* (Oxford: OUP, 1971).

'with much pain...': Hughenden Papers, 65/1–2, Disraeli to Rowton, 28/7/78; 'destroys my nights...': Blake, *Disraeli*, pp. 631–3; 'Look at Lord Roehampton...': Disraeli, *Endymion* (BiblioBazaar), p. 326; 'There is no gambling...': Monypenny and Buckle, *Disraeli*, vol. VI, p. 31; 'When?...Tomorrow...What is your security?': Monypenny and Buckle, *Disraeli*, vol. V, p. 447, and Blake, *Disraeli*, pp. 581–6; 'It is only by the amplification...': St John, *Disraeli and the Art of Victorian Politics*, p. 187; 'to me it appears...': Edward Stanley, 15th Earl of Derby, *Diaries*, ed. John Vincent (London: Royal Historical Society, 1994), vol. 4, p. 15; 'If foreigners can settle...': Derby, *Diaries*, vol. 4, p. 427; 'so far as I can make out...': Derby, *Diaries*, vol. 4, p. 257; 'the peasantry of Western Surrey...': Derby, *Diaries*, vol. 4, p. 423; 'In one word, he is not a gentleman': Derby, *Diaries*, vol. 4, p. 384; 'loss of a kind of employment...': Derby, *Diaries*, vol. 4, p. 369; 'He was a master...': Lady Gwendolen Cecil, *Life of Robert, Marquis of Salisbury* (London: Hodder and Stoughton, 1921–1932), vol. II, p. 114; 'It appears to me...': Monypenny and Buckle, *Disraeli*, vol. VI, p. 23; 'I really believe...': Blake, *Disraeli*, p. 575; 'When I entered political life...': Monypenny and Buckle, *Disraeli*, vol. VI, p. 13; 'England has been treated as though we were Montenegro or Bosnia': Taylor, *Struggle for Mastery*, p. 236; 'I look upon...': Monypenny and Buckle, *Disraeli*, vol.

VI, p. 31; Although the *Daily News* gave a figure of 25,000 women and children massacred, the number was generally thought to be around half that amount – see Blake, *Disraeli*, p. 592; 'Oriental people...': Hansard, House of Commons, 10 July 1876, vol. 230, col. 1182; 'I must again complain...': Monypenny and Buckle, *Disraeli*, vol. VI, p. 44; 'coffee house babble...': Hansard, House of Commons, 31 July 1876, vol. 2341, col. 203; 'those who suppose...': House of Commons, 11 August 1876, vol. 231, col. 1146; 'I rise at seven...': Hughenden Papers, 69/1, Disraeli to Corry, 13 September 1876; 'Let the Turks now carry away...': Blake, *Disraeli*, p. 598; 'one great anti-human specimen...': St John, *Disraeli and the Art of Victorian Politics*, p. 173; 'What a man is Gladstone...': Hughenden Papers, 69/1, Disraeli to Corry, 13 September 1876; 'may, I think, fairly be described...': Blake, *Disraeli*, p. 602; 'wisely & manfully...': Hughenden Papers, 69/1, Disraeli to Corry, 13 September 1876; 'repugnance to enthusiasm...': Monypenny and Buckle, *Disraeli*, vol. VI, p. 68; 'You have shown...': Monypenny and Buckle, *Disraeli*, vol. VI, p. 76; 'the probability or at least the chance of a breach...': Derby, *Diaries*, ed. Vincent, vol. 4, p. 337; 'Peace is especially an English policy...': Monypenny and Buckle, *Disraeli*, vol. VI, p. 92; 'clearness of vision...': Hughenden Papers, 69/1, Disraeli to Corry, 15 November 1876; 'an awful nuisance...': John Charmley, *Splendid Isolation?: Britain, the Balance of Power and the Origins of the First World War* (London: Hodder and Stoughton, 1999), p. 55; 'Also, personally for yourself...': Cecil, *Life of Salisbury*, vol. II, p. 95; 'Sal. seems most prejudiced...': Blake, *Disraeli*, p. 616; 'an army of European advisers...': Liverpool Record Office, *Papers of Edward Stanley, 15th Earl of Derby*, Salisbury to Derby, 26 December 1876; Disraeli's Cabinet Speaking notes are preserved in the Hughenden Papers; 'You must pardon...': Liverpool Record Office, *Papers of Edward Stanley, 15th Earl of Derby*, 920 Der (15) 17/2/3; 'What do you think...': Monypenny and Buckle, *Disraeli*, vol. V, p. 520; 'I should have felt sorry...': Monypenny and Buckle, *Disraeli*, vol. V, p. 520; 'Oh if the Queen were a man...': Blake, *Disraeli*, p. 637; 'This mawkish sentimentality...': Monypenny and Buckle, *Disraeli*, vol. V, p. 130; 'fortunately the middle classes...': St John, *Disraeli and the Art of Victorian Politics*, p. 176; 'the first thing...': Derby, *Diaries*, vol. 4, p. 392; 'bouncing and excited...': Derby, *Diaries*, vol. 4, p. 394; for details of Derby's 'wet-blanketing', see Bendor Grosvenor, 'Britain's "most isolationist Foreign Secretary": The Fifteenth Earl and the Eastern Crisis 1876–1878', as published in *Conservatism and British Foreign Policy, 1820–1920: The Derbys and their World*, ed. Geoffrey Hicks (Farnharm: Ashgate Publishing Ltd, 2011) p. 154; 'Her Majesty's Government are not prepared...': Kenneth Bourne, *The Foreign Policy of Victorian England, 1830–1902* (Oxford: Clarendon Press, 1970), p.

408; 'For my own part...': Hughenden Papers, 69/1, Disraeli to Corry, 20 October 1877; 'she urged strongly...': Blake, *Disraeli*, p. 622; 'What are you waiting for...': Blake, *Disraeli*, p. 653; 'I have a strong suspicion...': Morley, *Gladstone*, p. 552; 'Jew Premier': Blake, *Disraeli*, p. 605; 'Ill or well...': Derby, *Diaries*, vol. 4, p. 452; 'We can hardly make...': Liverpool Record Office, *Papers of Edward Stanley, 15th Earl of Derby*, Derby to Beaconsfield, 22 December 1877; 'it is clear enough...': Hughenden Papers, 92/4, Salisbury to Disraeli, 23 September 1876; 'He believes thoroughly in "prestige" – as all foreigners do...': Blake, *Disraeli*, p. 676; 'You and I must go together...': Monypenny and Buckle, *Disraeli*, vol. VI, p. 210; 'insane enough': Monypenny and Buckle, *Disraeli*, vol. VI, p. 213; 'We are on the eve': Hughenden Papers, Undated Cabinet Notes: B/XVI/B/60, ff. 191–4; 'What should – and does, I hope – absorb our attention...': Hughenden Papers, Undated Cabinet Notes: B/XVI/B66, ff. 214–15; 'I am a check...': Derby, *Diaries*, vol. 4, p. 493; 'a classic Victorian scoundrel...': Derby, *Diaries*, vol. 4, pp. 25–8, 461; 'excited and inclined to swagger...': Derby, *Diaries*, vol. 4, p. 505; 'to depress almost to the point of entire subjection...': Bourne, *The Foreign Policy of Victorian England*, p. 412; 'he is not really false...': Cecil, *Life of Salisbury*, vol. II, p. 287; 'Lord Beaconsfield can't negotiate...': Seton-Watson, *Disraeli, Gladstone and the Eastern Question*, p. 454; 'Cyprus is the key...': Monypenny and Buckle, *Disraeli*, vol. VI, p. 291; 'a sophistical rhetorician...': Monypenny and Buckle, *Disraeli*, vol. VI, p. 356; 'Great Britain won...': Taylor, *Struggle for Mastery*, p. 258; 'Her Majesty has fleets and armies...': Monypenny and Buckle, *Disraeli*, vol. VI, p. 354; 'As to Disraeli's firework...': Monypenny and Buckle, *Disraeli*, vol. VI, p. 359

Chapter XI: The Assiduous Mummy

'Had it been a routine age...': Monypenny and Buckle, *Disraeli*, vol. VI, p. 379; 'I have always been opposed...': St John, *Disraeli and the Art of Victorian Politics*, p. 194; 'When V-Roys and Comms-in-Chief...': Monypenny and Buckle, *Disraeli*, vol. VI, p. 382; 'I have now been here...': Monypenny and Buckle, *Disraeli*, vol. VI, p. 403; 'It will change everything...': St John, *Disraeli and the Art of Victorian Politics*, p. 192; 'Ld. B. is extremely dissatisfied...': Monypenny and Buckle, *Disraeli*, vol. VI, pp. 419–20; for detail on the lines of communication between South Africa and London see Monypenny and Buckle, *Disraeli*, vol. VI, p. 421, n. 1; 'My dear Sir Bartle Frere...': Hansard, House of Commons, 31 March 1879, vol. 245, cols 84–5; 'Lord Beaconsfield charges...': Monypenny and Buckle, *Disraeli*, vol. VI, pp. 459–60; 'a very remarkable people...':

Froude, *Beaconsfield*, p. 213; 'We may be said...': Monypenny and Buckle, *Disraeli*, vol. VI, pp. 447–9; for details of the economic deterioration see Blake, *Disraeli*, pp. 697–9; 'rusty phrases of mine': Blake, *Disraeli*, p. 698; 'day and night...': Monypenny and Buckle, *Disraeli*, vol. VI, p. 239; 'Remember that the sanctity of life...': Morley, *Gladstone*, p. 595; 'I never was a great admirer...': Monypenny and Buckle, *Disraeli*, vol. V, p. 270; 'A Prince, who really has seen everything...': Monypenny and Buckle, *Disraeli*, vol. VI, p. 472; 'policy of decomposition': Monypenny and Buckle, *Disraeli*, vol. VI, pp. 514–16; 'At home the Ministers have neglected legislation...': Monypenny and Buckle, *Disraeli*, vol. VI, p. 518; for details of Salisbury's wine and the scale of the election defeat see Monypenny and Buckle, *Disraeli*, vol. VI, p. 522; 'It seemed as if...': Blake, *Disraeli*, p. 711; 'She will sooner <u>abdicate</u>...': Blake, *Disraeli*, p. 717; 'without any of its excitement...': Monypenny and Buckle, *Disraeli*, vol. VI, pp. 531–2; 'Is it not possible...': Monypenny and Buckle, *Disraeli*, vol. VI, p. 530; 'in youth, a little fancy...': Disraeli, *Endymion*, p. 119; 'I cannot send you out...': Disraeli, *Endymion*, p. 119; 'The dinner was a banquet...': Disraeli, *Endymion*, p. 116; 'an insular country...': Disraeli, *Endymion*, p. 186; 'with a painful feeling...': Blake, *Disraeli*, p. 766; 'The matter [of the advance] rests entirely with Lord Beaconsfield': this letter can be found in the file of letters about *Endymion* in the Hughenden Papers; 'He was essentially a prig...': Monypenny and Buckle, *Disraeli*, vol. V, p. 549; 'I fully appreciate your feelings...': Monypenny and Buckle, *Disraeli*, vol. VI, p. 589; 'perpetual and complete reversal...': Blake, *Disraeli*, p. 743; 'I do not know...': Hansard, House of Lords Debates, 4 March 1881, vol. 259, col. 294; 'It is no easy thing...': Blake, *Disraeli*, p. 743; 'we have and have had for some days the climate of Cannes...': Blake, *Disraeli*, p. 742; 'an assiduous mummy...': Lytton Strachey, *Queen Victoria* (Teddington: Echo Library, 2006), p. 137; 'the most beneficent prince': Disraeli's last full speech in Parliament can be found in Hansard, House of Lords, 15 March 1881, vol. 259, cols 1044–5; his final words in the Chamber were spoken three days later, on 18 March, and are also in vol. 259 of Hansard, cols 1349–50; 'a confused brain...': Monypenny and Buckle, *Disraeli*, vol. VI, p. 449; 'I am blind...': Monypenny and Buckle, *Disraeli*, vol. VI, p. 609; 'I shall never survive...': Monypenny and Buckle, *Disraeli*, vol. VI, p. 611; 'No it is better not...': Blake, *Disraeli*, p. 747; 'I had rather live...': Blake, *Disraeli*, p. 748; 'He passed away...': Monypenny and Buckle, *Disraeli*, vol. VI, pp. 616–17; 'The last day and hours...': Monypenny and Buckle, *Disraeli*, vol. VI, p. 617.

Epilogue

For a superb analysis of the way Disraeli was resurrected as a political icon after his death, see John Vincent's *Disraeli*, p. 49. 'made England feared...': from *Lines on the Death of Lord Beaconsfield*, printed by John White and Son, Liverpool, in the Crawford Collections (on deposit from the Balcarres Heritage Trust) in the National Library of Scotland, available for viewing at http://digital.nls.uk/dcn9/7489/74893071.9.htm; 'I can scarcely see for my fast falling tears...': Blake, *Disraeli*, p. 749; 'All actors want to play Disraeli, except fat ones': we are grateful to Professor Steven Fielding for bringing this tribute to our attention. The quote can be found in Nora Johnson's *Flashback: Nora Johnson on Nunnally Johnson* (New York: Doubleday, 1979), p. 161; details of Disraeli's financial standing at his death can be found in Monypenny and Buckle, *Disraeli*, vol. VI, pp. 626–36; 'Men of action...': Monypenny and Buckle, *Disraeli*, vol. VI, p. 436; 'Sensible men...': Benjamin Disraeli, *Endymion*, p. 424; 'The greatest of legislators...': Disraeli, *Tancred*, p. 118; 'the greatest triumph...': Kirsch, *Disraeli*, p. x; 'I come from a race...': Blake, *Disraeli*, p. 706; 'I am only truly great in action...': Ian St John, *Disraeli*, p. 209; 'after sitting next to Mr Gladstone...': Aldous, *Lion & Unicorn*, p. 249; Vernon Bogdanor's pithy verdict can be found in his *Independent on Sunday* review of Stanley Weintraub's biography, 7 November 1993; 'We should always remember...': Blake, *Disraeli*, p. 389; 'I say you can have...': Hansard, House of Commons Debates, 30 August 1848, vol. 101, col. 706; 'I will rule without respect of party...': Hansard, House of Commons Debates, 22 January 1846, vol. 83, col. 122; for Bagehot's thoughts on Disraeli see *Bagehot's Historical Essays*, ed. Norman St John Stevas; 'the jewelled phrase...': Aldous, *Lion & Unicorn*, p. 249; for an account of Oscar Wilde's (unpublished) thoughts on Disraeli see Weintraub, *Disraeli*, p. 665; 'all the creative power...': Monypenny and Buckle, *Disraeli*, vol. VI, pp. 504–5; 'Dizzy has the most wonderful moral courage...': Weintraub, *Disraeli*, p. 352; '*Forti nihil difficile*': images of the chimney piece and the motto can be seen on the National Trust website, at http://www.ntprints.com/image. php?imgref=154134 ; 'I never listened to a speech of yours...': Letter from Count Vitzthum to Disraeli, 21 April 1867, as published in Monypenny and Buckle, *Disraeli*, vol. IV, p. 534.

ACKNOWLEDGEMENTS

Disraeli liked to say that he had been born in a library. In this way, he recorded his debt to his father Isaac who had spent his life in literature and introduced his eldest son to the delights of history.

This book about Disraeli was born in four libraries. The first and most important of these has been the Special Collections at Oxford University. These collections, which house Disraeli's papers, have temporarily been moved to the Radcliffe Science Library and we enjoyed spending time in these basement archives. We are greatly in debt to the curatorial team for their assistance, in particular Helen Langley, and to the National Trust for granting access to the files.

Our second library home has been Gladstone's Library at Hawarden. This remarkable institution lies close to Gladstone's estate at Hawarden Castle and houses his private library. It would, we think, have given Disraeli subtle pleasure, not without a dash of malice, to watch us search to solve the many riddles of his own life among the books of his greatest adversary – many of them filled with angry jottings in Gladstone's own hand.

Since our first visit to this library many years ago, a new Islamic Reading Room has been built which we have used as a base for our writing. The walls of this room are lined with books similar to those which Disraeli read during the

1850s. In particular, Disraeli would been intrigued by such esoteric titles as *The Jews of Islam*, *The History of the Mohammedan Dynasties in Spain* and *The Discontented Dervishes*. The library has been a haven of comfort and restful thought over the last two years, and we are grateful to all those who run this place, from Peter Francis, the Warden, to those in the kitchen who prepare the generous meals.

Two other libraries have been of great assistance. Once again, the British Library has been a hugely helpful resource, while many thanks are also owed to Tristan Garel-Jones who let us use his charming library at Candeleda in Castile to work on the manuscript. We write these words at Candeleda on a very hot summer day, protected from the heat by a rattan curtain, as we listen to the gentle splash of a fountain placed among the olive trees.

Part of the pleasure in writing about Disraeli was that after we had begun to tell people about our subject, we found that thoughts and findings flew in from all quarters, from enthusiasts and experts here in Britain as well as overseas. One such scribbler was Professor Steven Fielding who sent remarkable stories about early cinematic portrayals of Disraeli. We are also grateful to Sir William Gladstone who, after showing us round Gladstone's study, pointed us towards much useful reading matter on the relationship between his ancestor and Disraeli.

It was exceptionally good of Alistair Lexden, Andrew Gailey, John Jefferies and Ryan Tinggal to read the full text. Each reader provided much intelligent and entertaining feedback. Special mention must go to John Jefferies, who played a key supporting role in gathering together research on the way Disraeli's life developed into a series of myths after his death. We are also grateful to Frederick Mocatta, who read the early chapters of the manuscript and made pertinent points about Disraeli's ancestry.

Our agent Michael Sissons has again lent us his rich experience. Bea Hemming, our editor at Weidenfeld & Nicolson, has been an inspiration throughout the project, helping to refine our idea initially and providing much insight and illumination along the way. Linden Lawson has once again gone through our text in scrupulous detail, and we owe a particular debt to Pauline Glock, who managed to convert our wayward handwriting into orderly prose.

Disraeli in his own life liked to blend fact and fiction. His views on history were often dotty and unsound. We have tried in this book to avoid such confusion, but we apologise in advance for any errors which have crept through our defences.

In August 2011, Ed married Becky Jackson, whom he met at Cambridge ten years ago, and to whom this book is dedicated. Over the following two years, Becky has become an invaluable companion in this joint enterprise. Her suggestions and advice have greatly improved the manuscript, and once again, we were thankful for her fast typing skills. We are indebted to her for her love and support with this project. She is indeed more like a mistress than a wife.

INDEX

Works by Benjamin Disraeli (BD) appear under title; works by others under
author's name

blog and newsletter

For literary discussion, author insight,
book news, exclusive content,
recipes and giveaways, visit the
Weidenfeld & Nicolson blog and
sign up for the newsletter at:

www.wnblog.co.uk

For breaking news, reviews and exclusive competitions
Follow us 🐦 @wnbooks
Find us 📘 facebook.com/WNfiction